BORDER CITIZENS

Published in cooperation with the
William P. Clements Center for Southwest Studies,
Southern Methodist University

BORDER CITIZENS

The Making of Indians, Mexicans, and Anglos in Arizona

ERIC V. MEEKS

UNIVERSITY OF TEXAS PRESS, AUSTIN

Requests for permission to reproduce material from this work
should be sent to Permissions, University of Texas Press,
P.O. Box 7819, Austin, TX 78713-7819,
www.utexas.edu/utpress/about/bpermission.html

⊗ The paper used in this book meets the minimum requirements
of ANSI/NISO Z39.48-1992 (R1997) (Permanence of Paper).

LIBRARY OF CONGRESS CATALOGING-IN-PUBLICATION DATA

Meeks, Eric V.
    Border citizens : the making of Indians, Mexicans, and Anglos in Arizona /
Eric V. Meeks. — 1st ed.
        p. cm.
    Includes bibliographical references and index.
    ISBN: 978-0-292-71698-8 (cloth : alk. paper)
    ISBN: 978-0-292-71699-5 (pbk. : alk. paper)
        1. Arizona—Ethnic relations—History—19th century.   2. Arizona—
Ethnic relations—History—20th century.   3. Ethnicity—Arizona—History.
4. Indians of North America—Arizona—Ethnic identity—History.
5. Mexican Americans—Arizona—Ethnic identity—History.   6. Whites—
Race identity—Arizona—History.   7. Ethnic barriers—Arizona—History.
8. Social structure—Arizona—History.   I. Title.
    F820.A1M44 2007
    305.8009791′09034—dc22
                                                                    2007017833

FOR LEILAH

CONTENTS

LIST OF ILLUSTRATIONS

ACKNOWLEDGMENTS

Border Citizens: The Making of Indians, Mexicans, and Anglos in Arizona began as a dissertation at the University of Texas at Austin, where I had the pleasure of working with an extraordinary group of scholars. I wish to thank Neil Foley, my dissertation supervisor, for engaging me in hours of discussion as I developed my ideas, conducted research, and wrote and rewrote drafts of the manuscript. Special thanks also go to my dissertation committee, Gunther Peck, David Montejano, Pauline Turner Strong, and James Sibury, who helped me to grow as a historian and offered insightful critiques of seminar papers and dissertation chapters. I thank my fellow students at the University of Texas who took time to read and comment on many of the chapters—especially Sean Kelley, Marc McLeod, Matt Childs, Hal Langfur, Brian Larkin, and Leilah Danielson.

At Northern Arizona University I have continued to benefit greatly from the insights and support of colleagues and friends. Susan Deeds, in particular, took time out of an extremely busy schedule to read and comment on chapters and to write letters of support as I sought external funding to complete the manuscript. Many other members of the NAU faculty have also offered their support, and in the process have become enduring friends. I especially thank Sara Alemán, Sanjam Ahluwalia, Mike Amundson, Jeff Berglund, Monica Brown, Jennifer Denetdale, Sanjay Joshi, Cynthia and Peter Kosso, Scott Reese, Gioia Woods, and Miguel Vásquez. I also deeply appreciate the support of Aaron Cohen, Raquel Rotnes, and Jerry Thull, who have provided a much-needed refuge from academic life in Flagstaff.

I owe a special debt to those who shared with me their own experiences of living in Arizona's borderlands. Octaviana Trujillo taught me a great deal about Yaqui history and culture, both through personal conversations and by allowing me to sit in on her class in Guadalupe. Special thanks also to Dolores Huerta, who agreed to talk with me about her career as an activist at the end of a long day of energizing speeches and meetings at Northern Arizona University. Finally, thanks to Gabriel and Frances Alvarez, Tomasa Carpio, Esther and Frank Cota, Margo Cowan, Jimmy Molina, Henry Ramón, and Barbara Valencia, all of whom gave me new perspectives on the region I grew up in.

I could not have written this book without the staffs at numerous libraries and archives, especially the Special Collections at the University of Arizona; the Hayden Library at Arizona State University; the Arizona Historical Society in Tucson and Tempe; the Arizona State Museum in Tucson; the National Archives at Laguna Niguel, California; the Benson Latin American Collection at the University of Texas at Austin; the Salt River Archives in Tempe; and the Venito García Library in Sells, on the Tohono O'odham reservation. I give special thanks to Christín Marin and Patricia Etter for helping me navigate my way through the rich resources at the Chicano Research Collection and Labriola Center at Arizona State University; to David Shaul at the Venito García Library; and to Lisa Gezelter at both the Arizona Collection at ASU and the National Archives at Laguna Niguel. The staff of the Edwin J. Foscue Map Library, GIS Section, Southern Methodist University, also provided critical help in the production of all the maps that appear in this book.

At the dissertation and book stages, my work has benefited greatly from the financial support of several institutions. While I was a student at the University of Texas, a Thematic University Fellowship from the Graduate School and the Dora Bonham Fund and Walter Prescott Webb Dissertation Fellowship from the History Department were invaluable. I also thank the Southwest Center at the University of Arizona, which awarded me a Morris Udall research grant so that I could travel to Tucson to use their archival collections. At Northern Arizona University, two intramural research grants allowed me to conduct additional research as I revised my dissertation into a book.

A residential fellowship at the Clements Center for Southwest Studies at Southern Methodist University provided me time away from teaching and the intellectual space to transform a rough draft of the manuscript into a book. Thanks to David Weber, who carefully read every page and helped me to rethink my suppositions and refine my prose. Thanks also to Andrea Boardman and Ruth Ann Elmore for making my move and my stay in Dallas a pleasant one. I also am extremely grateful to Linda Gordon and

Sarah Deutsch, who traveled to Dallas in the middle of their semesters to participate in a workshop on the manuscript. Finally, I am indebted to all of those who read the manuscript and participated in the Clements Center workshop. In addition to those listed above, they are David Adams, Brian DeLay, John Chávez, Ben Johnson, Jeff Schulze, George Díaz, David Rex Galindo, Eduardo Morález, Don Coerver, and Daniel Wickberg.

Part of Chapter 2 was first published in *The Western Historical Quarterly* (Winter 2003) and was improved greatly by the close readings by anonymous reviewers and by David Rich Lewis. I wish to thank the Western History Association for recognizing this article with the Oscar O. Winter Award and the Bolton-Kinnaird Award, which gave me both well-needed encouragement and financial help as I revised this book into its final form. Portions of Chapters 7 and 8 first appeared in the journal *Reflexiones: New Directions in Mexican American Studies* (1997). Thanks to Víctor J. Guerra and Neil Foley for their insightful criticisms. Parts of Chapter 4 appeared in *The Journal of the Southwest* (Spring 2006), and I wish to thank Jeff Bannister and the anonymous reviewers for their helpful advice. I also thank all three of these journals for granting permission to reprint material from these articles in this book.

I greatly appreciate the patience and professionalism of editors William Bishel and Lynne Chapman of the University of Texas Press in helping to guide this book to its completion. Thanks also to Tom Lacey for his careful copyediting, which has resulted in a substantially more eloquent manuscript than the one I initially handed to him; and to Kay Banning, for her thorough and thoughtful indexing of the book.

Finally, I am extremely grateful to my family. Thanks to my parents, Ron and Maureen; to my brother and sister, Kevin and Deanne; to my parents-in-law, Susan and Ross; and my sisters-in-law, Eliza and Marah, for their encouragement and for bearing with many anxious, absentminded, and self-indulgent moments. My son, Adin, was born while I researched and wrote this book, and he provided many hours of joyful distraction. I dedicate the book to my wife, Leilah Danielson, who provided me with professional and emotional support through this long journey. I owe her incalculable intellectual and personal debts—for countless hours discussing ideas on long walks and reading drafts of the manuscript. I thank her most of all for her patience and love through sleepless nights and times of self-doubt.

BORDER CITIZENS

INTRODUCTION

In the mid-1960s a group of Yaquis in the Tucson barrio called Pascua took the first steps toward seeking federal acknowledgment of their status as American Indians. In part they hoped to obtain access to federal resources and an area of land outside the city. Since World War II, Tucson's warehouse district had enveloped Pascua, and the mechanization of agriculture had dramatically reduced the number of jobs on nearby industrial farms. Pascua residents lived in poverty, with dilapidated housing and worn-out and insufficient infrastructure. Catholic Yaquis also complained about excessive interference by local Protestant missionaries. They hoped that by moving outside the city they might be, as one contemporary ethnographer put it, "left alone with the traditional religious life of the Yaquis." The campaign to establish a new settlement sparked a rancorous debate about what it meant to be Yaqui, Indian, and ethnic Mexican in twentieth-century Arizona.[1]

Anselmo Valencia, a Yaqui war veteran, led the campaign to establish a new settlement after founding the Pascua Yaqui Association in 1963 "to maintain and enhance the Yaqui culture as it is found in the State of Arizona." Membership in the association was limited to "any person who has been ceremonially associated with the Yaqui Indians."[2] Valencia enlisted the help of Anglos living in Tucson, such as ethnographers Edward Spicer and Muriel Thayer Painter, who formed the Pascua Advisory Committee that same year.[3] Finally, declaring himself the chief of the Pascua Yaquis, he wrote to Rep. Morris Udall, explaining that Pascua had long been "the heart of Yaqui life and culture in Arizona" and that resettlement would empower them to protect their way of life.[4] Udall agreed to take up the cause, and he soon presented a bill before Congress to set aside an area of land in trust. He did so because he felt that "the Yaquis of Pascua Village are threatened with extinction as a tribe if a new home is not found for them."[5]

At the time, most Arizonans knew little or nothing about the Yaquis. Few were aware, for example, that thousands had first arrived in Arizona in the late nineteenth century, crossing the border to escape a war of attrition by the Mexican military to usurp and divide their lands in southwestern Sonora for private ownership and capitalist development. By the second half of the twentieth century, Yaqui families were settled throughout Arizona's borderlands. Because Yaquis were the descendants of immigrants who lived mostly in barrios or ethnically mixed rural towns rather than reservations, tended to speak Spanish as well as Yaqui, and shared many cultural traits and kinship ties with Mexicans and Mexican Americans, many Anglos assumed that they were Mexicans, and thought it incomprehensible that they could be American Indians.[6]

Opponents of Udall's bill sometimes expressed their opposition in explicitly racist and nationalist terms. Turney Smith, a rancher who lived near land sought by the Yaquis, explained his objections in a letter to Udall in 1964. "These so-called Indians," Smith argued, "are not Indians in the proper sense of the word. They are a mixture of several breeds—they have no nationality—no home and are not citizens of any country." To Smith the Yaquis defied the requisite characteristics of proper Indians, who were supposed to be indigenous to territory within the United States and culturally and racially pure. The bill also challenged his assumptions about Mexicans, since in Arizona the term *Mexican* had been imbued with derogatory meanings, implying a dangerous blending of races and alien status. How could a group of people from Mexico now claim to be pure Indians, let alone citizens of the United States?[7]

To complicate matters further, many Yaquis themselves showed little interest in the bill. Yaquis in the town of Guadalupe, in Maricopa County, were especially suspicious of intentions to seek benefits from the government based upon their status as Indians. One Guadalupano feared that the government would "tattoo a number on us and put us on a reservation." Others had simply never identified as American Indians but had developed strong ties to ethnic Mexicans, sharing a legacy of immigration, similar cultural practices, kinship ties, and a similar place within the socioeconomic order.[8] These ties became the basis for a collective identity that defied simple categories like Mexican and Indian. Gabe Alvarez, a Yaqui who had married a Mexican-American woman, put it this way: "I'm not an

American, I'm a Mexican. I'm from Mexico. . . . I speak Spanish, and I like Mexican music, so how can I be Native American?"[9]

In the end, Congress settled on an imperfect solution that left the official status of the Yaquis ambiguous. A revised version of Udall's bill (Public Law 88-350) passed Congress in 1965, placing 202 acres of land in trust as New Pascua, near the San Xavier Tohono O'odham reservation. The new law, however, fell short of recognizing Yaquis as equivalent to other American Indians. According to the law, "Nothing in this Act shall make such Yaqui Indians eligible for any services performed by the United States for Indians because of their status as Indians."[10] The bill thus recognized the Yaquis as Indians while refusing to endorse the idea that their Indianness entitled them to federal resources.

As this brief account suggests, the debate over Yaqui federal recognition raised fundamental questions about race, identity, and national belonging in twentieth-century Arizona. How could the descendents of immigrants from Mexico, many of whom spoke Spanish and shared many cultural traditions with ethnic Mexicans, be American Indians? The Yaquis were one of several indigenous groups in the region—the Tohono O'odham, Pimas, and Maricopas among them—who had experienced long histories of intercultural exchanges with Spaniards and Mexicans before the United States conquered the region in the mid-nineteenth century, and who continued to have economic, cultural, and kinship ties on both sides of the border. At a fundamental level, the debate over Yaqui federal recognition reveals the inadequacy of the standard terms of ethno-racial classification, such as Mexican, Indian, and Anglo, to capture the complex reality of people's experiences and identities. A central goal of this book is to interrogate how and why these ethno-racial categories and boundaries developed historically in the way they did, and to examine their evolving meanings.

In the past several years, scholars from a variety of disciplines have begun to explore similar questions in different contexts. Historians, anthropologists, sociologists, and others have come to a rough consensus that the meaning of categories such as Anglo, Mexican, and Indian change over time. They are not static, and they often hide more than they reveal about complex identities and intercultural relationships. Instead, it is now widely argued that both ethnic and racial categories are socially constructed, relational, and historically contingent.[11] Still, many scholars use such categories as a convenient way to identify different groups of people. While I, too, often find it necessary to resort to those terms in this book, I try to take more seriously the idea that we must question monolithic classifications and in the process, as two historians have recently put it, "give voice to silenced mestizo identities."[12] Arizona, with its diverse population of ethnic Mexicans and semi-Hispanicized indigenous peoples, provides an ideal arena in which to do so.

This book tells the story of Arizona's economic and political incorporation into the U.S. nation-state and of the ways in which race and ethnicity shaped labor markets, defined citizenship criteria, and inscribed national boundaries. This story is told from two interrelated perspectives. First, I explore how government officials, regional and national elites, and Euro-Americans attempted to comprehend and impose order on the indigenous and ethnic Mexican population beginning in the late nineteenth century by drawing boundaries of race, class, and citizenship. Before Arizona became a state, government officials struggled to integrate these populations into the developing industrial and extractive economy primarily as wageworkers. They would regulate their mobility and cultural development, promote assimilation or build and maintain hierarchical racial boundaries, and delineate who would or would not have access to full and equal citizenship.

Second, I examine how people of indigenous and Mexican descent struggled to maintain control of their own cultures and daily lives. As they interacted with one another, with the developing capitalist economy, and with the state, they created new institutions and practices that became the basis for challenging their exclusion from as well as their absorption into a monolithic national culture. These responses are best understood not as wholesale assimilation or resistance, but rather as resistant adaptation. As recent scholars have used the term, *resistant adaptation* refers to the unanticipated, resilient, and sometimes defiant ways in which people adapt to impositions by those in power.[13]

These two processes—classification by the Euro-American majority and resistant adaptation by subordinated peoples—were inextricably linked. Over time, ethnic identity took shape according to internal cultural factors such as language and religion and according to the differential relationships that various groups formed with one another, with the national economy, and with the nation-state. What made someone Mexican rather than Indian or white/Anglo, rather than nonwhite, evolved out of cross-ethnic interaction and stratification within the same, developing political and economic contexts.

To clarify this argument, it is necessary to define more precisely some of the key concepts and terms used in this book, beginning with *race*. Michael Omi and Howard Winant's definition is particularly salient: "*Race is a concept which signifies and symbolizes social conflicts and interests by referring to different types of human bodies.* Although the concept invokes biologically based human characteristics (so-called 'phenotypes'), selection of these particular human features for purposes of racial signification is always and necessarily a social and historical process" (emphasis added). Omi and Winant refer to this process as "racial formation." As Stuart Hall has argued, racial formation is also a hegemonic process in which, over time, racial categories become ingrained as "common sense" among those who use them—even those who have been racially classified. Still, such categories are always susceptible to challenges from below, so they are always unstable. They continually emerge, are redefined, or erode through historical processes of classification, oppression, resistant adaptation, and negotiation.[14]

Like race, *ethnicity* should be understood as a product of history, not simply as the static remnant of a primordial past. This is not to suggest, however, that ethnicity has no real content or that it is merely a "nexus of relations and transactions actively engaging a subject," as James Clifford has claimed. Rather, ethnicity must also be understood as a "mode of consciousness." This conception of ethnicity is strongly influenced by the work of Jean and John Comaroff. They argue that while ethnicity "has its origins in the asymmetric incorporation of structurally dissimilar groupings into a single political economy," it is also deeply felt. Ethnic identity is never static, but rather changes through time in a "dialectical relationship with the structures that underlie it: once ethnicity impinges upon experience as an (apparently) independent principle of social classification and organization, it provides a powerful motivation for collective activity." Ethnicity is different from race in that it is not necessarily linked to phenotype and it generally develops as a way for groups to define *themselves* in relation to those around them, rather than primarily as a way to impose control over others through the restriction of rights and privileges.[15]

As the Comaroffs' definition of ethnicity suggests, examining the process of racial and ethnic identity formation requires an understanding of the broader workings of political economy. Throughout this book *political economy* refers to the intersection between the forces of economy and government; more precisely, it is the economic milieu constructed largely by political processes, state institutions, and policies. It is a crucial concept because it implies that the economy does not simply develop naturally over time but through the explicit interventions of political actors and the state.

In Arizona the state played an enormous role in shaping the regional economy and in determining how certain groups would fit within it (i.e., as employers, property holders, wageworkers, or wards). I trace the evolution of Arizona's political economy over the course of a century, during which several state interventions stand out. In the 1870s and 1880s, government land grants to the railroads and subsidies to miners facilitated the first phase of modern industrial development, primarily in mining and agriculture. Simultaneously, the federal government helped to determine patterns of landholding through the reservation system, the Homestead Act, the Desert Lands Act, and the Dawes General Allotment Act.

In the twentieth century, the state continued to influence the character of the political economy. Most important for south-central Arizona was the Newlands Reclamation Act passed by Congress in 1902. It provided federal financing and a set of regulations for the construction of massive reclamation projects that fundamentally transformed south-central Arizona's desert ecology, economy, and social structure. During the Great Depression, federal New Deal programs dramatically impacted the economy, organizing the labor of thousands of Arizona residents—Anglo, indigenous, and ethnic Mexican alike—to further alter the region's infrastructure, ecology, and social structure. During and after World War II, government contracts attracted high-tech manufacturing firms to the region, resulting in unprecedented demographic and urban growth and laying the groundwork for the manufacturing and service economy to supersede the old extractive economy. Even as this new economy developed, however, agricultural production peaked in the 1950s, while the federal government continued to fuel its growth by recruiting Indians and importing thousands of Mexican braceros to work in the fields.

This book focuses on four contiguous counties that collectively experienced Arizona's most dramatic economic development and population growth from 1880 to 1980: Maricopa, Pima, Pinal, and Santa Cruz. In the late nineteenth and early twentieth centuries, copper was the backbone of Arizona's regional economy. By 1929, in fact, Arizona provided more than half of all copper purchased within the United States.[16] What truly differentiated the south-central Arizona counties from the rest of the state, however, was industrial agriculture. Indeed, it was the demand for farmworkers that drew the most immigrants from Mexico to settle in Arizona after 1910. In 1911 the completion of the Roosevelt Dam—among the first major reclamation projects built under the Reclamation Act—spurred the growth of a vast agricultural industry.[17] By 1920 the yearly harvest of Pima cotton, an extralong staple hybrid designed to be grown in the desert Southwest, reached about two hundred thousand acres, covering 70 percent of all irrigated lands.[18] Growers also planted everything from short-staple cotton to

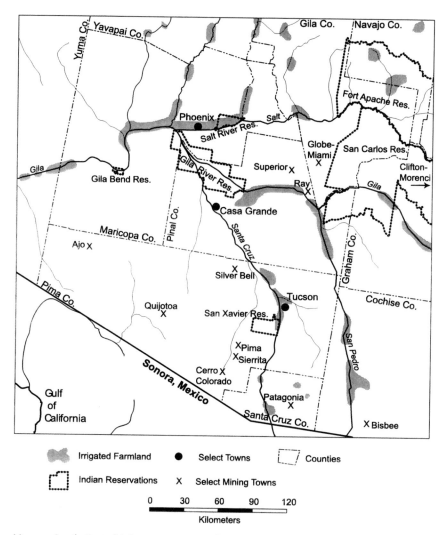

Map 0.1. South-Central Arizona, ca. 1900, with Mining Towns

alfalfa, citrus, and melons. With the completion of numerous other dams, a second major reclamation project in 1928 on the Gila River (the San Carlos Project/Coolidge Dam), and the installment of hundreds of groundwater pumps, Arizona's industrialized agricultural region eventually stretched from the Salt River valley (Maricopa County), into the Casa Grande valley (Pinal County), and along the Santa Cruz River into the vicinity of Tucson (Pima and Santa Cruz counties).[19]

South-central Arizona, because it is adjacent to Mexico, is also a fertile

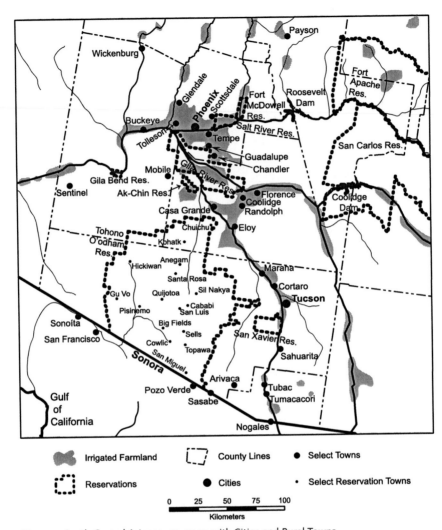

Map 0.2. South-Central Arizona, ca. 1940, with Cities and Rural Towns

site for exploring the production of racial, ethnic, and national boundaries. In many respects the boundaries of the nation-state are the most tangible and the most contested at its territorial borders. Physically, the U.S.-Mexico border has been marked by fences and enforcement mechanisms such as the Border Patrol. In a broader sense it has been an especially important site of cultural conflict through, for example, battles over immigration, language, and education. Throughout Arizona's history, this process would remain contested and incomplete, as a transborder regional community defied the efforts of the United States to promote a homogeneous national culture and enforce strict territorial and racial boundaries.[20]

Because ethnic and racial boundaries were so intricately linked to the construction of the nation, it is important to clarify the meaning of the term *nation*. Throughout this book the word refers to a cultural body that is, to quote two recent theorists, "in a perpetual condition of becoming."[21] While I use *state* to refer to the tangible institutions and bureaucracies that make up the federal and state governments, I view the nation as much more diffuse. It is, to use Benedict Anderson's classic formulation, an "imagined community" constructed both by state officials and the citizenry.[22] The nation-state's power consists in its ability to rule, regulate, and enforce, and to delineate cultural and social borders. Anderson is concerned with how elites and state officials construct the nation through printed media. I focus on how the meaning of the nation and the power of the state are contested by subordinated and marginalized peoples, often at the level of personal and community identity.

Just as it is necessary to distinguish between the state and the nation, it is helpful to differentiate between two forms of citizenship—one legal, one cultural. At one level, citizenship is a legal relationship between individuals and the state. The Anglo, ethnic Mexican, and indigenous populations of south-central Arizona each had a distinct and evolving legal status. Throughout the twentieth century, for example, unnaturalized Mexican nationals had no citizenship rights. They could not vote or sit on juries and could be physically removed from the country at the will of the U.S. government (as they were en masse in the 1930s and 1950s). Before 1924 most Arizona Indians were not citizens but had a special status as wards of the state. In that year the Indian Citizenship Act altered this relationship by recognizing all American Indians as citizens. Congress, however, left the specifics up to the states, permitting other restrictions on full membership in the body politic to remain in force.[23] In Arizona the 1912 state constitution specified that "no person under guardianship shall be qualified to vote in any election." Arizona's courts consistently applied this restriction to the indigenous population, although the line between who was and who was not Indian was not always clear. Until the Supreme Court struck it down in 1948, the Arizona law enforced the notion that Indians, as long as they remained dependent on the state, were not yet ready for full and equal citizenship.[24]

The residents of south-central Arizona also had changing cultural relationships with the United States. Recently, some scholars have begun to refer to these relationships as *cultural citizenship*. Renato Rosaldo and

William V. Flores have offered the simplest definition, writing that it refers to "distinctions in senses of belonging, entitlement, and influence that vary in distinct situations and in different local communities." In a sense, cultural citizenship is to the nation what legal citizenship is to the state. For example, while ethnic Mexicans and Indians have had distinct sets of political and civil rights as legal citizens (voting, serving on juries, etc.), they have also had distinct social and cultural relationships to the nation. Euro-Americans have variously regarded these groups as "savages" and/or foils to U.S. expansion, as aliens, as marginal to mainstream American culture, as wards or, more recently, as members of a diverse, culturally inclusive nation. And yet these groups have also struggled to define *their own* relationship to the nation, sometimes stressing their status as the original inhabitants of the region, sometimes as American citizens, and sometimes as members of their own, separate nations.

The meaning of cultural citizenship thus changes as people struggle to maintain, as Rosaldo and Flores have put it, their "right to be different (in terms of race, ethnicity, or native language) with respect to the norms of the dominant national community, without compromising [their] right to belong, in the sense of participating in the nation-state's democratic processes." The concept of cultural citizenship thus permits an examination of how different groups of people participated in the construction of their own identities while defining what it meant to belong to the nation in cultural terms. It also permits an exploration of how the meaning of citizenship evolved over time, and how it varied for different groups.[25]

In Arizona's borderlands, the project of nation building—incorporating the region economically and politically into the United States while defining the cultural and racial boundaries of full citizenship—became problematic just as the region entered a stage of rapid capitalist development through mining and reclamation and of political maturation through statehood in 1912. While expanding extractive industries demanded foreign labor, Euro-Americans in Arizona struggled to project an image of themselves as progressive, educated, and fully American—which usually meant being fully *white*—to the rest of the nation.[26]

This image was particularly important around the turn of the century, when regional elites engaged in a protracted struggle to shed Arizona's territorial status and gain admission as a state. One possible resolution to the problem presented by a large nonwhite population was to regulate immigration. Anglo employers and state officials did not want to shut off immigration entirely, since foreign labor was necessary for economic development. Instead, they attempted to manage immigration through legislation that was often contradictory. During debates over statehood, some sectors of Arizona's population pressed for a variety of anti-immigrant measures, including laws that would limit the number of immigrants who could work in hazardous occupations such as mining. Repeatedly, however, business interests—the cotton growers in Arizona were among the most vocal—defeated such legislation and secured exemptions from immigration restrictions for Latinos.[27]

Regulating immigration did nothing to address the problem of how to incorporate naturalized immigrants or indigenous peoples into the nation-state. In these cases, government officials and much of the Euro-American citizenry tried to ensure that the limits of full citizenship were maintained along lines of race and culture. Those who were perceived to have the potential to become fully assimilated were often coerced, particularly in the decades around the turn of the century. State and religious officials pursued this goal through, for example, Americanization programs and forced assimilation, boarding schools, and the banning of certain cultural practices.[28] Legislation and legal interpretations denied full citizenship to Arizona's indigenous population indefinitely.

The combined weight of restrictive immigration policy, racial segregation, and limits on citizenship relegated much of south-central Arizona's population to a second-class status. Groups such as the Yaquis, Tohono O'odham, and ethnic Mexicans became "border citizens"—people whose rights of belonging were in question, leaving them on the margins of the national territory and of American society and culture. Throughout the twentieth century, however, these groups would challenge the economic, political, and cultural boundaries that were being constructed around them, sometimes in cooperation with and sometimes in conflict with each other. They were "border citizens" both because of restrictions imposed on them and because they were redefining what it meant to belong to the U.S. nation-state from its borderlands. In the process they helped to redefine what it meant to be Mexican, Indian, and Anglo.

The relationships that these groups formed with one other and with the political economy substantially influenced how they identified themselves over time. Yaquis came to inhabit a liminal cultural and political space between two nations and between their status as Mexican and Indian. They lived and worked alongside ethnic Mexicans, shared their precarious legal status, and often spoke Spanish, while they shared close cultural and economic connections to indigenous groups in the region and were viewed as American Indians by most Anglo-Americans. Over decades these circumstances spawned tensions among the Yaquis themselves, especially between those who hoped to gain official legal status as American Indians and those who felt such a status would mean a *loss* of cultural independence and self-determination. Many of the latter built upon their interethnic ties and transnational culture to challenge existing ethnic boundaries and the cultural definitions of U.S. citizenship.

The Tohono O'odham also skirted national, racial, and ethnic boundaries, but in their own way. In 1854 the Tohono O'odham territory was split in half by the Gadsden Purchase/Mesilla treaty, the purchase by the United States of the territory that is now southern Arizona and Southwestern New Mexico. By the turn of the century, the vast majority of Tohono O'odham lived north of the border. Like the Yaquis, many spoke Spanish, worked together with ethnic Mexicans, and married across ethnic lines. The U.S. government, however, defined the Tohono O'odham, unlike the Yaquis, as American Indians, recognizing part of their homeland with reservations and subjecting them to distinct government policies. Over time, entanglement with federal bureaucracies such as the Bureau of Indian Affairs seriously affected their sense of themselves as a people.

Yet, Tohono O'odham fortunes were not solely determined from without. The Tohono O'odham found ways to manipulate their unique situation, building upon emerging tribal institutions to confront the hegemony of a monolithic U.S. nation-state, assert their rights as citizens and indigenous people, defend their economic interests, and express their cultural and political identities. In the process, old forms of village government by patriarchal consensus broke down, and women began to take an expanding role in government. They eventually challenged the validity of the geopolitical border itself, demanding that O'odham on both sides of the border be recognized, first and foremost, as citizens of the Tohono O'odham nation.[29]

Like "Mexican" and "Indian", "whiteness" was a fuzzy concept in the decades around the turn of the twentieth century. As historians such as Matthew Frye Jacobson, Linda Gordon, David Roediger, and Neil Foley have shown, the boundaries of whiteness were under constant negotiation, especially as immigrants from Mexico and Europe flooded into the United States. Italian, Spanish, and Slavic immigrants in Arizona fought to ensure that they would be counted as respectable white citizens in part by joining Anglo-Americans in their struggle to define Mexican immigrants as nonwhite aliens. In the 1930s the presence of a new class of Anglo migrants from the southern plains again challenged established boundaries between white and nonwhite. Since the so-called Okies often worked the same jobs and lived in the same labor camps as ethnic Mexican and indigenous workers, many Arizonans perceived them to be naturally inferior and not quite fully white. The concept of whiteness, then, was not monolithic. Its boundaries were periodically challenged or solidified in relation to evolving definitions of national citizenship.[30]

To reflect these shifts, I use several terms to refer to people of European descent. In the first four chapters, covering the period up to the 1930s, I use *Anglo* or *white* to refer only to those people who had adopted such an identity and whom others generally referred to with such terms. I use *Euro-American* to refer to people of European descent (excluding Mexicans), some of whom had been accepted as fully white, and others—like Italians and Slavs—who had not. For the post–World War II era, when sharp distinctions between different groups of European Americans subsided, I use Anglo and white to refer to a broader group of people, reflecting the fact that southern and eastern Europeans had generally been accepted as white.

Many Mexican Americans also made claims to whiteness. Armed with provisions in the Treaty of Guadalupe Hidalgo that guaranteed their access to U.S. citizenship and the weapon of legal (if not social or cultural) classification as white, Mexican Americans often challenged segregation and political and economic discrimination by struggling to gain acceptance as patriotic American citizens. At the same time, many Mexican Americans and Mexican nationals, the latter lacking legal citizenship, struggled to hold onto their own cultural traditions, joining *mutualistas* (mutual aid societies), labor unions, or other organizations to resist their subordination. In the 1960s and '70s, many Mexican Americans would assert an emerging ethnic identity as Chicano and embrace their indigenous heritage as a basis for empowerment rather than racial degradation. At different times and in different circumstances, then, they manipulated, sought inclusion within, or confronted existing standards of national belonging.[31]

To reflect the differing identities and legal statuses of people of Mexican descent, I reserve *Mexican American* for those with U.S. citizenship and *Mexican* for Mexican nationals. I use *ethnic Mexican* to refer to both groups collectively. At times I also use *mestizo* to emphasize the difference between those who identified with a specific indigenous group and those, most of them of mixed European and indigenous heritage, who no longer did so. I employ the term *Hispanic* only when making reference to external classification systems like the U.S. census, and *Spanish American* only when discussing either immigrants from Spain or individuals of Mexican descent who claimed to be Spanish largely as a means to claim whiteness. While even these terms do not adequately capture the diversity of the population, they at least provide a way to analyze the complexity of ethnic Mexican identity, and to distinguish between people lumped together too often by the national and racial designation of Mexican.

The diverse border citizens of south-central Arizona actively struggled to define their own identities. But the process of self-identification was deeply entangled with racial ideologies and government policies designed to construct their identities and their place in the nation for them. Ethnic and national identities were never autonomous; they were relational and historically contingent. The racial, economic, and political boundaries these groups faced, and the network of relations they formed with one another, played an extremely important role in shaping both their identities and their belonging to the nation-state. As they struggled to protect their own interests, their actions altered the blueprint drawn up by government officials and members of the Anglo majority for their assimilation and/or exclusion. Building upon a century of resistant adaptation, they would eventually alter the cultural meaning of citizenship, and the meaning of national belonging. By examining this process holistically we can begin to understand how and why certain groups were seen or came to see themselves as Mexican, Indian, or Anglo, or as having some other identity altogether.

▼ ▼ ▼ ▼ ▼ ▼ ▼ ▼ ▼ ▼ ▼ ▼ ▼ ▼ ▼ ▼ ▼ ▼

CHAPTER 1

DESERT EMPIRE

Shortly after the Mesilla Treaty (also called the Gadsden Purchase) transferred what would become southern Arizona from Mexico to the United States in the mid-1850s, hundreds of Americans moved into the territory to improve their fortunes.[1] Among them was Sylvester Mowry, a lieutenant in the army. Mowry was stationed at Fort Yuma when he began to dream about the potential that the new territory held for would-be entrepreneurs like himself. After resigning his commission in 1858, he began to prospect for gold and silver. He also served as a special commissioner in the Bureau of Indian Affairs (BIA),[2] with instructions to report on the region's indigenous peoples. In this capacity, he began to map and classify material resources and human inhabitants according to their value to U.S. interests and their potential for citizenship.[3]

As Benedict Anderson has argued, colonial states in the nineteenth and twentieth centuries imposed their rule in part by such mapping and classifying practices. They did so in an attempt to comprehend "the nature of the human beings [they] ruled, the geography of [their] domain, and the legitimacy of [their] ancestry." Census takers held onto the "fiction" that "everyone has one—and only one—extremely clear place," and therefore that people could not tolerate "multiple, politically 'transvestite,' blurred, or changing identifications."[4] James Scott has expanded on Anderson's argument, demonstrating that states in the twentieth century also attempted to create a "standard grid" to "monitor" populations and resources within their own borders. In the process, they often developed oppressive policies to regulate and transform indigenous social relationships and clarify the relationship of various groups to the state.[5]

Mowry's effort to map Arizona's geography and population exemplifies this process. As he surveyed the region, the peoples who seemed most similar to his own won highest honors. He described the Pimas (the Akimel O'odham, or "river people") along the Gila River as "a brave and hospitable race—they live in villages and cultivate the arts of peace. Their regular fields, well-made irrigating ditches, and beautiful crops of cotton, wheat, corn, pumpkins, melons, and beans have not only gladdened the eye, but also given the timely assistance to the thousands of emigrants who have traversed Arizona on their way to the Pacific." He had similar praises for the Maricopas, a smaller group who had moved from the Colorado River centuries earlier and had settled near the Pimas, adopting many of their economic and cultural practices.[6]

He judged the Papagos (today they prefer to be called the Tohono O'odham, or "desert people") who were closely related to the Pimas, to be "inferior to the Pimos [sic]" because they "do not cultivate so much, and live in scattered villages in the Central and Western parts of the Territory." For the nomadic Apaches he expressed only opprobrium: "They are best compared to the prairie wolf, sneaking, cowardly, revengeful, quick to assassinate the weak, and to fly from or yield to the strong." It seemed impossible that Apaches would ever become independent farmers or workers, and he saw only two options for them: "They must be fed by the Government, or exterminated."[7]

Mowry also suggested that certain groups—such as the Yaquis and Opatas in Sonora—were more naturally suited for manual labor than others. Mowry purchased a mine in the Patagonia Mountains, just north of the new international border, which supported four hundred workers by 1862.[8] He wrote that the full potential of Arizona and Sonora had yet to be tapped, from the Salt River valley in central Arizona to the Yaqui River delta in southwestern Sonora, where indigenous and mestizo farmers grew wheat, maize, beans, squash, peas, and cane. To exploit these resources, labor would be provided by those peoples who had proven themselves, in Mowry's eyes, to be "cheap, and under proper management, efficient and permanent" workers: "My own experience has taught me that the lower class of Mexicans, with the Opata and Yaqui Indians, are docile, faithful, good servants, capable of strong attachments when firmly and kindly treated. They have been 'peons' for generations. They will always remain so, as it is their natural condition."[9]

At least two other scholars have quoted Mowry to argue that by the 1860s Anglos in Arizona already viewed Mexicans and Indians in strict racial terms that justified their subordination.[10] Indeed, Euro-Americans moving into the territory already tended to view the existing regional population as inferior. By taking Mowry's words out of context and by neglecting to emphasize that he characterized each group differently, these scholars imposed a biracial model onto a much more complex process of racial formation. In fact, like other travelers to the region, Mowry was careful *not* to lump all of Arizona's indigenous and Mexican inhabitants together. His respect for the Pimas, for example, because their farms were productive and they had helped in the fight against the Apaches, led him to condemn the government's failings in its dealings with them. He singled out "lower-class" Mexicans, Yaquis, and Opatas as naturally inferior, and thus as ideal workers.[11]

It is misleading, therefore, to suggest a clear racial order among monolithic groups labeled Anglo, Mexican, and Indian in the early territorial period. Mowry drew careful distinctions between the different mestizo and indigenous populations. Neither could the regional Euro-American elite be accurately defined as Anglo. Some of Arizona's mine owners and other economic elites were of German, eastern European, and/or Jewish ancestry. Ethnic Mexicans were also divided along lines of culture, national citizenship, and class. Tucson, which was the largest town in Arizona at the time of the Gadsden Purchase, remained, in the words of one historian, "a haven for upper- and middle-class Mexican society in the southwestern United States."[12] At least through the 1870s, ethnic Mexicans who had earned their fortunes through ranching, freighting, and mining maintained substantial influence in local and territorial politics. This political power would be chipped away in subsequent decades, but at least until 1880, while the people of the region spoke of "cultivated" versus "lower-class Mexicans" and "peon," "savage," or "industrious and independent" Indians, these classifications had not become a strict racial divide.[13]

This chapter examines why and how permeable racial lines began to close up during the half century that constituted Arizona's territorial period—particularly after 1880, as the pace of economic development accelerated. Emerging boundaries of race, class, culture, and language would determine who would have access to resources, who could work where, who could join craft unions, who would be accepted as first- or second-class citizens, and who would be excluded from citizenship altogether. Some, like the Chiricahua Apaches, would be banished from the territory. Other groups would find ways to survive in Arizona. By the time Arizona became a state in 1912, those survivors would develop a variety of relationships with the U.S. nation-state, as defined in part by the perceptions of elites such as Mowry but also by their own cultural patterns and strategies of resistant adaptation.

DESERT PEOPLES

When the region that would become Arizona was acquired by the United States, most of its territory remained under indigenous control. After decades of neglect by the newly independent nation of Mexico and renewed raids and resistance from the Apaches, only about one thousand Mexicans remained in the area, most of them in Tucson and on ranches along the Santa Cruz River. The lives and identities of the regional population were in a state of constant flux, defying the neat classifications made by Euro-Americans like Mowry. Groups traded with one another, adopted certain cultural practices from one another, raided and warred against one another, or engaged in all of these practices simultaneously. As incorporation into the U.S. nation-state proceeded and a new industrial economy began to develop, the rate of cultural change would accelerate—but it is important to recognize that cultural adaptation had been occurring continuously for centuries.[14]

As Mowry noted, the border between Arizona and Sonora was all but meaningless in terms of ecology and culture in the late nineteenth century. Most of south-central Arizona and central-western Sonora make up a distinct and uniform ecological zone called the Sonoran desert. While *desert* brings to mind, for many, the image of a wasteland, the Sonoran is an arboreal desert that includes a wide variety of grasses, shrubs, and low-growing trees, myriad forms of cacti, and diverse fauna. Its biological diversity is due largely to its low elevation and to heavy rains in the late summer and lighter rains in the winter when evaporation rates are low. This rich natural world allowed the Sonoran desert to become, according to one botanist, "by far the richest in number of life forms and in variety and development of communities" of the North American deserts.[15]

In the northern reaches of the Sonoran desert, in what is central Arizona, lie the basins created by the Salt and Gila rivers—rivers that once flowed freely out of the semiarid mountains to the east through the arid basins and intermittent mountain ranges of the desert, eventually merging with the Colorado River and the Gulf of California. Farther south, in Sonora, several rivers flowed out of the Sierra Madre Occidental and cut across the state, running generally southwest toward the Gulf of California.

While the semiarid mountainous regions to the east contain small patches of flat, irrigable land, the arid deserts of the central and western regions of both states are interrupted by rich alluvial floodplains and river deltas. Historically, most desert streams were dry for much of the year, carrying water only intermittently during heavy summer downpours. As one

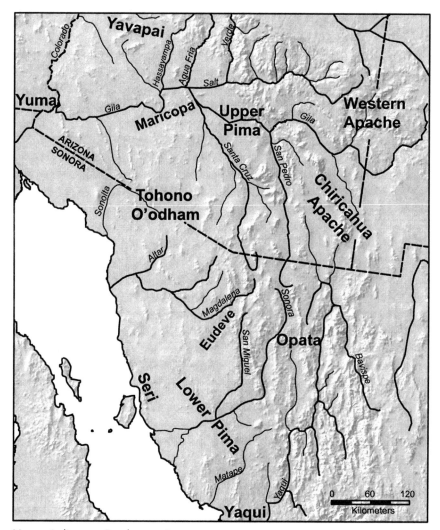

Map 1.1. Indigenous Peoples, ca. 1854

botanist explains, "fresh water has always been at a premium in western Sonora." Water could be found in natural and man-made water holes, or *charcos*, and in mountain springs.[16]

The diverse flora and fauna have provided food and building materials for the region's inhabitants for many centuries. The ubiquitous mesquite tree produces pods rich in protein and carbohydrates that can be used to make breads and porridges. Desert peoples collected cactus fruit, such as the *pitahaya*, and the agave plant for its leaves and edible heart. For over a thousand years they used the fibers of the yucca plant to weave fine baskets for storage. Durable ironwood was ideal for crafting utensils, and the trunks of other trees, such as the mesquite, were used to construct family dwellings. They hunted large and small game, including mule deer, white-tailed deer, pronghorn antelope, bighorn sheep, javelinas, and jackrabbits. They used the animals for both their meat and hides, using the skins to make shoes, sleeping mats, and other items.[17]

When Jesuits established missions in Sonora in the seventeenth century, one of the groups they came across were the O'odham, who lived in villages and *rancherías* stretching from the Gila River for approximately one thousand miles to the south. The O'odham language is a part of the Uto-Aztecan family, which includes Nahuatl, the language of the Aztecs.[18] O'odham speakers came from widely varying cultures, ranging from the seminomadic Hia C'ed O'odham of the extremely arid region northeast of the Gulf of California to the sedentary agriculturalists known as the Akimel O'odham or Pimas living along the banks of the Gila and other rivers. Distinct group identities were discernible through variations in regional dialects, economic practices, and cultures, but any notion of a tribal political entity was foreign to the O'odham. Villages and scattered rancherías were largely autonomous political units, with temporary unions formed only in times of war or for intervillage meetings. Residents of each ranchería were related by kinship. Councils of village men made decisions by consensus about when to plant and harvest, hunt, engage in war, or practice a variety of seasonal rituals. These councils were loosely led by individuals called keepers who retained their power only as long as they earned the respect of their communities.[19]

Two centuries of Spanish colonial settlement affected groups of O'odham differently, creating further cultural divisions among an already diverse people. In the late seventeenth and early eighteenth centuries, the Jesuit Eusebio Francisco Kino established missions among the O'odham who lived along the Magdalena and Altar rivers, in present-day Sonora, and among a group of O'odham known as Sobaipuris along the Santa Cruz River in present-day Arizona. These included the missions at San Xavier, Guévavi, and Tumacácori. Over time, the O'odham nearest the missions and Spanish settlements adopted certain Spanish linguistic traits, crops (such as wheat), and livestock. They also merged indigenous religious practices with Catholic practices, helping to create a distinct brand of folk Catholicism. Some of the villages adopted political offices introduced by the Spanish, such as the *gobernador* (village-level governor). *Gobernadores* came to rival or even replace the keepers and served as intermediaries between O'odham villages and the Spanish government. Unfortunately, Spaniards also introduced devastating diseases which disrupted many of the old villages and spurred new migrations. Over time, this process created a broad cultural division between the more Hispanicized O'odham to the south and along the Santa Cruz River and the relatively isolated O'odham to the north and west. This new division would remain important well into the twentieth century.[20]

The northernmost O'odham, who remained outside of areas of Spanish colonization altogether, were the Akimel O'odham or Pimas, who lived along the Gila River and its tributaries. They were among the most sedentary O'odham, building diversion dams of mud, logs, and brush, and distributing water to their fields using networks of canals and ditches. The Pima river settlements were larger and more permanent and had greater and more reliable supplies of food and water than those of the semisedentary and nomadic O'odham, who lived in the open desert or along ephemeral desert streams. The Pimas also required less hunting and gathering and thus had more leisure time and specialized in trades more than did their desert cousins. They grew cotton, wove cotton clothing, and made ornaments of imported turquoise and shell.[21]

South of the Gila River, the O'odham retained a variety of other cultural patterns as they interacted to greater or lesser degrees with Spaniards and mestizos. The Sobaipuri, who lived in or near the missions along the Santa Cruz River, found themselves in the worst position, serving as a buffer between Spanish settlers and Apache peoples who moved south into the region after the mid-seventeenth century. The Apaches came into conflict with both mestizo settlers and the O'odham, leading to a state of open warfare. By the late eighteenth century, a combination of disease, Apache raiding, and warfare had decimated the Sobaipuri villages.[22]

Further to the west, however, groups who were not as sedentary, such as the Tohono O'odham, fared much better. Historically, the Tohono O'odham were semisedentary farmers and hunters. In the late summer they took advantage of storms to raise crops of corn, tepary beans, squash, and cotton in the floodplains of ephemeral desert streams—a type of farming they referred to as *ak chin*. Once they harvested these crops, they would migrate either to villages near mountain springs for the winter or live among more sedentary O'odham, such as the Pimas along the Gila River or the Sobaipuri along the Santa Cruz. Tohono O'odham men supplemented agriculture with hunting, and women supplemented it with the gathering of seeds and cactus fruit. Ultimately, the Tohono O'odham living in what is now southern Arizona were much more successful at preserving aspects of their indigenous ways of life—which they called the *Himdag*—than either the O'odham farther to the south or the Sobaipuris to the east.[23]

A linguistically unrelated group called the Maricopas lived just to the west of the Pimas along the Gila River. The Maricopas were Yuma speakers who had migrated from the Colorado River not long before Spaniards arrived in the region. As early as the 1690s, as Eusebio Kino made his first *entradas* into the Sonoran desert, he made contact with "Opas and Coco-Maricopas" who lived near the Pimas. Opa and Coco-Maricopa were probably Piman terms for these newcomers. As anthropologist Paul Ezell suggests, "It is more than probable that the Yuman peoples did not regard, until very late in historic times if then, the Piman names as their proper appellatives."[24] It was only in relation to other ethnic groups that identities such as Maricopa were established.

Even farther to the south, in what is today Sonora, Mexico, the influence of Spanish and Mexican culture was much greater than among the indigenous peoples of what would become south-central Arizona. By the end of the seventeenth century, the Opatas and Eudeves of central Sonora found themselves in the midst of a new mining frontier, and by the middle of the eighteenth century, silver, gold, and lead attracted mestizo settlers to the region. Edward Spicer suggests that by this time "no important part of Eudeve and Opata territory was without Spanish inhabitants." Both of these groups intermarried with mestizos with greater frequency than did the O'odham to the north, and they accepted Christianity in greater numbers. While certain segments of the Opata population would revolt periodically, by the nineteenth century many worked for wages and increasingly came to recognize (if not to fully accept) the political authority of the regional and town governments.[25]

To the west of the Opatas, in the fertile Yaqui and Mayo river valleys of southwestern Sonora, lived Cahitan-speaking peoples, thousands of whom would migrate north into Arizona during the upheavals of the late nineteenth century. They became known in Spanish and Mexican accounts as the Mayo and Yaqui Indians. Their location away from the primary areas of European and mestizo settlement allowed them to control their interaction with the incoming colonists to a greater degree than the Opatas and Eudeves could. Yaquis and Mayos lived on scattered rancherías in the floodplains, hunting, growing crops, weaving native-grown cotton, producing baskets and pottery, and engaging in limited trade. Their language, also a part of the Uto-Aztecan language family, was related to O'odham, but the two were not mutually intelligible.[26]

After initially fending off Spanish incursions in the sixteenth century,

Yaquis accepted Jesuit missionaries between 1614 and 1617, probably to find an alternative to the impending threat of further military attacks and slave raids. Traditionally, the Yaquis lacked both a full-time, professional priesthood and a permanent tribal political body, and village councils made decisions for their individual communities through consensus. The Jesuits, however, introduced baptism and pressured the Yaquis to construct denser pueblos than the traditional rancherías. New villages emerged, each arranged around a Catholic mission. Simultaneously, new civil officials such as the Jesuit-appointed *gobernador* rivaled the old councils. For the Yaquis and Mayos, then, the process of *reducción* (concentration into mission communities) was more complete by the nineteenth century than it was among the Tohono O'odham and the Akimel O'odham living on the Gila River.[27]

Consequently, Yaquis and Mayos became entangled in the expanding market and wage economy more quickly than did the Tohono O'odham and Pimas. The Jesuits instructed the Yaquis in the construction of a system of dams and canals and introduced the practice of long-term storage and marketing of their surplus harvest. As early as 1645, Yaqui men began to leave the pueblos temporarily to work in the Sierra Madre mines, using their earnings to purchase horses, clothing, and other items. By the eighteenth century, miners, *hacendados* (owners of haciendas), and Jesuits competed for Yaqui labor. The Yaquis took advantage of these competing interests by engaging in what Evelyn Hu-DeHart has termed "rotational migration" between villages, missions, and mines. Yaqui men engaged in temporary stints away from the mission pueblos while the women and children, for the most part, remained in the villages.[28]

In an unusual reversal of the colonial process, the Yaquis briefly gained more autonomy in the late eighteenth century when the Spanish crown expelled the Jesuits from its empire. In their absence, Spanish-introduced civil and religious offices continued to evolve. Ironically, a colonial system initially intended to promote cultural assimilation had the opposite effect, as the new civil and political institutions brought a greater sense of cohesion across village lines. The captain-general of the militia, for example, who presided over all of the Yaqui pueblos collectively, became increasingly powerful, while the responsibilities of the village *gobernadores* expanded to include the oversight of community plots and livestock. The growing sense of collective identity among the Yaquis and their determination to resist incursions onto their land would continue to frustrate Mexican *vecinos* (settlers or residents) and officials, prompting periodic rebellions throughout the nineteenth century and into the twentieth.[29]

In the three decades after Mexican independence in 1821, political turmoil led to the decline of Mexico's hold on the northern borderlands. In the territory that would become south-central Arizona, Apaches repeatedly undermined Mexican colonization efforts. As a result, between 1821 and 1848, the Mexican government approved only twelve relatively small land grants—far fewer than in the other northern borderland states and territories of Nuevo Mexico, Alta California, and Coahuila y Tejas. Over time, the recipients of these grants either sold some of their land or divided it among members of their extended families. By the time of the war between the United States and Mexico in 1846, there were ninety-eight ranches in the fertile land along the Santa Cruz River, many of which were periodically abandoned due to warfare with the Apaches.[30]

During the Mexican period the indigenous peoples of northern Sonora increased the intensity of their resistance to Mexican incursions. The declining military presence and a lack of resources to support the missions and peace camps led to new tensions between Mexican mestizos and Indians, particularly with respect to the Apaches, who were renewing their raids and resistance with vigor in the 1820s. The O'odham also rose up in the 1840s, gaining a degree of autonomy they had not enjoyed since the seventeenth century. Because of widespread hostilities, Mexican *vecinos* in what would become Arizona were periodically forced to abandon their ranches, and only a total of about one thousand non-Indian settlers lived near Tucson or along the Santa Cruz River. For the most part, the Arizona portion of the Mesilla tract, acquired with the Gadsden Purchase, remained in the hands of its diverse, indigenous peoples.[31]

A MINING AND RAILROAD EMPIRE

In the two decades after the Gadsden Purchase, a small class of Anglo, Euro-American, and Mexican-American elites came to dominate Arizona politically and economically. These elites often justified the subordination of their Mexican and Indian workers by claiming superiority because of their European or American heritage and their lighter skin. Sonoran Mexicans had long pointed to their Spanish heritage as a mark of their superiority. In fact, many Sonoran Mexicans who were actually the offspring of mixed marriages denied being so, claiming, as one historian has put it, to be "Spaniards from Europe" and "disdaining anyone who was not white." As the United States tightened its grip on the region through railroad construction and the industrialization of mining, and because of migration from states to the east, the economic and political power of the

Mexican elite would erode. In the process a somewhat more distinct racial divide would emerge.[32]

Partly because of diversity within the elite class, it would be inaccurate to suggest that there was a clear racial order between Anglos, Mexicans, and Indians before 1880. A small class of ethnic Mexicans shared with the growing Euro-American elite a high social status and a substantial degree of economic and political power well into Arizona's territorial period. As late as 1881 the Tucson city directory was careful to distinguish between classes of ethnic Mexicans and Indians. It stated that Barrio Libre, just south of central Tucson, was a "slum district" inhabited by "Papago Indians" and "lower-class Mexicans," and that it was not a suitable area for "cultivated Mexicans."[33]

Some Mexican Americans, like Estevan Ochoa, initially prospered because of the developing industrial economy and remained an important political force. Into the 1870s Ochoa and Mariano Samaniego largely controlled the freighting industry on both sides of the Arizona-Sonora border, while others made their fortunes ranching and as merchants. In 1870 Leopoldo Carrillo, a Sonorense (native Sonoran), was the wealthiest person in Tucson. Federico Ronstadt, the son of a German immigrant and a Mexican woman from a landholding Sonoran family, emigrated from Sonora in 1882 and founded a successful wagon-and-carriage business. This economic strength translated into political clout. In 1875 Tucson citizens by a vote of 187–40 elected Estevan Ochoa mayor.

Mexican-American involvement in territorial politics was less impressive but still significant. On the first Territorial Assembly of Arizona (1864), two of nine members were Mexican Americans—Francisco S. León of Tucson and José Mariá Redondo of Arizona City.[34]

Some of the elite investors who transformed Arizona into a mining empire were neither Anglo nor Mexican. One of the most important, Henry Lesinsky, was a Jew from central Europe. He had emigrated first to the Australian gold mines before eventually making his way to the United States. In Las Cruces he began building up his fortune by buying grain from Hispanic farmers and selling it to the U.S. government. He delivered mail and opened a store in Silver City before moving to Arizona. He soon established the Longfellow Copper Mining Company, hired a party of skilled Mexican miners, and founded the town of Clifton at the junction of Chase Creek and the San Francisco River in 1873.[35]

The first Euro-American mining entrepreneurs attempted to adopt the Mexican system of peonage. Until 1863 southern Arizona was still a part of the New Mexico territory, which had passed a bill legalizing peonage in

1851.[36] Charles Poston and Samuel Heintzelman, who organized the Sonora Mining and Exploring Company, were among the first to hire Mexican workers. In 1856 they paid a party of Mexican miners to help clear out some Spanish mine shafts near Tubac to explore for new silver veins. They soon operated two mines in the vicinity, which along with Mowry's Patagonia mine drew hundreds of Mexican workers from Sonora.[37] Poston initially purchased the laborers' debts from wealthy Sonoran *hacendados* and then employed the men in his mine. One traveler to the region commented that the *hacendados* sold "their peons—debts—and do not even take the trouble to notify the peons of the changes which has taken place in their condition, much less take into consideration their will and consent."[38]

Before 1880 the considerable agency of the ethnic Mexican and indigenous workers themselves prevented the formation of a strictly racialized class system. Many Mexicans worked only for brief periods in the mines before returning to their fields in Arizona and Sonora. They sometimes stole some of their employer's livestock as payment for their labor. If the mine owners or overseers attempted to subdue them, the result could be a violent confrontation. As a result, the practice of peonage was always unstable.[39] Legal peonage ended altogether when Congress passed a law in 1867 banning it.[40]

Some Tohono O'odham also worked in the mines, but because they retained vast territory, farms, and livestock, their lives were not circumscribed by their experiences as mine workers. In 1864 forty-two Tohono O'odham men worked at the Cerro Colorado mine. Indian agent John Walker indicated that Tohono O'odham men often sought employment wherever they could when the water dried up in their villages. Some went to Tubac "where they [had] the confidence of the Sonora Mining Company, and readily [found] employment," while others worked in various capacities in Tucson. Others worked at mines at Picacho, Fresnal, and Quijotoa. Poston, however, suggested that the O'odham "would not submit to the regimentation of the mines and were never any serious challenge to the Mexicans' almost complete monopoly of mine labor." The evidence suggests that the O'odham could have worked in greater numbers had they so desired. Poston's statement that the O'odham did not like the "regimentation" of mining and Walker's that they could "readily find employment" suggest that the O'odham *chose* to participate at a limited level in the developing wage economy.[41]

A lack of transportation to national markets kept mining operations small before 1880, and Lesinsky's mine at Clifton was no exception. Clifton, which was on territory recently captured from the Apaches, remained relatively small before 1880. Lesinsky responded by building his own narrow-gauge railway to carry unrefined ores to the reduction works, but throughout the 1870s, he never employed more than a few hundred miners. Only in 1877, after considerable lobbying by Arizona capitalists, did Lesinsky's future look brighter. That year, Estevan Ochoa sponsored a bill in the territorial assembly that granted the Southern Pacific Railroad a charter to build a route across the Arizona desert.[42]

The construction of the Southern Pacific and a new network of smaller railroads rapidly altered the economy and social structure of the Arizona borderlands, connecting regional mines to a transnational economy controlled largely by U.S. capitalists. In addition to the Southern Pacific, which traversed Arizona in 1880, several others connected the mines and smelters in Arizona and Sonora to national and international markets. These lines facilitated the movement of cattle, mining ore, and people back and forth across the border.[43]

Ironically, Ochoa's bill to bring the Southern Pacific to Arizona rendered freighting, which was his and many of the Mexican-American elites' most lucrative business, obsolete. The railroad thus accelerated the development of a more strictly defined, racialized class system in which Mexican nationals and Mexican Americans alike found themselves subordinated. By the latter 1880s, Mariano Samaniego was the only Spanish-surnamed individual remaining on the territorial assembly; by shortly after the turn of the century, there was no Mexican-American representation in territorial government. Some Mexican Americans, like Federico Ronstadt in Tucson, would preserve their relative affluence by finding ways to adapt (see Chapter 3), but the clear trend after 1880 was toward the erosion of their economic and political power.[44]

The development of highly industrialized and capitalized mining ventures also undermined the ability of Mexican and indigenous workers to negotiate the terms of their labor. Unlike Poston's and Mowry's early ventures, the new projects were characterized by a stricter, racialized class system. In the 1870s and early 1880s, Chinese immigrants provided most of the manual labor on the railroads. When the work was completed, some of them remained and were hired by mining companies, but a wave of nativist resentment over their arrival soon resulted in their expulsion.[45] The large copper companies began to utilize labor contractors, or *enganchadores*, who traveled into Mexico to sign up displaced Mexican peasants. The workers no longer emigrated solely from Sonora but also traveled up the Mexican Central Railroad to El Paso, and then over the Southern Pacific to the Arizona copper mines.[46] By the 1880s the railroads and copper companies imported their own skilled labor and managers from other U.S. states and from Europe, while ethnic Mexicans and Indians filled the lowest-paid, unskilled positions. As a result, in 1890 a journalist for the *Arizona Daily Citizen* could write that at Clifton, which had reached a population of two thousand, ethnic Mexicans and Indians were relegated to manual labor, and "all skilled workers are white."[47]

Still, even by the turn of the century, it would be inaccurate to characterize the racialized class structure in the mining towns as a binary system. According to a government study on immigration called the Dillingham Report, the workforce remained stratified between Irish- and Anglo-American citizens, southern and eastern European immigrants, ethnic Mexicans, and Indians. The complex nature of this racial hierarchy was apparent in the wage levels in the Clifton-Morenci-Metcalf mining district. There, in 1909, 94 percent of native-born workers whom the Dillingham commission identified as white earned $3.50 per day or more. What Canadian, English, German, and Irish immigrants earned was comparable with the wages of native-born, Euro-American workers. In stark contrast, 93 percent of Mexican-born workers earned between $1.50 and $2.50. According to historian James Kluger, two hundred Yaquis also worked at the mines by 1915. If this number is accurate, the Dillingham commission likely combined the Yaquis with ethnic Mexicans in its figures, making it impossible to compare wages between the two groups. In the middle of the wage hierarchy were Italian immigrants, 78 percent of whom earned between $2 and $3 (Figure 1.1). (The racial classification of eastern and southern Europeans is discussed in Chapter 4.)[48]

Wage stratification was not based simply on different skill levels but on race and nationality. Native-born and Canadian, English, German, and Irish employees described as miners and general laborers earned up to twice the wage of the ethnic Mexican workers in the same positions, and substantially more than Italians.[49] At the smelters at Clifton and Douglas, where much of Clifton-Morenci's copper was processed, the Dillingham Report explained that "the Mexicans are employed largely at common labor, but whether employed at this or at work of higher grade, most of which is done by native-born and north Europeans, they are paid, as a rule, lower wages than those received by 'white' laborers engaged in the same or similar kinds of work." Sixty-five percent of U.S.-born Mexican Americans earned less than $2.50 per day, while 85 percent of foreign-born western and northern Europeans earned $3 or more (Figure 1.1).[50] Racial classification, rather than nationality, language, or degree of skill, structured the wage hierarchy. Moreover, this was a multitiered rather than a binary or dual-wage system.

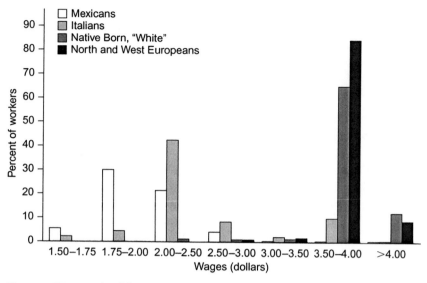

Figure 1.1. Wages at the Clifton-Morenci Mines, 1909. Source: Senate, *Reports of the Immigration Commission*, 61st Cong., 2d sess., 1911 (Washington, DC: Government Printing Office, 1974), 125–133.

Indigenous workers—a group almost wholly ignored by most historians of Arizona labor—were often relegated to the lowest-paid manual jobs, below southern Europeans and ethnic Mexicans alike. Such stratification occurred on both sides of the border. On Sonora's rail system, for example, according to an 1883 census, 810 Yaquis, 664 Mexicans, and 475 Euro-Americans made up the workforce. Even in Mexico, Euro-Americans held most of the skilled positions and office assignments, while most Mexicans worked in construction or as translators. Yaquis held only the lowest-paying jobs as track repairmen and construction workers.[51]

The subordinate status of indigenous workers was perhaps clearest at the Cornelia Copper Company's mines in Ajo, located within traditional Tohono O'odham lands near the border with Sonora. There, hundreds of Tohono O'odham men lived and worked under highly segregated conditions. The 1920 census lists the majority of "Papagos" at Ajo as general laborers in the copper plant, "Mexicans" as miners and mine laborers, and "whites" as skilled workers, managers, and foremen. As in other mining communities, the company maintained racial boundaries both in the mines and in town—not only between whites and nonwhites, but also between Indians and Mexicans. The O'odham were restricted to an area that became known as Ajo Indian village. Unlike in the Mexican section, the company did not even provide housing for the O'odham workers, justifying that practice by suggesting that the O'odham were ephemeral workers, wanting only to earn a little cash before returning to their own rancherías—a claim that will be interrogated in later chapters.[52]

AN AGRICULTURAL EMPIRE

Mowry's vision of an agricultural empire stretching from the Salt River in Arizona to the Yaqui and Mayo rivers in Sonora was slower to develop than the mining empire, but by 1880 it was well under way. U.S financing again largely fueled the transformation in both the United States and Mexico. In Arizona, agencies such as the Geological Survey, the Army Corps of Engineers, and the Reclamation Service (renamed the Bureau of Reclamation in 1923) determined where agricultural development would take place and who would benefit from it. Race played a significant role in these decisions. As large-scale irrigation projects led to the rise of mechanized commercial farms, many ethnic Mexican and indigenous farmers lost access to water through upriver diversions and erosion. Thousands would find themselves with little choice but to work for wages in the burgeoning mining industry, on the railroads, and on new commercial farms. By the first decade of the twentieth century, then, it became clear that agriculture in the transborder region would mirror, in many respects, the structure of the copper mines: large, capital-intensive farms would rely upon a mobile, racially stratified workforce to produce staple crops for market.[53]

Even with these substantial changes in Arizona's economy, many ethnic Mexicans held onto their lands well into the twentieth century. During the territorial period, the U.S. government confirmed as valid approximately one hundred thousand of the eight hundred thousand acres of land grants that had been made before the Gadsden Purchase, most of them along the Santa Cruz and San Pedro rivers.[54] Moreover, between 1875 and 1901, Hispanic-surnamed individuals—some of whom had roots in the region stretching as far back as the eighteenth century—received 259 patents for homesteads in the territory.[55]

On both sides of the border, ethnic Mexican landholders continued to practice traditional forms of open-range ranching and farming into the 1900s. Along the San Pedro and Santa Cruz rivers, members of extended families took possession of contiguous homesteads, often leaving the land unfenced, mingling their herds, and cooperating in yearly *corridas* (roundups). Longtime resident families included the Sozas, who owned fourteen homestead patents in one contiguous area, and the Pachecos, whose cattle brand dated to 1818 in the Tucson and Tubac areas and who owned at least four different patents. Antonia Wilbur-Cruce wrote in her memoir that three generations of her family lived together on her father's ranch just north of the border, raising goats and running cattle on the open range and growing subsistence crops in their own *milpa* (a large garden or small farm). Like other large Sonoran ranchers, her father claimed pure Spanish ancestry, boasting that he was the descendent of the "very last conquistador to come to Arizona."[56] Such claims were not just about land; they were also about race. By claiming pure Spanish ancestry, wealthier Mexican Americans also claimed whiteness and thus attempted to distinguish themselves from the surrounding population of mestizos and Indians.[57]

Industrial agribusiness would soon begin to replace this older pattern of landholding on both sides of the border. In Sonora, Mexican officials and U.S. investors alike viewed the fertile Yaqui River valley as a potential center of commercial agriculture in northwestern Mexico. When the Mexican government took a comprehensive survey of Sonora in 1849, it found that there had been very little encroachment into the homeland of the Yaquis. They had been working for wages in the haciendas and mines near Alamos, Buenavista, and Hermosillo but still maintained a largely autonomous political and cultural existence along the river. In the next couple of decades, Mexican officials began to work concertedly toward ending this older pattern of communal landholding in favor of private ownership.[58]

The Yaquis resisted this federal privatization project as best they could. Throughout the latter nineteenth century they periodically fought armed battles to maintain control of their territory, while adopting new, collective means to manage their lands. In the 1870s and '80s, under the leadership of the military captain Cajeme, they consolidated their operation of large community plots, collectively stored their grain, governed themselves by consensus through a panvillage council, instituted the first Yaqui tax system on imports, and charged a toll (often paid in weapons) to traders and travelers. Thousands of Yaquis held their ground until the late 1880s, but a growing number of mestizos and immigrants moved into the Yaqui valley. Three permanent garrisons of Mexican soldiers protected the settlers. The Yaquis faced increasingly miserable conditions, and many Yaqui fighters began to give themselves up. Cajeme continued to lead attacks against the military forts from his base in the Bacatete Mountains north of the river, but the military responded with a war without quarter. By 1887 four thousand Yaquis had surrendered, and Cajeme was captured in April and executed in Cócorit.[59]

The Comisión Científica de Sonora proceeded to survey the Yaqui River valley and to divide it into private plots. Despite promises to the contrary, little of this land went to the Yaquis. While the Yaquis fought a guerrilla war against the government for decades, hundreds of families began to leave the river permanently to work on the railroads, mines, and ranches, often crossing the border into Arizona.[60]

The Tohono O'odham also faced increasing incursions onto their lands to the northeast, but they were protected somewhat because their drier lands were not as suited to large-scale irrigation or farming as Yaqui lands. Still, in the 1870s and '80s as the Apache wars came to a close, growing numbers of Anglo and Mexican-American ranchers moved onto O'odham land. At the time, the relatively large defensive villages that the O'odham had formed in the eighteenth century to protect themselves against Apache attack were once again dispersing into clusters of smaller rancherías, to take better advantage of land and water resources. This resulted in thirteen distinct village clusters, each with somewhat different dialects and cultural patterns.

Euro-American ranchers from the United States threatened the O'odham by digging wells and raising cattle near a number of Tohono O'odham villages southwest of Tucson. These villages were inhabited by the distinct dialectal and cultural group of O'odham called the Ko-lo:di—a group that had been much closer to the Spanish missions and to Mexican settlement than other groups of O'odham farther to the west and north. The Ko-lo:di, along with some nearby villages of another group, the Aji, to the west, had already adopted elements of Spanish material and nonmaterial culture, including cattle ranching and language. These O'odham now adapted further by taking some of the newcomers' livestock for themselves and substantially increasing their own herds. U.S. government officials complained that thousands of head of cattle disappeared from Euro-American ranches in the 1890s. Incursions by Euro-American ranchers stalled temporarily when a devastating drought struck the region in 1899, but they continued with the return of wetter weather after 1905.[61]

The threat to O'odham land was renewed with the end of the drought. Several wealthy Sonoran landholders expanded into Tohono O'odham territory from the south, digging wells and grazing cattle directly adjacent to O'odham rancherías. By the turn of the century, the U.S. government had established only two small reservations for the Tohono O'odham, leaving most of their lands open to exploitation by non-Indians. These were the 69,000-acre San Xavier reservation, founded south of Tucson along the Santa Cruz River in 1874, and the 10,297-acre Gila Bend reservation, established in 1882 to protect a small, seasonal farming village along the Gila River. The majority of the Tohono O'odham, however, lived outside these

two reservations. Incursions by non-Indians had important cultural and social consequences for the Tohono O'odham. Those Ko-lo:di who lived along
the Altar and Magdalena rivers in Sonora, and those Aji who lived east of
the Santa Cruz, bore the brunt of the incursions. While a few responded
with violence, most did not. Instead, hundreds of Ko-lo:di from northern
Mexico fled north across the border into Arizona, where they joined existing O'odham villages or established new ones. These groups were among
the most Hispanicized Tohono O'odham, and they often looked down upon
other groups of O'odham who retained more indigenous cultural and economic practices to the north and west.[62]

While the groups generally coexisted, these divergent cultural patterns
would promote the development of two broad factions in future years. The
southeastern O'odham, largely made up of Ko-lo:di and some eastern Aji,
tended to borrow more readily from Euro-Americans, and they became
the most economically prosperous by developing substantial cattle herds
and engaging in the market economy. The western and northern groups of
O'odham lived farther away from Euro-American settlement and tended to
reject more vehemently outside influences. Both groups, however, whether
they liked it or not, became increasingly entangled in the expanding capitalist economy, either by raising livestock for market or taking up wage
work on the ranches and in the mines.[63]

By 1900 the most important region of industrial agricultural development in Arizona lay farther to the north, in the Salt River valley. Americans had begun to establish farms there in the mid-1860s, and at an accelerated pace in the 1870s, to take advantage of the new demand for produce
by the military and the mining towns. As late as 1870, two companies had
attracted only 240 inhabitants (of whom 115 were ethnic Mexicans) and
had opened only fifteen hundred acres to cultivation. That same year, however, the federal government opened the Salt River valley to homesteading,
and in February 1871 Phoenix became the seat of Maricopa County, which
encompassed the entire river basin.[64]

Corporate interests and speculators dominated farming in the Salt
River valley from the beginning, building a modern infrastructure that
linked the area to the world market and demanding an increasing number
of manual workers. The population of the region grew steadily despite periodic and sometimes disastrous floods. In the 1870s promoters built the
Maricopa and Grand canals. The passage of the Desert Lands Act in 1877
increased the size of homesteads and thus provided a further draw to the
region. In 1882 the Arizona Canal Company financed the 41-mile Arizona
canal by selling bonds as far away as London and Edinburgh. Finally, the

Maricopa and Phoenix Railroad replaced the freighting road from Phoenix to the Southern Pacific depot at Maricopa and provided a crucial link to national markets. By 1890 four canals irrigated fifty thousand acres north of the Salt River and supported a population of eleven thousand.[65] While some families managed to establish small homesteads, an elite class of investors dominated the valley, largely through their ability to control the limited water supply.[66]

The development of industrial agriculture and mining proved a devastating blow to the Pimas (Akimel O'odham) and Maricopas, who had become commercial farmers in their own right by the mid-nineteenth century. Beginning in the 1840s, Pima and Maricopa villages had become safe havens for travelers en route to the Pacific. They supplied wheat and other produce and served as allies against the Apaches. By 1870 the Pimas produced over three million pounds of wheat per year, much of which they sold or traded to market.[67] Their material and military aid, along with their sedentary, agricultural way of life, prompted many Euro-Americans to view them as among the "better class" of Indians and to praise them as allies who should be defended by the U.S. government.[68] In 1872 a BIA official reported that "they are industrious, agricultural people, who pride themselves on being self-supporting." These traits made them appear racially different from other Indians. Many Euro-Americans agreed that, unlike less sedentary groups, they could one day be incorporated into a nation of independent citizen-farmers and workers.[69]

All of this began to change, however, in the mid-1860s, when non-Indian settlers diverted water from the Gila River above the Pima and Maricopa farms. The federal government established one of the first reservations in Arizona for the Pimas and Maricopas in 1859. Encompassing sixty-four thousand acres, it was far smaller than the one hundred miles of riverfront that these groups claimed. More important, they were not guaranteed priority water rights to the river. Soon, diversions in towns such as Florence and Safford, deforestation, livestock, and mining caused severe erosion of the watershed. In the late 1890s, in a period of drought, the hydrographer in charge of a geological survey noted that "the result of the diversion was to deprive the Indians of the greater portion of their water supply during the period when the water was most needed to mature their crops."[70]

Euro-American depictions of Pimas and Maricopas changed dramatically as conditions on the Gila reservation deteriorated, revealing how the process of racial formation was linked to changes in the political economy. In the years after upriver diversions and erosion reduced the flow of the river, BIA agent John Stout declared that "not a drop of water" reached the Pima fields, and agent Frederick Grossman complained that Pimas and Maricopas began to leave the reservation to steal cattle and horses and destroy the crops of nearby farmers. (His report supported his proposal to remove the Pimas to Indian territory and therefore must be read with skepticism.) Newcomers in the irrigated lands of the Salt and Gila also began to complain, characterizing the Pimas and Maricopas as "uncommunicative," untrustworthy, and degenerate. When families began moving off the reservation in search of water and irrigable land—to the Blackwater district south and east of the reservation, to Gila Crossing to the west, and north to the Salt River valley—the complaints grew louder. Residents of both areas sent petitions to the Indian commissioner about their "troublesome and dangerous neighbors."[71]

In subsequent years the Pimas and Maricopas were able to secure protection of more land, but without the protection of their water. In an attempt to ameliorate their problems without taking water from Euro-American settlers, President Rutherford Hayes created a new reservation on the Salt River south of Fort McDowell, and hundreds of Pimas and Maricopas settled there permanently. President Chester Arthur increased the Gila reservation to 360,000 acres in 1882. More land, however, did nothing to resolve the water problem, and Pimas and Maricopas sunk further into economic despair. Their cultivated acreage decreased from an average of about nine thousand acres per year in 1880–1889, to 6,700 per year for the following half decade, to 3,600 per year up to 1899. In 1904 a federal investigating committee determined that the Pimas along the Gila had raised no crops for the previous five years due both to upriver diversions and drought. Many Pimas survived by selling their cattle and gathering mesquite to sell as firewood in Phoenix and other nearby towns. By 1905 the Pimas were cutting and selling nearly twelve thousand cords of wood per year.[72]

In 1902 federal officials had a chance to rectify the dire situation on the Gila reservation with the passage of the Newlands Reclamation Act, but they chose not to. Once again, racism and a lack of economic and political influence severely disadvantaged the Indians. In the 1890s Frederick Newell, a hydrologist for the Geological Survey who would later become the first director of the Reclamation Service, investigated a plan to build a major dam either on the Gila or the Salt. Newell revealed his racial bias when he argued that if a dam were to be built on the Gila "several acres well-tilled by white men would be destroyed for the benefit of one acre poorly worked by the Indians." Due in part to such biases, the Pimas and Maricopas were unlikely to win a battle against the intense lobbying effort sustained by Maricopa County growers to locate the project on the Salt.

Land speculators such as A. J. Chandler organized the Salt River Valley Water Storage Committee to lead the charge, and in 1903 the effort paid off. The Salt River Project, whose centerpiece was the Roosevelt Dam, became the first major project to be planned under the Reclamation Act. The Pimas and Maricopas would have to wait another three decades for a reservoir.[73]

The completion of the Roosevelt Dam, a part of the Salt River Project, capped off a dramatic transformation of south-central Arizona's desert ecology and political economy. The dam was completed in 1911, and water from the new reservoir flowed into an extensive network of canals and onto the fertile soils of the Salt River valley. Combined with a new hybrid of long-staple cotton, federal reclamation allowed a vast agricultural industry to flourish.[74] By 1920 the yearly harvest of Pima cotton in Arizona reached about two hundred thousand acres, with 142,322 of those in the Salt River valley—a remarkable 70 percent of all land irrigated via the new reclamation project. While in subsequent years the proportion of long-staple cotton would decline as farmers planted everything from citrus and melons to alfalfa, long- and short-staple cotton would remain a staple of the regional economy for the next fifty years.[75]

As competition in the agricultural market throughout south-central Arizona intensified, and as fences were erected and ranching or farming required greater amounts of moveable capital and connections to national markets, many Mexican-American landholders found themselves with little choice but to sell. Antonio Córdova, whose family owned a ranch in southern Arizona, recalled that his family sold their ranch to "an American" in the 1920s. "Can you imagine," he exclaimed, "all that land, the house, the well and the equipment, for $3,000! A lot of people sold their ranches that way. . . . Then we would end up with nothing—no land, no cattle, no money." Herminia Córdova, whose family owned a ranch seventy miles south of Tucson, remembered that "it was hard to make it on the little ranches when there was not much land, especially when they began to fence the range. The big ranchers could make it, but the little ranchers could not, so the little ranchers began to sell off their land."[76] Many of these ranchers would soon find themselves working for wages alongside Indians and Mexican immigrants on farms owned by Euro-Americans.

RACE, STATEHOOD, AND CITIZENSHIP

As industrial mining and agriculture expanded at the turn of the century, Arizonans argued that the economy and population of the territory had matured enough to warrant full statehood. Without it Arizona residents—

Anglo and non-Anglo alike—lacked the power to elect their own governors or voting representatives to Congress. Yet, as Howard Lamar has shown, statehood was repeatedly postponed because of disagreements over the conservation of federal lands, political competition between congressional Democrats and Republicans, and the belief, which is most important for this study, held by many national political leaders that New Mexico's and Arizona's populations, because they were largely made up of Mexicans and Indians, were not fit for self-government. Due largely to the territory's ethno-racial makeup, powerful government officials such as Indiana Senator Albert Beveridge hoped to maintain an imperial relationship with Arizona, explicitly comparing it to new overseas possessions like the Philippines.[77]

Throughout the two-decade struggle to become a state, Anglos in Arizona honed an argument for an end to territorial status based on the ideas that the majority of residents were white, educated, and civilized and that the indigenous and ethnic Mexican populations would have little role in government. As Arizonans sat down to write a constitution, this argument manifested itself in explicit, exclusionary policies designed to relegate nonwhites and those who did not speak English to second-class citizenship. In large part, then, the quest for statehood led to the development of a clearer definition of the ideal Arizona citizen in cultural, historical, and racial terms. Racial inequality was not simply an unfortunate corollary to full statehood; it was built into the very identity of Arizona from its inception.[78]

Arizonans began to press for statehood in earnest in the 1880s and '90s. In 1889 Congress initially included Arizona in an omnibus bill to admit the Dakotas, Wyoming, and Washington as states, but it soon dropped Arizona from the bill due in large part to the objections of Republicans who did not want to admit what would likely become a Democratic state. After Arizona was excluded from the bill in 1891, a group of twenty-one Arizona men decided to move forward anyway. The spokesman for the effort was Mark Smith, Arizona's delegate to Congress. When Smith presented his case before Congress and President Benjamin Harrison, however, the president responded that the Republicans were "opposed to the free coinage of western senators." This response, combined with the national panic of 1893, ended the territory's chances to achieve statehood in the nineteenth century.[79]

In the first decade of the twentieth century, the statehood campaign picked up steam, and statehood was reconnected to the idea of the acquisition of full citizenship. In 1901 numerous editorials appeared in Arizona newspapers connecting statehood to "full enfranchisement" and freedom from "territorial vassalage." As the secretary of Arizona's Territorial Democratic Committee said, "We are all anxious to acquire the full privilege of American citizenship, to increase our opportunities and to substantially build up the country of our choice." He argued that territorial status deprived the region's inhabitants of their full liberty as members of the national body politic: "During this struggle I am seeking citizenship, and I feel as though I express the heartfelt will of all democrats when I say, 'God speed the day.'"[80] In late October the participants in a convention held in Phoenix voiced a similar sentiment. Pointing out that the region had been in a territorial status for five decades, convention attendees couched their quest for statehood in the discourse of liberty, citizenship, and self-government.[81]

Statehood proponents contended that the educated "American" population—which, it became clear, did not include the indigenous and Mexican-American populations—would dominate Arizona culturally and politically. When Congress considered a new bill to admit Oklahoma, New Mexico, and Arizona as states in 1902, congressional delegate Mark Smith declared before the U.S. House, "The fact is, that excluding the reservation Indians, who are not and cannot become citizens, Arizona has the best generally educated population in the United States." Smith pointed out that most people in the territory had been born in the eastern part of the country—a fact that distinguished Arizona from neighboring New Mexico, which had a much larger Mexican-American population. "The large body of our people," he said, "came when fully grown from the different states of the union. They know the duties of citizenship as well as the members of this house, and they have attended to those duties with a modesty and propriety which I am justified in commending as an example for the emulation of eastern states."[82]

Smith's reference to Americans from eastern states served to delineate racial and cultural boundaries—a discourse that would manifest itself in a series of restrictive laws passed in the early 1900s by the territorial assembly. First, the assembly passed a $2.50 poll tax, which undermined the right of many working-class people, and thus many Mexican-American people, to vote. The Daily Enterprise, a progressive newspaper, complained that the law opened a door that might "disfranchise all save the wealthy and privileged classes" to no avail. Over the next several years, the assembly passed even more explicit discriminatory legislation. In 1909 it passed an English literacy test for voting. The Democratic governor at the time, Richard Sloan, protested the measure, declaring, "It is a wholesale disfranchisement of the respectable element of our Mexican population who, by all rights of birth, ancestry, identification with country and treaty rights as well, have a just claim to consideration in any scheme looking to the curtailment of the privileges of citizenship." The measure passed despite his protests.[83] That same year, the assembly passed a law that segregated "students of the African race" into their own schools. (The population of blacks in most of Arizona was extremely low—with the exception of black soldiers stationed in Santa Cruz County.) In 1914 Phoenix would put teeth into the ruling by establishing a separate "colored High School." While Hispanic students, whom the courts generally defined as white, could not legally be segregated by race, they were often segregated by other means, particularly by the justification that they were deficient in the English language.[84]

Despite such measures, opposition to statehood at the federal level remained strong. The most powerful opponent was Senator Beveridge, who served as the chairman of the Senate Committee on Territories. Beveridge used his position to hold up the omnibus statehood bill in the Senate. In part, his opposition reflected his Republican Party affiliation, since he feared that Arizona would tip the balance of power in the Senate toward the Democratic Party.[85] Beyond that, Beveridge viewed the territories of the Southwest in the same vein as he viewed the territories of Guam, Puerto Rico, and the Philippines—in short, as imperial possessions that were inadequately prepared for self-government. "We govern the Indians without their consent, we govern our territories without their consent," he explained in 1898, because "it is ours to save that soil for liberty and civilization."[86]

In December, due largely to Beveridge's concerted opposition, the omnibus bill died in the Senate. According to the Arizona Democrat, Beveridge told President Theodore Roosevelt that New Mexico and Arizona were similar to the "Negro section of the south," and he suggested that the Mexican population was indifferent both to democratic institutions and to the English language.[87] He then submitted a new Senate bill to admit Arizona and New Mexico as a single state. Joint statehood would not change the racial demographics of the two territories, but it would likely subordinate Democrats within a Republican majority.[88]

In the years that followed, rather than directly challenge Beveridge's characterization of Indians and ethnic Mexicans, Arizona's political and economic elite argued that if the territory were admitted separately, these groups would have little cultural or political influence. The Twenty-Second Territorial Assembly resolved that it was "unalterably opposed to the admission of Arizona and New Mexico into the union as one state under any terms or conditions whatsoever."[89] Arizona was not like New Mexico, opponents of "jointure" protested. As the *Arizona Democrat* declared, "Its Mexican population is less than 51,000, for the Indians who held that portion of Mexico before American annexation, never permitted Mexicans to get a foothold."[90]

Proponents of separate statehood bolstered their case by clearly defining, in cultural, racial, and historical terms, the ideal Arizona citizen. The territorial assembly told a racist and gendered story of the region's frontier history, in which manly pioneers had wrested control of the territory from its uncivilized and unmanly Indian and Mexican predecessors. House Resolution XIV stated:

> In behalf of that band of pioneers who have wrung from the savage
> this fair land of Arizona, in behalf of the citizens of Arizona who have
> fought its battles and developed those conditions under which we now
> happily exist, this House resents the imputation that our members
> or the people of this territory will ever submit to the proposition that
> Arizona will consent to any scheme by which it will lose its identity
> and name and its grand history that has been marked by the expendi-
> ture of blood, treasure and privation.

The territorial governor added that if the two territories were combined, "the delegates from New Mexico, in a convention thus constituted, could form and adopt a constitution repugnant in every particular to the people of Arizona, subversive of their interest, impeding their progress, offending their pride, and humiliating them to the last degree against the will and protest of every delegate from Arizona."[91]

When a jointure bill passed the House in 1906, Arizona delegates refined their race-based argument for separate statehood and clarified who would and would not be eligible for full citizenship. In February they presented a lengthy protest to the Senate. On the front page of the document they explained that they would not accept jointure because of "the decided racial differences between the people of Arizona and the large majority of the people of New Mexico, who are not only different in race and largely in language, but have entirely different customs, laws, and ideals and would have but little prospect of successful amalgamation." The protest placed the racial boundaries of American identity in stark relief. It maintained that at least certain European immigrants, who were more similar in their racial and cultural makeup to Euro-American Arizonans, would likely become good citizens. The same could not be expected of those of Mexican descent. "Arizona's population is distinctly American," the document read, "composed of people from all parts of the United States and the *best type of immigrants from other countries*. Their ideas of social conditions, Christian civilization, modern progress, and future development are of the highest" (emphasis added). By contrast, New Mexico's much larger ethnic Mexican population could never be expected to assimilate fully.[92]

The statehood debate was ultimately decided by popular referendum. The Senate, which remained deadlocked on the issue, finally allowed Arizona and New Mexico to vote on whether to accept jointure after the territorial assembly's 1906 protest. Arizonans soundly defeated the measure. Less than two years later, President Roosevelt declared in his annual address before Congress that Arizona and New Mexico should be admitted separately. Finally, in 1910, Congressman Ed Hamilton of the House Committee on Territories introduced a new bill enabling Arizona and New Mexico to be admitted as separate states.[93]

Arizona's constitutional convention and new state legislature fulfilled implicit promises to limit political and economic rights along racial and cultural lines. During debates over the constitution, the number of Mexican immigrants in Arizona grew, driven largely by the upheavals of the Mexican Revolution and a rising labor demand. One organizer for the Western Federation of Miners complained that "the American citizen, to a large extent, had been driven out of these mining communities." Sentiments such as this fueled the rise of a new coalition, made up of craft union members, small farmers, and merchants, who led a nativist assault against Mexicans. As the delegates met to write up a constitution, they designed more policies to restrict noncitizen and nonwhite workers from the right to vote and work.[94]

Ethnic Mexicans were not the only targets of the nativist assault. Many Anglo, Irish, and Cornish union men expressed concern about "the lowest type of Europeans," referring to the newest wave of European immigrants who were populating the mining towns. Italian, Spanish, and Slavic workers received, on average, much lower wages than did native Euro-Americans and northern and western Europeans. Nativist discourse and unequal wage structures revealed that the boundaries of whiteness itself were still under contention, with some groups hovering on its margins. The idea that whiteness would be made less permeable over the following decades will be discussed in detail in Chapter 4 as will the fact that even into the 1930s, some Euro-Americans remained questionably white.[95]

Conservative craft unionists petitioned the constitutional convention to limit the rights of newer immigrants to work in the mining towns. In 1910 four hundred primarily Cornish, Anglo, and Irish residents of the mining town of Globe sent a petition to the convention to require employers of more than five workers in hazardous occupations to hire no less than 80 percent "native-born citizens of the United States" and "qualified electors." Workers in Bisbee and Douglas filed a similar petition. The petitions were not only directed at Mexican immigrants, but also at Italians, Slavs, and Spaniards. Arizona's Immigration Restriction League supported the measures, declaring "that some large industrial concerns have denied to American workingmen their God-given privilege to work in their own country under their own flag," and that unless the government acted, "in a very few years Arizona will be an alien state peopled by an alien race." In the end, the measure did not pass, but it would be resurrected shortly after the passage of the constitution (see Chapters 3 and 4).[96]

The new constitution also included a measure denying suffrage to Indians, more explicitly excluding them from full membership in the national polity than any other ethnic group. The clause read, simply, "No person under guardianship shall be qualified to vote in any election." This clause became especially relevant after 1924, when the national Indian Citizenship Act granted citizenship to all American Indians, whether or not they had accepted allotment or continued to live on reservations. Theoretically, the Indian Citizenship Law, combined with the Fourteenth and Fifteenth amendments to the U.S. Constitution, should have protected the voting and civil rights of Indians. However, until the late 1940s Arizona courts would apply the "guardianship" clause to all of Arizona's indigenous population, regardless of political and economic status.[97]

The new state legislature also reaffirmed the English literacy law with a new law in 1912 that restricted voting rights to those who could "read the Constitution of the United States in the English language in such manner as to show he is neither prompted nor reciting from memory, and to write his name." It should be noted that while the law referred to men, a referendum would extend full suffrage to Arizona women later that year. The law was designed to disenfranchise ethnic Mexicans and southern and eastern European immigrants, and it fulfilled that basic goal to great effect. In 1910 Cochise and Pima counties had the largest concentration of ethnic Mexicans and European immigrants in the state. In the former, 50 percent of the foreign-born population was ethnic Mexican. Due to voting restrictions, the electorate in almost half of the precincts in both counties was not large enough to hold primary elections in 1912.[98]

Arizona's incorporation into the national political economy relegated much of the state's nonwhite (or questionably white) working population to unskilled, low-wage work and to second-class citizenship. By the first decade of the twentieth century, from the Yaqui River to the Salt River, most indigenous inhabitants of Sonora and Arizona had lost their ability to subsist without working at least part time for wages. The same corporate mining, railroad, and agricultural ventures that undermined their ability to subsist created an insatiable demand for their labor. Still, most Indians resisted abandoning traditional subsistence strategies for full participation in the developing wage economy. Pimas, Maricopas, and Tohono O'odham struggled to maintain other means of subsistence, whether through raising cattle, gathering and selling wood, marketing crafts, or farming (whenever conditions improved enough to allow it). Thus, as of 1912, thousands of indigenous people in southern Arizona survived not so much at the bottom of the wage labor hierarchy as on its margins—a topic that will be discussed in much more detail in the next chapter.

Mexican Americans faced a different set of obstacles to full and equal status as citizens and workers. The decline of the Mexican-American elite and the influx of Yaqui and mestizo immigrants from Mexico helped to solidify an increasingly impermeable, racially defined class structure in which ethnic Mexicans, whether Arizona natives or immigrants, were subordinated. While some Mexican Americans continued to build a life around independent livestock operations or, especially in Tucson, craft and merchant activities, they were a small minority. Anglos had promoted an image of Arizona's citizenry as white, progressive, and racially and culturally homogeneous. Full political and economic incorporation was thus intricately tied, from the state's inception, to racial, economic, and political inequality. Such restrictions were not simply unfortunate aberrations within an otherwise free society. They were integral to the very identity and political economy of the new state.

▼ ▼ ▼ ▼ ▼ ▼ ▼ ▼ ▼ ▼ ▼ ▼ ▼ ▼ ▼ ▼

CHAPTER 2

FROM NOBLE SAVAGE TO SECOND-CLASS CITIZEN

In the 1880s the government of the United States reformed its well-worn policy of concentrating Indians onto reservations into a new campaign designed to assimilate them into the nation. Federal officials allotted reservation lands for private property and strove to educate and detribalize Indians in government schools, to integrate them economically as farmers, ranchers, and wageworkers, and to pave the way for them to become citizens.[1] BIA officials in Arizona soon discovered, however, that federal policies had to be revised to meet regional conditions, such as the aridity of the Sonoran desert, the labor demands of cotton growers and other employers, and the agency of the indigenous peoples themselves.

In Arizona the BIA also had to contend with the fuzziness of the boundaries between Indian and Mexican identity and the proximity to the international border. BIA officials struggled to keep the regional indigenous population away from ethnic Mexicans, fearing that such contact would degrade the Indians' industry and purity and interfere with the process of assimilation. Tapping into the noble savage trope, local officials tended to characterize the Tohono O'odham, Akimel O'odham, and Maricopas as proud people who had avoided the racial and cultural "pollution" that had stricken the regional Mexican population. They viewed allotment of communal lands into private property, as well as education and, increasingly, wage labor, as the most likely means to convert this innate pride and industriousness into the necessary characteristics for good citizenship.

By the turn of the century, however, the goals of the national assimilation policy began to change, ironically leading to the exploitation and segregation of Indians as a racialized minority rather than to their integration as equals. While some BIA officials remained optimistic about converting

Arizona's sedentary and semisedentary indigenous groups into equal citizens, others were much less sanguine, viewing them as racially inferior and thus incapable of ever becoming full citizens.[2] As one historian has put it in reference to Indians in the Pacific Northwest, the laws and institutions that emerged after 1900 ironically "tended to perpetuate the racial category they aimed to eliminate."[3] While the assimilation policy before 1900 was ethnocentric, in later decades it was often unabashedly racist.

The indigenous peoples of Arizona in their diversity developed varying strategies to cope with the government's assimilation policies, depending upon their specific circumstances and cultures. The Tohono O'odham, who had long engaged in a pattern of seasonal migration, most readily adapted to wage work by migrating between villages, industrial farms, railroads, and mines. Some managed to survive by raising cattle for market, but most owned only a few head. Instead, they began to move in and out of the wage economy while preserving kinship ties and indigenous agricultural practices on their *rancherías*. In so doing they followed a pattern familiar to peoples in other regions around the world. Indeed, what Frederick Cooper has found for South Africans who moved in and out of reserves to find wage work could just as well apply to south-central Arizona. As colonizers attempted to institute a new labor regime, they had to reckon with "people who were themselves trying to keep the labor market from absorbing their being and their communities" with "their own work ethics, their own conceptions of when it made sense to put out energy and when—and for whom—it did not."[4]

Other indigenous groups in south-central Arizona developed somewhat different strategies. While many Akimel O'odham (Pimas) and Maricopas took up wage work, most tried instead to live off sporadic farming, livestock operations, and wood gathering. The waters of the Gila River, however inconsistent and unreliable, made this more possible than it was in the Tohono O'odham's desert rancherías. (The Yaquis, who had no lands of their own in Arizona and were not subjected to the new assimilation policies, will be discussed elsewhere). While their strategies differed, all of these groups resisted assimilation and racial discrimination and actively shaped their relationships to the emerging political economy and the nation. In so doing they also began to redefine what it meant to be Tohono O'odham, Pima, or Maricopa.

ASSIMILATION POLICY IN SOUTH-CENTRAL ARIZONA

In the late nineteenth century, as the federal government began to implement its new assimilation policy, many local BIA officials had high hopes for the Pimas, Maricopas, and Tohono O'odham. Euro-Americans tended to view these groups as among the so-called better class of self-supporting and independent Indians, in large part because they were sedentary or semisedentary farmers. Still, even the most generous characterizations tended to depict these groups more as noble savages than as modern, independent citizens. Their reputed vitality, independence, and love of freedom was laudable, but it was also dangerous because it existed outside the social, political, and economic fabric of the nation. Whether these characteristics could be remolded to conform to the modern demands of citizenship and competition in a capitalist economy remained an open question.

One of the central tools of the assimilation policy was allotment. In 1887 Congress officially endorsed a new policy of dividing reservation lands in severalty with the passage of the General Allotment Act, often called the Dawes Act. According to the new law, each head of family was entitled to a tract of land and each dependent to a smaller parcel. Any Indian who received an allotment would become a U.S. citizen with "equal protection under the law," echoing the language of the Fourteenth Amendment. The government would hold the allotment in trust for at least twenty-five years, or for longer periods if the president deemed it necessary. The interior secretary reserved the right to sell any lands not allotted in negotiation with each tribe. At the end of the trust period, individual Indians would receive fee-simple patents. The law also authorized the Interior Department secretary to "secure a just and equal distribution" of water—an element of the law that was especially pertinent in Arizona's arid environment, where irrigation was imperative for farming.[5]

In the nineteenth century the BIA allotted only one reservation in south-central Arizona, the San Xavier. It seemed well suited to allotment because the Santa Cruz River allowed the Tohono O'odham who lived there to maintain relatively prosperous farms. Beginning in 1890 the BIA allotted 41,600 acres on the reservation, leaving 71,090 as communal property. The final step of the allotment process, however—the transfer of allotted lands into fee-simple property—would never occur. The aridity of the Sonoran desert, combined with the resistance of O'odham and Euro-Americans alike, would serve to alter allotment plans of Tohono O'odham lands.[6]

Allotment was not the only element of the federal government's assimilation program. The BIA also used a system of boarding schools, day schools, and industrial training schools to promote assimilation, often coercing indigenous children to attend. In 1881 the BIA established its first boarding school in Arizona at Sacaton, on the Gila reservation, near a government-subsidized Presbyterian school that had been established over a decade earlier. The facility, however, proved adequate to serve only a small number of students. Therefore, in the 1880s and '90s, BIA officials sent hundreds of Pimas, Maricopas, and Tohono O'odham to schools in other states. A few went to large boarding schools like Carlisle in Pennsylvania and Hampton in Virginia, but most went to industrial and vocational schools in western cities and towns, such as Albuquerque, New Mexico, Genoa, Nebraska, Chilocco, Oklahoma, and Grand Junction, Colorado. Some also attended private institutions such as the Presbyterian school in Tucson. In the meantime, federal policymakers suggested that a much larger boarding school should be built somewhere in central Arizona to serve the entire territory. In 1891, after years of debate over the best location, the Indian Office opened a school just south of Phoenix.[7]

While BIA officials touted Phoenix Indian School as a means to assimilate the Indians, many of those who lobbied for the school had less-philanthropic goals. In fact, Salt River valley growers supported the idea of a boarding school primarily as a potential source of Indian labor. Colonel William Christy and William Murphy, who owned thousands of acres of land and controlled much of the water supply through the Arizona Improvement Company, were two of the schools' most influential supporters. An editorial in the *Arizona Republican* anticipated a need for workers the school might produce: "In a few years our lands, now being so extensively planted with fruit trees and vines, would give employment to many of the pupils." And after the first class of thirty-one Pimas and ten Maricopas enrolled in 1891, an official noted that "the farmers and fruit growers in the vicinity of the school are ready to employ these boys and girls as soon as their labor becomes sufficiently skillful to pay them." Within the first weeks of enrollment, local landholders asked Superintendent Wellington Rich for workers for the upcoming harvest.[8]

BIA agents hoped that wage labor would help to assimilate the Indians and train them to work in an industrial economy. It would also serve a cultural function, encouraging, for example, a sexual division of labor that approximated that of the Euro-American majority. The BIA placed women called field matrons in communities such as South Tucson to that end, arguing that domestic labor would train Indian women in the domestic arts, preparing them for their future as wives in nuclear family households. Such households were deemed crucial in preparing Indians to be good citizens, since women would provide a clean home and moral guidance to their children, while eventually the men would earn a family wage. According to Janette Woodruff, who served as Tucson's field matron from 1915 to 1930, the Indians' position as "servants of the white employer class . . . was an essential steppingstone from the desert camps to a more comfortable life." To help promote the formation of proper households, Woodruff held training sessions in children's health and in domestic skills such as sewing. She also organized a "girls' day" in which she attempted to impart Anglo standards of social behavior and provided marriage guidance to end the common indigenous practice of forming conjugal unions without legal sanction (see Chapter 3).[9]

Predictably, rather than assimilate indigenous men and women, the school outing system tended to segregate them permanently into specific kinds of low-paid, manual labor. In fact, Wellington Rich, the Phoenix Indian School superintendent, felt that Indians did not have the intellectual capacity of whites, and he doubted whether the students could ever "compete successfully with the white youth of the community in any of the mechanic arts, mercantile pursuits, or professions." He felt that it was better to place the Indians in unskilled and semiskilled positions than to harbor such lofty goals. Thus, in the spring of 1893, he agreed to hire out a few older boys to local farms and construction projects and eleven girls to work in Phoenix homes as domestic servants. Rich also supported the desire of Phoenix residents to maintain racial segregation and declared, "I have no sympathy with the scheme of diffusing the educated Indian youth among the whites. They should as a rule, in my opinion, return to their people and assist in the civilization of the latter."[10]

Rich's successor, Harwood Hall, carried on a similar program. He understood that "the hiring of Indian youth is not looked upon by the people of this valley from a philanthropic standpoint—it is simply a matter of business," but he still enthusiastically treated the school as an "employment agency, whereby the desiring pupil can secure employment as soon as qualified." In 1896 Hall refined the program so that local families would pay nothing other than "board, proper care and instruction" for female domestic workers. Over the next year, he hired out almost two hundred students as domestics and farm workers.[11]

The development of this "outing system," as school officials called it, signaled a gradual shift in the goals and tactics of the assimilation policy. Indeed, by 1900, vocational training and wage labor recruitment would largely replace the older goal of converting Indians into small farmers. On one hand this was a pragmatic change reflecting a national shift toward an industrialized, wage economy. On the other hand, it reflected a more sinister change in how government officials viewed Indians. Many officials publicly expressed their views that Indians were inherently inferior and could never compete with whites in the capitalist economy. Francis Leupp, who became Indian commissioner in 1905, argued that Indians were racially inferior, and he pointed to the labor system in the South as a model to emulate: "Our first duty to the Indian is to teach him to work. . . . Even the little papoose can be taught to weed the rows just as the pickaninny in the South can be used as a cotton picker." He soon established a regional employment bureau in the Southwest to carry out the plan.[12]

Reforms in the allotment policy also made it more likely that even individuals who received allotments would have to work for wages. By the turn of the century, many policymakers began to argue that allotment was failing to assimilate the Indians. While some blamed the policy, others blamed the limited potential of the Indians themselves. Commissioner Leupp explained his philosophy in his 1905 annual report: "The commonest mistake made by his white well-wishers in dealing with the Indian is the assumption that he is simply a white man with red skin." This mistake ignored inherent racial differences and led to the erroneous conclusion that Indians would all become self-sufficient farmers.[13]

This shifting philosophy underlay a series of laws that undermined federal protections of allotments just as the BIA began to target the Arizona reservations for severalty. Among the most important reforms was the Burke Act of May 1906, introduced by future Indian Commissioner Charles Burke. The new law eliminated the mandatory twenty-five-year trust period of the Dawes Act, allowing the Interior Department secretary to grant immediate fee-simple titles to those allottees deemed "competent and capable of managing his or her affairs." Once these lands were taken out of trust status, they would be subject to taxation and could be sold to any buyer. The new law also made full citizenship contingent upon the transition of allotments to fee-simple status.[14] These policies thus both delayed the granting of citizenship and made indigenous landholdings more vulnerable due to the new expense of maintaining them and their susceptibility to unscrupulous land buyers.

In 1901 the federal government began to develop a plan to allot the rest of the reservations in south-central Arizona (only San Xavier had been allotted). The new campaign began with a request by the Arizona Territorial Assembly, which hoped to absorb "surplus" Indian territory as public lands or for private development. Federal officials first turned their attention to the Gila River reservation where the Pimas and Maricopas lived. William H. Code, the irrigation engineer on the reservation, proposed that a system of pumping stations might eventually furnish enough water to irrigate about ten thousand acres of allotments and common lands.

The catch was, the stations would have to be paid for by selling off the rest of the reservation, which amounted to 180,000 acres. Code was a former employee of A. J. Chandler, one of the most successful land speculators in the Salt River valley, and it was not likely a coincidence that these lands were adjacent to Chandler's 18,000-acre ranch. The rest of the reservation would be allotted into 5-acre plots—far smaller than the 60-acre farms that many Pimas and Maricopas traditionally operated, or that the Dawes Act had intended. If implemented, the net effect of Code's plan would be to drastically reduce Pima and Maricopa landholdings, transferring most of them to Euro-American growers like Chandler.[15]

While Code began to drill wells on the Gila reservation in anticipation of his plan being carried through, BIA officials debated how to proceed with Tohono O'odham lands. It bears repeating that the federal government had designated only two small reservations for the Tohono O'odham in the nineteenth century, at San Xavier and Gila Bend, but the vast majority of the population (estimates average around six thousand) lived in desert rancherías stretching from northern Mexico to the Gila River. The BIA sent a special allotting agent to south-central Arizona in 1909 with the intention of dividing Tohono O'odham lands into 80-acre parcels of farmland and 160-acre plots of grazing land. The plan had the support of some Tohono O'odham leaders in the southeastern district, which was occupied primarily by the distinct cultural and dialect groups, the Ko-lo:di and the eastern Aji. Many were government school graduates and/or had become Presbyterians. They also owned most of the cattle. Most Tohono O'odham in other regions, however, showed little interest in allotment, and they pressured the government to change its plans.[16]

Along with the new campaign to allot Indian lands, the BIA continued to encourage Indians to supplement agriculture with wage work. While the Phoenix Indian School continued its outing system, in 1901 Indian agent J. M. Berger of the previously allotted San Xavier reservation arranged to have Tohono O'odham work on the railroads stretching from California to New Mexico. By 1901 as many as 180 Tohono O'odham were employed by the railroads, and Berger praised them for their "peaceable and quiet" acceptance of low-wage labor ($1.75–$2.25 per day) and for not joining labor unions.[17]

The completion of the Salt River Project in Maricopa County in 1911 and the subsequent cotton boom dramatically expanded this nascent labor recruitment program. In 1914 Commissioner Cato Sells assigned Frank Thackery, superintendent of the Gila River Indian School, to take "general supervisory charge of the Indian labor problem in the Salt River valley, particularly as it relates to the growing cotton industry among the white farmers." Sells directed Thackery to cooperate with the Salt River Valley Egyptian Cotton Growers Association to "affect a stable system in the employment of Indian labor with a view of building up a large and permanent market for such labor."[18]

In assigning Thackery the role of labor agent, Sells simultaneously accommodated politically influential growers and implemented an evolving assimilation policy. The federal government, which had already transformed the regional political economy by financing the massive Salt River Project and granting land to railroads and mining companies, now worked to ensure that growers would have access to labor for their newly irrigated fields. Sells explained in a letter to the superintendent of the Phoenix Indian School, "The growing of Egyptian cotton in the Salt River valley and vicinity has been developed to a point where its further success depends largely upon the ability of this Bureau to supply the growers with a dependable amount of Indian labor to assure the proper picking of the increased acreage." Sells felt that accommodating the growers went hand in hand with the goal of assimilating the Indians.[19]

While many BIA officials doubted the inherent abilities of the indigenous population, others remained more optimistic, suggesting that wage labor would supplement farming on the reservations and encourage assimilation. These officials tended to emphasize the natural independence, adaptability, and relatively sedentary nature of south-central Arizona's indigenous population, suggesting that these qualities made them good candidates for eventual status as independent citizen workers.

In the multiethnic environment of Arizona's borderlands, this optimism took an interesting twist. Local BIA officials frequently drew sharp distinctions between Indians and mestizos, thus helping to construct stricter racial boundaries between them than actually existed (see Chapter 3). Mexicans, they argued, had already been degraded by centuries of racial mixing and subordination by oppressive Spanish and Mexican political and economic systems. The Indians, by contrast, remained racially, culturally, and economically unpolluted, and thus had a promising future as equal members of the nation-state.

The boundaries between Indian and ethnic Mexican identity were quite fuzzy in Arizona's borderlands, and drawing them was no easy task. Field matrons and other BIA officials struggled to keep the Indians away from the corrupting influence of mestizos who often lived in the same towns, barrios, and even households. San Xavier Superintendent Henry McQuigg clarified this goal when he first recommended that a field matron position be established in Tucson. According to McQuigg, the presence of Mexicans, along with that of some poor whites, would threaten the purity of the Indian women and their chances for cultural and economic assimilation. In his words, "There are many worthless Mexicans and Whites who drift in here for a time; and with the pleasure resorts, the wide-open policy of Tucson, etc., the temptations in the way of the Indian girls are pronounced."[20]

The field matrons worked within the barrios to identify those whom the government recognized as Indians, such as the Tohono O'odham, and those it did not, such as Yaquis from Mexico. Jannette Woodruff recalled in her memoir that when she first moved to Tucson to take up her post as field matron in 1915, a Tohono O'odham police officer showed her around the barrio, pointing out where the O'odham lived. When Woodruff asked about an adobe house they were passing by, he turned to her and said, "Not stop here . . . Mexican. Over there don't matter neither. Yaqui. He don't matter to Uncle Sam." Woodruff found these distinctions confusing because "these foreigners were scattered all through the village, and since their houses were of the same style as the Papagos, I had no way of making distinctions. I was concerned with the Papagos only."[21] In other words, she recognized at least in vague terms, that "Indian" was an artificial racial distinction that overlooked the similar conditions, close proximity, and ties of kinship, language, and culture that many barrio residents shared.

According to certain BIA officials, Mexicans presented a special threat to Indians because of their supposedly degraded and immoral character and their propensity for interracial mixing.[22] Woodruff soon caught on to this racial logic. She often complained about Indian girls who were seduced and impregnated by "half-breed Mexicans." She encouraged them to escape relationships with unseemly Mexican men, and instead urged formal, government-sanctioned marriages with other Indians. In one case, for example, she complained of a Tohono O'odham woman who married an "uneducated and uncouth . . . swarthy half-breed" who worked and lived in a local graveyard. To Woodruff's relief, the woman eventually left him.[23]

Frank Thackery, who had been assigned the role of Indian labor agent for Arizona cotton growers, also struggled to ensure that Indians kept a safe distance from Mexican workers. Using the trope of the degraded Mexican, he implied that the threat of wage labor was not so much in low pay or poor working conditions but in the character of the Mexican workforce. In May 1916, for example, acting upon a request by the New Cornelia Copper Company, Commissioner Cato Sells wrote to Thackery and asked if any Indians could be supplied for the mines at Ajo. Thackery responded, "If our Pima and Papagoes [sic] are to secure employment in the mines they must come in contact with the very worst element of labor, which will contaminate and degrade them to the extent of making very undesirable citizens." He suggested that of all the inhabitants of Ajo "fully eighty percent are Mexicans and many of them of the very worst type, whose morals are very detrimental to any people who continue to associate with them." Thackery felt that the O'odham would be better served if they continued to work in agriculture, and he pointed out that Salt River valley growers were clamoring for more workers. He reminded the commissioner, "Our Pima and Papago Indians have always been an agricultural and stock raising people." He thought that sending them to the mining camps would be a step backward, while training them in more efficient farming methods through agricultural wage work "will make of them a hardy and honorable body of people of which some day the state of Arizona will be proud to recognize as citizens."[24]

At times the O'odham themselves manipulated such nativist, anti-Mexican discourse to their own ends. Edwin Santeo, a Tohono O'odham who obtained a job as labor recruiter for cotton growers and the BIA, strategically deployed such rhetoric to press his case for the preservation of jobs for O'odham workers. Santeo complained to Thackery that some employers were hiring Mexicans and ignoring the rights of the Tohono O'odham in "their own land." He berated the "so called U.S. Indian employment agents" for not adequately informing the villages of available work. As he put it, "We can not afford to overlook the labor question for our people . . . so let us join together and try to save our people and friends from hard times before them." Speaking in nativist terms, Santeo explained, "I don't like to see the cheap labor in the valley by foreigners. It means that the Indians will not be able to make their living when hard times come on." Santeo thus joined the rising groundswell against Mexicans as aliens who had no right to take the jobs of legitimate members of the U.S. nation, which, he asserted, included the Tohono O'odham.[25]

LAND, WAGE LABOR, AND RESISTANT ADAPTATION:
THE TOHONO O'ODHAM

In the fall of 1925, a missionary living among the Tohono O'odham wrote that most of the residents of Anegam, Cababi, and Santa Rosa left the villages for several months every year to work for wages on Anglo-owned cotton fields. "So great is the demand for their labor and so poor the quality of their lands," he explained, "that they are forced to leave their habitat annually during November, December, and January."[26] Only a few years later, ethnographer Ruth Underhill offered a seemingly contradictory picture of the very same villages, characterizing them as the most "isolated" and "traditional" of all the O'odham communities. Indeed, when Underhill arrived in Arizona in 1931 to study the O'odham, she was attracted to the Santa Rosa district precisely because she perceived it to be secluded and culturally pristine. As she would explain, these villages were the "stronghold of the old morality and ceremonies." "There," she wrote on another occasion, "Papago was spoken in its ancient dialects. There I might find parts of the past, still alive."[27]

These two observations may seem contradictory on the surface, but only if modernization and tradition are understood as dichotomous. As commercial cotton-farming boomed in the 1910s and '20s, growing numbers of Tohono O'odham began to move seasonally between their villages and the cotton fields. Most returned frequently to their desert rancherías where they continued, when conditions allowed it, to farm, raise cattle, and re-establish cultural and kinship bonds. The BIA policy of encouraging the Tohono O'odham to take up wage work thus failed to assimilate or integrate them into the surrounding society, instead permitting them to create a unique niche within the political economy of south-central Arizona—one that would ultimately reinforce, rather than undermine, their sense of themselves as a distinct people.[28]

Of course, long before the BIA developed a system of labor recruitment at the turn of the twentieth century, the Tohono O'odham had engaged in a pattern of rotational movement between villages, missions, and Euro-American-owned mines and farms. The Tohono O'odham historically practiced *ak chin* agriculture (see Chapter 1), planting a variety of crops in the deltas of ephemeral desert streams in order to take advantage of summer rains, and then moving between mountain spring villages and desert gathering camps for the remainder of the year. As early as the late eighteenth century, the O'odham of northern Sonora worked in mission communities such as San Xavier del Bac and Tumacácori, but the number of individuals residing at the missions never exceeded much more than one hundred at a time, and most lived in the missions only temporarily before returning to their home villages.[29] Many Tohono O'odham also historically worked for other O'odham for payment in kind. Alonso Flores, whose family owned an allotment on the San Xavier reservation at the turn of the century, recalled how "the Santa Rosa people, that's what they call those people out there in the country . . . used to come down and help us, because we raised wheat and barley and beans." To reimburse them, he and his family would either pay them with a "share of the crops" or "if we had the money to pay them, we would go ahead and pay them with the money."[30]

From the Spanish occupation to the U.S. territorial period, more and more Tohono O'odham took up wage work. As early as the 1850s, O'odham men often worked in mines at Patagonia, Tubac, and Ajo.[31] Hundreds also worked for Mexican and Anglo ranchers who lived along the San Pedro and Santa Cruz rivers, where women would work as domestics, grind wheat, and/or carry wood and water, and men would handle the cattle. By the end of the century, others worked on the railroads and in other capacities throughout the Southwest.[32]

Only in the southeastern districts of the Tohono O'odham territory, which was occupied mostly by the distinct cultural and dialect groups of the Ko-lo:di and the eastern Aji, did significant numbers of Tohono O'odham manage to avoid wage work by raising large cattle herds. Around the turn of the twentieth century, many Mexican Ko-lo:di moved north to Arizona from Sonora, bringing cattle and ranching skills with them. Livestock would help this group avoid dependence upon the wage economy. Their distinct economic niche also had cultural significance, since those families who engaged in commercial ranching were generally more receptive to the prospect of private property and began to abandon the older practice of village government by consensus. By the early 1900s, many Ko-lo:di and eastern Aji in the district were also becoming Presbyterians, responding to missionaries who were active in the area.[33]

The growing divergence between O'odham who depended upon a combination of ak chin farming and wage work and O'odham who had become commercial ranchers in their own right led to disagreements over the future of Tohono O'odham lands. In the first decade of the century, a Presbyterian missionary named Frazier Herndon persuaded some converts among the Ko-lo:di and Aji to press for allotment as a way to protect their lands from outside encroachment. Herndon hoped that allotment would concentrate the population and thus facilitate conversions, and he helped to convince the BIA to send an agent to initiate the process. Soon, however, the allotment agent ran into resistance from O'odham from other districts, including Aji villagers further to the west and north, where ak chin farming remained common. Some of these villagers actively resisted allotment by pulling up survey markers.[34]

By 1913 the BIA put its allotment plans on indefinite hold for several reasons. First, those O'odham who had resisted allotment surveys made it clear that the process would be more cumbersome than anticipated. Second, some local BIA officials questioned whether the arid desert lands of the Tohono O'odham lent themselves to severalty, since irrigable land was scarce and even lands along ephemeral streams were only productive for short periods of time before the O'odham had to move to the winter villages. More important, however, was that in 1913 Arizona Senator Marcus Smith, with the support of Arizona's newly organized state government, successfully added a clause to the 1913 Indian Appropriations Act declaring that no more land would be allotted on Arizona's public domain. The new state government argued that enough of its lands was already controlled by the federal government, and it hoped to reserve Tohono O'odham lands for exploitation by commercial ranchers and miners.[35]

Still, it became increasingly clear to both the Tohono O'odham and local BIA officials that something had to be done to protect O'odham lands. Many Mexican-American and Anglo ranchers were claiming Tohono O'odham lands as their own. Moreover, conditions for those who lived on previously designated reservations or allotted lands were rapidly deteriorating. At San Xavier, allottees suffered from a decreasing water supply due to overgrazing, dredging, and diversions from the Santa Cruz River. The Gila Bend reservation was in even worse shape because of upriver diversions.[36]

The BIA assigned the superintendent of the Gila River reservation, Frank Thackery, to seek a new solution. Thackery, who already felt that the arid lands of the Tohono O'odham were unsuited to allotment, helped to organize a committee of eight members to study conditions in the rancherías. The Committee of Eight was made up of Thackery himself, Tohono O'odham leaders Jose X. Pablo and Hugh Norris, and both the Presbyterian missionary Frazier Herndon and the Catholic missionary Bonaventure Oblasser, among others. Both Norris and Pablo had been educated in government schools and were Presbyterian Ko-lo:di who had earlier supported allotment but now hoped to find another way to protect O'odham lands from non-Indian incursions. To enlist the support of other O'odham, they worked through a new organization of southeastern Aji and Ko-lo:di called the Good Government League (GGL). The GGL called public meetings and convinced 111 O'odham to sign a petition asking for protection by the federal government. The Committee of Eight then presented a joint recommendation to the Indian commissioner in August 1915, arguing that the best way to protect grazing lands and to preserve dispersed Tohono O'odham farmlands was to establish a new reservation. They stressed the point that the Tohono O'odham had always avoided dependence on government annuities, and that a reservation would ensure that they could continue to do so.[37]

The politically savvy Thackery courted Salt River valley growers for support, reminding them of their dependence upon seasonal Indian labor. Since cotton growers only needed pickers for several months out of the year, the committee reasoned that the rancherías should be protected, offering the Tohono O'odham a place to return when the picking season ended. They explicitly linked the idea of a reservation to the larger goal of encouraging work discipline and proper gender roles, arguing that a reservation, combined with seasonal wage work, would promote the "industry, individuality, and manhood" of O'odham men.[38]

The committee's report persuaded Indian Commissioner Cato Sells to recommend the creation of a new reservation, but this was not the end of the story. President Woodrow Wilson established a reservation by executive order in January 1916, but soon thereafter a coalition of Arizonans, primarily from Pima County where most of the reservation was situated, protested the move. Euro-American and Mexican-American cattlemen, the Tucson and Casa Grande chambers of commerce, and the Chamber of Mines led the assault, complaining both about the loss of access to O'odham lands and about the loss of potential tax income. Race was central to their argument. In a 61-page report they argued that "just as many white people, every whit as industrious and deserving as these Indians, would appreciate a similar princely gift from the government. . . . If this land is ever to be made worth a dollar for any purpose whatever, enterprising, hustling, go-ahead white men will do it."[39]

To challenge the opposition, Thackery intensified his effort to enlist support from cotton growers who employed Tohono O'odham workers. In a letter to Bonaventure Oblasser he asked for assistance in recruiting "at least 1,000 Papago pickers by the latter part of September or the first part of October," arguing that "the amount of cash they will receive in wages is not nearly so important to their people as it will be to further establish a good name for themselves as morally strong people who are honest and efficient workers." He concluded that "it is an opportunity to prove that no mistake was made in recently recognizing their landed rights by giving them a large reservation."[40]

As Thackery had hoped, Arizona cotton growers provided decisive political support for a reservation. John Buchitt of the Tempe Cotton Exchange wrote personally to Senator Carl Hayden, arguing that without the reservation, "the Papagoes [sic] would be compelled to move, and as they are needed, in fact necessary, in the development of our cotton industry I sincerely hope that you will do all you can to prevent any reduction in the size of their holdings."[41]

In 1917 President Wilson signed a compromise measure to resolve the conflict over the reservation once and for all. Wilson issued a new executive order that cut the reservation into two parts divided by a 475,000-acre strip that was to serve as the site of a new road between Tucson and Ajo. He also removed several other sections from the reservation that had been occupied by Mexican-American and Euro-American ranchers and left the reservation open to non-Indian mining patents. Even with the reduction in size, the new Papago or Sells reservation represented a significant—if only partial—victory for the Tohono O'odham and their supporters. In their struggle to protect their lands, the Tohono O'odham had succeeded in establishing one of the three largest reservations in the country in the middle of the allotment era. Perhaps counterintuitively, it was the actions of Anglo cotton growers that proved decisive. In June an assistant to the state attorney general proclaimed that Thackery's enlistment of support by cotton growers had been critical, since he had "demonstrat[ed] that the Papago Indians are of economic value to Arizona through getting them to become cotton pickers."[42]

After the reservation was established, other contentious issues remained. The BIA planned to make cattle ranching, rather than farming, the economic foundation of the reservation even though many villagers preferred to continue traditional forms of ak chin agriculture. Throughout the 1910s government surveys estimated that the O'odham planted between nine to ten thousand acres using ak chin methods. To encourage a transition to ranching, the government dug twenty-nine new deep wells, four shallow wells, and thirty-one *charcos* (water tanks for cattle) on the Sells and San Xavier reservations between 1917 and 1933. While some O'odham, such as the cattle-ranching Ko-lo:di and Aji on the southeast portion of the reservation, encouraged this economic program, others put up concerted resistance.[43]

Some Tohono O'odham objected to the construction of wells altogether, since they understood that it was the first step in preparing the villages for conversion to a livestock-based economy. For example, at the western Aji village of Ge Oidag (Big Fields) the O'odham complained both that a new well would cost too much and that it was designed to put an end to ak chin farming methods. Such practices had cultural as well as economic significance. Big Fields was the location of one of the largest yearly *nawait* ceremonies, which many O'odham viewed as essential to their way of life (the Himdag) because it ensured that the rains fell on their fields every summer. During the ceremony, O'odham men drank saguaro cactus wine, called *nawait*, produced by O'odham women and then purged themselves with vomiting in order to "bring down the clouds." The O'odham at the village refused to cease the practice despite persistent calls by BIA officials to end it, and they viewed plans to build the well as part of an attack on their culture. Only after persistent pressure, and after the BIA retracted its demand that the villagers would have to pay for the new well, did the local headman agree that the government could proceed to build it.[44]

Because of the ephemeral nature of ak chin agriculture, which relied upon the rainwater runoff from later summer storms, the Tohono O'odham from farming villages increasingly supplemented their household economies with off-reservation wage work. Those who owned little or no cattle were most receptive to working for wages, but only if the work did not undermine the viability of the villages. As Tohono O'odham labor recruiter Edwin Santeo began to seek potential workers for the cotton industry in the mid-1910s, he found that local headmen were willing to encourage the residents in their rancherías to work off-reservation only if they were permitted, in Santeo's words, "enough time to make arrangements for their own crops before they go."[45]

Tohono O'odham from Mexico also responded to the demand for wage-workers, ignoring the international boundary that divided their homeland. In Mexico, Tohono O'odham lived in communities such as Sonoíta, El Carrizo, and Pozo Verde, just south of the border. Johnson José remembered, "O'odham would cross the boundary to the north, work and earn their money. There were no problems crossing the boundary. When the harvest was over they would return south." Reyes Salcido, who grew up in Sonoíta, remembered similarly that her father crossed the border frequently to work in Arizona: "The boundary meant nothing to us. We would travel back and forth, north to south and south to north, in wagons and later in cars without any problems."[46]

Off-reservation wage work thus did not fundamentally undermine the cultural or political structure of the villages. Within families that combined ak chin farming with seasonal wage work, traditional patrilocal residence patterns remained common. In Santa Rosa, which produced cotton pickers in large numbers, women continued to move into or near the households of their husbands' families well into the 1930s. The distribution of fields among the villagers was still the responsibility of all-male village councils. Rather than a strict division between male producer and female homemaker, husband and wife tended to the family field together. Women also continued to gather cactus fruit and trade pottery, baskets, and other items, while other family members worked for wages in the cotton fields and mines, on the railroads, and in Tucson. These adaptations defied the BIA's policy of transforming the O'odham economy and encouraging nuclear family households with a stricter division of labor between male breadwinners and female homemakers. They also explain why Ruth Underhill could describe Santa Rosa as one of the most "traditional" villages on the reservation.[47]

James McCarthy's family provides a good example of how off-reservation wage work and a flexible, sexual division of labor could preserve rather than undermine ties to the reservation villages. In the 1920s McCarthy (who had adopted this name as a soldier during World War I) left the reservation to work along the Pacific coast from California to Alaska, sending wages back to his family in southern Arizona. Meanwhile, his mother, sister, and brother remained in Arizona, farming and raising a few cattle on the ranchería while seasonally picking cotton for the Goodyear Company farms in the Salt River valley. Eventually McCarthy returned to his family. He explained that "as farm workers, we were paid $1.50 a day and board. All the money we made we put into one bank—my mother. Any time one of us needed some money, we went to her." McCarthy supplemented his family's agricultural income with more lucrative work in the copper mining town of Ajo. Throughout the 1920s and into the 1930s, this pattern allowed the family to retain close ties to the reservation, and thus to resist BIA attempts to assimilate them.[48]

Some families depended more upon the wage work of women than men. The records of Tucson field matrons reveal that while some work was available to O'odham men in the city, almost twice as many positions were open to women. In 1913 the superintendent at San Xavier noted that field matron Lydia Gibbs had helped over sixty O'odham women to obtain jobs in Tucson homes. As he explained, "There are 31 girls and 32 women working in town. The women are married and do washing at their homes and also work at times in private families."[49] One Tohono O'odham woman who lived and worked in Tucson in the 1900s and 1910s recalled, "I guess there was lots of work for women because everybody worked. . . . They worked out among the people, like I said, washing and ironing and all that stuff—making maybe tortillas for the Mexicans and . . . for the white people."[50]

Janette Woodruff noted that work in Tucson was a part of a larger economic strategy. In 1918 the O'odham population in Tucson varied seasonally from about 175 to 275. As she explained it, "From January until along in the spring it is on the increase . . . many coming from the country to work in town. . . . All found steady work and good wages, saving their money and buying what they need when they return to their homes in the country." As the cotton industry boomed a decade later, Woodruff noted that the majority of those households added a new element to this seasonal pattern, with entire families leaving to work in the cotton fields during the harvesting season from October through January.[51]

Women who lived for extended periods in Tucson and those who worked there only briefly often retained close connections to their home villages, where extended family members remained to care for livestock and/or subsistence farms. One girl who periodically moved to Tucson so that her mother could work as a domestic recalled that they would return every year to Santa Rosa for All Souls' Day and again during the August rainy season to help their relatives plant beans and other crops. A woman named Frances Manuel left her children on the reservation in the care of her mother-in-law while she took up domestic work in Tucson and while her husband worked for the railroad. As Manuel recalled, "I came back to the village every weekend, then pretty soon we went every two weeks. . . . I had my house there on the reservation; everything was the same because we had my mother-in-law there, and the beds were made."[52]

The extra income provided O'odham women with the opportunity to help their families in the villages or to escape their family's strict oversight of their behavior. In one case, according to Janette Woodruff, a woman "had saved money enough to build a house for her parents on the reservation." In another a woman who "was put out of her home by her father because she bobbed her hair . . . came to my place and stayed with me all night. Her father came to try and have her return home, but she would not." On the same day, "another girl went to her home in the village with the understanding if her people were not good to her I could put her in a home where she could earn good wages and have a good home." While Woodruff's interpretations of these women's actions must be read critically, since one of her goals was to loosen their ties to the reservation, it appears that domestic labor served as an important alternative for some O'odham women to dependence upon their families or on O'odham men, and as an inroad to the diverse social and cultural life of the cities.[53]

Many Tohono O'odham women who worked in Tucson continued to attend seasonal fiestas and ceremonies outside of town, often to the consternation of both their employers and BIA officials. One Tucson field matron noted in frustration that during a December fiesta at San Xavier she received many complaints about Indians who did not show up for work. During the week of December 3–7 she found the O'odham village in South Tucson almost deserted. Complaining that "the Indian . . . lacks application or 'sticking' qualities," she noted that he/she "will leave a good job, to attend a fiesta, or picnic, regardless of the plight in which he leaves his employer."[54]

Tohono O'odham women thus often resisted the strict work regimen encouraged by BIA officials and informally negotiated the terms of their labor with their employers. In one case, Woodruff complained that "five girls . . . hired an auto and went . . . to San Xavier to a dance, returning at 5 o'clock in the morning" and "not one of their employers knew they were gone." Other O'odham women took frequent sick days off, quit without notice, or simply disappeared for several days. Exasperated, Woodruff exclaimed, "It is surprising what some of the white women take from the Indian girls in order to be nice to them so they will not leave."[55]

While women were more likely than men to find wage work in Tucson, men were more likely to find it in the mining towns. Men living in Mexican border towns such as Sonoíta, and in the western rancherías on the Sells reservation, could earn some of the highest and steadiest wages available to them just west of the reservation at Ajo (though they earned lower wages there than any other ethnic group). As with agricultural or day labor, many men worked at Ajo only temporarily and then returned to their villages or left to find other jobs. Into the 1930s the New Cornelia Company capitalized on this tenuous connection with the mining towns by not building homes for its O'odham workers. Instead, it leased plots of undeveloped land to the Indians, who had to construct their own housing at Ajo Indian village.[56]

While these conditions were highly exploitative, the availability of wage work outside of Ajo at least allowed O'odham men to protest with their feet when they no longer were willing to tolerate poor treatment. In the late 1920s James McCarthy was injured three times doing heavy work such as drilling, shoveling, and moving track. Because "the company did not give me any pay while I was resting," he left to work in the San Joaquin Valley in California for a season before returning to Arizona to work on the railroad and in the cotton fields. Peter Blaine, who would serve as the chairman of the Papago Tribal Council in the 1940s, recalled similar experiences at Ajo. After repeatedly being denied a job as a driller, he too eventually left to take up wage work elsewhere.[57]

In at least one case, the Tohono O'odham at Ajo put up more direct resistance to the unequal working and living conditions. In early December 1916 over one hundred O'odham workers went on strike, joining Mexican American and Euro-American workers to protest low wages and poor working and living conditions. According to the *Arizona Labor Journal*, 130 O'odham joined the local union. Eventually, the strike was put down when 150 troops from the 14th Infantry entered Ajo on December 20 (see Chapter 4).[58] While there is no recorded evidence that the Tohono O'odham participated in organized labor activism at Ajo again, in the years after the strike, they resumed their practice of periodically working in the mines while dividing subsistence and wage labor responsibilities between family members and preserving ties to the rancherías.

WATER, ALLOTMENT, AND RESISTANCE
ON THE GILA RIVER RESERVATION

The BIA's policy of using allotment and wage labor as the best way to free the Indians from ward status and to promote independence and citizenship was perhaps most paradoxical in its application to the Pimas and Maricopas. For these groups, independence had always been based upon access to the free-flowing waters of the Gila River and its tributaries. It was difficult to deny the role that upriver diversions in towns like Solomonville, Florence, and Safford had played in disrupting the river's flow. Some Pima and Maricopa leaders exploited this contradiction by directly confronting the federal government, and by skillfully utilizing the BIA's own assimilation rhetoric to point out that it was government policy, or government inaction, that was undermining their independence and industry.

As the name Akimel O'odham (river people) suggests, a certain kind of labor, namely, farming with the natural flow of the river, was an important element of Pima identity. George Webb, a Pima who grew up on the Gila reservation, remembered the critical role that the river played for the Pimas before upriver diversions and erosion. He explained that every morning as the sun began to rise, "the Pimas were out in the fields with their shovels. They would fan out and lead the water to the alfalfa, along the corn rows, and over to the melons." Webb used the metaphor of a blackbird that would not sing without the sound of the flowing river to explain the impact that the dying Gila had on his people. When the river still flowed, "the red-wing blackbirds would sing in the trees and fly down to look for bugs along the ditches. Their song always means that there is water close by, as they will not sing if there is not water splashing somewhere."[59]

Even as the Gila's waters fell to a trickle in the 1890s and early 1900s, most Pimas and Maricopas initially rejected wage work, choosing to remain on their reservation to attempt either to farm or to subsist from the land through other means, such as cutting and selling mesquite for fence posts and fuel. As early as 1905, Pimas and Maricopas were cutting and selling nearly twelve thousand cords of wood every year.[60] Some tried paid farmwork only to reject it and return to the reservation. George Webb, for example, worked in 1917 as a ranch hand in the Glendale area of the Salt River valley. He soon quit his job and returned to Gila Crossing—one of the few places where the Gila still rose to the surface through an alluvial spring—to attempt to farm and raise cattle. In his memoir, while he acknowledged that much of the Gila reservation had been reduced from a rich agricultural area "where everything used to be green" to "acres of desert" and "miles of dust," he explained that most Pimas "had never worked for wages. They chose to stay on the Reservation. It was their home."[61]

A few, usually those who had attended government schools, followed another path, choosing to abandon the reservation altogether. Despite the severe problems on the reservation, this decision was never easy. Anna Shaw, who had attended the Gila River Indian School, felt that the decision she and her husband made to move to Phoenix in 1920 involved the rejection of an important part of their identity. As she would later explain in her autobiography, "Back in 1920 when Ross and I were hopeful young newlyweds, we had but two alternatives—farming in wretched poverty on the reservation or working hard to get ahead at a city job in the white man's world." Shaw recalled with regret that the economic situation on the reservation gave them no real option. In her own words, "We, of course, chose the latter, but in doing so we had to give up the opportunity to be with other Indians on our own land and share in our proud Pima-Maricopa heritage. We had to live like white men."[62]

Still, Pima and Maricopa identity was not as inflexible as these stories might seem to suggest, and many reservation leaders attempted to find a middle ground between the extremes of either wholesale abandonment of or persistence in an unchanging way of life. By the early twentieth century, Pimas and Maricopas had already undergone dramatic changes. They had been actively engaged with the American market economy for sixty years through their production of wheat and other crops. Many had become Presbyterians, and hundreds had attended government day schools and/or boarding schools. Change did not necessarily imply an abandonment of their identity. They were asking for a reasonable federal policy that would preserve their access to the Gila River's water and allow the reservation to remain economically viable.

Unfortunately, what the government had in mind was far from reasonable. Throughout the first decade of the twentieth century, the BIA prepared to enact William Code's 1902 plan to allot the reservation into 5-acre plots and sell off 180,000 acres of so-called surplus lands on the western portion of the reservation to pay for groundwater pumps to the east. The Pimas and Maricopas put up a concerted fight against the plan. Antonito Azul, who by the turn of the century had become known as the head chief of the Pima nation due to his visible public role as a negotiator with the surrounding Euro-American population, adamantly rejected the land-for-water deal. In 1906 Azul argued that 5-acre allotments, without a substantial area of common grazing land and sufficient access to river water, were too small to ensure independence from government support. He protested to

Congress in 1906, "All our people ask for is enough of water to irrigate from 25 to 30 acres to the family and enough of desert land to supply them with firewood and some pasture, so that they, as formerly, can earn their living." He also argued that if the Pimas were forced to rely on groundwater pumps, as Code hoped, their farms would suffer from alkali buildup and lose the benefit of the river's natural fertilizers.[63]

Azul and other Pima leaders skillfully used the rhetoric of early-twentieth-century Indian policy—about the importance of avoiding dependency on the government—to make their point. "Of course," he said, "we want the Government to give us water, but we want good river water—a water that will fertilize land and produce good crops, by which we can make our own living and be independent. We do not want to be dependent upon the Government for subsistence."[64] He thus turned the rhetoric of the assimilation policy on its head, arguing that it was government policy, and not Indian laziness, that threatened to undermine the very qualities that Euro-Americans touted as necessary for full citizenship.

In 1911 the issue of water allocation and allotment became urgent as Commissioner of Indian Affairs R. G. Valentine began to enact a slightly revised version of William Code's plan. Valentine ordered Charles E. Rioblin, a special allotting agent, to begin allotting five acres each to heads of family on the Gila reservation and five acres to the spouse of each household head. Once these lands were allotted, five acres would be distributed to single men with "preference being given to those able to utilize the allotment"—a vague stipulation that Pimas and Maricopas interpreted to mean that some men, children, and single women might end up with nothing. Water would be supplied through a series of groundwater pumps, rather than from the natural flow of the Gila.[65]

Pima and Maricopa leaders once again sharply condemned the plan. Many of them farmed sixty acres or more, so five-acre allotments would drastically reduce their holdings. In 1911 Azul wrote Congress an "appeal to justice" in which he directly criticized W. H. Code, the irrigation engineer, and J. B. Alexander, the Indian agent who had been stationed at the Gila reservation between 1902 and 1911. Specifically, he condemned both men's claims that "the east end of the reservation [was] enough for the Indians, leaving the west end—the best part, and that near the ranch of some 18,000 acres belonging to Code's friend and business associate, Chandler—for the white people." Azul's claim that the western portion of the reservation had the best lands was confirmed by Willis Lee, an engineer with the Geological Survey. Lee argued that pumps would best be installed in the west because underground water sources were closer to the surface there.

But Code ignored such concerns, seemingly confirming Azul's accusations that he was more interested in opening the reservation to land barons like Chandler than solving the water crisis on the reservation.[66]

The Pimas and Maricopas had the support of some Euro-Americans in the Casa Grande valley, who agreed that federal reclamation policy had primarily helped large land speculators like Chandler rather than smaller farmers. Thomas Weedin, a journalist in the Casa Grande valley, argued that the nature of the commercial agricultural boom in Arizona was a threat to the Indians and white small farmers alike. Moreover, he argued that, by usurping the Indians' rights to the Gila, Euro-Americans in effect encouraged the Indians to resort to "mendicancy and vice." Weedin correctly pointed out that the depressed status of the indigenous population was not due to racial inferiority but was rather the result of the government's ill-advised policies and the nature of industrial agriculture. He reminded his readers that the Pimas and Maricopas had until recently been "the only successful irrigators in Arizona." Their crisis, he explained, had begun with the diversion of the Gila's waters. The Reclamation Bureau had passed up its chance to rectify this situation when it constructed a dam on the Salt River rather than the Gila, largely because of the lobbying power of commercial growers like Chandler and the influence of William Code. In the case of the Pimas and Maricopas, then, the government was engaged not in "elevating a savage tribe" but in promoting "the destruction of a civilization already attained."[67]

Some Pima and Maricopa leaders also astutely recognized that they would strengthen their hand by linking the interests of Euro-American farmers to their own. The politically savvy Azul argued that there was enough water in the Gila to "mak[e] thousands of happy homes for us Pimas and for the whites besides, at a small expense to the Government, which years ago was the steadfast friend of the Pimas, but not of late years."[68]

Not all indigenous leaders, however, conformed to this strategy. Others demanded that their access to the free-flowing river be renewed, regardless of the impact on Euro-American farmers. In 1908 the U.S. Supreme Court had decided in *Winters v. the United States* that Indians enjoyed "reserved rights" to the waters on their homelands. This decision, in theory, should have allowed the Pimas and Maricopas to sue upstream diverters. Following the Winters doctrine, 444 Pimas and Maricopas signed a petition demanding the restoration of "our river water." Pima leaders such as Kisto Morago and Harvey Cawker formed the Pima Business Committee in December 1911, arguing that the Winters doctrine guaranteed an amount of water equal to the free flow of the Gila: the water was "still ours, and such water would cost us nothing."[69]

In response to the outcry by hundreds of Pimas and Maricopas, the BIA, Arizona's attorney general, and Senator Carl Hayden explored the possibility of using the Winters doctrine to file suits against those who had diverted the Gila's water. Both the BIA and Senator Carl Hayden, however, decided not to support litigation. Hayden did not want to pit the claims of Indians to water against Euro-American claims. He was so adamant on this point that he argued, despite evidence to the contrary, that it was solely environmental change and not upriver diversions that had disrupted the flow of the river.[70]

Indian resistance, however, did persuade the federal government to suspend Code's allotment plan. In 1912 the House Subcommittee on Expenditures in the Interior Department began its own investigation of conditions on the reservation. Shortly thereafter it concluded that A. J. Chandler and other speculators had indeed influenced Code to act on their behalf. In 1913 Code resigned. Senators Hayden and Ashurst then pushed a new, joint-use solution that would theoretically address the problems of the indigenous and Euro-American farmers alike. In June 1914 they introduced a bill to pursue the construction of a major dam and reservoir on the Gila to be called the San Carlos Project. Hayden asserted that the interests of Euro-American farmers would be advanced by publicizing the Indians' crisis on the reservation. "Our best, and in fact our only avenue of approach," he declared, "is by reason of the fact that the Pima Indians will be benefited." He hoped that such an approach would win over Western politicians who might otherwise oppose a second major federal reclamation project in Arizona.[71]

Meanwhile, the government initiated a new allotment program that would protect a far greater area of land. While Code's plan had called for only 5-acre allotments totaling ten thousand acres, between 1914 and 1922 the government divided more than ninety-six thousand acres into allotments, with most Pimas and Maricopas securing rights to two 10-acre allotments each. Only one of each of the allotments had water rights, leaving the other for grazing cattle. The allotments were to remain in trust for twenty-five years, meaning that the Indians could not sell the land, and the property could not be taxed or mortgaged. The latter stipulation, from the Dawes Act, was designed to protect the allotments while the Indians began their farming operations. These allotments represented a victory over Code's much less generous plan. Still, for many Pimas and Maricopas, 20-acre tracts were far smaller than the 60-acre farms they had maintained in the past.[72]

Unfortunately, the BIA failed to secure the other crucial ingredient for successful farming: water. As World War I began, Congress shifted attention from domestic to international concerns, and interest in the San

Carlos Project waned. Eventually, even Carl Hayden pressed for a more modest proposal that would combine smaller dams and ditches with groundwater pumping. Over the next ten years, the government constructed two new diversion dams as a part of the Florence Casa Grande Project, but upriver diversions, flooding, and the failure to recognize Pima and Maricopa reserved water rights left only a minority able to make a living by farming throughout the 1920s. Only in 1924 would discussion of the San Carlos Project resume.[73]

Partly because of the new irrigation works and partly because of a period of increased rainfall, Pima and Maricopa allottees managed to cultivate an average of sixteen thousand acres between 1910 and 1914 and thirty-two thousand acres between 1915 and 1919. Some even began to grow their own long-staple cotton and sell it on the market.[74] Thus, at the precise moment that the demand for their labor skyrocketed, many Pimas and Maricopas could once again subsist without resorting to wage labor in large, Euro-American–owned cotton fields.[75]

By the early 1920s, however, declining conditions on the Gila reservation once again put new pressures on Pimas and Maricopas to work for wages on off-reservation farms. The decade began with an economic depression (1920–1921) followed by several years of drought. The new superintendent of the Pima agency, A. F. Duclos, pointed out that the renewed water crisis resulted in the decline of the indigenous system of production and distribution. The Pimas and Maricopas had once operated an efficient system whereby "each village had a subchief, a water boss, and necessary assistants" who organized and oversaw field production, permitting them to raise "thousands of bushels of grain and beans." Now, no amount of exposure to the agricultural techniques of the Euro-American commercial growers could rectify the underlying problem: "The water of the Gila River that made their field production possible is no longer available."[76]

Predictably, without a solution to the water shortage, allotment failed to solve the problems of the Pimas and Maricopas—or, for that matter, to assimilate them. Rather than question the allotment policy and the diversion of the Gila's waters by Euro-Americans, Commissioner Burke explained that off-reservation cotton-picking would "very largely solve the problem [of] frequently recurring periods of distress"—distress that he admitted was due to the lack of water. As a warning to those who refused to accept his offer to make "a better living outside," Burke explained that he would no longer "continue to ask Congress for relief." He thus continued to follow the logic that had spurred him to sponsor the Burke Act of 1906, which had ended the mandatory twenty-five-year trust period for recipients of allotments. In effect, he viewed the combination of the crisis on the reservation and the labor demand on nearby industrial farms as an opportunity to convert the Indians into wageworkers, and thus to end the ward status of the Pimas and Maricopas.[77]

Despite ever-worsening conditions, many Pimas and Maricopas continued to avoid seasonal cotton-picking. In 1923 Duclos granted the Indians under his jurisdiction the right to cut and sell wood, "which has enabled them to come through the winter with very little assistance." According to Duclos, only a small number of Indians were willing to work as farm laborers. Other Pima and Maricopa wageworkers sought better-paying jobs closer to home—on the new federally funded irrigation works, on the railroads, or in the construction of a new smelter for the Magma Copper Company in Superior, Arizona. For the time being, then, the Pimas and Maricopas avoided the same kind of large-scale participation in the agricultural wage economy as the Tohono O'odham, maintaining a distinct niche in the regional political economy.[78]

In 1924 Congress passed the Indian Citizenship Act. Some scholars have viewed the law as a big step toward admitting Indians into the national polity as equals. As historian Frederick Hoxie has pointed out, however, the law did not guarantee equality; instead, it capped off a series of reforms that relegated much of the indigenous population to a subordinate status within the nation-state. The law did nothing, for example, to guarantee Indians the right to vote. In Arizona the courts continued to define them as people "under guardianship" who were ineligible to participate in elections. Moreover, nothing in the law prevented states and private citizens from segregating Indians, or from discriminating against them as racialized minorities. Quite the contrary, the net impact of the reforms associated with the assimilation policy was to relegate Indians in Arizona to the bottom rungs of a racial and class hierarchy. At best, then, the Indian Citizenship Law guaranteed second-class citizenship.[79]

Still, the Tohono O'odham, Pimas, and Maricopas had their own ideas about their future place in the socioeconomic order and the national polity—ideas that differed substantially from the blueprints drawn up by federal bureaucracies and regional employers. Most Pimas and Maricopas, for example, refused to leave the reservations to take up wage work. Instead, they continued to eke out an existence with the increasingly unreliable flow of the Gila River and groundwater pumps, or by harvesting and selling mesquite.

Even for those who worked off the reservation, wage work did not generally lead to cultural assimilation as the BIA had hoped. Instead, most indigenous people found a variety of means to negotiate the shifting contours of the political economy. Those Tohono O'odham who worked in the mines organized the most direct resistance to the exploitation of their labor, working across ethnic lines to combat poor wages and working conditions. Others simply refused to engage in wage work altogether. Thousands of others moved annually from villages into the agricultural fields, mines, and towns. Such a pattern allowed them to return periodically into desert rancherías where they farmed, raised cattle, reinforced kinship bonds, and participated in rituals and fiestas. In each case, they played an active role in defining their place in American society, negotiating, as best they could, the rapidly changing economic and social terrain.

CHAPTER 3

▼ ▼ ▼ ▼ ▼ ▼ ▼ ▼ ▼ ▼ ▼ ▼ ▼ ▼ ▼ ▼ ▼

CROSSING BORDERS

Rosalio Moisés Valenzuela and his older sister, Antonia, both of them Yaquis, were born in Colorada, Sonora, where their father worked as a miner in the mid-1890s. Their parents and grandparents had fled the Yaqui River to escape the ongoing war with the Mexican army. In his memoirs Rosalio recalled how "many friends and relatives from the Rio Yaqui worked in the Colorada and Suviete mines or at the Minas Prietas five miles away where they dug for graphite." Most of the boys and men over the age of ten worked for eight pesos a day for eight-hour shifts, which was substantially more than they might earn working on the haciendas. Men and women with land, livestock, or special skills contributed to the family income in other ways. Some of Rosalio and Antonia's relatives owned cattle, and their grandfather, Abelardo, was a full-time shoemaker. María, their grandmother, was a *curandera*, tending to the spiritual and physical health of the community. The Valenzuelas supported themselves in this way until 1900, when war between the Yaquis and the Mexican military erupted once again. Many men left the mine, returning to the Yaqui River to help defend the villages. "From this time on," Rosalio recalled, "our lives changed."[1]

The events of 1900 propelled Rosalio and Antonia toward a series of moves that would eventually take them across the border into Arizona. That year they moved with their grandparents and several other family members to an orchard in Hermosillo. Their mother, Cecilia, left their father, Miguel, during this tumultuous period, and both children lost contact with her. Miguel obtained a new job at the Sierrita mine, while Rosalio began to work in the orchard, and Antonia helped to support the family by selling tortillas and taking in laundry. Soon, however, their lives were disrupted again. In 1903 Mexican soldiers searched Hermosillo for Yaqui insurgents. They captured and executed Rosalio's baptismal *padrino* (godfather) and rounded up their grandfather, Abelardo, and shipped him to the Yucatán to work as a peón. Miguel then temporarily returned to the Yaqui River to resume the fight against the Mexican army, but fearing for the lives of himself and his children, he soon crossed the border into Arizona. Rosalio and Antonia waited in a small house in Ranchito, Sonora, as their father looked for work north of the border. Finally, in 1905, having found a job at the Silver Bell mine near Tucson, Miguel called for his children to join him.[2]

After crossing the border, Rosalio and Antonia lived in a home constructed by their father in Barrio Anita, a multiethnic Tucson neighborhood. There, hundreds of ethnic Mexicans, Yaquis, and Tohono O'odham, among others, lived and worked together, attended the same churches and fiestas, and formed ties of kinship and culture. Miguel worked alongside other border crossers from Mexico on the railroads, on the farms in the Salt River valley, and in mines and smelters stretching from Arizona to California. Eventually, Rosalio followed the path of his father, earning wages in the mining towns and on the railroads and industrial farms. Antonia married Ignacio Villegas and soon gave birth to three children delivered by her grandmother, María.[3]

Throughout their years in Arizona the Valenzuelas retained close ties to Sonora. They had little sense of a national identity relative to either Mexico or the United States. Instead, their life histories are filled with references to kin and local communities scattered around both sides of the border. In Arizona they worked the same kinds of jobs and lived among a similar mix of ethnic groups as they had in Sonora, including mestizos and O'odham. Miguel occasionally supplied arms to Yaquis who fought against the Mexican army in Sonora. Antonia and Ignacio eventually moved to Chandler, where they worked in the cotton fields and had more children together. Rosalio continued to work a variety of jobs, while making personal visits to Mexico for events such as the feast day of San Francisco at Magdalena. Finally, in 1932, after the Yaqui wars died down and the Great Depression seriously disrupted Arizona's extractive economy, he moved permanently back across the border to the Rio Yaqui. Neither Antonia nor Rosalio ever applied for U.S. citizenship.[4]

Rosalio and Antonia's story illustrates several important themes concerning border crossing and border culture in Arizona and Sonora. First, it raises questions about the adequacy of the word *immigration* at least as it was applied to the U.S.-Mexican borderlands. Historians have often suggested that immigrants to the United States were uprooted or pushed out of their home country by poverty and/or political oppression, while being pulled by economic and/or political opportunity in the United States. While there is some truth in this formulation, the experiences of the Valenzuelas and thousands like them reveal its shortcomings. In fact, as I demonstrated, the same basic forces altered the political economies of Sonora and Arizona simultaneously, displacing small farmers and ranchers on *both* sides of the border while creating a demand for their labor. Displaced peasants and ranchers had little choice but to travel from town to town working for wages. They rarely made a single, clean break with Mexico, making their way across in stages, while often maintaining transnational relationships for decades after entering the United States. Thousands, like Rosalio, eventually returned to Mexico permanently.[5]

The story of the Valenzuelas also offers a glimpse into the rich social world of the Sonora-Arizona borderlands, in which many different groups worked the same kinds of jobs on both sides of the border, came together in diverse communities, and formed intimate, interethnic ties. As historian David Gutiérrez has written, "In response to their increasingly sharp experience of racial, cultural, and class difference, ordinary working-class ethnic Mexicans were forced to develop new mechanisms of adaptation—mechanisms that drew on sources of collective identity and solidarity that were only tangentially related to notions of formal nationality or citizenship."[6] In Arizona these identities transcended not only the international boundary but ethnic boundaries as well. A transnational, inter-ethnic regional culture flourished in communities such as Barrio Anita, where Miguel Valenzuela built a home for his family. Individuals constructed broad social and cultural networks through marriage, fictive kinship, religion, and reciprocal exchange, defying both the international border and strict ethno-racial boundaries.

Still, this story should not be generalized too far. Many border crossers followed a different path, expressing interest in permanent residency and full citizenship soon after entering the United States. Most Mexican Americans were sharply aware of the forces that excluded them from full citizenship status, and many of them worked continuously to differentiate themselves from recent border crossers in order to claim their rightful status as equal citizens, even going so far as to support legislation restricting Mexican immigration. For them, the presence of thousands of immigrants who bypassed official channels to emigrate and naturalize complicated their own attempts to become fully American.[7]

CROSSING THE INTERNATIONAL BORDER

In the decades after the Gadsden Purchase, many Mexicans who moved into what would become Arizona stayed only for brief periods. The first substantial movement occurred in the late 1840s and early 1850s, when over ten thousand Sonorans moved to, or traveled through, the region on their way to California to find gold. Most, however, failed and eventually made their way back to Sonora. In the 1860s, perhaps another seventy-five hundred Sonorenses entered the United States, largely to escape civil war and the French invasion of Mexico. Like the first wave of border crossers, many returned to Mexico when some semblance of stability returned.[8] In the 1880s, however, a new network of railroads and industrial mines spurred a more sustained movement between nations. Moreover, the completion of the Southern Pacific from Arizona to El Paso in 1880 began to bring Mexicans to Arizona from regions other than Sonora. Labor contractors recruited thousands from Chihuahua, Durango, and central Mexico. From there, they crossed through El Paso to Arizona by rail.[9]

Still, until about 1910, most Mexicans remained in the southern and southeastern parts of Arizona, from whence they could easily move back and forth across the border. This area included Pima, Cochise, and Graham counties, where most of the state's major mines were located (Figure 3.1). By the turn of the century, Mexican nationals made up the majority of the workforce in mining towns such as Clifton-Morenci and Ray, and on rail lines such as the Southern Pacific.[10] An anthropologist who has studied the region during this period found that "kin living in the two nations were not clearly differentiated by official citizenship status in their fates, their working opportunities, and their personal security."[11] In towns directly on the border, such as Nogales and Douglas, barbed wire fences were often the only divider between the two nations, and individuals could walk back and forth with ease. As a result it is impossible to determine gross immigration figures over this period. In 1907 Arizona Governor Joseph Kibby said, "What proportion of those Mexican immigrants remain here permanently is impossible to say. They are passing to and fro all of the time between Sonora and Arizona."[12]

The case of Carlos Cordoba serves as a good example of such transborder migration. Cordoba was born in 1909 in the mining town of Cananea, Sonora, but in 1914, in the middle of the Mexican Revolution, he moved north with his family to the Sonoran border town of Agua Prieta. There he worked in his uncle's shop where he learned machining, drilling, and the art of forging iron tools. At the age of fifteen, after attending a vocational school in Hermosillo, Sonora, he began to cross periodically into the

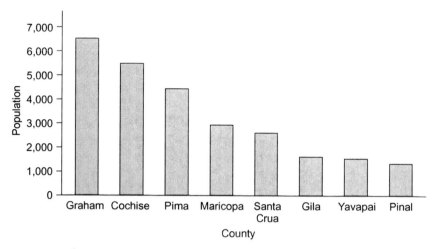

Figure 3.1. Eight Arizona Counties with Largest Mexican-Born Populations, 1910. Source: University of Virginia Geospatial and Statistical Data Center http://fisher.lib.virginia.edu/census/ (accessed August 2004).

United States, like many other young men his age. He did so because, as he said, in Mexico "they paid less, you had to look for work in other places, and jobs were scarcer." Cordoba soon joined a Mexican friend in Douglas, just north across the border from Agua Prieta. His first job in the United States was at a quarry, halfway between Douglas and Bisbee. At $2.50 per day his earnings surpassed what he could have made in Mexico. Because the quarry was so close to the border, it was easy for him to travel to Agua Prieta on the weekends. After three years at the quarry, Cordoba moved on to the Phelps Dodge Copper Queen mine in Bisbee, where he could earn even higher wages and still remain close to his family in Mexico.

Cordoba continued to work in Arizona through the 1920s, but like so many other Mexican border crossers, he never became a U.S. citizen. His last job in the United States was at a small mine in Cochise County near Bisbee. There he managed to save one hundred dollars before the mine closed at the beginning of the Great Depression in 1929. Like Rosalio Moisés, he did not bother to notify U.S. or Mexican officials but simply moved back to Agua Prieta to rejoin his family.[13]

Many Mexican Tohono O'odham—whose homeland had been bisected by the Gadsden Purchase—also periodically crossed the border to live and work in Arizona. Julia Bustamante's experiences were similar to those of many Tohono O'odham. Born in the Sonoran town of Pozo Verde, Bustamante married a Tohono O'odham man from Arizona. "My husband was born on my Nation's lands to the north and worked on both sides," she recalled many decades later. "I remember when there was no boundary. We O'odham just came and went as we pleased." Another Tohono O'odham woman, Silvia Parra, was born in Pisinemo, on the U.S. side of the border, but her family traveled every year back to their fields in San Francisco, Sonora. "We never had problems coming and going on our O'odham lands. There was no fence. My grandparents had no idea of United States lands and Mexican lands. They only knew O'odham lands. . . . They had no idea of United States or Mexican citizenship."[14] Indeed, for most Tohono O'odham, the border meant very little, and they had no clear identification with either the Mexican or U.S. nation-states.

Not all of those who crossed from Mexico into the United States in these early years did so with the intention of returning to Mexico. Many thousands of Mexicans followed a different path, eventually settling permanently in Arizona and calling for their families to join them. This became increasingly true in the 1900s as Mexico slipped into economic and political turmoil. In 1908 a railroad official noted a significant change in the resident Mexican population. Men who had worked in the United States for years "began to bring back their families. . . . Most of the men who had families with them did not go back the following season, but some of the men without their families did, and some of them came back the next year with their families." As the Mexican Revolution devolved into civil war in the 1910s, Mexican communities around Arizona took on a more settled character, although individual family members, particularly men, continued to move around in search of work.[15]

Tucson, which had harbored a substantial Mexican population since the eighteenth century, remained the most established ethnic Mexican community in the early years of the twentieth century. The Mexican Revolution led to a new influx of Mexican nationals into Tucson in the 1910s. Only 270 foreign-born persons with Hispanic surnames settled in Tucson between 1900 and 1910, but during the next ten years the population of foreign-born Hispanics grew from 2,441 to 4,261—an increase of 75 percent. This growth was largely confined to segregated areas of the city. As the railroads drew urban development to the north and to the east, where Euro-Americans dominated, most ethnic Mexicans and indigenous people remained concentrated in the barrios to the south and west.[16]

In an environment less and less friendly toward Mexicans, Tucson served as a refuge for a substantial ethnic Mexican elite and middle class. The revolutionary leaders Plutarco Elías Calles, Adolfo de la Huerta, and Alvaro Obregón, for example, stayed in Tucson as a temporary place of exile. A small, relatively well-off class of ethnic Mexican merchants also chose Tucson as their permanent home. For this group of ethnic Mexicans, crossing the border generally meant something quite different than it did for thousands of peasants, workers, and temporary expatriates. They tended to have a greater stake in establishing themselves as U.S. citizens than less affluent Mexicans, since doing so would help to secure crucial economic ties and respect from Euro-Americans.[17]

Federico Ronstadt's story illustrates this point. Rondstadt, who was born in Sonora, was the son of a wealthy German father and a Mexican mother who claimed pure Spanish ancestry, in part, as a claim to whiteness. He crossed into Arizona through the border town of Nogales in 1882 at the age of fourteen. As he remembered it, his father told him, "Now you are in the United States of America, without any question the greatest nation in the world. You will enjoy great liberty and protection under the American government and you must always feel and show deep appreciation for that." Whether or not Ronstadt recalled his father's exact words, the crux of the conversation stuck with him and instilled a desire to become a U.S. citizen. After negotiating with the Mexican government of Porfirio Díaz concerning surveys of several Sonoran ranches owned by his family, he fulfilled his desire. "When these matters were out of the way," he explained, "I promptly applied for citizenship to carry out my dream and ambition of years."[18]

Ronstadt's wealth, light skin, education, and personal connections through his father earned him a level of acceptance in the United States that most Mexicans would never enjoy. He was quite successful at adapting to the changing economy of the early-twentieth-century borderlands. As he recalled in his memoirs, "By 1906, we had built up a good trade for custom made wagons and other lines in Southern Arizona and in the state of Sonora, Mexico." He signed a contract with William Greene to provide wagons and transportation to Greene's company town of Cananea, Sonora, and he "also had subagents in Nogales, Hermosillo, and Guaymas." As the wagon trade declined, he diversified his operations, building electric streetcars and selling automobiles, auto parts, and general hardware. His successes allowed him to establish himself as a respected citizen and businessman, even among the Anglo community. The necessity of maintaining a good name for himself also gave him an incentive to declare his allegiance to the United States, unlike most Mexican border crossers whose loyalties tended to be to their families and immediate communities rather than to either the Mexican or U.S. nation-states.[19]

While a few Mexicans like Ronstadt became respected merchants, most were less fortunate. In the 1910s the violence of the Mexican Revolution

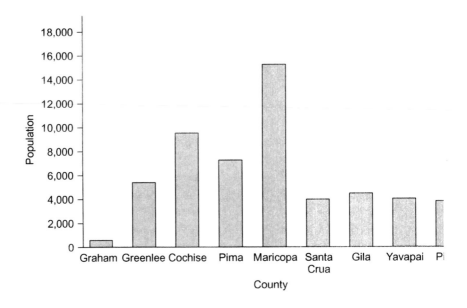

Figure 3.2. Nine Arizona Counties with Largest Mexican-Born Populations, 1920.
* Source: University of Virginia Geospatial and Statistical Data Center http://fisher.lib
.virginia.edu/census/ (accessed August 2004).

*Graham County was divided into Graham and Greenlee counties since the previous census
in 1910.

and an agricultural boom in the Salt River valley (spurred by the completion of the Roosevelt Dam) enticed more Mexicans into Arizona than ever
before. In 1914 the Salt River Valley Egyptian Cotton Growers Association hired labor recruiters to travel to the border towns to entice workers
into the valley. These *enganchadores*, as they were known, arranged transportation to the labor camps, where the workers reimbursed the growers
for transportation, food, and provisions out of the wages they earned picking cotton. The newly irrigated farmlands in Maricopa County surpassed
the rest of south-central Arizona as the primary destination for Mexicans
by 1920 (Figure 3.2).[20]

The growing presence of Mexican workers sparked a rancorous, racist
debate about immigration. Many Arizonans felt that Mexican "peons"
threatened to "degrade" and "pauperize" Euro-American workers by undermining their ability to maintain an honest living.[21] Ironically, U.S. employers also invoked racial stereotypes to argue that the border should be
kept open. Mexicans, from their point of view, were docile and tractable
and had few ambitions, making them a perfect source of cheap labor. More-

over, the exploitation of their labor did not require that they be naturalized as citizens, since they could easily return to Mexico when their work was done. Both sides of the immigration debate thus tended to characterize Mexicans as racially inferior.[22]

The growing demand for labor during World War I at least temporarily tipped the balance toward those who wanted an open border. The changing opinions of Arizona Congressman Carl Hayden reveal the thinking behind this policy. Before the war Hayden defended Arizona's Alien Labor Law, which would have restricted alien mine workers to no more than 20 percent of the total workforce had it not been declared unconstitutional by the federal district court in San Francisco. As Hayden put it, "I say that if mining can not be carried on except by employing aliens who will work long hours for little wages in mines where men are cheaper than mine timbers, we had better let the ore lie in the bowels of the earth where nature placed it."[23] Hayden revised his position, however, during Arizona's wartime cotton boom. Speaking before the House Committee on Immigration and Naturalization in 1919, he explained that the labor demand in the long-staple cotton fields doubled during the harvesting season from late October to January. "As a practical proposition," he argued, "the necessary temporary labor can come from but one source and that is Mexico." These workers would not be permitted to remain in the United States permanently or to naturalize as citizens. Instead, southwestern states should "admit temporarily seasonal laborers from Mexico, who are citizens of that Republic, to engage in agricultural work only." Upon the completion of their work, they would be expected to return to Mexico.[24]

Hayden and other proponents of temporary admittance of Mexican workers persuaded Labor Secretary William Wilson to exempt Latin American immigrants from the restrictive immigration law of 1917. The 1917 law mandated that immigrants pay a head tax and pass a literacy test to enter the country, but Wilson's so-called ninth proviso waived these requirements for immigrants from the Americas. It also loosened nineteenth-century restrictions on recruitment of Mexican contract labor. The exemption allowed Salt River valley growers to recruit around thirty thousand Mexican nationals between 1918 and 1920 alone. As a result, by 1920 Maricopa County, where Phoenix is located, far outpaced all other Arizona counties in its Mexican-born population, surpassing even Pima County, where Tucson is located, and mining counties like Cochise and Greenlee (Figure 3.2).[25]

Among those who moved into the Salt River valley were hundreds of Yaquis. Dozens of families moved into "Yaqui town," soon to be known as Guadalupe, just south of Tempe, and in 1917 Goodyear Tire and Rubber Company enticed hundreds of Yaquis to move to its cotton camp in Chandler.[26]

Several years later, the Salt River Valley Water Users Association began to hire Yaquis as their primary full-time labor force for canal maintenance. By 1920 the association established a labor camp southwest of Scottsdale occupied by about four hundred Yaqui men, women, and children, and a second southside camp with about thirty-five Yaqui families. They also picked up Yaqui workers every morning from Guadalupe. Approximately four hundred men, divided into five work crews, held relatively steady jobs, and many others worked seasonally during the summers to clear grass from the canals.[27]

By 1930 at least twenty-five hundred Yaquis lived in about ten communities in south-central Arizona. Besides the Salt River valley settlements, Yaqui communities developed in Yuma, Marana, and Eloy, all of which became important centers of industrial agriculture. Near Tucson were two areas of Yaqui settlement. About five hundred Yaquis lived in Barrio Libre, as a section of South Tucson was known, amid a substantial population of Tohono O'odham and ethnic Mexicans. Hundreds of others lived in the more ethnically homogeneous community of Pascua, adjacent to a primarily ethnic Mexican barrio called Belén.[28]

Thus, the diversity of the barrios, rural towns, and labor camps of south-central Arizona countervailed the tendency of Anglos to view their residents monolithically, through racial blinders, as Mexican aliens and peons. Within the camps lived not only Mexican mestizos but also families and individuals who identified as Yaqui, Tohono O'odham, Pima, Opata, Mayo, or otherwise. Moreover, the residents of these communities included native Arizonans, naturalized citizens, and more recent border crossers who formed a dense network of economic, cultural, and kinship ties that transcended both international and ethnic boundaries.

CROSSING ETHNO-RACIAL BORDERS

Most ethnohistorians and ethnographers of Arizona's borderlands have focused their attention on individual ethnic groups (or on white/Indian or Anglo/Mexican relations) rather than on the bonds that tied these groups together. For example, the best history of the Mexican-American experience in Tucson, Thomas Sheridan's *Los Tucsonenses*, provides a rich account of daily life in the city but says little about the close ties that ethnic Mexicans had with Yaquis and Tohono O'odham who lived among them.[29] There have also been numerous tribal histories of the Yaquis, Tohono O'odham, and Pimas, among other groups who lived in Arizona's borderlands. Most of the histories tightly focus on the persistence or evolution of single tribes over time, thus underemphasizing the cultural, economic, and kinship ties that these groups often shared with one another. While such studies are important in their own right, they tend to reinforce the notion that ethnic boundaries and identities are natural and self-contained, if not static, rather than to examine these identities as historically contingent and relational.[30]

One of the most basic interethnic ties in the barrios was marriage, although marriages that crossed the racial line between white and nonwhite were technically illegal in Arizona. The territorial assembly first passed an antimiscegenation statute in 1865, prohibiting marriage between whites and Indians, Mongolians, or blacks. Over time the law was amended to be even more restrictive. By 1913 it said that "all marriages of persons of Caucasian blood, *or their descendants,* with negroes, Mongolians or Indians, *and their descendants"* were null and void [emphasis mine]. Finally, in 1931 Hindus and Malays were added to the list of people "Caucasians" could not legally marry.[31] These statutes illustrate the state's intolerance for blurred ethnic identifications, particularly when marriage threatened the boundaries of whiteness.

Significantly, the antimiscegenation statutes did not prevent marriage between Anglos and ethnic Mexicans—a testament to the ambiguous racial status of the latter. The courts generally defined ethnic Mexicans as white, regardless of social custom. This also meant that ethnic Mexicans could not legally marry Indians, blacks, nor any of the other groups named by the law.

Two court cases demonstrate the legal system's tendency to draw strict racial boundaries, even in cases where social reality was much more complex. In 1921 Joe Kirby, whose mother was Mexican and whose father was Irish, went to court to annul his marriage to his wife, Mayellen, by claiming that he was white and she was "a person of negro blood." Mayellen's lawyers did not challenge the accusation that she was partly black, but they did challenge Kirby's claim that he was white, since his mother was Mexican. If both marriage partners were nonwhite, the marriage was legal. The judge in the case, however, refused to accept this argument, stating that "Mexicans are classed as of the Caucasian race. They are descendants, supposed to be at least, of the Spanish conquerors of that country, and unless it can be shown that they are mixed up with some other races, why the presumption is that they are descendants of the Caucasian race." He found Kirby to be white and Mayellen black and annulled the marriage.[32]

Two decades later, in 1942, the courts made another revealing ruling when Frank Pass, an accused murderer, tried to stop his wife, Ruby

Contreras Pass, from testifying against him at his trial. Arizona law did not allow spouses to testify against one another. To get around the law, Ruby's lawyers argued that the marriage was null and void because Frank had one Paiute grandparent and thus was racially Indian, while Ruby was Mexican American and therefore Caucasian. The court agreed to annul the marriage on this basis and allowed Ruby to testify. When Pass appealed the decision, the appellate court confirmed that the marriage was null and void because Frank was part Indian and Ruby was Caucasian.[33] Once again, the courts made a complicated case of marriage between people of mixed ethnic heritage simple by classifying the marriage partners in starkly binary racial terms, with Mexican-Americans falling into the "white" category.

Not only were marriages between ethnic Mexicans and Anglo-Americans legal, but in the nineteenth century they were common—suggesting that Anglo-Americans did not yet view ethnic Mexicans as clearly non-white. Intermarriage was particularly common in communities with large, ethnic Mexican populations such as Tucson and in rural areas near the border. Up to 1879, of all marriages in Tucson, 23 percent were between Anglo-Americans and ethnic Mexicans.[34] Moreover, in rural areas such as the Tres Alamos region along the San Pedro River, interethnic marriages remained the norm until about 1900.[35]

Still, as historians such as Deena González, Al Hurtado, and Katherine Benton have suggested, mixed marriages did not necessarily imply racial egalitarianism. Most were between Anglo men and ethnic Mexican women, and their frequency in part reflected the high proportion of Anglo-American men to women. Such marriages allowed these men to gain access to land owned by ethnic Mexican families. Some of them may have even viewed these marriages as a form of sexual conquest—in essence, as a way to solidify their own sense of racial superiority by asserting white, male authority over Mexican women. Yet, as Katherine Benton has argued in the case of Tres Alamos, "These kinds of marriages offered at least the potential for some kind of power balance between the Anglo husband and the family of his wife." Some women owned their own land and cattle, and they may have viewed their marriages to Euro-American men as a way to secure their own economic and social status, perhaps even to secure their racial status as white.[36]

In any case, it is clear that a steep decline in marriages between ethnic Mexicans and Anglo-Americans between 1880 and 1910 reflected a sharpening of ethno-racial boundaries. This was a period of rapid industrialization, increased immigration by Mexicans, Europeans, and Anglos, increased competition for resources, and the emergence of a strictly racialized class structure. By 1910 only 10 percent of Tucson marriages involved mixed ethnic Mexican and Anglo partners.[37] Interethnic marriages also declined sharply in rural Cochise County, where such marriages had been common before 1900. Katherine Benton has found that even the daughters and sons of nineteenth-century interethnic marriages tended to marry only ethnic Mexicans in the twentieth century, so "these intermarried families became more 'Mexican' than 'American.'" By 1910, then, there was less social interaction between the two groups and more segregation into distinct rural and urban enclaves.[38]

While marriages between ethnic Mexicans and Anglo-Americans declined, unions between Mexican Americans and Indians remained common and can be seen as an implicit form of resistance to Arizona's imposed racial boundaries. Yet, evidence suggests that such marriages were sometimes prevented based on the miscegenation law. In 1930, for example, a BIA field matron complained that she was "trying to have marriage consummated between an Indian woman and a Mexican man who are living together." Because of the state's miscegenation law, she found that "the authorities [would] not grant them a license." Still, because Anglo-Americans had come to view Mexican Americans as nonwhite (socially if not legally), the antimiscegenation statute was only sporadically enforced when the respective partners were Indians and ethnic Mexicans, as evidenced by the fact that both the Kirby and Pass marriages went unchallenged until one partner decided to seek an annulment.[39]

Genetic evidence, life histories, and observations by government officials and ethnographers suggest that conjugal unions between ethnic Mexicans, Yaquis, and Tohono O'odham were common. Recent genetic evidence, for example, shows that 39 percent of today's Tohono O'odham population carries nonnative, Y-chromosome markers, suggesting that a large number are the offspring of interethnic unions with people of European descent.[40] This research says little about when the mixing occurred, but anecdotal evidence suggests that such unions were frequent in the early twentieth century. In 1913, for example, a BIA official cited several known cases of "illegitimate babies . . . whose fathers [were] either white or Mexican" as a primary motive for placing a BIA field matron in Tucson.[41] Because the field matrons were assigned the task of ensuring that Indians went through the proper legal channels to legitimize their marriages, their records are filled with accounts of interethnic affairs. A field matron reported, for example, on a family that employed an O'odham woman as a domestic, complaining that she had "been having a Mexican come to her room." After the field matron called on her intending to stop the affair, she reported that "instead she took an evening train and got away from me. We are trying to find her in Phoenix."[42]

Yaquis also commonly married illicitly across imposed racial boundaries. Spicer cited five cases of intermarriage between Yaquis and ethnic Mexicans in Pascua in the 1930s, and these numbers would likely have been much higher had he also looked at ethnically mixed communities like Barrio Libre, Barrio Anita, and Guadalupe.[43] Another anthropologist has noted that "it is usual, in fact, for many Mexicans of the regions of Arizona/Sonora to be of Spanish/Mexican/Yaqui/Mayo/Pima ancestry."[44] Over time such unions created a dense network of interethnic ties—a network often overlooked by outside observers who viewed Indians and Mexicans as members of sharply designated racial groups.

Marriage was not, of course, the only way to form interethnic ties. The system of *compadrazgo*, or fictive kinship, was often as important as were ties of marriage and blood. Under this system, individuals sponsored their neighbors as *padrinos/madrinas*, or godparents, for events such as weddings, baptisms, and the fulfillment of ritual vows.[45] Compadrazgo often crossed ethnic lines, since the region's ethnic Mexicans, Yaquis, and O'odham shared the tradition. Spicer indicated that Yaquis were "constantly drawing on their Mexican-American neighbors to serve as madrinas and padrinos," and he observed that probably "every family in Pascua [had] links with neighboring Mexican Americans through the ceremonial sponsorship system." The Tohono O'odham, too, shared in the practice, primarily for baptisms and for blessings of *santos*, or figures of the saints. *Compahlis* or *comahlis* (O'odham for *compadres* and *comadres*) carried medals in the images of saints to be blessed by a priest for their owners. Compadrazgo thus inextricably linked the indigenous and mestizo populations, blurring the lines between supposedly rigid racial boundaries while reinforcing a shared sense of difference from the surrounding Euro-American majority.[46]

Compadrazgo often connected members of the ethnic Mexican and indigenous working classes to wealthier families who provided financial help in times of need. Again, these ties often crossed ethnic lines. Lolita Ochoa, for example, a Tohono O'odham woman, remembered that it was very common for Tohono O'odham in Tucson to have Mexican-American compadres. Ochoa, who spoke to her interviewer through a Tohono O'odham interpreter, felt that many Tohono O'odham and Mexican-American families became "like relatives, really close relatives and real good friends." Joe McCarthy, a Tohono O'odham, recalled in his autobiography that "most of the Papago women worked for Mexican people," and that these economic relationships often led to more intimate ties. McCarthy's mother had a relatively well-off Mexican-American comahli who lived north of Tucson's railroad tracks, and whose family owned a ranch outside of town. Her comahli sometimes helped provide goods such as dried meat, cheese, or other products from the ranch, and she would reciprocate to the best of her ability. In one instance, McCarthy recalled, "While I was back home, Mother wanted me to take some cactus syrup to her Mexican godmother, who lived across the railroad tracks. . . . There were a few Mexican houses around there, and sometimes she sent me over there to give them something." He remembered his compadres as "very good people."[47]

Interethnic bonds also developed through joint participation in regional parish and mission churches. In 1903 the Presbyterians established their first permanent mission in South Tucson. While the mission was initially intended exclusively for the Tohono O'odham, Yaquis, ethnic Mexicans, and a few Chinese residents soon attended services and Sunday school classes.[48] In 1914 Catholic missionaries from San Xavier also began offering multiethnic masses and classes in South Tucson. One of the priests explained that every Sunday afternoon a missionary from San Xavier conducted Mass and held classes in Tucson using "the Spanish language as his audience speaks one of three languages, viz., Spanish, English, and Papago. So you see it is a difficult task, requiring the patience of Job."[49] In 1926 the Catholic missionaries built the San José mission, which became a meeting place for ethnic Mexicans, Yaquis, and Tohono O'odham alike.[50]

Of course, other institutions and cultural practices served to reify, rather than break down distinctions *between* ethnic groups, such as the Tohono O'odham *nawait* ceremony described in Chapter 2. Yaquis also continued to hold the ethnically exclusive Lenten and Pascua ceremonies in the barrios. Since Arizona Yaquis were not physically separated from the surrounding ethnic Mexican population as they had been in Sonora, their seasonal ceremonies became an important public affirmation of their distinct cultural values and identity. While they often received the sacraments in ethnically mixed churches, they also constructed their own separate church buildings and plazas where they housed the *santos* and carried out various seasonal rituals. They expressed their religious devotion by serving in a number of different ceremonial institutions—as *maestros* (lay prayer readers), *koparim* (ritual singers), *matachin* dancers who dedicated their work to the Virgin Mary, and *fariseos,* who were responsible for organizing the annual Pascua ceremonies. They also served as deer and *pascola* dancers at Yaqui ceremonies and at multiethnic events.[51]

Besides such ethnically exclusive institutions, an array of seasonal fiestas and institutions brought Yaquis, Tohono O'odham, and ethnic Mexicans together. In Tucson, for example, a fiesta honoring St. Augustine, the patron saint of the town, began on August 28 and ended on September 16, Mexican Independence Day. The festival drew hundreds of Indians and ethnic Mexicans from Tucson and elsewhere. Among other interethnic seasonal ceremonies and events was All Souls' Day on November 2 and the Fiesta of San Isidro on May 15. During that event, ranchers and farmers marched in a procession and then offered vegetables at an altar to San Isidro to ensure a bountiful harvest. Jacinta Jacobo Carranza, who was born in 1902, remembered, "On St. Isidro's Day, May 15, all of the farmers in the area where we lived made a procession through the milpas—they made the procession praying and singing praise so that God and San Isidro would help them—that a year's planting might be successful so that they might have crops to sell."[52]

One of the most important and persistent transnational and transethnic rituals in the Sonora-Arizona borderlands was—and remains to this day—the feast day of San Francisco in Magdalena, about sixty miles south of the Arizona-Sonora border. The festival's origins reflect a long history of colonialism and intercultural exchange. As designated by the Franciscan order, October 4 is the feast day of Saint Francis of Assisi, yet the focal point of the annual pilgrimage to Magdalena was an image of Francis Xavier, the Jesuit patron saint. The Jesuit missionary Eusebio Francisco Kino founded the mission in the late seventeenth century, but the town gained its significance as the center of Franciscan rather than Jesuit mission activity after the Jesuits were expelled from what was then called New Spain in 1767.[53] Thousands of ethnic Mexican and indigenous Sonorenses and Arizonans made an annual pilgrimage to this holy center to marry or have their children baptized there, or in the hope that it would cure their illnesses. Others simply went to participate in the festivities, which included music and dancing with performances by deer and *pascola* dancers from both sides of the border.[54]

The festival drew thousands of ethnic Mexicans and Indians from both Sonora and Arizona to Magdalena. In her memoir about life on her father's ranch near the Arizona-Sonora border at the beginning of the twentieth century, Antonia Wilbur-Cruce remembered that many Yaquis, Tohono O'odham, and Mexicans passed by her father's ranch "on their way to Magdalena, Mexico, to visit San Francisco."[55] According to Alberto Alvaro Ríos, a Mexican American who lived in Nogales, the festival was alive and well fifty years later. As he described it, "Starting late in September, for two weeks, I remember seeing hundreds and possibly thousands of native Indians, Mexicans, and Arizona residents as they walked, along the river and along the road, the sixty-five miles from Nogales to Magdalena. It was a show of penance or devotion, and timed so that they would all arrive there on October 4, the feast of San Francisco."[56]

The Magdalena festival also carried political significance. Because those who attended the festival generally crossed the international border without proper authority or documentation, government officials repeatedly tried to end the practice. In 1913 a BIA official warned Frank Thackery, the superintendent of Pima Indian School, that hundreds of Tohono O'odham planned to make the trip despite the dangers posed by the Mexican Revolution. He explained, "Their trips are mostly made for debauchery anyway, and most any year they go they only lose their money, but this year they may lose everything they love." Thackery responded quickly, writing, "I have decided to forbid their going, and I wish you would please advise them to that effect, saying further that in case any of them should attempt to go, it would be necessary for me to ask the authorities of the emigration or other Government Service to bring them to trial for their conduct in disobeying our instructions and the laws governing."[57]

Despite repeated warnings and restrictions, hundreds of Tohono O'odham, Yaquis, and ethnic Mexicans continued to make the trip. In 1919, for example, a BIA field matron noted that she had tried to obtain passports for three Tohono O'odham who wished to attend the festival, but "as they only permitted them forty miles on the other side of the border, and the distance they wished to go would be about sixty-five miles . . . the Indians have decided that . . . passports will not be needed." Indeed, many Tohono O'odham continued to attend the festival without state sanction, and there was little government officials could do to intervene.[58] Eventually, employers and state officials would recognize that they could not stop the annual pilgrimage. Henry Dobyns, who conducted fieldwork among Tohono O'odham cotton pickers around 1950, noted that the O'odham "made plain to growers . . . that the Magdalena pilgrimage took precedence over even national patriotism and personal gain. Faced with Papago intransigence, most growers decided to haul their Indian pilgrims to Magdalena in trucks rather than let them spend time making the trek in slow horse-drawn wagons."[59]

The Magdalena festival thus illustrates, in the most direct way, how the persistence of certain transnational and interethnic cultural practices challenged U.S. laws designed to solidify both national and racial borders. Scholarship that focuses solely on the histories of individual ethnic groups, while important, can also reinforce a tendency to overlook the intimate bonds that tied these groups together. Examining these interethnic ties reveals that the process of *mestizaje* (intercultural and biological mixing) continued despite both legal and social prohibitions. Such processes could work to blur ethnic margins and defy racial boundaries. It was therefore uncertain whether separate group identities such as Yaqui, Tohono O'odham, or Mexican would persist over time. Rather than presume that people within these groups identified along such rigid lines, we need to understand how and why these identities emerged, endured, and/or evolved through history.

FAMILY ECONOMIES, GENDER, AND IDENTITY

A flexible division of labor between men, women, and children sustained indigenous and ethnic Mexican families in the rapidly evolving economy of the Arizona/Sonora borderlands. Most men held a wide variety of jobs outside the barrios and rural towns during their lifetimes, and even over the course of a single year. Men might work in urban construction, in the yards of city households, on railroad maintenance crews (commonly known as *el traque*), in nearby mines or smelters, and in agriculture all over the span of a couple of years. Women generally bore the primary responsibility for caring for their homes and their children, and often took care of *milpitas* (small garden plots) nearby. They also earned income by working as domestics, by producing and selling tortillas, tamales, and crafts and, increasingly, by picking cotton. Over time such adjustments led to cultural shifts in the meaning of manhood and womanhood. They also changed the relationship between various ethnic groups in the barrios, affecting the way those groups defined themselves and each other.[60]

Many families who lived in Mexico supplemented their income with wages earned by husbands and sons in the United States. The family of Carlos Cordoba, whose story I introduced earlier, provides a good example. Carlos worked periodically in mining towns, smelters, and quarries in Arizona while his family tended to their household in Agua Prieta, Sonora. He handed much of his earnings, after paying for his own room and board, to his mother and sisters in Mexico. Over the years he earned enough to purchase and install a new floor and roof for his mother's house. He also was able to buy her a variety of appliances, including a sewing machine and a cast-iron stove.[61]

Cordoba's experiences were quite common. Katherine Benton has found that, in the late nineteenth and early twentieth centuries, Mexican men in Arizona sent as much as 40 percent of their wages to support families, households, and farms in Mexico. Their employers often assumed that these were single, unattached men, and they justified paying them less by suggesting they did not need a family wage. Anglo-American workers, they argued, required higher wages to support their wives and children, who more often lived with them in the mining camps. In the process, employers and Euro-American workers alike reinforced the racial notion that Mexicans were inherently unsettled and transitory—a racial stereotype that would endure even after more Mexican men brought their families with them across the border.[62]

For those indigenous and ethnic Mexican families who lived within Arizona, a similar division of labor was common. For example, the Yaqui men of the Savala family, after moving to South Tucson, continued a pattern that had begun in Sonora, working outside the barrio for the railroads, mines, and industrial farms. Women and children contributed to the family income through an alternative economy, largely controlled by non-Anglos, in Tucson and the surrounding region. As Refugio Savala recalled, "My mother [Thomasa], being so active, soon found a way to put us two younger boys to work to bring in food. She made tortillas and tamales and we sold them among the people in the neighborhood. With the money, she bought the material to keep her laundry business going." Members of the Savala family also harvested wheat seasonally on the Tohono O'odham San Xavier reservation south of Tucson. They were often paid in kind and sold the wheat to a local Mexican-American merchant for cash.[63]

Although many ethnic Mexican and indigenous women worked for wages, the male-operated, Spanish-language press encouraged an idealized patriarchal household in which men should serve both as the breadwinners and the final decision makers. Spanish-language newspapers such as *Las Dos Repúblicas* and *El Tucsonense* featured frequent articles that urged women to retain "a more sedentary life" and to keep charge of "the interior arrangement of the house, the purchase of provisions, the care of animals, the maintenance and cleaning of the furniture, the supervision of domestic help and the early education of the children." Women's only "weapons" in the household should be their "sweetness, persuasion and cunning." According to this conservative ideal, the daughters of ethnic Mexican families should remain home until married, engage in social activities only in the presence of chaperones, and preferably not engage in wage work outside the home.[64]

Only a minority of prosperous ethnic Mexican farmers and merchants could approach this ideal. And in reality, pronouncements about proper gender roles were a response to changing circumstances, rather than accurate descriptions of the structure of most ethnic Mexican households. In the early decades of the century, most working-class families could not sustain themselves without taking advantage of all potential wage earners.

Among poorer families, entire households often participated in seasonal cotton-picking from October through January. By the mid-1920s, many working-class barrios witnessed an almost wholesale exodus to the cotton fields during the picking season. Janette Woodruff witnessed this phenomenon in the 1925–1926 season, when most of the homes in South Tucson were closed because "the people were working in the cotton fields." [65] Edward Spicer observed a similar practice in the village of Pascua, finding that men, women, and children alike moved to the labor camps in family units in September to pick cotton. As he explained, "This is cotton-picking season, and most of the families leave the village to take up residence on cotton ranches. They return at certain times for ceremonies, such as All Souls' Day in November, and a few families drift back before the cotton-picking is finished because they are tired of it or because of illness, but during this period of three or four months, the village has the air of being deserted." [66]

By the 1920s, growing numbers of women, particularly unmarried daughters who still lived with their parents, worked outside of the home year-round as domestics, saleswomen, laundresses, telephone operators, and dressmakers. In sixty-one contiguous ethnic Mexican households in a Tucson barrio enumerated in the 1920 manuscript census, seventy-eight men and nineteen women worked regularly for wages outside of the home. The majority of these women, thirteen in all, still lived with their families. Three were unmarried household heads, while two were unmarried and living with their siblings rather than their parents. Only one of the women was married, indicating that the ideal of nonworking wives held substantial sway. Yet the census tells us nothing about other income-producing work these women might have performed, such as petty trade or seasonal wage work in the cotton fields. [67]

Ethnic Mexican daughters worked outside the home for both economic and sociocultural reasons. As Mexican-American women took up wage jobs and participated in urban social life and consumer culture, they also began to challenge the gender roles prescribed for them by their parents and by the Spanish-language press. The decline of chaperoning was one manifestation of these changes. Traditionally, many ethnic Mexican families expected young women to be accompanied by male kin when they attended dances or other social functions with men. In interviews of Mexican-American women who came of age between the two world wars, Vicki Ruiz found that "every informant who challenged or circumvented chaperonage held a full-time job, as either a factory or service worker. In contrast, most women who accepted constant supervision did not work for wages." [68]

Anecdotal evidence from Arizona is consistent with this larger pattern. For many families, particularly in smaller rural towns, chaperoning remained common well into the twentieth century. For Ruby Estrada, who lived in a small, rural Arizona town, chaperoning "wasn't devastating at all. We took it in stride. . . . It was taken for granted that that's the way it was."[69] In contrast, Livia León Montiel, who lived near Tucson and who participated often in the social life of the city, felt that her parent's insistence on chaperones had become "old-fashioned" by 1930. Montiel recalled feeling that her mother "was very strict and straitlaced. . . . She felt that we had to be chaperoned, but at that time chaperones were already a thing of the past." Montiel's parents also refused to allow her to attend Tempe Teacher's College in 1931. As the Great Depression dragged on, however, Montiel eventually persuaded her parents to allow her to go to school and obtain a job. In 1933 she attended Cox Commercial School in Tucson to learn clerking and stenography, then began working as a secretary for the Alianza Hispano-Americana, a Mexican-American mutual aid society. Although her taking on a full-time job diverged from idealized gender roles, her decision to work with the Alianza reinforced her connection to the ethnic Mexican community in a new, public way.[70]

While gender roles among ethnic Mexican families were slowly changing, Yaquis generally maintained a stricter sexual division of labor, and the adherence to this gendered ideal became an important indicator of Yaqui identity. In Yaqui households in the early decades of the twentieth century, the primary wage earners were men. In the forty occupied Yaqui households in Pascua enumerated in the 1920 manuscript census, not a single woman held a nonseasonal wage job. Because the census was taken in January during the cotton-picking season, these numbers do not reflect the fact that by 1920 Yaqui families, including men, women, and children alike, seasonally left the barrios to engage in farmwork. Yaqui women also earned money by selling tortillas or occasionally taking in laundry. Still, very few worked for wages year-round.[71]

Spicer noticed this persistent trend in the mid-1930s. While conducting fieldwork in Pascua, he found that during most of the year, with the exception of the picking season, "remunerative labor is engaged in almost exclusively by men, the women occupying themselves only with house work." He found only a few exceptions to this rule, as four women who were "all under thirty" worked as maids and laundresses for other Tucson families.[72]

Yaqui women who strayed too far from this ideal might find their very identity as Yaquis questioned by the surrounding community. Revisiting the story of Antonia Valenzuela provides one such example. Valenzuela was living in Chandler (in the Salt River valley) when her husband, Ignacio, became ill and died. Now a widow with three children, she decided to move to Pascua after learning that she might find employment as a housemaid. According to an ethnographer who recorded her life history, Valenzuela worked "in Mexican homes washing and cleaning" while her brother's wife cared for her children and her own family in a one-room house. Free from the oversight of her husband and her mother-in-law, and for the first time earning her own income, Valenzuela soon began to exercise here newfound independence. "For the first time in her life, Antonia had no older, dominant woman or hard husband to direct her behavior. She exercised her freedom by discarding the traditional skirt and blouse, adopting instead one-piece cotton dresses with full, gathered, shorter skirts. Rebozos were replaced by handkerchiefs tied over her hair. She retained this style of dress until she died, noting that if [Ignacio] had lived, she could not have done so." [73]

Soon, however, Antonia learned through the grapevine that a woman named Josefa González "began talking badly about her and her children, saying they had 'become Mexicans.'" When Antonia confronted her, Josefa criticized her for wearing "modern dress" and scolded her children for speaking Spanish, rather than Yaqui, in public. Antonia responded that her children spoke Yaqui in the household, but Josefa continued to talk badly about her for years. Antonia's adoption of a nontraditional role for Yaqui women, and her use of her wages to purchase nontraditional clothing, made her susceptible to accusations that she was adopting the identity of a Mexican. Even this small rebellion proved to be temporary because, within a couple of years, Antonia married another Yaqui man with "a good job"; thus, according to the ethnographer, "of course, [she] immediately stopped working." [74]

In the cities, Tohono O'odham practiced a gendered division of labor that was different from that of either the Yaquis or ethnic Mexicans.[75] BIA field matrons actively recruited Tohono O'odham women from the reservations to work in the cities—something they did not do for Yaquis, who were not recognized by the federal government to be an American Indian tribe. This distinct, federal classification had a very real impact on the sexual division of labor in O'odham families. Often it was women who could best support their families in the cities, while men remained on the reservation to farm or raise cattle or traveled to find work on railroads, ranches, and in the mines. By contrast, without a reservation, most Yaqui and ethnic Mexican men had no alternative but to work for wages.[76]

By the 1940s these factors helped to create the racial stereotype in Tucson that O'odham women were particularly fit to work as domestics. Just after World War II, one researcher found that O'odham women made up the bulk of the domestic service workforce for local businesses and private homes, while a smaller proportion of ethnic Mexican women, and very few Yaquis, held such positions. In fact, by that time many felt that Tohono O'odham women had an inherent affinity for domestic labor. Employers chose to explain the overrepresentation of these women in paid domestic work as a natural phenomenon, suggesting they were "much superior" to other ethnic groups in such positions. But, for O'odham women, recruitment by the BIA had encouraged a situation in which domestic wage work was becoming an accepted occupation, while it remained a questionable way to earn a living for Yaqui women.[77]

In sum, for the Tohono O'odham, Yaquis, and ethnic Mexicans in the barrios, distinctly gendered patterns of wage work—patterns that emerged only as they became entangled with the developing wage economy—became markers of ethno-racial identity. Over time these differences became, along with religion, kinship, and ethnic institutions, social markers of ethnic difference. Those who strayed too far from established patterns (such as Antonia Valenzuela) risked accusations of improper behavior; or worse, of forsaking their kin in order to achieve status in the eyes of another ethnic group.

MEXICAN-AMERICAN RESPONSES TO IMMIGRATION

Not all ethnic Mexicans were immersed in the transnational folk culture of the Arizona-Sonora borderlands. By the 1910s many Mexican Americans, particularly those from the middle class, hoped to distinguish themselves from the growing population of Mexican nationals in order to secure a cultural and social status as fully American. Since Anglo-Americans often failed to differentiate between Mexican Americans and Mexican nationals, the tenuous higher social position that some middle-class Mexican Americans had established seemed threatened. These Mexican Americans worried that the new immigrants might undermine their own struggle to achieve acceptance and national belonging.[78]

Mexican Americans were sharply aware of the growing threats to their own social, economic, and political status. After 1880 intermarriage between Anglos and Mexican Americans became less common. Between 1900 and 1910 ethnic Mexicans became a numerical minority even in Tucson. By the beginning of World War I, they no longer served as mayors, sheriffs, or legislators and experienced many kinds of institutional discrimination. They were rarely called to serve on juries, were the first to be laid off during economic downturns, and when tried in the courts were more often convicted and served longer sentences than Anglo-Americans. To many Mexican Americans the presence of thousands of Mexican nationals seemed to threaten any chance that they had of reversing these trends.[79]

Indeed, some Mexican Americans placed much of the blame for their own precarious social status on Mexican nationals. In Arizona an ambivalent stance toward immigration was particularly apparent within the *mutualistas,* or mutual-aid societies. Historically, the mutualistas had embraced the principle that ethnic Mexicans shared a cultural heritage and a mutual responsibility to come to one another's aid, regardless of national citizenship. The oldest and largest mutualista in the state, the Alianza Hispano-Americana, was formed in 1894 by members of Tucson's declining elite, but its members included both a newer class of small businessmen and a large number of immigrants. In time the Club Latina, Club Azteca, Sociedad Mexicana-Americana, and the Liga Protectora Latina joined the Alianza in organizing social events, offering low-cost life insurance, and providing financial aid. Still, in their struggle to be accepted as respectable, patriotic citizens, many Mexican-American members of these mutualistas grew to resent Mexican nationals who lived in the rural towns, mining centers, and barrios. As one historian has explained, while the mutualistas agreed on the importance of uplifting the dignity of "those of our race," most also held firm the principle of self-improvement and the "love of work," and persistently encouraged the Mexican working class to "moderate its customs."[80]

Certain mutualistas more than others actively served the interests of Mexican nationals. In 1915, for example, Mexican Americans in the Salt River valley organized the Liga Protectora Latina (often called simply the Liga or LPL) as a direct response to the alien labor bill passed by referendum the previous year. Pedro G. de La Lama, an educated immigrant who had crossed the border in 1886, was the driving force behind the LPL and its resistance to the proposed legislation. In February 1915 he and a few other influential ethnic Mexicans in Phoenix called a mass meeting to voice their opposition to the law. Hundreds of Mexican miners signed a petition opposing the new legislation and subsequently began forming local lodges of the Liga in their own communities. Like most mutualistas, the Liga provided health and funeral benefits and encouraged the ethnic Mexican population to become educated. But its more inclusive rhetoric, reflected in its slogan *Uno para todos, todos para uno* (One for all, all for one), and its more explicitly confrontational stance attracted discontented working-class immigrants more successfully than other mutualistas. As a result, in only two years, the Liga grew to rival the Alianza as the second largest mutualista in the state, with thirty lodges. Ultimately, the Liga's opposition failed to overturn the Alien Labor Law, but the federal district court subsequently declared it unconstitutional.[81]

An internal struggle within the Liga revealed how the growing influx of Mexican nationals forced Mexican-American members to take a clearer position on immigration in the Salt River valley. On May 15, 1919, Pedro de la Lama sent a written complaint to Arizona Governor Thomas E. Campbell charging the Arizona Cotton Growers Association (ACGA) with manipulating, exploiting, and mistreating thousands of Mexican farmworkers. De la Lama claimed that the ACGA and the growers were not fulfilling the stipulations of their contracts and of the regulations under the ninth proviso. Most of the pickers, he charged, lived in tents clustered in unsanitary camps, and they were paid less than had been promised in their contracts. He also claimed that many growers had either deducted wages from the workers to pay for their provisions or had paid the workers with purchase orders at company stores.[82]

Ironically, two of the stores singled out by de la Lama as the worst perpetrators were those owned by the Mexican-American founders of the first Liga lodge in Tempe, the Estrada family. Rafael Estrada was a Pima County native who owned a substantial amount of farmland in the Salt River valley. He and his sons had founded Liga Lodge No. 1 in Tempe in 1914. The Tempe lodge had become one of the most active in the state, providing financial assistance and serving as an employment agency. In fact, the Estradas had become full-time *enganchadores* for the ACGA. Rafael traveled to Sonora, Sinaloa, Nayarit, and sometimes Zacatecas, earning four dollars for each worker he recruited. His sons, Pedro and Ramón, managed two family stores from which they sold food and provisions to the workers once they arrived in the Salt River valley.[83]

In 1919 de la Lama accused the Estrada family of engaging in dishonest recruitment tactics and forcing workers to buy overpriced goods from their stores. Euro-American ranchers and farmers near Tempe had come to depend on the Estradas as important mediators with their Mexican workers. Pedro Estrada would later explain that his father was well liked by the Anglo community in Maricopa County, who affectionately referred to him as Guero because, according to Pedro, he had ruddy skin and sandy hair. In early-twentieth-century Arizona, the name also implied that Estrada's status as a landowner and a contractor whitened him in the eyes of the regional elite. To de la Lama and others, however, he was a power-hungry sellout. The Mexican consul from Los Angeles, who conducted an investigation of the Estradas upon de la Lama's request, criticized Rafael Estrada for exploiting Mexican nationals in order to achieve personal status. As he put it, Estrada was a "renegade Mexican" and a "blond Christ who is the epitome of a *cacique*" (a boss/tyrant).[84]

The accusations signaled a growing rift among Mexican-American leaders in the Salt River valley. In 1919 and 1920 the Liga was hobbled by an internal struggle for control between those who wished to serve as advocates for the immigrant poor and those who wished to promote an image of middle-class respectability and patriotic citizenship. Those in the latter group were especially concerned about the growing nativism and fear of radicalism that was sweeping the nation after World War I. By the end of the year, they emerged victorious, and the LPL took a decidedly conservative turn. An increase in its initiation fees resulted in a predictable exodus of the poorer, largely immigrant members. When José Castelán, a member of Tucson's Lodge No. 8, protested the change, the lodge expelled him. With the new leadership in control, Liga membership rapidly dropped, and by the mid-1920s it ceased to function as an active organization.[85]

The Liga's demise left the immigrant working class with little effective support among the Mexican-American leadership of the mutualistas in their battle against systematic discrimination and labor exploitation. Throughout the 1920s the Alianza Hispano-Americana and other mutualistas suggested that Mexicans could best gain acceptance and citizenship through hard work and education, rather than through organized protest. Reflecting this belief, the Alianza worked with the Phoenix Americanization Committee to establish a new social center, called Friendly House, in south Phoenix. Its purpose was primarily to turn Mexicans into Americans by instilling civic virtue and teaching home economics, hygiene, and English. As Adam Díaz, a Mexican-American board member, recalled, Friendly House "was for teaching the immigrants how to cope with a country as strange as America. . . . They would take them in and orient them, and help them with the Constitution and help with their English" in order to make them "ready for their citizenship."[86]

Perhaps the majority of Mexican immigrants had no desire to assimilate. Manuel Gamio, in a series of interviews conducted in the latter 1920s, found this to be a common perspective among Mexicans in Arizona and throughout the Southwest. Among those he interviewed was Carlos Morales, who had been born and raised in Sonora in the 1880s and '90s before moving to Tucson during the Mexican Revolution. Morales told Gamio, "I haven't wanted to, nor do I want to learn English, for I am not thinking of living in

this country all my life. . . . I don't like anything about this country, neither its customs nor its climate, nothing, that is to say." Like many border
crossers, Morales had first entered Arizona to escape the violence of the
revolution, and he had remained because of the economic opportunities
he found there. Some day soon, however, he hoped to return to Mexico to
rebuild his life as a Mexican citizen.[87]

Indeed, for those Mexican nationals who had no intention of becoming
naturalized American citizens, Americanization was both undesirable and
irrelevant. Thousands either held on to their national identity and citizenship as Mexicans or felt little loyalty to either the Mexican or the U.S.
nation-states. For many, connections to kin and to multiethnic local communities of O'odham, Yaquis, and ethnic Mexicans remained more salient
than national belonging. Instead, they maintained their own ethnic and
interethnic cultural and social networks in barrios and rural towns, shel-
tering themselves from or struggling against discrimination and exclusion.

In the early decades of the twentieth century, both the territorial border
between the United States and Mexico and the ethnic boundaries between
indigenous peoples and ethnic Mexicans remained fuzzy and permeable.
Movement back and forth across the border and transnational cultural
practices defied the line on the map separating the two nations, while intermarriage, *compadrazgo,* interethnic cultural and religious practices,
and shared language (Spanish) and class status, among other factors, belied
stark ethno-racial classifications.

During this same period, however, the U.S. government began to police the territorial border, restrict immigration, and prevent interethnic
mixing through miscegenation laws and other policies directed at specific,
racialized ethnic groups. The government, for example, viewed the Tohono
O'odham as American Indians, but not the Yaquis, dramatically affecting
each group's place in the regional order (as "American Indians" with a reservation versus landless refugees from Mexico). Moreover, some Mexican
Americans defined themselves as fully American and/or as white to distinguish themselves from Indians and Mexican nationals. Even variations
in gendered patterns of wage work became markers of ethno-racial identity. Over time, divergent positions within the regional political economy,
along with emerging racial ideologies and state policies that were intoler-
ant of blurry ethnic categories, influenced how the residents of Arizona's
borderlands *defined themselves*—albeit, as will become apparent, often in
unanticipated ways.

▼ ▼ ▼ ▼ ▼ ▼ ▼ ▼ ▼ ▼ ▼ ▼ ▼ ▼ ▼ ▼ ▼ ▼

CHAPTER 4

DEFINING THE WHITE CITIZEN-WORKER

As the Great Depression descended on south-central Arizona in June 1930, the Arizona State Federation of Labor (ASFL) called for new restrictions on Mexican immigration to protect "white citizen-workers of Arizona and other Southwestern states."[1] Such explicitly racial calls for shutting the border were nothing new, dating back to the early part of the century. Arizona's trade unions had long conflated national identity with race, using *white* and *American citizen* interchangeably. From the time Arizona became a state, many native Anglo, Irish, and Cornish Americans fought to restrict full citizenship rights to white Americans and English speakers. They lobbied for the 1909 English Literacy Law and the 1914 Alien Labor Law in order to protect the boundaries of the white citizen-worker and to ensure their own inclusion within those boundaries.

Still, the definition of *white citizen-worker* remained permeable as employers, politicians, Mexican nationals, Mexican Americans, European immigrants, and Anglos negotiated and struggled over the cultural and racial meaning of citizenship. In the years leading up to World War I, Italian, Spanish, and Slavic immigrants fought to ensure that they would be counted as industrious white citizens. They did so, in part, by joining Euro-Americans in fighting to define Mexican immigrants—and not themselves—as nonwhite aliens. However, when ethnic Mexican workers actively challenged their own subordinate status by organizing and striking, European immigrants and Euro-Americans were forced to reassess their own racial exclusionism.[2]

The boundaries of whiteness remained somewhat permeable, although less so, into the 1930s. The Depression amplified fear that Mexican workers were degrading the economic and social status of the Euro-American working class. Pressure from Arizona and other southwestern states compelled the Labor Department to restrict Mexican immigration and initiate a nationwide repatriation campaign in the 1930s. Ironically enough, after the Mexican workforce thinned out, Euro-American migrants from the Plains states began working under the same substandard conditions (often for even lower wages) familiar to Mexicans and Indians. The boundaries of whiteness blurred once again as incoming migrants were labeled Okies and white trash, were shuttled into poor neighborhoods, and faced the contempt of many native, Anglo Arizonans.[3]

While scholars such as Noel Ignatiev, David Roediger, and Linda Gordon have focused on how various groups of European immigrants "became white" in the late nineteenth and early twentieth centuries, this chapter demonstrates that, rather than making unidirectional progress toward whiteness, some groups would move into and out of its circle.[4] Still, by the end of World War II, the boundaries of whiteness would become more fixed as Mexican immigrants grew to far outnumber other immigrants, as many Okies moved into more skilled positions or out of agricultural work altogether, and as the Bracero Program reinforced the idea that migrant farmwork was nonwhite, noncitizen labor. Historian Neil Foley has argued that, in Texas, whiteness remained fractured when white yeomen farmers lost status by falling off the agricultural ladder to become "off-white" farmworkers.[5] In Arizona, however, there was a relatively small class of Euro-American family farmers and no comparable ladder from which to fall. By the end of the war, the boundaries of whiteness would become less permeable than ever.

COPPER AND THE LIMITS OF INTERETHNIC ORGANIZING

As World War I raged in Europe, Mexican, Spanish, Italian, Slavic, and indigenous miners throughout southern and central Arizona organized a series of strikes, initially without the support of Anglo, Irish, and Cornish (referred to collectively here and known as Anglo) trade unionists. These workers directly confronted both their unequal treatment by the mining companies and a racialized discourse that labeled them as lazy, tractable, and degenerate. For Anglo trade unionists, recognition of the new labor movement would imply a rejection of the principle that so-called foreigners were the source of their own precarious economic status and an acceptance of an identity based on the shared experience of class exploitation. The implications of these strikes thus reached well beyond the mining towns, since they would help to define white citizen-workers throughout the state for decades to come.

Since the late nineteenth century, the boundaries of whiteness had been in flux. Linda Gordon's study of turn-of-the-century Clifton-Morenci, a mining town in southeastern Arizona, convincingly demonstrates that Spaniards, Italians, and eastern Europeans "were not (yet) clearly white or nonwhite." Anglo-Americans viewed Catholic "Euro-Latins," to use Gordon's term, as alien because of their religion, language, darker skin, and lower economic status. When a local police officer referred to a crowd of workers as consisting of "Dagoes, Bohunks, and foreigners of different kinds—no whites at all," he was expressing a common sentiment that some Europeans were not quite white.[6]

Anglos viewed Euro-Latins and Slavs in other mining towns similarly. In Globe the editor of the *Arizona Silver Belt* suggested in 1902 that eastern and southern Europeans were excessively "clannish," and "ignorant of our language, of our customs and of our laws."[7] Others referred to them as "less intelligent whites" who, like Mexicans and Indians, did not have the character to make good unionists or citizens.[8] Katherine Benton found the same to be true in Bisbee: "Children who grew up in Bisbee remembered the stinging epithet of 'Bohunk' heard in the street and schoolyard."[9] As these examples suggest, Anglo-Americans often identified themselves as white in opposition to Mexicans, Indians, and to recent southern and eastern Europeans alike.

The wage structures in the mines were clearly biased against those deemed foreigners and/or nonwhite. In Clifton Morenci, for example, both native Anglos and immigrants considered "old-stock" (a racial term referring primarily to the Cornish, English, Irish, and Germans) earned the highest wages, while Italian immigrants earned substantially less (see Figure 1.1, page 29). In Bisbee, Slavs and Italians were in the middle of a multitiered wage scale. In what were called white men's camps like Bisbee, Anglo workers came to an agreement with management to retain such a wage structure, making organizing between these groups unlikely.[10]

Gender in the mining camps was also intertwined with the racialization of those thought of as foreigners. Anglo workers claimed that they had families to support and homes to maintain but that Mexicans, Slavs, and Euro-Latins could survive on lower wages because they were supposedly more transitory. By about the turn of the century, many Mexican and Italian men had left their families in their home countries, sending their wages back to support them. Even when these groups began to bring their families with them, however, the myth persisted. As a Bisbee resident declared, "The foreign element can live on a mere pittance to what a white man can. . . . All that is necessary [to demonstrate this fact] is for a man to go up north of the Catholic Church and in an oblong building he will find a bunch of Italians living as no white man can." Comments such as this implied that all Italians were single men with no desire to improve their condition or raise families in their own homes.[11]

Early in the twentieth century, southern and eastern European immigrants occasionally joined with Mexican workers to protest unequal wages and working conditions. In June 1903, for example, the Arizona and Detroit Copper Company in Clifton-Morenci reduced the workday for underground miners to eight from ten hours—a move that might have been welcomed had it not meant a decrease in the daily wage from $2.50 to $2.25. In response, thirty-five hundred Mexican, Italian, and Slavic workers walked out and demanded a return to the higher wage, better safety, health benefits, a closed (union) shop as well as, more broadly, *igualdad* (equality) and *justicia*. Neither the Anglo-dominated trade unions nor the state government offered support. Territorial Governor Alexander Brodie dismissed the strikers as members of an amorphous "foreign element among the miners," while press reports blamed the strike on "Mexicans, Italians and other foreigners."[12] The Western Federation of Miners (WFM) offered verbal encouragement but no material support. Just when the strikers approached a showdown with the Arizona Rangers and the territorial militia, the town was flooded by a downpour of rain and hail in which thirty-nine people died and because of which the strike ended.[13]

Linda Gordon has identified the Clifton-Morenci strike as a turning point in the history of Arizona's racial order. Intimidated by the nativist rhetoric against the strike, many Italians, Slavs, and others not from western Europe attempted to disassociate themselves from the ethnic Mexican population. Some Italians married into established Anglo families and worked their way into Anglo fraternal lodges and craft unions to distinguish themselves from the ethnic Mexican population. Women as well as men found ways to prove themselves to be white citizens. Gordon uses the example of Luisa and John Gatti, who attempted to enhance their own social positions during a local dispute concerning the adoption of Irish-American orphans by Mexican-American families. After the families adopted the children from a New York orphanage, Louisa Gatti, manipulating the discourse of both race and motherhood, protested that the children were white and did not belong in Mexican homes. The Gattis helped to organize a vigilante effort to "rescue" the children and to challenge the adoptions in court. Eventually, the dispute was resolved in the Supreme

Court, and the Gattis won custody of one of the children. By 1905, Gordon argues, "the Gattis were unquestionably Anglos."[14]

It would be a mistake, however, to overstate the extent to which Euro-Latins and Slavs became white after 1905. Rather than there being a strict Anglo/Mexican racial binary, "Americans" (including English-speaking immigrants), "foreigners," (including Slavs and Euro-Latins), Mexicans and, at the bottom, Indians all were separated. Anglo, Cornish, and Irish organizers dominated the craft unions, which were associated with the American Federation of Labor (AFL), as well as the Western Federation of Miners (WFM). Philip Mellinger has shown that at mining towns such as Bisbee, "labor peace was based upon an understanding between the older, settled mining workers" and company officials. Managers tolerated Anglo union membership only if unskilled eastern and southern European workers were kept out. Thus, when Slavic workers at Bisbee demanded to be admitted into the WFM in 1907, most Anglo workers refused to join them. When Slavic and Italian workers went on strike anyway, they were quickly defeated.[15]

More than a decade after the 1903 Clifton-Morenci strike, Euro-Latins still had not been fully accepted as white. In 1915, for example, in the mining town of Ray about one thousand Spanish immigrants lived segregated in a neighborhood called Barcelona, adjacent to the Mexican section known as Sonoratown. Wages for Mexican and Spanish workers alike were only $2.25 for muckers and $3 for machine workers, significantly lower than wages for Anglos in "white men's camps" such as Miami where, due to the efforts of the WFM, muckers and machine workers earned $3.75 and $4.15, respectively.[16]

Anecdotal evidence suggests that Anglo workers were more likely to classify Spanish immigrants as akin to Mexicans than as white because of the similarities in language, religion, and cultural and kinship ties between the two groups. In Miami, Enrique Pastor's experiences serve as an example. He was born in 1915 to a Spanish father, Antonio, and a Mexican mother, Isabel. Antonio, despite being Spanish, had moved with his new wife into what was known as Mexican Canyon. There, Enrique recalled, Anglo employers restricted both Spanish and Mexican workers to one side of the local Catholic Church. "You would go into the church, and the left side was [for] the Mexican people. The Anglos [sat] on the right. . . . You have to remember that my father came from Spain, a very religious country. Yet, any Spaniard you might not see in church."[17]

Their often-intimate relationships and the similarities in the patterns of discrimination against Mexicans, Spaniards, Italians, and Slavs provided an impetus for these groups to form alliances and, at times, to protest collectively. An incident at Ray began two years of sustained labor activism throughout the southern half of the state. The Ray Consolidated Copper Company and the local sheriff's department were keeping a stranglehold on the workers, intimidating, ejecting, or jailing purported troublemakers. In 1914, when the mining companies slashed wages throughout southern Arizona by 10 percent, the workers began to organize. Copper prices rebounded dramatically the next year due to wartime demand, and the mostly Anglo/Irish/Cornish WFM local at Miami won a wage increase in the form of a sliding scale that tied their wages to the rising price of copper. Euro-Latin and Mexican workers at Ray soon decided that they should benefit similarly. Despite lacking the support of the WFM or of local Anglo workers, about one hundred ethnic Mexican miners went on strike. Spaniards soon joined them to form a workingman's committee, demanding that they be placed on the higher wage scale and that the company conduct a "proper inspection and an amount of repair work sufficient to render the mine safe."[18]

The mainstream press declared that the strike was mostly the result of racial tension, and historians have accepted this view all too readily. During the strike, the conservative Arizona press fought an ideological battle to appeal to Anglo perceptions of the strikers as degenerate "bandits" and "revolutionaries" who were "easily swayed by radical orders." Newspaper accounts raised fears about the possibility of an imminent "race war." These accounts capitalized on violence between a few Mexican and Anglo workers, border skirmishes associated with the Mexican Revolution, and rumors of impending war with Mexico. In particular, they raised fears about the Plan of San Diego, a document found by authorities in Texas that called for an uprising against the United States. Yet, in stark contrast to these reports, the Ray strikers remained orderly and peaceful, while demanding higher wages, better working conditions, and equality. I have found nothing other than these newspaper accounts to suggest that the workers intended to engage in a revolution.[19]

The activism of Mexican and Spanish workers at Ray challenged the nativism of Anglo union leaders. The national leadership of the AFL had been particularly guilty of alarmist, racist rhetoric, and the recently organized Arizona State Federation of Labor (ASFL) followed suit. In the WFM, meanwhile, a new group of organizers struggled against older leaders to make the union more inclusive. In 1915 these younger, regional leaders actively supported the Mexican and Spanish workers, discounting claims that the strikes were solely a matter of racial strife. Even the ASFL, in a marked shift in its rhetoric, refused to endorse press reports that blamed the Ray strike on racial antagonism and Mexican nationalism. Contributors to the ASFL's *Arizona Labor Journal* ridiculed accounts in the *Silver Belt* and the *Arizona Republican* that blamed the strike on interracial conflict, suggesting instead that "the spreading of the rumor that racial trouble had arisen in Ray" was merely a strategy to delegitimize the strike. They argued further that the press was trying to "appeal to American 'patriotism' to 'defend' the country against Mexican conquest." ASFL and WFM organizers thus explicitly rejected a nationalist and nativist justification for crushing the strike, implying—at least for the time being—that workers' rights transcended lines of race, culture, and citizenship.[20]

Some Anglo organizers, in fact, viewed the Ray strike as an opportunity to press for higher wages and working conditions in *all* of the mining camps, for *all* ethnic groups. Anglo representatives from the Globe-Miami WFM local, in their words, "found conditions much as they had been described by the visiting Mexicans." Unlike in previous years, the WFM took concrete steps to aid the strikers, granting a local charter to eight hundred mostly Mexican and Spanish workers. Even the ASFL decided to support the strike, listing the workers' five demands in its newspaper. The demands included the adoption of the Miami wage scale, an eight-hour day, lunch breaks, an end to labor contracts, and the "right to speak freely on all subjects at meetings held at their own pleasure."[21]

The Ray strike ended after two weeks with only a partial victory, but the support from the Anglo-dominated unions that had been adversarial before the strike made it much more significant than the immediate gains might suggest. The company agreed to a new wage scale, but at only sixty cents above the current wages, rather than the $1.50 increase for muckers and $1.15 for machine men originally demanded. It offered a vague promise not to discriminate against union men in the future, provided that the Ray workers agree not to form their own WFM local. Instead, seven hundred mostly Spanish and Mexican workers joined the overwhelmingly Anglo local at Globe-Miami. The workers also won the right to hold meetings without company interference, and underground workers won thirty-minute lunch breaks. This was clearly only a partial victory, but the ASFL considered it an important step forward. An ASFL organizer declared in the *Arizona Labor Journal*, "Great credit should be given to the Mexican strikers who closely followed the advice of their committee, which discountenanced all forms and attempts at disorder." Such descriptions were a direct refutation of claims in the mainstream press of an imminent, revolutionary race war, or of an anarchical Mexican population that was "easily swayed" by radical orders.[22]

The Ray strike, and a strike at Clifton-Morenci a few months later, demonstrated that interethnic industrial unionism had taken hold, directly challenging the enforced racial divisions between ethnic groups in the mining towns. At Clifton-Morenci, five thousand ethnic Mexican, Spanish, Italian, and Anglo workers went on strike together. The WFM locals at the Anglo-dominated Globe and Miami districts offered $15,000 in support.[23] Like the strike at Ray, it remained mostly peaceful, and in the end the strikers won a minimum wage of $2 per shift and a sliding wage scale. In return, however, the company demanded that the workers abandon their new WFM locals and receive a much smaller wage increase than they had demanded.[24]

The importance of these strikes in ethno-racial terms is apparent in union membership roles. In Globe-Miami, for the first time, Italian, Slavic, and Mexican workers together made up the majority on the local WFM board. Some local union men protested that the board was now "alien," and Samuel Gompers of the AFL accused the leadership of the union of harboring "pro-German" and IWW (Industrial Workers of the World) sympathies. In reality, in 1916 the IWW had a substantial presence only in Bisbee. The local WFM and the ASFL had themsleves become more confrontational and inclusive. The ASFL increased its power relative to other unions, particularly after internal disputes within the WFM in 1916. That year the more radical members of the WFM branched off from the union and changed their name to the International Union of Mine Mill and Smelter Workers (Mine-Mill) to send a message that the union would no longer fight only for those workers deemed fully American. The new level of cooperation between workers of various national and ethnic backgrounds signaled the emergence of a powerful, multiethnic labor movement.[25]

Middle-class Mexican Americans in Phoenix and Tucson found their own loyalties tested by the strikers. Much of the Spanish-language press and many *mutualistas* disapproved of the strikes, insisting on the importance of order and patriotism at a time of international crisis. Having come to resent the lack of distinction that many Anglo-Americans made between Mexican nationals and Mexican-American citizens, some tried to distance themselves from the strikes.[26] One mutualista—the Liga Protectora Latina—initially bucked the trend by offering moral and material support to the strikers. A local lodge of the Liga in Ray, while apparently not directly involved in planning the strike, provided some financial support for the strikers.[27]

In early December 1916 the wartime labor movement became even more inclusive when Tohono O'odham laborers joined a general strike at Ajo—an important fact that existing accounts of strikes in the World War I era have overlooked. The Ajo strike began after the local carpenters and electrical workers sent a petition to the company demanding that they be placed on the sliding-wage scale. When the company offered only a 50-cent increase, the carpenters and electricians appealed to the unorganized, largely ethnic Mexican and indigenous workers for their support. Hundreds of ethnic Mexican and Tohohno O'odham workers joined the strike the next week. Ed Crow, a Mine-Mill organizer, traveled to the district and helped to form a strike committee which demanded full recognition of the union and wages equal to those paid at Miami and Douglas. The ASFL urged all Arizona locals to support the strikers, optimistically predicting that "the prize, if we do this and put all our strength and resources behind the strike at Ajo, will be the first closed camp in the state."[28]

Over one hundred Tohono O'odham participated in the Ajo strike, defying contemporary stereotypes of Indians as passive, pliant, and dependent. Shortly after the strike began, Mike Curley, the superintendent of the New Cornelia Copper Company, complained to Rev. T. Wand on the Tohono O'odham reservation that "the majority of the men working for this company went out on a strike. Among them were the Indians and the Mexicans." Curley requested that Wand persuade the O'odham to return to work, but there is no evidence that Wand fulfilled his request. Instead, according to the *Arizona Labor Journal*, 130 O'odham joined the union, representing "perhaps the first instance on record where any body of Indians has ever joined a labor union."[29]

The sheriff again intimidated the strikers with arrests, and the company and the mainstream press fed fears of racial violence, Mexican bandits, and revolutionaries in order to persuade the federal government to intervene. Purportedly to protect the American residents of Ajo from these impending threats, 150 troops from the 14th Infantry entered Ajo on December 20. The publisher of the company-run *Ajo Copper News* justified the move in an editorial the following Saturday, invoking the Villista raid on Columbus, New Mexico, several months earlier. "It would be an easy matter for a few hundred Mexican bandits to surprise the camp at any time and loot it, or worse, and get away before U.S. troops could possibly reach the camp. The *News* does not expect a raid, but, for that matter, neither did the people of Columbus, N.M.—it came, nevertheless. Preparedness is wise." Ed Miller of the ASFL ridiculed the claim that the military was there to protect the camp from Mexican bandits. He pointed out that the soldiers were not stationed in a position to protect the town from an external threat, but rather "right between Superintendent Curley's house and the company boarding house."[30]

Unlike the Clifton and Ray strikes, the Ajo strike was a complete failure, brought about by the strategic use of rhetoric by the press about Mexican "bandits" and intimidation by the sheriff's department and the U.S. Army.[31] Once the troops were in place, the company published a notice that all workers who desired to return to work would be permitted to. Many strikers held out for a while, but by the end of January, all had either left town or trickled back to work.[32] The company continued to capitalize on fears of a Mexican raid in order to persuade the army to remain encamped in town. In March the *Ajo Copper News* suggested that "any person, company or corporation having influence should use every means possible to have the company of soldiers here now remain."[33] By July, Anglos in the town had organized the Citizens' and Property Holders' Protective Association and the Workman's Loyalty League. The *Copper News* was happy to announce that "there is intense earnestness manifest and grim determination that does not augur well for any disturbers in our midst." The members of these organizations painted themselves as the true citizens of the mining town, while characterizing Mexicans, in particular, as radical, disorderly aliens.[34]

By April 1917 the entrance of the United States into World War I put a new premium on national loyalty and patriotism, prompting many supporters of the labor movement to reverse their positions. Middle-class Mexican Americans, particularly after the recent nativist assault in the mainstream press, were under the greatest pressure to reassert their loyalty as citizens. Even the Liga Protectora Latina, which had supported the 1915 strike at Ray, printed a pro-war, antistrike message on all of its stationery: "Help our country by co-operating in all industries without giving any cause of any disturbance between capital and labor. . . . It will help win the war."[35]

Wartime demands for patriotism contributed to the most egregious instance of union busting in the World War I era: the Bisbee deportation. IWW organizers had decided to make Bisbee a test case of industrial unionism in Arizona, and for six months after the Ajo strike they catalyzed worker discontent. In July 1917 the strike began. Ethnic Mexican and Slavic workers at the mines called for a substantial increase in wages for surface workers and an end to the blacklisting of union members by Phelps Dodge. While the IWW was more concerned with national worker solidarity than local circumstances at Bisbee, the Mexican, Slavic, and Finnish workers at the Copper Queen saw the strike as an opportunity to end the inequalities in Bisbee's so-called white man's camp. About 90 percent of the workforce joined the strike.[36]

The strike explicitly aimed not only to equalize wages but to challenge the racialized and gendered ideology of Bisbee's white man's camp. Non-Anglo workers were no longer willing to tolerate the fact that white men received higher wages—a practice justified by their supposedly higher standard of living and greater need to care for their families. In short they rejected the notion of a superior white manhood and sought to challenge Anglo perceptions that they were irrational and unmanly transient workers. The strike was thus about race, gender, and class simultaneously.[37]

Phelps Dodge refused to tolerate the challenge to its racially ordered camp. In a scene comparable to Ajo, the local Workers' Loyalty League and Citizens Protective League, along with the local sheriff and company managers, were determined to be rid of local agitators. The sheriff deputized hundreds of Anglos in these organizations who then invaded the workers' homes at dawn and marched twelve hundred of them onto twenty-three boxcars, deporting them to Columbus, New Mexico. Most of the deported workers would never return to Bisbee. More than twenty years would pass before mine workers in Arizona would successfully begin to organize a new series of strikes to challenge the racialized class hierarchy.[38]

Despite the defeat, Euro-Americans from eastern and southern Europe had taken a large step toward acceptance by Anglo workers as white citizen-workers through their growing involvement in the regional unions. From 1915 to 1917 strikes improved wages and chipped away at racial inequalities. The Miami sliding-wage scale became common in many of Arizona's copper towns, and Euro-American workers in select camps, such as Bisbee, enjoyed higher wage scales. The gap between the pay for Euro-Latins and Anglo workers narrowed. In certain camps, such as Clifton-Morenci, Spanish-surnamed men retained their positions as officials of ASFL union locals, and Spanish-surnamed workers made up half of the union rolls. Still, the copper companies continued to enforce segregation and discrimination against ethnic Mexicans. Moreover, both in the ASFL and Mine-Mill organizations, anti-immigrant forces pushed their agenda. Eastern and southern European immigration declined substantially in the years after the strikes—particularly after the national origins laws in 1921 and 1924 initiated restrictive quotas on the number of people that could emigrate from these countries. In the meantime, Mexican immigration continued to climb.[39]

From 1915 to 1917 Mexicans had made convenient scapegoats, both because the radicalism and violence of the Mexican Revolution helped to justify a hard line against the strikes and because Mexican immigration was far outpacing that of any other group. In 1910 Mexican immigration to Arizona already outpaced immigration from all other nations *combined* (Figure 4.1). A decade later the federal census indicated that the number of Mexican nationals had doubled to about sixty thousand, a number that certainly undercounted undocumented Mexican immigrants (Figure 4.2). This influx made Mexicans appear to be a far greater threat than other national and/or ethnic groups. In 1925 one ASFL organizer complained that Arizona's mining camps had come to be dominated by *"campesinos and peons from the farms and haciendas"* of Mexico, who depressed the wages of the American workers. A Mexican/Anglo dichotomy was becoming clearer than ever before, while racial distinctions between eastern and southern Europeans and Anglos were becoming much less common.[40]

The fact that some Mexican Americans attempted to pass as eastern or southern Europeans to avoid discrimination demonstrates this point. Carlos Contreras, who grew up in Tempe before he took a job in Ajo, recalled that in the 1930s he and his family almost managed to enter a public swimming pool by claiming to be southern European. "Our parents told us we couldn't go swimming because we were Mexicans but if we tried we might pass for Italians or Greeks. Well we almost made it. Two or three of the family had gone thru when I came up to pay. The man asked me if I was Mexican and I answered no, then he said *'Como te llamas?'* I answered immediately without thinking, 'Carlos.' You can imagine how low my heart sank." Contreras's mistake marked itself indelibly in his consciousness, clarifying for him on what side of the boundary between white and non-white he fell.[41]

This is not to suggest that an Anglo/Mexican dichotomy was so hegemonic that other ethno-racial distinctions disappeared. Indians still found themselves relegated to a third-tier position in both the mining and agricultural sectors. And many Spaniards in places like Ray-Sonora-Barcelona continued to live segregated within their own neighborhoods or together with ethnic Mexicans. Many of them, due largely to linguistic and religious affiliation, identified more with ethnic Mexicans than Anglos.[42] Only in the 1930s would rising fears about Communism lead some Arizonans to become suspicious once again of eastern Europeans, but this was generally no longer a racial designation. After 1920 the brunt of nativist sentiment fell on the backs of ethnic Mexicans alone.

NATIVISM, REPATRIATION, AND MEXICAN AMERICANS

In the three years after the 1917 defeat of industrial unionism in the mining towns, south-central Arizona saw the greatest influx of Mexican workers yet. While some crossed to work for the mines or the railroads, the majority came to work in the agricultural economy, which boomed after the completion of the Salt River Project. The rapid increase in the importance

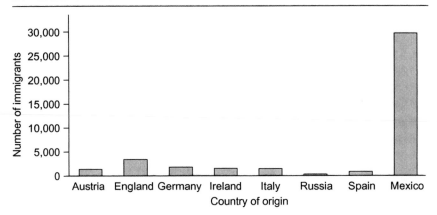

Figure 4.1. National Origin of White Immigrants in Arizona, 1910. Source: University of Virginia Geospatial and Statistical Data Center http://fisher.lib.virginia.edu/census/ (accessed August 2004).

of industrial agriculture forced everyone, including Arizona's politicians, Mexican Americans, and the labor unions, to re-evaluate their stance on Mexican immigrant labor. Cotton growers promoted the stereotype of the tractable Mexican sojourner who had no interest in American citizenship, wishing instead only to earn a little money by doing work that Anglos shunned. For ethnic Mexicans, this argument created a new ideological obstacle to full membership in the nation-state, since Mexicans were expected to return to Mexico, not become citizens. And for Arizona's mostly Euro-American trade unionists, the new influx created yet another period of crisis, in which union leaders had to decide whether to organize Mexican workers or redouble their efforts to restrict immigration. Their decisions were influenced by fears that Mexican workers threatened the manhood of yeoman farmers and white citizen-workers.

In 1920, when cotton prices, cotton acreage, and Mexican immigration peaked, the ASFL briefly experimented with organizing Mexican farmworkers. It did so not simply out of empathy for the Mexicans but to ensure that white farmers and farmworkers, most of whom were employed in supervisory and semiskilled positions, did not sink into the "barbarous" condition of the Mexicans. An editorial in the *Arizona Labor Journal* declared, "Officers of the Arizona State Federation of Labor realized that American labor must either lift the Mexican laborer somewhere close to its own standards or it would be dragged down to the level which the cotton companies have attempted to establish for this farm labor, which is an unthinkable condition."[43]

Even as some ASFL leaders supported Mexican workers, others continued to argue that Mexicans were themselves the source of the problem. An editorial in the *Arizona Labor Journal* suggested that "by adding thousands of an inferior race to our population, every form of vice and crime is promoted that a few rich men may grow richer." ASFL officials complained that Mexicans recruited under the ninth proviso had "been farmed out to other farmers and miscellaneous employers . . . in violation of federal agreement," rather than being "sent back to their own country." [44]

Still, in 1920 ASFL leaders began to organize in the Salt River valley during the late spring and summer. They timed the campaign so that most of the workers in the fields were year-round employees rather than seasonal laborers. In May, after a six-week campaign, ASFL organizer Lester B. Doane (who had helped to organize Mexican miners three years earlier) claimed to have enrolled thousands of men into union locals in "practically every town in Maricopa County." To allay growers' fears, Doane assured them

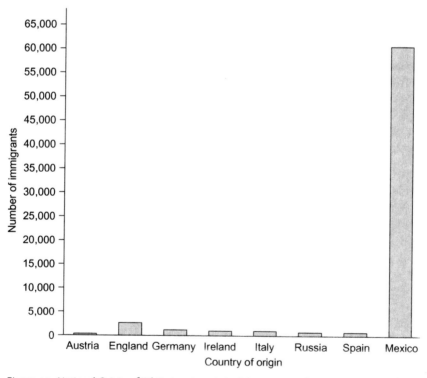

Figure 4.2. National Origin of White Immigrants in Arizona, 1920. Source: University of Virginia Geospatial and Statistical Data Center http://fisher.lib.virginia.edu/census/ (accessed August 2004).

that the workers were not planning to strike. Rather, he hoped that common "business principles" would convince the "reasonable majority" of growers of the need for "fair prices for the necessities of life." The ASFL planned to establish cooperative stores so that the workers would no longer have to buy goods at inflated prices from labor contractors.[45]

Rather than cooperate, the growers fought back, and they generally had the courts and the local police on their side. Police responded to grower complaints by jailing and deporting Mexican organizers. According to the *Arizona Labor Journal*, when six Mexican farmworkers in Glendale asked the Arizona Cotton Growers Association for higher wages, they were quickly arrested, sent to a Tempe jail, and then deported the next morning, leaving the eight-year-old son of one of the workers behind. In July another worker was deported from Tempe without his family, after he complained that he earned inadequate wages. Finally, in November the local police arrested R. M. Sánchez, the secretary of the Phoenix Federal Labor Union, on charges of avoiding Selective Service. The police held Sánchez in Nogales without a hearing until the end of the picking season in February and then released him without comment. An editorial in the *Arizona Labor Journal* drew a direct connection between the ACGA's tactics and those of Phelps Dodge three years earlier: "If the people of Arizona think that the deportation of nearly twelve hundred miners from Bisbee on July 12, 1917, was an unusual case, they are very much mistaken. It was unusual only in the point of numbers and brutality displayed."[46]

A national recession and a precipitous fall in cotton prices struck the final blow to the 1920–1921 organizing campaign—a blow that would effectively end interethnic union organization in Arizona's fields for over a decade. That year, cotton growers were shocked to find that sales fell $20 million below the previous year's level. Since cotton acreage in the Salt River valley had doubled over the previous year, the bust hit valley growers especially hard. As one historian has explained, "Many growers, unable to sell their crops except at a great loss, merely cut their pickers adrift, often without final pay." The *Tucson Daily Citizen* reported that thousands of Mexicans were stranded in the Salt River valley, and the Nogales Chamber of Commerce reported that thousands more were returning to the border, causing overcrowding and unsanitary conditions in the city. The ASFL established a breadline to help feed the stranded workers until the Mexican government could arrange for their transportation back to Mexico, but the crisis decimated the union locals in the fields.[47]

After the failure of the 1920 campaign, most ASFL leaders abandoned hopes of organizing Mexican farmworkers, instead renewing their gendered and racist calls for immigration restriction. In 1920 John Bratton of the ASFL suggested that Mexicans threatened the independence and manhood of the family farmer. Not unlike the Anglo workers in the mines, he suggested that Mexican immigrants undermined the white farmer's ability to provide for his wife and his family, and thus deprived him of the "one thing above all others that distinguishes the civilized man from the savage . . . his habit of looking ahead and making provisions for the future." Since "the Mexican" supposedly had little inclination to plan for his future or for his family, but instead was content with "only enough to clothe, feed and shelter himself," he supposedly lacked the character necessary to become a good citizen-worker. He also endangered white Americans who had larger ambitions.[48]

The demand for seasonal workers remained relatively weak in the early 1920s. Between 1921 and 1924 the price of Pima cotton fell, and acres in production declined from two hundred thousand to nine thousand. Many growers switched back to alfalfa, barley, wheat, citrus, melons, and lettuce; others, to short-staple cotton. In 1921, when Secretary of Labor Wilson failed to renew the ninth proviso for the first time since 1917, growers did not put up much of a fight. Throughout the first half of the 1920s, the regular flow of Mexican immigrants, combined with out-of-state workers and indigenous workers, provided enough workers to handle the newly diversified fields. Only in 1924–1925, when acreage planted in short-staple cotton climbed to over 150,000, did the demand for labor increase once again.[49]

Calls for the restriction of Mexican immigration intensified once again, however, as the economy stagnated in 1927 and especially in 1929, when the Great Depression dramatically impacted both the cotton and the mining industries. The acreage planted in cotton soon fell to about 113,000, and cotton prices fell once again. As prices plummeted, standard picking rates declined from $1.50 to 50 cents per hundredweight. Mining was also hit hard. Early in the Depression many copper mines, including those at Ray and Ajo, shut down entirely, and copper sales declined to only about $10 million. Only thirty-three hundred workers remained employed in the mines.[50]

The Great Depression amplified long-standing fears that Mexicans would compete for jobs and degrade the economic, cultural, and racial status of the Anglo working class. The Central Labor Council of the Globe-Miami mining district wrote to the president of the AFL that the "industrial, social and educational standards of Americans" were being dramatically undermined by the "Mexican influx." J. H. Francis, an Arizona legislator, expressed the feelings of many of his constituents when he complained about "the terrific drain imposed upon Arizona taxpayers through the admission of thousands of indigent Mexicans annually into this state." The ASFL, in turn, repeatedly called for greater enforcement of the border.[51]

Nativist rhetoric again transcended economic concerns to imply that Mexicans could not be assimilated and that nationality was determined not only by birthplace but also by race. In March 1930 the *Arizona Labor Journal* printed what it called a "splendid article," using inflammatory language to support immigration restriction. The article suggested that "American standards of citizenship" were threatened by "the permanent addition to our population of a great mass of the least intelligent and the least assimilable of all the alien groups which have settled among us." The author complained not only about job competition and low wages but more generally about the "further Mexicanization of the Southwest."[52]

Arizona politicians who had once supported temporary admittance of Mexican nationals changed their minds in response to the growing cry for restriction. U.S. senator Carl Hayden stated in April 1930, "No large number of aliens should be permitted to become permanent residents of the United States, whose children will not look the same, act the same, and have the same ideals, as other Americans." In December Hayden introduced a resolution to appropriate funds for a full count of the undocumented Mexicans who remained in the country. He enthusiastically endorsed President Herbert Hoover's nomination of William Doak to be secretary of labor, embracing Doak's promise to intensify immigration restrictions.[53]

Hayden's actions were part of a growing national groundswell in support of federal action. In March 1930 the United States stopped issuing visas altogether to "common laborers" from Mexico, and the Congress made illegal entry a misdemeanor punishable by jail time. An active campaign was begun to deport undocumented border crossers, while cities and states took it upon themselves to encourage and intimidate even legal immigrants to return to Mexico. Under Secretary of Labor Doak, immigration agents carried out raids in cities across the country, entering into communities and workplaces to arrest and deport those without proper documentation.[54]

Thousands of Mexican nationals were either forcefully deported or chose to leave "voluntarily," though even such repatriations were often the result of employers' active intimidation or discriminatory treatment. Maximo Alonzo, who lived in the mining town of Miami in 1931, remembered the deportations well. "There was no work, no nothing here," he recalled. "The government brought trains to haul people away—at that time there was mainly Mexican people here—and they were loading them in boxcars and trains, putting them back out to El Paso to the frontier." Alonzo acknowledged that mining employers and government officials did not force Mexicans onto the trains, but the hostile atmosphere and the lack of work gave them little choice but to return to Mexico.[55] Between 1930 and 1932 it is estimated that 18,520 Mexicans were deported from Arizona.[56]

Whether or not they were U.S. citizens, people of Mexican descent were treated as unwanted aliens. Rosalio Frolian Muñoz, a Mexican-American student at the Arizona State Teacher's College, wrote in 1938, "The attitude toward Mexicans changed very decidedly after 1929, and repeatedly one hears politicians, miners, and farmers who previously justified the contracting of Mexican labor at starvation wages denouncing the children or grandchildren of those immigrants and demanding that they be sent back to Mexico 'where they belong.'" Muñoz contrasted this anti-Mexican sentiment with attitudes toward European immigrants and their children: "Members of other nationalities are considered Americans after the second generation, but the Mexicans seem to be discriminated against and labeled with derogatory terms on all occasions." His comments suggest that the Anglo/Mexican dichotomy was much clearer than it had been earlier in the century when immigrants from southern and eastern Europe had often been lumped together with Mexicans as foreigners and aliens.[57]

Mexican Americans struggled over how to respond to the rising nativist tide. *El Tucsonense,* a Spanish-language newspaper, published frequent editorials condemning the treatment of Mexican nationals. In 1937, when Arizona stopped providing emergency aid to unnaturalized immigrants (except for those with dependent children born in the United States), *El Tucsonense* called the action "cruel, brutal, anti-social, and un-Christian." It also applauded the resolution of the local Club Democrático Hispano Americano to gather funds for *"nuestra raza"* (our race/people) to make up for the withholding of aid. In so doing, the editorial acknowledged Mexican Americans' cultural and kinship connections with Mexican nationals.[58]

Other Mexican Americans chose instead to draw a clear line between themselves and Mexican nationals, often asserting that they were white. Mexican Americans worried about the negative stereotypes that new, uneducated, working-class immigrants reinforced in the minds of the Anglo majority.[59] One researcher found that, for the most part, Tucson's Mexican Americans objected when "Mexican" was used "in contrast to the term *white* for the English-speaking group." They accepted Mexican as a designator of culture and national origin, but not as a marker of race. Mexican-American claims to whiteness sometimes took even more explicit forms. A prominent Mexican-American businessman in Tucson explained that he preferred to be called Spanish American because, in his words, Mexican was appropriate only for "Mexican nationals or for the pure Indians from Mexico." Claiming pure Spanish descent had long served as a way to gain entry into the circle of whiteness, and the rise in anti-Mexican nativism made such claims seem urgent.[60]

Some Mexican Americans organized politically to secure their status as citizens. In 1932, for example, Luis Cordova, a Southern Pacific Railroad worker, organized the Latin American Club in Phoenix to encourage voter registration and to endorse political candidates. Adam Díaz, who played an important role in the Phoenix registration drive, remembered walking "from house to house, door to door [to] explain to people what we were trying to do."[61]

Voting restrictions and intimidation, however, limited the effectiveness of the registration efforts. A 1937 case from South Tucson is instructive. That year, local property holders and entrepreneurs incorporated the barrio as an independent municipality. Ethnic Mexican leaders in the barrio hoped to elect a majority to the council in the first election of April 1937. Thirty Mexican-American residents organized the Club Hispano-Americano Independiente de la Municipalidad de Sur Tucson. They walked door-to-door to register voters. The editors of El Tucsonense asked that South Tucson residents "unen fuertemente (strongly unite)" to elect members of "nuestra raza" to the city council, and the Club Hispano-Americano hosted gatherings that included free food and dancing to encourage voting.[62] Ultimately, these tactics failed. In the election only one in five of the winning candidates was a Mexican American. The results illustrate how obstacles to voting limited the ability of Mexican Americans to achieve political change through voter registration alone.[63]

Many middle-class Mexican Americans saw naturalization and self-improvement, rather than political activism, as the best way to help Mexican immigrants. The Alianza Hispano-Americana argued that ethnic Mexicans could best gain acceptance and citizenship through hard work and education. Reflecting its belief in this principle, it joined forces with the Phoenix Americanization committee to establish Friendly House in the early 1920s. Friendly House's primary motive was to encourage the Americanization of Mexican immigrants and to help them find jobs. In the 1930s Friendly House attempted to instill civic virtue and to teach home economics, hygiene, and the English language to Mexicans who lived in the Salt River valley.[64]

Ironically, its emphasis on Americanization eventually evolved into active support for repatriation. In 1931 the Mexican consul in Phoenix reported that seven thousand Mexicans were being processed for deportation. Rather than protest the move, Friendly House helped to repatriate some 130 Mexican families to Mexico in 1933.[65] Its support for deportation reveals that, in the struggle to be considered American and/or white, Mexican Americans sometimes accepted discriminatory policies against Mexican nationals. It also reveals how difficult it was for ethnic Mexicans, except for a few who were light-skinned and/or middle class, to follow in the footsteps of European immigrants who had gained acceptance as white citizens.

THE QUESTIONABLE WHITENESS OF OKIES

Ironically, while the deportation of Mexicans was designed, in part, to protect white citizen-workers from a further slippage in their economic and social status, for some it had precisely the opposite effect. In the years following deportation, migrant workers from the south-central plains increasingly found themselves working under the same substandard conditions their Mexican and indigenous forebears had experienced. Most of the newcomers refused to see Mexican and indigenous workers in the labor camps and barrios as their equals, holding on to the notion that their whiteness made them superior. Many, if not most, viewed their unfortunate circumstances as temporary; they held onto their faith that they could work their way up the agricultural ladder or into new occupations altogether. Their experiences, and their attitudes toward Mexicans and Indians in Arizona, expose how the boundaries between white and nonwhite functioned in midcentury Arizona.[66]

An influx of workers from the south-central plains began in the 1920s. Arizona growers began recruiting in the plains as early as 1924, when highway construction linked Arizona to the region for the first time. Most of the migrants ended up in Pinal and Maricopa counties, where four-fifths of the state's cotton crop was produced. Between 1929 and 1933 many of these newcomers were disappointed to find relatively little work available after the dramatic cut in cotton prices and acreage. By 1933, however, Arizona cotton production was on the rebound, and regional growers who no longer had access to the thousands of Mexicans who had been deported once again were searching for a cheap labor source.[67]

One reason the cotton industry in Arizona recovered early was that the Coolidge Dam on the Gila River was completed. Combined with a proliferation of groundwater pumps, it led to an expansion of irrigated acres in the Casa Grande valley from about fifty-five thousand to eighty thousand in a few short years. Ironically, another cause of its recovery was the federally subsidized crop reduction measures of the Agricultural Adjustment Act. The act resulted in higher prices for cotton, so it also led to an increase in acreage under production. In 1937 Arizona growers planted almost three hundred thousand acres of cotton, breaking a state record.[68]

While workers from Arizona's reservations, towns, and barrios still filled some seasonal jobs, Anglos came to make up the largest farm labor force for the first time in the state's history. In 1936–1937 about two thousand Tohono O'odham moved from their reservations into the cotton fields every picking season and twenty-five hundred to three thousand ethnic Mexican and Yaqui workers came from towns and cities within Arizona. Two thousand Anglo workers traveled to Arizona from California, where the peak season occurred earlier, ending by November. The greatest number of seasonal workers, however, came from Texas, Arkansas, and Oklahoma, totaling some eighteen thousand. A 1941 study found that 90 percent of those who migrated to Arizona in the 1930s and remained over the course of the decade were "white," while only 6 percent were from Mexico and 4 percent were black.[69]

Repatriation succeeded in opening up jobs for white citizen-workers, but such jobs represented a jolting decline in their economic and social status. As white tenants in the plains and the South became wageworkers, their status as white came into question.[70] The process of moving out of the south-central states and into Arizona had a similar effect. A study of migrant workers in Arizona by the Works Progress Administration noted negative attitudes toward the newcomers. It found that residents throughout southern Arizona "universally applied . . . the term poor white trash" to the incoming migrants. Just as they had historically viewed Mexicans as inherently degraded, many Arizonans viewed the new migrants' poor condition to be the result of their innate inferiority. According to the report, "In the cotton towns where the pickers go on Saturdays to buy their supplies, the permanent residents—merchants, restaurant waiters, delivery boys, police officers, etc.—regard the cotton pickers with a feeling closely analogous to racial prejudice. Though there appears to be no overt social segregation in the cotton towns, the pickers are thought of as naturally inferior, particularly when they have no money to spend—as they frequently do not."[71]

While the WPA study found no "overt social segregation," there was de facto segregation. Many impoverished migrants had no choice but to move into the poor areas of the small towns and cities. Father Emmett McLoughlin, a Catholic priest who lived in Phoenix at the time, suggested that residents encouraged this pattern of social segregation in order to present Phoenix as a modern, clean city and to shed its image as a "cow-town." Phoenix "was trying to bolster the social status of its citizens by shunting across the tracks the immigrants from Oklahoma, Arkansas, and Texas and by veneering itself with the gloss of a symphony orchestra, a Little Theater, and necklace of resort hotels." While the newcomers moved into shoddy neighborhoods filled with "shacks . . . without electricity, most without plumbing and heat," most Phoenix residents chose to ignore the problem. "Phoenix did not know—or pretended not to know—that it had slums. But in them lived the Negroes, the Mexicans, and the 'white trash.'" [72]

Many black migrants also made their way into central Arizona to work in the fields during the 1920s and 1930s. In 1920 there were fewer than two thousand blacks in Maricopa, Pima, and Pinal counties combined. By 1930, however, that number rose to 6,364 and by 1940, to 10,402. Most of these newcomers came to Arizona for reasons similar to those of the Anglo migrants—because they, too, had lost their position as tenants or share-croppers and were in search of a better life in the West. [73]

The status of black workers, when compared with that of the incoming Anglos, says much about where the boundaries of whiteness lay in the years between world wars. In Arizona, black newcomers faced much clearer and more explicit forms of discrimination and segregation than those faced by Anglo migrants. African Americans had no choice but to move into completely segregated communities, such as south Phoenix, Mobile, and Randolph. Deed restrictions in Randolph explicitly reserved all of the lots on the west side of Highway 87 for whites and lots on the east side for nonwhites. In the schools black children were completely segregated from white children. A resident of Randolph who suggested that the black side of town was "just like an Indian Reservation" was using Indian/white seg-regation as a reference point for understanding black/white segregation, which was relatively new. In any case, white Arizonans made ample dis-tinctions between black and white migrants, a fact that suggests that Ok-ies remained white, if not fully equal. [74]

The depressed status of the incoming migrants proved disturbing to many Anglos. In Arizona many of the farm operators had origins in the south-central states, and some even had relatives among the Depression-era migrants. [75] Moreover, many native Anglos felt an ideological impera-tive to ensure that white citizen-workers did not sink to the degraded level of nonwhite workers in the fields. Mexican repatriation, it turned out, had failed to secure the status of Arizona's Anglo population, and in fact had the opposite effect once the cotton market rebounded. As a result, the perceived line between respectable white citizens and nonwhite Mexican, Indian, and black workers seemed at risk of dissolving.

Stanley Rider, a member of the Citizens' Civil Liberties Committee of Arizona, expressed the views of many Anglo-Arizonans concerning the degraded socioeconomic status of the incoming migrants. In a Tucson radio address toward the end of the decade he declared, "Now the foreign racial groups are gone, or rapidly going. In their places have come the people from the 'Dust Bowl,' native white Americans, who trace their ancestry back to the patriots of revolutionary days." Their poverty, he insisted, unlike the poverty of the nonwhite population, was not the result of natural inadequacy, but of economics and technology: "'Tractored off' their places at home, as Steinbeck so graphically describes it in *The Grapes of Wrath*, they faced destitution, when, lo, they were offered manna in the promised land." While he exaggerated the degree to which "foreign racial groups" had disappeared, his point was clear. Mexicans were foreign not simply because they were from another country, but because they were racially different. On the other hand, the newcomers from the plains, due to their whiteness and their former status as farm owners and operators, were true Americans. As such they did not deserve to withstand the poor treatment that had been acceptable when it primarily affected the Mexican and indigenous populations.[76]

As the decade progressed, it became clear that race and culture worked to the benefit of the incoming migrants. Historian Marsha Weisiger has found that most of the newcomers eventually worked their way into more permanent, well-paid positions. She accounts for this success by suggesting they benefited from "gumption, hard work, perseverance, and a bit of luck." In making this argument, however, she overlooks the fact that many ethnic Mexican and indigenous workers worked just as hard, yet most of them failed to achieve the same results. The best explanation for that discrepancy is racial discrimination.[77]

Employers maintained a double standard in the treatment, hiring, and promotion of their workers. Growers often segregated Mexicans and Indians in the camps from the Okies and were less likely to promote the former into positions such as timekeeper or weigh boss. The son of one farm owner recalled that his family employed Mexicans, Indians, and Anglos alike, but they promoted only the latter into better-paying, year-round positions. He drew distinctions between those he judged to be responsible farmworkers and those he called the "dregs of humanity," including Mexicans and Indians and some transient Okies. Over time, he suggested, "the good ones integrated in the community and raised families, and they became part of us." The bad ones, implicitly, did not fulfill their manly responsibilities as citizens to settle down and provide for their families.[78]

Many Anglos enjoyed quick promotions and integration into their communities. Among these was Dennis Kirkland, who was recruited by Casa Grande landowner Pete Ethington. Kirkland recalled that "there was a lot of segregation" in the cotton camp in which he first lived, and that there were a couple rows of cabins "for the Mexicans . . . in the backside." The Indian workers, he added, "were treated the worst, in terms of working conditions." Kirkland was promoted to weigh boss, and his father, who had only a third-grade education, was soon promoted to timekeeper. This was not unusual among the Anglo newcomers. Lloyd Hamilton, who arrived in 1937 to pick cotton, secured a job with the Buckeye Irrigation Company within a year after his arrival and was soon operating his own 40-acre farm. Sam Cambron, who moved into Arizona in 1936, was hired by C. O. Vosburgh as a weigh boss, and eventually became Vosburgh's superintendent. Vosburgh later granted Cambron 120 acres of land, which the latter expanded to some two thousand.[79]

As Arizona's economy began to improve, Anglo workers also received the most stable, skilled, and best-paying jobs on vegetable and fruit farms. In 1933 the vast majority of the packing-shed workers in south-central Arizona were Anglo. According to a contemporaneous study by Stuart Jamieson published by the Department of Labor, "White shed workers . . . generally refused to work beside members of a nonwhite race or even to allow them to work inside a packing shed." Shed workers feared that allowing "one or a few to work in a shed . . . would be a 'thin edge of the wedge,'" thus jeopardizing their monopoly on such better-paying jobs. Anglo agricultural workers used race to explain why ethnic Mexicans made up the majority of workers in the vegetable fields surrounding the sheds. One worker from Oklahoma argued that Mexicans and other nonwhites were racially better suited for work in vegetable fields because they "could stoop down better" and thus "go right through the field."[80]

Some Anglos managed to overcome such racism and tried to organize unions with the state's Mexican and indigenous populations. Other workers' insistence upon racial exclusion and separation, however, partly explain why Arizona's modest labor movement had only limited effectiveness. As shed workers began to unionize in 1933, they did so separately from the fieldworkers, reflecting their own anxieties about their occupational and racial status. The National Industrial Recovery Act (1933) had excluded farm laborers from the right to engage in collective bargaining. Shed workers were protected under the new law as processors, and they feared that farmworkers would jeopardize their status. Jamieson observed at the time that this refusal reflected "racial as well as occupational differences." Anglos insisted upon a separate union not only to avoid the "lack of legal protection suffered by field workers" but also to avoid the "discrimination" and "low social status" suffered by Indians and Mexicans.[81]

There were exceptions to this rule. Organizers from California's Cannery and Agricultural Workers Industrial Union (C&AWIU) made inroads among the fieldworkers in 1933–1934, when wages failed to reflect the rebound in the cotton market. That year, picking rates reached a nadir of 50 cents per hundredweight. C&AWIU organizers made regular visits to the migrant camps around Maricopa and Pinal counties, and they established an office in Coolidge. The union had organized a successful strike in Yuma (on the border between Arizona and California) in September, and since there was little doubt that the 50-cent wage was no longer justifiable, the state arbitration board was able to negotiate a 10-cent increase for the 1933 season. Since this wage was still far below what the union and the pickers felt was adequate, many pickers still refused to work.[82]

Unfortunately, by the spring of 1934, the C&AWIU pulled out of Arizona to counter a campaign of violence and intimidation in California by the growers' association there. In its absence the ASFL attempted to continue the organization campaign, but aggressive recruiting by the Arizona Farm Labor Service in the southern plains and the out-migration of thousands of workers to California undermined the effort.[83]

Organizers again made ephemeral progress in 1937–1938. Arizona growers had recruited a surplus of workers, and flooding in California prevented them from moving west. Recognizing their chance to make inroads into Arizona, California's United Cannery, Agricultural, Packing and Allied Workers of America (UCAPAWA) signed up many of the stranded pickers onto the union roles and organized a march in Phoenix to demand commodity aid. Lacking the support of Arizona's more stable, mostly Anglo shed workers, however, the unskilled, seasonal workforce could not maintain an effective movement. While the shed workers made some compromise gains in the following year, by the end of the decade, UCAPAWA lost its foothold altogether in Arizona. In the postwar period, only the sheds would remain unionized, and the highest paying shed jobs would remain the exclusive domain of Anglo workers. Ammon Hennacy, who began working in the Arizona fields in the 1940s, verified Jamieson's earlier observations in saying, "In the packing sheds here I never saw a Negro, Mexican or Indian have a good paying job."[84]

Such racial favoritism was not limited to agriculture. Employers in other industries were more likely to hire migrants from the south-central states than longtime Mexican and indigenous residents. As early as 1931, BIA field matrons in Tucson began to notice that Tucson residents were hiring unemployed Anglo workers for odd jobs such as lawn work instead of the Mexicans and Indians who had held such jobs for decades.[85] Such favoritism remained widespread during World War II. Tucson's Brotherhood of Locomotive Firemen and Enginemen, for example, explicitly barred Mexicans and Indians from the union in its 1941 constitution.[86]

Federal New Deal agencies also practiced racial discrimination. In the Civilian Conservation Corps, recruitment was disproportionately swayed toward Anglos. The Pima County Welfare Board was given a quota of one thousand CCC recruits in 1933. According to the Club Hispano-Americano, most of them were Anglos, while only one-fifth were of Mexican descent. These figures were vastly out of proportion with the Mexican-American population in the county. When the mutualista criticized the uneven figures, county officials responded that it would be socially disruptive to raise the standard of living of Mexicans while allowing that of whites to decline.[87] Blacks and Mexican Americans were segregated into separate barracks in the camps. According to federal policy, Mexican Americans were not to be segregated, but when local whites insisted that they live in separate quarters, segregation of Mexicans became standard in Arizona's CCC camps.[88]

The federal government responded to the poor working conditions of the nation's farmworkers more directly in 1935 by establishing the Resettlement Administration, which within a year was renamed the Farm Security Administration (FSA). The FSA began to construct and operate labor camps throughout the country to ameliorate the poor living conditions of migrant farmworkers, restore order to the nation's industrial farming areas, and resolve the ongoing conflicts between growers and organized workers. To this end it instructed its camp managers to discourage union activity.[89]

Anglo reactions to the camps reveal much about the identities of white migrants and how the boundaries of whiteness functioned. Ironically, the new level of federal aid made Anglo residents, and especially Anglo men, especially sensitive to charges that they were not behaving like good citizens. Federal guardianship might be appropriate for nonwhites, but it was not an acceptable position for Arizona's white male citizens. In response, Anglo workers insisted that they were self-reliant, manly, and independent and did not need government handouts.

Decades later many would deny that they ever received federal help. One man who eventually established his own farm insisted with pride, "I tell you, my folks never got any welfare, or any commodities. It was just against their principles, they wouldn't do it." Another explained that his family had little choice but to accept public assistance, and to live in an FSA camp but that they always felt "really, really bad" about their position. He explained further that despite the fact that "all of us at that time had to take it . . . the minute we could all get off of it, we got off of it." Another former cotton-picker explained that he had never accepted public assistance and felt that most people who wanted to work could do so. Many, he argued, were simply lazy. "They preferred to stand in that line and get it," he explained, "and I'd rather work."[90] Each of these men defined the white citizen-worker as one who was highly industrious, could provide for one's own family, and would avoid dependency at all costs, thus emulating the mythical ideal of the yeoman farmer or craftsman.

Gender was inextricably linked to the concept of the white citizen-worker. Aware of the stigma attached to cotton picking, many of the newcomers drew distinctions between themselves and other workers, suggesting that because their own condition was purely circumstantial and temporary, they did not fit the profile of the typical Okie, who was usually described as a single, transient man or as a man incapable of caring for his family. One woman whose family had operated tenant farms in both Oklahoma and Texas before moving to Arizona to pick cotton explained that she and her family had never really been Okies because that term referred to "people that moved around from job to job; they never stayed anywhere any length of time." In contrast, her father was able to build a house for his family so that they could move out of the tents. Within two years her husband secured a job at a cotton gin so that she wouldn't have to pick cotton anymore. In her telling, men had to achieve financial independence to secure the social status of the women in the family, allowing the women to take on their proper roles as homemakers. As another ex-farmworker explained, only "transient laborers," not those families who settled down to stake new roots, were the true Okies. In his words, "a lot of them, that's all they ever wanted, they wanted a job for a few days and then they wanted to move someplace else and they didn't want any responsibility. Those were really the Okies."[91]

Self-consciousness about accusations of dependency was an important cause of the ultimate failure of one particularly ambitious FSA project in Arizona—a 3600-acre cooperative farm in the Casa Grande valley. Founded in 1935, the farm was occupied by up to sixty families on contiguous 2-acre tracts. Each family earned wages and split the annual profits after deductions for capital, management, and nonmember employee expenses. The FSA revealed its own racial biases by selecting fifty-six Anglo families—no ethnic Mexican or indigenous families—in the first two years of the project.

From the outset, residents of Pinal County expressed concern about the character of the migrants, about the government's overt role in establishing such a venture, and about its cooperative nature. Some Pinal County residents called the farm Little Russia, and derided the settlers, calling them Reds. The local press derisively described the settlers as "cotton pickers" who lived in "shacks," and the editor of the *Casa Grande Dispatch* asked, "Are these people Americans or do some of their names end in '-vitch' or '-insky'?"[92] The comment reveals how the ideal of the independent family farmer remained closely linked to definitions of good American citizenship—even if fewer and fewer families actually met such an ideal.

Sensitivity about their status bred a deep resentment among many of the settlers, which in turn led to factionalism and to a defensive expression of their own whiteness. While the farm was initially conceived as a self-contained venture in which women and children would aid the male household heads in certain tasks like the cotton harvest, by the third or fourth year, many of the men refused to allow their wives and children to engage in manual labor. According to political scientist Ed Banfield, who personally interviewed many of its participants, "Cotton-picking was associated with a class status which the settlers wished to escape," and so the settlers "used Indians, Mexicans and other 'Okies' for low-caste jobs almost exclusively [by] 1942."[93]

Banfield also found that the settlers preferred to keep a social distance between themselves and resident Mexicans, Indians, and Okies who still worked as cotton pickers. Instead, they preferred to associate with the more stable class of resident Anglos. For this reason, he suggested, they were most comfortable in the town of Florence, where "the underlying population of farm laborers . . . was Mexican," while the "Anglo-Saxons" were "teachers, prison guards, highway employees, and county office clerks." Growing increasingly dissatisfied with government interference and the social stigma attached to manual labor (particularly the manual labor of women and children), many had abandoned the farm by 1943. In 1944, with little support from the residents, the FSA put the land up for sale.[94]

By 1942–1943 so many Anglo farmworkers found new jobs in war industries or joined the military that growers once again faced a labor shortage. As many Anglos abandoned the FSA camps, ethnic Mexicans took their places. Once again, a castelike distinction between unionized, white citizen-workers, and seasonal, nonunionized, nonwhite and largely noncitizen workers emerged. No longer did Arizonans view people of Slavic and Italian ancestry as distinct races. Since the end of the copper strikes in 1917 and the boom in Mexican immigration that followed, such distinctions hardly seemed relevant.

While the Okies seemed to lose some of their whiteness in the 1930s, a reemerging, racialized class structure was bolstered in 1942, when the War Department initiated the Emergency Farm Labor Program, the Bracero Program, to import Mexican workers. The Bracero Program would help to firmly reestablish the notion that farm labor was a job for Mexicans and other nonwhites, and not for white citizen-workers.[95]

Decades later a farmer in Buckeye, in Maricopa County, recalled that when he had first arrived in the 1930s "it was mostly people from Oklahoma and Texas and Arkansas. Then, as things began to get better after the Depression, and those people that had any ambition went on to better things, why they started using more coloreds and Mexican laborers." Implicit in his narrative was the idea that blacks and Mexicans lacked ambition and were thus to blame for their own failure to achieve upward mobility. This thinking, as it turned out, had only temporarily been threatened in the 1930s by the appearance of Okies. After World War II, seasonal labor continued to be labeled as a natural occupation for Mexicans, Indians, and, increasingly, African Americans. White workers, so the myth went, had demonstrated their greater worthiness for better jobs and for first-class citizenship by independently working their way out of poverty. It was precisely this myth that would remain at the heart of the racially ordered class system in Arizona for years to come.[96]

▼ ▼ ▼ ▼ ▼ ▼ ▼ ▼ ▼ ▼ ▼ ▼ ▼ ▼ ▼ ▼ ▼

CHAPTER 5

THE INDIAN NEW DEAL AND
THE POLITICS OF THE TRIBE

In 1902 Peter Blaine was born to a Tohono O'odham mother and a mestizo father (part O'odham) in South Tucson. In the early years of his life, his mother, like many other urban O'odham women, supported her family by cleaning houses. When Blaine was six his mother died, and he moved into the home of his aunt Josefa and her husband, a Yaqui. He grew up speaking both Yaqui and Spanish, only later becoming fluent in the O'odham language his mother had spoken. In his memoir he recalled the neighborhood he was born in thus: "In the scattered houses, not only were there Papagos, but also Yaqui and Mexican families. The Spanish word *barrio* was used to describe those houses south of 17th Street. No whites lived there, just a mixture of Mexicans and Indians." From an early age, his environment and his identity were clearly multicultural, as illustrated by his trilingualism, his interethnic family, and his intimate ties to the diverse peoples of Tucson and southern Arizona.[1]

Eventually, Blaine moved from the multiethnic barrios of Tucson to the relatively homogeneous Tohono O'odham reservation at San Xavier. There he came to see himself unequivocally as Papago rather than Yaqui or Mexican. Still, this was a localized identity, and his sense of himself as a member of a tribe was tenuous. Blaine retained close ties to Tucson while he moved from job to job around southern Arizona. In the latter half of the 1920s he served as the "delegate . . . for the Mexican people" on the Tucson Trades Council—a position he obtained through his involvement with the construction workers' union. Only during the 1930s, when he began to work with the Indian branch of the Forest Service, a centerpiece of the Indian New Deal, did Blaine's conception of belonging to a larger tribal community solidify.[2]

This brief account of Blaine's life demonstrates how the development of a tribal identity was not simply the product of biology, language, kinship, or cultural tradition but also of engagement with the multiethnic regional community, the political economy, and the nation-state. For the Yaqui- and Spanish-speaking child of a mixed marriage there was no guarantee that he would identify unequivocally as Tohono O'odham. In the mid-1930s, though, while working under the Forest Service's Indian branch, Blaine was propelled into a position of leadership among the Tohono O'odham because of his trilingualism and experience with the union. As he explained in an oral history, "The people didn't know nothing about organizing a government. There was only the chief's organization in each village. There were no elections. What the chief said was law. The people had accepted this way of village government for who knows how long." Blaine began to direct the organizing skills that he obtained as a unionized worker and Forest Service employee toward the creation of a new tribal government.[3]

The Indian New Deal was designed, in part, to encourage tribal cohesion—in many cases among peoples who had never conceived of themselves politically as tribes. Under the direction of Commissioner John Collier, the Bureau of Indian Affairs relaxed its policy of forced assimilation, ended and even reversed the allotment process, reformed its education program, and encouraged economic development on the reservations. It also created a process whereby Indians would vote within one year to reorganize politically and then write constitutions, elect tribal councils, and form tribal governments. Most of these reforms were passed by Congress as the Indian Reorganization Act (IRA) in June 1934.[4]

The implementation of the IRA was often far more complicated than Collier had hoped and was contradictory in its outcomes. In Arizona the economic programs of the Indian New Deal, which were intended to make tribes more self-sufficient and reservation economies more viable, tended instead to make growing numbers of Indians dependent upon wage labor. The reforms also often presumed a level of homogeneity among indigenous groups that had never existed. According to one historian, the IRA "ignored Indian socio-historical realities," and "formalized a political unity superimposed on cultural and political diversity within single reservations."[5] It also often ignored intimate ties, such as Peter Blaine's, that transcended both ethnic boundaries and those of the reservation.

In Arizona's borderlands the Indian New Deal included an extra level of complexity. Because the international border had artificially divided peoples of similar cultures, languages, and traditions and because Indians lived with, worked alongside, and frequently married non-Indians, decisions about who would or would not be eligible for reorganization seemed arbitrary. Were the Yaquis, for example, who had origins in Mexico and who spoke Spanish, to be recognized as American Indians or should they be defined as Mexican immigrants and thus be subject, as other Mexicans were, to the repatriation program of the 1930s? And what would become of Tohono O'odham who still lived on the Mexican side of the border? How the U.S. government chose to define these groups, and how the Indians responded to and/or attempted to influence those decisions, would profoundly shape their place in the United States and their sense of themselves as peoples.

THE INDIAN NEW DEAL, ECONOMIC REFORM, AND WAGE LABOR

The economic centerpiece of the Indian New Deal was the Indian Emergency Conservation Relief Program established in 1933 by Congress and later renamed the Indian Civilian Conservation Corps (CCC-ID). The program was intended not only to promote economic self-sufficiency but also to integrate Indians fully into the national political economy while promoting tribal cooperation. According to Commissioner Collier, the primary architect of the program, emergency conservation work would improve reservation lands while providing jobs for many thousands of Indians. Indians were trained in what were called leader camps (two of which were in Arizona) to work as group leaders, foremen, and project managers. In addition, a branch of the federal Civil Works Administration employed Indians in jobs ranging from clerical work to various types of skilled and common labor. Others worked for the Works Progress Administration, the Public Works Administration, and the Forest Service. Collier hoped the programs would foster self-reliance by training Indians in management skills and would encourage rather than condemn reservation-wide cooperation and organization, thus preparing the way for political reorganization and the formation of tribal governments.[6]

In practice, however, the most immediate result of these economic programs was to integrate thousands of Indians into the wage economy, often to the detriment of their economic self-reliance. In the early years of the Depression, many indigenous people who had come to depend on wage work had lost their jobs. In Arizona, cotton agriculture and mining were devastated after 1929. Mining towns such as Ajo, which had employed hundreds of Tohono O'odham, shut down. Moreover, wages for picking cotton declined from $1.50 per hundredweight to a mere 50 cents, and even those Pimas, Maricopas, Tohono O'odham, and Yaquis who continued to work as pickers could no longer rely on this income as they had in the 1920s. Unemployment was also severe in Tucson and Phoenix. In 1931 BIA field matrons began to notice that residents of these cities were hiring unemployed white workers for day labor instead of indigenous workers who had held such jobs for decades. In February a field matron in Tucson complained, "Four men here for work, but I have no calls for them. There are about 1800 hundred men and women in Tucson and vicinity seeking employment, and many jobs that formerly went to Indians are now given to whites."[7]

In the cities, indigenous women were often the hardest hit by the Depression. Many indigenous families, both in the cities and on the reservation, had come to depend upon the relatively steady work done by young women in Phoenix and in Tucson. The files of field matron Gracie S. Taylor, who served in both Phoenix and Tucson in the early 1930s, contain dozens of letters from women seeking work as well as replies from Taylor that no work was available. A letter written in March 1933 by Agnes Vavages is representative of the desperate circumstances many Indians faced. Vavages had worked as a domestic for two families over the course of the previous four years in Coolidge, but had recently lost her job. Because her father had just passed away, she needed a job more than ever to support her family. As she explained, "I have just lost my father and so I have to work again and support my mother, and little sister. . . . I don't care if I get six or seven dollars a week for cooking and house work it is alright so please write and let me know if you can help me." Despite her pleas, Taylor could do nothing to help her. "At present I have nothing, but if I should have would be glad to send for you," she replied. "Times are so hard that many people are doing their own work and those who are hiring do not want to pay very much."[8]

In response, beginning in 1933 the new federal work relief programs provided many Indians with desperately needed wage jobs. Over the next two years, hundreds applied for emergency conservation work.[9] On the Pima, Maricopa, and Tohono O'odham reservations, the government's public works program included the "remaking" of the reservations and the improvement of transportation and communication. By October 1933 on the Tohono O'odham reservations, 891 men were already working under the direction of the Sells agency. They constructed telephone lines, fire lookout houses, *charcos*, wells, horse and foot trails, fences, and cabins. They dug new wells and *charcos* in many of the reservation villages, continuing a program initiated over a decade earlier and rendering the movement between summer and winter villages obsolete. The BIA built a new road from Tucson through Sells to Ajo in 1929, making travel from the reservation to these two towns much easier. Seventy miles of new primary roads facilitated contact and communication between villages. Two hundred miles of truck roads provided access to areas that could previously only be reached on horseback. BIA official Harwood Hall declared that these improvements, and the experience Indians from different villages had working with one another, would not only improve economic conditions but would help to promote tribal cooperation and acceptance of political reorganization under the IRA.[10]

Government-directed relief programs on both the Salt and Gila River reservations were extensive as well, substantially altering the political economies there. Federally directed programs had perhaps their most dramatic impact on the Gila River reservation community and were intricately linked to the completion of the San Carlos Reclamation Project. On June 7, 1924, Congress finally passed a law approving the construction of a major dam and reservoir on the Gila River—a project that was billed as a rival to the Salt River Project constructed two decades earlier. Between 1925 and 1929 the Pimas and Maricopas had farmed only between five thousand and twelve thousand acres of land along the Gila. Now they hoped that the new project would enable them to become prosperous farmers once again. Pima leader Hugh Patton exclaimed optimistically at the dedication of the new Coolidge Dam on March 4, 1930, that the project's completion was the "brightest page in the long, varied history of the Pima people."[11]

The settlement in 1934 of a lawsuit by the Justice Department against upriver diverters seemed, at first, to provide even more reason for the Pimas and Maricopas to be optimistic. Under the agreement the Gila reservation was to receive enough water to irrigate fifty thousand acres, nearly matching the 49,896 acres that had been allotted to individual Indians.[12] The BIA felt that Pimas and Maricopas would enthusiastically take up farming once the project was completed. A local BIA official expressed this view in essentialist terms, declaring that the Pimas had a "natural instinct to till [the soil.]" Ironically, though, the work programs on the reservation would remove agriculture further from "nature." BIA officials paid little heed to the recommendations of Pima and Maricopa leaders, rendering knowledge and farming techniques developed over centuries largely obsolete.[13]

Rather than permit a return to widespread farming, the San Carlos Project and the New Deal work-relief programs made the Pimas and Maricopas increasingly reliant upon wage labor, much as the Tohono O'odham now were. In the late 1920s some Pimas and Maricopas had worked for wages on the construction of the San Carlos Project itself. In the 1930s the BIA oversaw the construction of an extensive network of canals and deep wells and the clearing and leveling of over thirty thousand acres of what government officials referred to as raw desert land (land that had once been irrigated by small diversion dams and the natural flow of the river). Pimas and Maricopas provided most of the common labor on the project as well as a portion of the skilled labor, working as foremen, carpenters, mechanics, and truck and tractor operators. According to C. C. Wright, an agricultural extension agent, the Indians were beginning to rely on the steady wages they obtained through such work. As Wright explained, "Any man could make a better living at $2 a day on a job than he could by farming his land in the ordinary way." The disappointing performance of the dam itself contributed to this growing reliance on wage labor. The reservoir could not reach its total capacity because of silt buildup and a permeable riverbed. Even within the San Carlos irrigation district (which provided water for both Indian and non-Indian farms), from 40 to 69 percent of the water (96,225 acre-feet) came from the ground rather than from the reservoir.[14]

Indigenous farming of traditional crops such as corn, native cotton, and wheat was also complicated because the new project wrought dramatic changes on the reservation's ecology and encouraged the leasing of land to outsiders. To prepare the land for modern agricultural methods, work crews used steel drags to completely remove the indigenous flora. They burned the brush piles, leaving the ground completely bare, and operated about thirty rotary fresnos and hydraulic dirt-movers to level the ground to an irrigable grade. Finally, they constructed new borders and ditches and cut and hauled fence posts to completely enclose previously allocated allotments. The result was an increased level of government control over Pima and Maricopa agriculture.[15]

High operating expenses and debt also prohibited most Pimas and Maricopas from making a living by farming. Under the government's program, the Indians were to purchase seeds and tools and pay for the maintenance of their wells and for the operation of the Coolidge Dam itself beginning in 1937. As one BIA official admitted, "The chief weakness of the method was that it left the Pima in debt for his equipment." The new reservationwide Pima-Maricopa council, which was formed in 1934 after the passage of the IRA, refused to pay the expenses for the operation of the dam when payments of $2.80 per acre were scheduled to begin in 1937. BIA agents explained that the payments were not for the water itself but for operating expenses. Such a distinction was irrelevant to most Pimas and Maricopas who argued that they should not have to pay for what had already been theirs. To get around the problem, the BIA took control of twelve thousand acres of unallotted farmland and used the profits to pay for the maintenance of the reclamation project.[16]

The new level of federal involvement meant that Pimas and Maricopas had little control over decisions about agriculture on the reservation. They had almost no modern farming equipment, and prices for crops such as cotton were at their lowest ebb. In 1932 BIA and agricultural extension experts decided, without the Indians' consent, that alfalfa would be a preferable alternative to wheat and cotton. C. C. Wright felt that alfalfa would help revitalize the productivity of the soil and that it would "enable the Indian farmer to hold down his job and farm his land at the same time." Like the concurrent, BIA-directed reductions of sheep on the Navajo reservation in northern Arizona, decisions about what would be planted and how it would be grown and marketed were made by government officials.[17]

Class divisions on the reservation grew deeper as a select few Pimas and Maricopas managed to prosper under the new conditions. Juan Patterson, a Phoenix Indian School graduate, for example, returned to the reservation, opened a store, and soon was operating a commercial ranch with about six hundred cattle.[18] The majority, however, owned very few cattle, having sold herds to survive the diversion of the Gila's waters. Hundreds grew alfalfa and leased their allotments or charged grazing fees to non-Indian cattle companies, while working for wages for the same companies on their own land. By 1935 there were sixty-nine hundred cattle owned by non-Indian ranchers on the allotments, with more than 450 families participating in leasing and working for the companies. This produced income of about seventy thousand dollars. To pay for alfalfa seed on their own lots, Pimas and Maricopas often had to take out loans from the same companies who fed their cattle on the reservation, which further increased their debt.[19]

With little access to capital and little say in the decision making regarding agriculture on their lands, many Pimas and Maricopas grew cynical about the Indian New Deal. Nathan Allen, who grew up on the Gila reservation during this era, recalled that "there were not many of the O'odham farming during the time I was growing up because farming had become very expensive. . . . Most of the people had jobs off the reservation, mostly farm laborers because this was the only skill they knew. The purchasing of fuel-powered farm machinery was next to impossible. . . . There was nothing to put up for collateral, no cattle, no horses, and no land because it was held in trust by the federal government." Rather than directly condemn the BIA for these problems, Allen said simply that "the days of horse-drawn farm equipment were long gone, fond memories in the minds of the elders of our community. Perhaps this will give you a clue as to my feelings."[20]

These problems also led many Pimas and Maricopas to reject the authority of the new reservation-wide councils. The diverse population of Pimas,

Maricopas, and a few Tohono O'odham on the Gila reservation formed one tribal community, and those on the newer Salt River reservation formed another—an example of how the Indian New Deal often ignored traditional ethnic boundaries, while creating clear divisions where none had existed. Those on the Gila reservation voted to approve a new constitution and by-laws in March 1936; shortly thereafter they received a corporate charter for what became known as the Gila River Pima-Maricopa Indian Community. Most Pimas and Maricopas, however, paid little attention. Their lack of interest was exacerbated by the fact that Congress did not grant the Pima and Maricopa council the right to attend hearings and defend Pima water rights in the courts. For this reason and because the IRA economic policies failed to revitalize farming on the reservation, the council "lost prestige with the Pimas [and] was not regarded by Indians as an effective represen-tative organization." [21]

Meanwhile, BIA officials encouraged Indians who could not live off of their land to take up wage work off the reservation. During the 1936–1937 picking season, "considerably more than two thousand O'odham" moved into the labor camps to pick cotton from October though January.[22] Peter Blaine, who worked as a recruiter for the BIA in the latter part of the decade (after cotton production had rebounded), recalled, "In those years we used to have a lot of calls from cotton farmers, clear up to Buckeye and all the way down to Sahuarita. . . . I was sent out [by the BIA] to see this village and that village and tell them about cotton-picking jobs."[23] Myrtle Jordon, a Pima, remembered, "Indians picked cotton. Oh, yeah, they picked cotton. . . . I always wondered why they had to go out and pick." Ironically, then, the New Deal economic policies, which had purportedly been designed to promote economic self-dependence, instead increased reliance on leasing and low-paid wage labor on farms and ranches off the reservation.[24]

TRIBAL REORGANIZATION: THE CASE OF THE TOHONO O'ODHAM

The Tohono O'odham offer a particularly interesting example of tribal re-organization because, for them, the concept of a tribal political body had no precedent. The scattered villages and *rancherías* were each tradition-ally governed by a headman and a council of village men. Still, as Peter Blaine's story suggests, political reorganization would begin to accelerate a process whereby the Tohono O'odham would view themselves as a whole, as a more united group distinct from nearby peoples such as the Akimel O'odham (Pimas) with whom they were closely related. The new institutions would also sharpen ethnic lines between the Tohono O'odham and the diverse mestizo population with whom they had historically worked, worshipped, and intermarried.

By the early 1930s, the idea of a tribalwide political body had the open support of only a small number of mostly Presbyterian Aji and Ko-lo:di leaders in the southeastern districts of the Sells reservation. This group, which had formed the Good Government League (GGL) in 1911, often claimed to speak for the Papago tribe as a whole. Many other O'odham, however, such as the Ko:adk in the northwest and most of the Aji, remained suspicious of the federal government's plans. For them the concept of a tribal government remained foreign, since no legitimate political body had ever governed above the village level. Moreover, the economic interests of the some seventy villages varied widely. Some relied primarily on livestock, while others had come to depend on a combination of wage labor, petty trade, and subsistence farming. Divisions between those who owned cattle and those who did not were particularly salient. In 1930 the average herd consisted of about twenty-five to thirty cattle, but many owned far fewer and some owned far more. In the southeastern districts, for example, José Pablo owned 250 and the Toros family owned two thousand. Class thus compounded religious and cultural differences and intensified the debate over the federal government's plan for the formation of a tribal government.[25]

Outside observers labeled as progressive those Tohono O'odham who were most entangled with the BIA bureaucracy, particularly those in the largely Presbyterian, cattle-rich sections in the southeast, to differentiate them from those they labeled conservative, who generally hoped to retain village autonomy. Progressive and conservative were heavily biased terms, reflecting the imposed idea that those who accepted Anglo ideas and institutions were more advanced. The issues dividing these groups were, in fact, far more complex. Factions formed around a combination of issues, including religion, degree of education in government schools, class, and geographical proximity to the agency at Indian Oasis, which had come to be known as Sells after the former Indian Commissioner.[26]

Those villages and rancherías that outsiders labeled conservative or traditional tended to identify primarily with their own, kin-based local communities much more than with a tribe. Most sustained themselves through a combination of subsistence agriculture, seasonal wage labor, gathering and selling wood, petty trade, and perhaps by raising a few cattle. Children from these areas attended nearby Catholic mission day schools or did not attend school at all, thus retaining close ties both to their families and villages. They tended to resist BIA attempts to recruit their children into government schools and to put an end to native rituals such as the *nawait* ceremony. (The BIA periodically arrested leaders who made saguaro cactus wine.) Many O'odham in these villages, unable to afford the larger cattle herds of the southeastern districts, maintained their own farms. In fact, as late as 1936, Tohono O'odham farmers cultivated about 12,900 acres on the San Xavier and Sells reservations, with 80 percent practicing some form of subsistence agriculture.[27]

Still, it would be inaccurate to suggest that the Tohono O'odham who were labeled traditionalists or conservatives were isolated from the modern world. Since farming was not sufficient to sustain them, most of these families relied increasingly upon wage labor. The O'odham of the Santa Rosa district, for example, in the central to northeastern part of the reservation, had fully adapted seasonal migration to the cotton fields into village life by the mid-1920s, without abandoning their historic sociopolitical structure in their village. Those in the western reaches of the reservation also worked for wages in agriculture, and hundreds of men from this sector worked in nearby mines such as Ajo—except when the mines temporarily closed in the early 1930s. Families brought cash earned through picking or mining back to their villages, made periodic trips to Tucson for material goods or bought from local traders on the reservation.

Residents of these villages were also politically creative, and not simply wedded to static traditions. In 1928 they formed their own intervillage organization, the League of Papago Chiefs (LPC), which was headed by a Catholic Aji named Juan Joaquín, to counter the influence of the GGL. Ironically, then, headmen who had insisted on village autonomy and had resisted the authority of one panvillage organization now decided to form another, signaling a new level of regional cooperation even among so-called traditionalists. They were especially concerned about the GGL's claims to speak for all Tohono O'odham and its willingness to become deeply entangled with Anglo institutions. They worked closely with Catholic missionaries such as Bonaventure Oblasser to help them oppose the largely Protestant GGL's claims of tribal authority.[28]

The LPC had other concerns as well. Perhaps the most important of these was its disapproval of federal plans to make livestock, rather than farming, the basis of the O'odham economy. In 1928 Juan Joaquín explained in a letter to Commissioner Charles Burke that the LPC chiefs wanted the government to stop building so many *charcos* for cattle, which the O'odham would have to pay to maintain. He wrote, "The rich Papagos get their own bulls, to make their cattle better. The rest of us are too poor to pay for so many. . . . We do not want to be like the Pimas. They have many things that they have to pay for and they are going to lose all their land to the Americans." The LPC also wanted the BIA to return lands to the O'odham that had been removed from the reservation in 1917, including the 475,000-acre strip that divided the reservation and that had since been occupied by Anglo and Mexican-American ranchers. It also protested BIA interference with cultural rituals such as the *nawait* ceremony.[29] In fact, the LPC was so successful at stirring up opposition that by 1930 the GGL, which supported the federal government's plans, had lost most of its influence. In its place, however, some of its members formed a new organization called the Papago Council, again without the consent of most Tohono O'odham.[30]

Disagreements over these issues revealed how complicated the process of weaving many dozens of disparate villages into a unified tribe would be. The villages had long governed themselves as independent units, and each had its own traditions, dialect, religious practices, and economic base. Anglos, including many BIA officials, often presumed that the Tohono O'odham already thought of themselves as a unified tribe. In reality, the BIA was asking for a substantial reconceptualization of Tohono O'odham identity as a single people, rather than as a more loosely associated group of autonomous villages. Many Tohono O'odham would continue to fight to protect village autonomy, and in the process they would substantially revise the BIA blueprint for tribal reorganization.

New concerns, such as non-Indian mining claims on the reservation, also contributed to divisiveness there. Families in cattle-poor villages depended not only on wage work in nearby industrial cotton ranches or in Ajo and Tucson, but also upon reservation mining. In 1932 C. J. Rhoads, commissioner in the land office, reported that 122 patents for reservation mines had been issued to non-Indians, each covering about twenty acres. Fifty-eight more were under consideration.[31] The Papago Council hoped to gain authority over the reservation's mineral rights—an authority that had been excluded from the executive order creating the reservation in 1917. O'odham workers who depended upon wage income, however, were concerned that such a change might lead to the closing of the mines. The LPC, distrusting the motives of the Papago Council, also challenged the move. Ignoring its concerns, the council hired three lawyers to seek control over reservation mineral rights. In October 1932, after extensive lobbying and pressure by their lawyers, the Interior Department secretary responded by withdrawing all Tohono O'odham lands from mineral entry until further notice.[32]

The mining issue compounded the distrust that many Tohono O'odham felt for both the BIA and the Papago Council. Peter Blaine stressed the fact that those who relied upon wage labor had different interests than cattle owners who controlled the council. "A lot of old people hardly had a way of earning a living," he said. "No cattle, only a little farming when it rained. So they worked the mines." More broadly, he criticized what he called the "so-called council" for supporting the mining moratorium, arguing that "there was no such thing as an official council representing the people."[33]

As the IRA was being considered in Congress, conflicts over mining and the direction of economic development on the reservation became intertwined with debates over political reorganization. In 1934 Peter Blaine traveled to Washington, D.C., with a delegation to protest the moratorium on reservation mining. While there he learned about the Indian Reorganization Act for the first time. Not surprisingly, he was wary of it, since the mining moratorium seemed to illustrate perfectly how a reservation-wide tribal council might threaten the interests of individual villages. Blaine spoke about the issue in a hearing before Congress, and he submitted a petition with some four hundred O'odham signatures in support of his position. He also had the backing of Arizona's mining interests, the Tucson Chamber of Commerce, and Arizona Senators Hayden and Ashurst. While the Arizona delegation was less concerned about the O'odham than they were about pleasing powerful mining interests, they did share a common interest with those O'odham who wanted to keep the mines running.[34]

To ensure that the mining moratorium did not create a stumbling block to O'odham acceptance of the Wheeler-Howard bill, Congress wrote language into it that revoked the 1932 moratorium. The new language was enough to persuade Blaine, among others, to back away from his objection to political restructuring.[35] Still, Congress offered a small fig leaf to the Papago Council, demanding that miners compensate the O'odham for any damage done to reservation lands and permitting the O'odham to charge five cents per acre per year for use of the lands. Leasing would remain a central issue in reservation politics for years to come.[36]

Several other factors helped to reduce O'odham opposition to the Indian Reorganization Act. By 1934 hundreds of Tohono O'odham were participating in work-relief programs on the reservation. These programs helped to alleviate the crisis brought about by the Depression. Moreover, the federal government, responding to a lobbying campaign by the LPC and following a shift in policy toward a reconsolidation of tribal territory, had begun to purchase much of the land that had been excluded from the Sells reservation in 1917. By 1933 the government had already purchased 360,000 acres, reuniting the southern and northern sections of the reservation. Over the next few years, more purchases were made. In 1940 the new boundaries of the reservation were finalized with the purchase of the San Joaquín and

Romero ranches. The purchases made the Tohono O'odham reservation the second largest in the country.[37]

Combined with the federal relief program, the land purchases helped to build support among the O'odham for tribal reorganization. In 1934, after the government had reunited the southern and northern parts of the reservation, the BIA sponsored a referendum on reorganization. A majority of 1,443 approved the formation of a tribal government, while only 188 voted against it. These numbers, however, must be considered skeptically. Those who participated in the referendum represented a minority of the total Tohono O'odham voting population (about 47 percent), indicating a lack of interest in the whole affair by many and/or a physical inability to participate in the election. Many hundreds, in fact, were living and working away from the reservation when the vote took place, but only ten people sent in absentee ballots.

An analysis of the election returns reveals that majorities in the eastern part of the reservation voted for reorganization, while support in the west was slim. Almost all of the districts to the east supported reorganization with majorities of 80 percent or better. By contrast, the western sections had both the least participation and, among those who did participate, the largest number of votes in opposition. In the Hickiwan district in the northwestern section of the reservation, only nineteen people voted. In Gu Vo, the southwestern district, not a single person cast a ballot. Directly east of Gu Vo, in Pisinemo, sixty-seven ballots were cast, but forty-seven of the sixty-seven, or 70 percent, were against reorganization.[38]

Over the next two years, a debate ensued over what shape a new tribal constitution would take. One of the biggest issues remained the BIA's desire to make cattle ranching the major economic enterprise on the reservation. Superintendent Hall wanted to construct reservation fences, prepare the range for cattle operations, and control the size of reservation herds in order to reduce erosion possibly through livestock reductions. Many Tohono O'odham, however, resisted. Some wanted to continue farming and resented interference by the BIA in their affairs. Some commercial cattle ranchers feared Hall's plan to institute grazing fees, fence the range, and possibly engage in a reduction program. Hall's insistence on linking the issue to tribal reorganization thus threatened to unravel support. John Collier advocated decoupling the two issues. In the end the O'odham themselves, with support from Collier, managed to expunge Hall's range management plan from the constitution, removing a significant obstacle against its acceptance.[39]

Perhaps the most important effect of the Indian work relief programs was that they facilitated intraethnic cooperation between villagers who had interacted with one another infrequently, creating more support for the idea of a tribal government. About twelve hundred men (including many Indians from other reservations) worked on the various relief programs on the Tohono O'odham reservations. The expanding infrastructure that resulted served to connect distant villages, dialect groups, and districts. The new roads also facilitated movement between villages and to towns outside of the reservation, such as Tucson and Ajo. Equally important was the experience of working alongside hundreds of others from villages throughout the O'odham territory. Henry Dobyns, an ethnohistorian who conducted fieldwork among the O'odham around 1950, wrote, "The psychologically rewarding CCC work experience conditioned most of those Papagos who participated in it toward seeking reservation-wide solutions to what they could perceive as reservation-wide problems, using forms of social organization and technology novel to Papago historic experience up until that time."[40]

Indeed, the camps became centers of interaction between residents of the various districts, blurring divisions between distinct dialects and cultural groups. Peter Blaine, who worked with the Indian branch of the Forest Service on the reservation, personified this process. As he recalled, "Every camp had boys from different villages. . . . I had been around and pretty well knew all the dialects of the reservation." Blaine had come a long way from his childhood in a Yaqui-mestizo household to become a leading advocate of a new, panvillage, Tohono O'odham identity. His experiences made him an avid promoter of the idea of a tribal government, and he used his position in the Forest Service "to travel and to talk to the people" about the idea.[41]

Deep disagreements remained over how much authority the new tribal government should have. Many of those who participated in the writing of the constitution were concerned that the new government would undermine village autonomy, and they worked diligently to protect it. José Anton of the Pisinemo district—the only district that had emphatically rejected reorganization in 1934—decided that because reorganization was inevitable, he would actively participate in the process to protect the authority of the villages. Anton promoted a federation of reservation districts, with separate governing bodies for the eleven districts of the three reservations. Each district, in addition to choosing a representative and alternate to the new tribal council, would also elect its own five-member council. This resolution—"Each district shall govern itself in local matters in accordance with its old customs"—became article IV, section 2 of the proposed constitution.[42]

The 1936 referendum on the constitution revealed that the efforts of

Anton and others to preserve village and/or district autonomy paid off because 58 percent of eligible Tohono O'odham voted—an increase of over 10 percent from the vote in 1934. The new constitution was approved by 1,340 voters; 580 voted against. Many villages that had distrusted the idea of a tribalwide political body supported the new constitution. In Anton's village of Pisinemo, which in 1934 had soundly rejected reorganization, forty-nine people, or 53 percent, favored the new constitution. In the purportedly traditional Aji village of Santa Rosa, 128 votes were cast, and eighty-two, or 64 percent, supported the constitution. Still, on the reservation as a whole, it is important to note that 42 percent of eligible Tohono O'odham did not vote, and more O'odham voted against the constitution than had voted against reorganization two years earlier. Because the election took place during the cotton harvest on December 12, hundreds of Tohono O'odham, including many from Santa Rosa, were working off the reservation at the time. And yet relatively few votes were cast from agricultural regions outside the reservation (about thirty from the polling station in Eloy).[43] It appears, then, that many O'odham remained alienated from the process.[44]

Still, many leaders who had once doubted the efficacy of reorganization embraced the constitution and became active in tribal politics. Rather than supersede the authority of local village headmen, the Tohono O'odham elected many traditional village leaders onto the councils. Superintendent Hall noted that village headmen were elected to the district councils "in practically every instance." At the tribal level, Ida N. Wilson, an O'odham woman who served as the first secretary to the Papago Tribal Council, claimed in 1939 that "since January 30, 1937, the date of its first meeting, the Papago Tribal Council has assumed a definite place in the handling of tribal affairs, and under the leadership of its officers, the Council has made great progress in welding the Papagos into a tribe which is now closely consolidated. . . . It is learning the values of cooperation, of following through on its aims and goals with a singleness of purpose which no one previously thought possible." While such claims were too sanguine, they indicated a desire among some O'odham to embrace the political and cultural concept of the tribe.[45]

That a woman serving in a position of power would make such a statement demonstrates that the O'odham were adapting in other ways as well. Into the 1940s, ethnographers such as Ruth Underhill and Rosamund Spicer noted that, in many villages, patrilocal residence patterns, patriarchal families, and all-male village councils remained standard. The new tribal council, however, began to counter the authority of village patriarchal councils, and in the process provided a new avenue for women to become active in public affairs. Even though she was relegated to the highly gendered position of secretary, Ida Wilson became the first of a growing number of women who would serve in tribal government.[46]

Tohono O'odham who remained in Sonora, Mexico, remained alienated from the debates over tribal reorganization in the United States. As Bernard Fontana has explained, "Mexican law . . . did not recognize any special 'Indian' status. Indians were, and are, regarded as Mexican citizens on par with everyone else. Papagos received no reservations or land titles by virtue of their 'Indianness.'" As early as 1900, hundreds of Mexican O'odham had either moved to the United States, particularly to the Chukut Kuk district of the Sells reservation, or had begun to identify more as Mexican than Indian. Mexico encouraged this process through its postrevolutionary ideology of *mestizaje*, which held that Mexicans were a greater people because of rather than despite interethnic mixing. Carl Lumholtz counted twenty-three occupied O'odham villages in Mexico in 1910, consisting of approximately nine hundred people, but he found that most O'odham were "no longer able to keep up their native feasts and are rapidly disappearing into the body of Mexican laborers." By 1930 perhaps five hundred to seven hundred individuals who continued to identify as Tohono O'odham lived in Sonora.[47]

By the 1930s the geopolitical border between the United States and Mexico began to have a more profound effect on Tohono O'odham communities. Beyond the growing efforts of the U.S. government to police the border, O'odham on different sides of the line found themselves negotiating with two very distinct political systems. In 1928 Mexican President Elías Calles proclaimed the creation of an *ejido*, an area of communally held land, for the Tohono O'odham at Pozo Verde, thus recognizing a small portion of traditional O'odham lands in Mexico (7,675 acres). This land, however, was not a reservation in the way that term was used in the United States. Instead, the government of Mexico treated the O'odham just like any other group of peasants and small farmers. Over several decades the O'odham land base in Mexico would continue to face incursions by non-Indians, threatening their viability as a people. Mexican O'odham received little to no help from the tribe in the United States to challenge such incursions. While many Mexican O'odham traveled frequently across the border to take advantage of economic and educational opportunities in the United States, not until many years later would the U.S. tribal council reach out to those who lived on the other side of the border.[48]

Even in Arizona the influence of the new tribal institutions was limited. In the short term, the Indian New Deal's economic policies, including the expansion of wage jobs, had a far greater impact than did political re-organization. Into the postwar period, a growing number of O'odham participated in seasonal agricultural labor. An economic study by the tribal council in the 1940s found that while wage labor had provided less than 30 percent of total income on the reservations in 1937, it provided 56 percent of total O'odham income only a decade later. Ethnographer Henry Dobyns estimated that 50 percent of wage income was derived from picking cotton in 1950. Until picking machines began to replace manual workers late in the 1950s, many villagers, including some from Mexico, continued a pattern of moving into the fields during the picking season and then back to their home villages to farm or to towns and mines off the reservation for the remainder of the year. For thousands of O'odham, such a pattern became a primary marker of the passing seasons, impacting their lives far more than the new, remote tribal institutions. Only in the longer term would the tribal government begin to take on greater relevance.[49]

Nevertheless, tribal reorganization began to promote a greater sense of a unified "tribal" identity while reinforcing ethnic boundaries between the Tohono O'odham and other ethnic groups in Arizona's borderlands. For Peter Blaine, who would soon be elected as the second chair of the tribal council, it drew attention away from the multiethnic world of his childhood in South Tucson and toward the new institution of the tribe. This is not to suggest that the adoption of a more coherent tribal identity was a smooth process. To the contrary, many challenged the BIA's conception of a tribe every step of the way, and in the end what they would develop was not what the BIA bureaucrats had intended. The tribal government would eventually begin to challenge certain BIA policies head-on and promote greater political, cultural, and economic self-determination for the Tohono O'odham as a whole.

NOT FIT TO BE A TRIBE: THE CASE OF THE YAQUIS

In 1930 the relationship between the Yaquis and the U.S. government remained far more ambiguous than that between the government and the Tohono O'odham, Maricopas, and Pimas. U.S. law unequivocally defined Indians as nonwhite, so Indian immigrants were ineligible for naturalization. Because citizenship (or the intent to become a citizen) was required in order to apply for a homestead, the first generation of Yaqui immigrants also had very little chance of acquiring their own land.[50] As immigrants from Mexico, they constantly faced the threat of deportation, especially during the repatriation campaigns of the early 1930s. At the same time, the federal government refused to recognize them as a tribe or to establish a reservation for them, since they were not indigenous to the United States. This ambiguous legal and social position had a significant impact on how Yaquis came to define themselves.[51]

In the 1930s a group of Anglos in Tucson attempted to persuade the government to recognize the Yaquis as an American Indian tribe so that they could benefit from new protections under the Indian New Deal. A Baptist missionary who visited the Yaqui community of Pascua in the 1930s "did not see why these people had to pay taxes when the Pimas and Papagos didn't, and he thought that he might, through the proper sources, have their taxes exempted."[52] Ruby Haigler Wood, who worked in the Yaqui community of Guadalupe as a teacher and social worker in the same decade, was also perplexed about the status of the Yaquis. As she put it, "Because they're born here, although they are Mexican Indians . . . it looks to me like they should be classed as Indians."[53]

Requests for federal recognition of the Yaquis as an Indian tribe were ironic. Before 1924 Indians had been required to disassociate from their tribal communities and communal lands in order to become U.S. citizens. Now some Anglos perceived tribal recognition to be the best means to make Yaquis full American citizens. To understand the implications of these efforts, it is necessary to look back at how Yaqui identity and sociopolitical organization had changed in Arizona before 1934 and the passage of the IRA.

The Yaquis, like the Tohono O'odham, historically lacked permanent tribal organization. Moreover, for complex reasons, some Yaquis identified more with their Mexican than with their Indian heritage. At times, intermarriage and intercultural ties with mestizos led to acculturation—a continuation of a process of *mestizaje* that had proceeded for centuries in Mexico. Other Yaquis, however, shed their Indian identities for more strategic reasons. Before 1930 Yaquis were reluctant to divulge their identities due to fear of reprisal by the Mexican government. As Evelyn Hu-De-Hart explains, "Yaquis quickly learned not to divulge their true identities, claiming, instead, to be Opatas, Pimas, or Mexicans."[54]

In the United States there were other reasons to claim to be either Mexican American or a member of some other indigenous group. During the repatriation era in the 1930s, fear of deportation led some Yaquis to claim they were O'odham. Still others hid their identities to avoid racial discrimination from Anglos and Mexican Americans alike. While BIA officials often declared that Indians were more "pure" than ethnic Mexicans and thus more capable of becoming citizens, many Anglos placed Indians at the bottom of the race hierarchy. While many Anglos viewed Mexicans as racially degraded through miscegenation, many paradoxically viewed them as superior to Indians because they were at least partly white. Moreover, because Mexican Americans were defined as Caucasian by the courts, claiming to be Mexican American could have legal advantages for Yaquis.

The story of the Chavarría family provides more intimate insight as to why some Yaquis publicly shed their Yaqui identities. Born in 1884 in the community of Pueblo Viejo near Solomonville, Arizona, Pablo Chavarría grew up and married Dolores Amado, a Mexican American whose ancestors had lived in Arizona since before the U.S.-Mexican War. In Solomonville, Pablo and Dolores had two sons, Paul and Ralph, whom Pablo supported by working on nearby ranches and as a musician. Around 1920, as the cotton boom attracted tens of thousands of Indians and Mexicans from Sonora and southern Arizona into the Salt River valley, the family joined the migration by relocating to Tempe. Dolores died there, and Pablo continued to support his two sons by working on nearby ranches and farms. They lived in Los Arribeños, one of the two largest ethnic Mexican barrios in Tempe.[55]

Pablo mostly disassociated himself from other Yaquis in Los Arribeños, but he made close connections to the surrounding Mexican-American community. He supported his family financially by working as a musician in the rural towns scattered around Maricopa and Pinal counties. He and his sons also worked periodically for wages on commercial farms until Pablo was able to buy a small ranch of his own just west of Tempe. Eventually, he met Rita Moreno, a Chiricahua Apache, and the two soon married. Pablo and Rita had five children together—Roberto, Rodolfo, Ray, Josephina, and Antonio.[56]

Throughout this period, Pablo's children, including those from his second marriage with Rita, grew up identifying themselves as Mexican Americans rather than as Indians. According to Ray, who was born in 1927, Rita and Pablo kept their Indian heritage secret even from their own children. Not until many years later did Ray discover his true family background. Looking back at his childhood, he recalled that his father rarely associated with Yaquis who lived in nearby Guadalupe. "Knowing that Guadalupe consisted more of the Yaqui Indian, they stayed away. So they—what would you say?—ostracized the barrio completely out." As he grew older, Ray asked his father why he had disowned his Yaqui ancestry. His father answered that Mexican Americans did not want to associate with the Yaquis because "they were ashamed of their own race, they didn't want to mingle with the Indian, with the Yaqui, because then people would say that they were also Indian." Reflecting on his father's decision, Ray thought that "the reason that we didn't find out 'til later that we were American Indian was due to the discrimination of races. The Indian was looked down upon, like today. And Dad didn't want us to suffer through any of that. So he would always say that he was a Mexicano."[57]

The Chavarrías, in fact, became well-known and well-respected members of Tempe's Mexican-American middle class. Paul eventually became a member of the leading *mutualista* in the state, the Alianza Hispano-Americana, and played in its orchestra. Over the years he played frequently at *fiestas patrias* (patriotic festivals). Later he became a leading organizer of the Sociedad Mutualista Porfirio Diaz—ironically, a mutualista named after the Mexican dictator who bore much of the responsibility for dispossessing the Yaquis in Sonora.[58]

While others certainly followed a similar path as the Chavarrías, thousands continued to identify as Yaquis, and they gained the support of some influential Anglo-Americans in their attempts to secure a distinct relationship with the U.S. government. Many Anglos saw the Yaquis as American Indians, and they drew sharp distinctions between them and other immigrants from Mexico. They were especially impressed by their religious ceremonies, particularly with their indigenous *pascola* and deer dances. According to Edward Spicer, who lived among and studied the Arizona Yaquis in the 1930s, "The prompt and concrete result of the reintroduction of the old ceremonies was the Anglo-American recognition that Yaquis were different from Mexicans. . . . It resulted very soon in the establishment of an identification of Yaquis with other American Indians in the minds of a number of Anglo-Americans. This, in turn, was associated with reservations, and so we see Anglo-Americans attempting to develop a sort of reservation system for all Yaquis in Arizona."[59]

Anglo recognition of the distinct Indian cultural practices among the Yaquis helped lead to the founding of two of the largest Yaqui settlements in Arizona: Pascua, near Tucson, and Guadalupe, south of Tempe. In Guadalupe, Lucius Zittier, a Franciscan priest, helped to secure an area of trust land for about thirty Yaqui families who worked on nearby ranches and railroads in the 1910s. Zittier hoped to protect Guadalupe, then known only as Yaqui Town, as "a pure Indian settlement without any admixture of whites or Mexicans." He invoked the discourse of Indian purity and Mexican impurity, warning that any influx of Mexicans would "ruin the settlement." With the proper guidance and insulation from the other farmworkers around them, the Yaquis might successfully be converted into good Roman Catholics and good citizens.[60]

Salt River valley employers also drew racial boundaries between Yaquis and ethnic Mexicans. Some explained the willingness of the Yaquis to work on their farms with mythical ideas about their cultural and racial purity as Indians, and their legendary resistance against the Mexican army. Invoking the trope of the noble savage, they suggested that the Yaquis had a unique reverence for independence and freedom, and thus had a drive that mestizo workers supposedly lacked. In the starkest of racial terms, one cotton grower commented, "The Yaquis aren't as much like niggers as the Mexicans, because they haven't been peons and had to act that way."[61]

Ironically, such characterizations served the interests of employers who could argue that because the Yaquis were strong and warriorlike, they were perfectly suited to dangerous and physically demanding manual labor. Howard Ruppers, a foreman for the Salt River Valley Water Users Association (SRVWUA) in the 1920s and '30s, characterized the Yaquis as one of the "last tribes of unconquered Indians." He drew an explicit connection between their Indian status and their purportedly superior work habits. In his words they "possessed a skill along with a dexterity unexcelled" and they were "not only good soldiers in a military sense, they are also most reliable in times of emergencies such as flash floods and storms." Such qualities made them "the finest type of labor obtainable."[62] Others went so far as to suggest that the Yaquis were immune to hot weather and scorpion stings.[63]

Anglo perceptions of and actions toward the Yaquis were colored by their preconceived notions about Indians in other ways as well—ways that, over time, influenced how the Yaquis would define *themselves*. Anglo officials sometimes called certain prominent Yaquis "chief," reflecting their assumption that Yaqui social and political organization was similar to that of other American Indians. Some Yaqui leaders, in turn, adopted the term. This is not to say that the concept of chief was entirely foreign to the Yaquis. In part, it built upon the tradition of village headmen and *gobernadores* in Mexico and upon the title of military captain, which had taken on greater power under the Yaqui leader Cajeme in late-nineteenth-century Mexico. The term was thus a syncretic blending of Anglo expectations about how Indians should behave and of leadership positions long recognized by the Yaquis in Sonora.

The political discourse of tribes and chiefs became most significant for those Yaquis who lived in the barrios near Tucson, especially in the largely homogeneous community that would come to be known as Pascua. Juan Muñoz, better known as Juan Pistola, was the first in Arizona to take Chief of the Yaquis as a title. Pistola established his leadership during the national recession of 1920–1921, when he helped to obtain federal relief and jobs for Yaquis living near Tucson. He was instrumental in working with a real-estate agent so that Yaquis could rent property in Pascua. As a result some Yaquis recognized him as the leader of the village.[64] Refugio Savala explained that his family favored Pistola's leadership in large part because "he got employment for us during this period of depression after the war" and because he helped to send Savala and his siblings to school.[65]

By 1930 Pascua and Guadalupe were the two largest and most stable Yaqui settlements in south-central Arizona, and they served as the primary sites for the practice of annual fiestas and ceremonies such as Holy Week. The word "Pascua" came from the Spanish term for the ceremonial processions of Easter weekend. The Lenten and Easter ceremonies played a significant role in shaping the distinct relationship between Yaquis and Anglo-Arizonans. Beginning in the 1920s, for example, the Tucson Chamber of Commerce promoted the Pascua ceremonies as a tourist attraction. According to a newspaper article in 1925, "Their religious devotions are performed with a sincerity that is unquestionable, even to the most casual observer." It went on to suggest that Yaquis had a natural love of independence: "The Yaqui Indian is a Mexican Indian driven from his native land by a long series of wars and persecutions because he has steadily refused to subdue an inherent independence and love of liberty. . . . Like all children of nature these people worship God in the great open spaces." The Chamber of Commerce capitalized on this reputation, promoting the event as "one of the outstanding folk festivals of the Southwest" and providing chairs and assistance with managing the large crowds that flocked to Pascua to observe the ceremonies every year.[66]

Guadalupe was also a relatively stable community, but it was less ethnically homogeneous than Pascua. Local missionaries such as Lucius Zittier had hoped that Guadalupe would remain an exclusively Yaqui community, but growing numbers of ethnic Mexicans settled in and around the original 40-acre town site and the 92-acre Biehn colony, which was held in trust by the Presbyterian Church. Some of the ethnic Mexican residents were immigrant agricultural workers who simply squatted on unoccupied land around the forty acres. Others, such as A. C. García, Maximo Solarez, and Louis Gastello, purchased substantial areas of land (totaling 280 acres) in the immediate vicinity of the original Yaqui Town in the 1920s and '30s. Over time, they sold individual plots of land to other ethnic Mexicans, who eventually surrounded the Yaqui settlement in several new neighborhoods.[67]

Still, Guadalupe Yaquis managed to retain an identity distinct from the growing ethnic Mexican population. Every year they practiced the Lenten and Easter ceremonies on a plaza at the center of the original 40-acre town site. They continued to maintain their own ritual sodalities (organizations responsible for certain ritual tasks) and to hold their own seasonal ceremonies. Eventually, they constructed their own separate church building directly next to the Catholic mission—a building that housed the images of saints and became the focal point of religious processions.[68]

By the 1930s Guadalupe served as the most important anchor community for Yaqui farmworkers who lived and worked in the Salt River valley. Hundreds of Yaqui men worked as full-time employees for the SRVWUA, living in Guadalupe and in two labor camps, one in Scottsdale (the northside camp) and one in Chandler (the southside camp). In all three communities, men generally worked year-round while women and children often participated in seasonal cotton chopping and picking. This arrangement, while highly exploitative, was also conducive to continued participation in important cultural events in Guadalupe. Every year, hundreds of Yaquis from the two SRVWUA camps, as well as those who were scattered among some seventy other camps throughout the valley, converged in Guadalupe for the Easter ceremonies.[69] Ruby Wood, a social worker who moved into the community in the 1930s, recalled how "a lot of them, during that week, would get off if they happened to be head of the ceremonies, and they'd give them that time, that could be their vacation period." While employers sometimes protested the practice, it became clear that any attempt to crack down would result in an exodus from the fields. Thus, the Yaquis, in at least one small way, forced the hands of the growers, giving them little choice but to accede to their insistence that they continue certain sacred practices. As Wood put it, their employers would "take it that way so they didn't just quit."[70]

The Yaquis selected their own local leaders in Guadalupe, Pascua, and similar towns, continuing in a less organized form a long tradition of village-level autonomy. In Pascua, after Juan Pistola's death in 1922, other Yaqui men attempted to take up the mantle of chief. In the late 1920s and early 1930s, the state district attorney, the INS, Arizona's governor, and the Pima County sheriff all referred to Cayateno López as chief of the Yaquis. Many Yaquis, however, adamantly contested the claims of anyone to speak for them as a collective whole—a fact that was consistent with the Yaqui tradition of government by village headmen selected through consensus.[71]

Nevertheless, leaders such as Pistola and López played important roles in helping the regional population adapt and defend their interests in Arizona. López helped to protect Arizona Yaquis from deportation. In 1927 a Yaqui from Sonora named Guadalupe Flores encouraged Arizona Yaquis to buy up plots of land in Sonora and take up farming there. Most Arizona Yaquis rejected the plan. Cayateno López traveled from settlement to settlement to build up resistance to Flores. With the backing of both Pascuans and Guadalupanos, López wrote letters to the governor and to President Herbert Hoover explaining that most Arizona Yaquis wished to remain in Arizona. He pointed out that a majority of them had been born in the state, and that "there wasn't anything to do in Sonora. This is the only country we know."[72]

Fortunately, into the mid-1930s most local and federal officials tended to view the Yaquis as political refugees and did not seek to deport them. In 1932, in the midst of the national repatriation program, Arizona Governor George Hunt declared that those Yaquis who had secured steady work would not be deported. In his words, those who demonstrated "their fitness for citizenship and did not become a burden on public systems" would not "become subject to deportation."[73] Edward Shaughnessy of the INS explained several years later, in a letter to Senator Hayden, "As they were not in possession of the documents required by the Immigration Act of 1924, their presence in the United States was considered to be illegal for immigration purposes, but this Department took no steps looking to their deportation because of their status as refugees."[74] Still, these were not unequivocal guarantees of federal protection. What would happen if government officials did, in fact, decide that the Yaquis had become a burden on public systems? By the late 1930s, the INS provided an answer by actively pursuing a deportation plan, just as it had deported over half a million Mexicans.

Mexican President Lázaro Cárdenas and the governor of Sonora encouraged the return of both mestizos and Mexican Indians to help revitalize the Mexican economy and strengthen the Mexican state. To reassure Arizona Yaquis, Cárdenas established a *zona indigena* (communal *ejido* land) along the Rio Yaqui in 1937. The governor of Sonora informed U.S. officials that the Yaquis would not be subject to reprisals if they returned to their homeland along the river. Whether the Sonoran government could guarantee these claims, however, was unclear. According to the Spanish-language newspaper *El Tucsonense*, Mexicans who had taken up landholdings along the Yaqui River in Sonora pleaded with the government not to permit the Yaquis to return, fearing that they might raise a "series of problems for small farmers in the Yaqui River valley."[75]

Some Yaquis returned to Mexico voluntarily as the Depression dragged on. Rosalio Moisés, for example (see Chapter 3), decided in 1932 to return to the Rio Yaqui while eking out an existence on $1.80 per day working for the SRVWUA. As he remembered it, "I got to thinking about the Rio Yaqui in Sonora and all the stories I had heard about the place. The valley lands were rich, and there was gold in the mountains. The lands needed little water; all kinds of seeds would grow very fast. . . . A man could live there without working for wages." In early October he sold a gallon of bootleg whiskey in the Salt River camps, and he used the profits to cross back into Sonora. He then hopped a train for Nogales and hitched a ride with a truck driver to Magdalena, where the feast day of San Francisco was under way. There, after praying and lighting a candle in front of the statue of Saint Francis, he took a train to Vicam station, in the Yaqui River valley. Sadly, despite his dreams of life as a farmer, he soon found himself working for meager wages in someone else's bean fields. Many other Yaquis whose stories remain unrecorded must have followed a similar path with similarly disappointing results.[76]

To certain concerned Anglos in the United States, federal recognition as an Indian tribe seemed a perfect way to protect the Yaquis from deportation, since it would secure their status as U.S. citizens. In 1934 Arizona Congresswoman Isabella Greenway and University of Arizona Professor John Provinse wrote letters to BIA Commissioner John Collier requesting federal aid for the Yaquis under the Indian New Deal. Collier responded, "It has long been the opinion of our legal advisors that this office has no direct legal authority to make provision for these Indians, and that the situation would have to be met by a special act of Congress." While Collier's response was disappointing, it at least left open the possibility that Congress might consider a law to recognize the Yaquis as American Indians.[77]

Simultaneous with these new efforts, INS officials began deporting Yaquis, though doing so proved difficult. While government officials still tended to view the Yaquis as foreign nationals and permanent aliens—or, as Senator Carl Hayden put it in 1936, "Mexican citizens in this country under sufferance"—by the late 1930s many hundreds of Arizona Yaquis had been born in the United States and were automatically U.S. citizens.[78] As Edward Shaughnessy of the INS explained in a letter to Carl Hayden, "It is only when we have some definite information that they have gone to Mexico and returned unlawfully that deportation proceedings can be successfully instituted." To encourage Yaquis to move to Sonora, the INS developed a strategy of deporting certain leaders who had crossed the border in recent years. Over the next several months they deported thirty-four Yaquis.[79]

For some Anglo supporters of the Yaquis the need for securing Yaqui citizenship now seemed more urgent than ever. In 1937 a group of Tucson residents protested the deportation efforts and lobbied to secure an area of trust land for the Yaquis. Thamar Richey, an elementary school teacher in Pascua, headed the effort. Richey urged the government to resettle Tucson's

Yaquis on irrigable land away from the Tucson city limits, and away from the supposedly corrupting influence of the urban Mexican population. There they could once again take up farming and become stable citizen farmers, rather than be further degraded by low-wage day labor and agricultural work. Although the Resettlement Administration had already established a collective farm exclusively for Anglo workers in Casa Grande, it refused to establish a similar settlement for the Yaquis, claiming it did not have adequate funding.[80]

The Tucson group then tried another angle, arguing that the Yaquis should be formally recognized as an American Indian tribe. Mrs. J. R. Fitzgerald of Tucson, who became the spokesperson for the group after Richey's death, requested that "the Yaquis now in this country be brought in under the Indian service and given the benefits of protection of our government" so that they would have "an equal chance with their neighbors round about to become American citizens." The Yaquis, according to Fitzgerald, were experiencing difficult times because of the Depression, but they were "freedom-loving, independent people who have always made their own way." With the right economic opportunities, which she believed federal acknowledgement as Indians would assure them, the Yaquis would make ideal, productive citizens.[81]

Again federal officials denied the request, leaving the status of the Yaquis unresolved. When Senator Hayden forwarded Fitzgerald's requests to Collier, his response was more emphatic than it had been in 1934. Ignoring the fact that many Yaquis had been born in Arizona, Collier wrote, "Since under existing law these people may not be naturalized" (because they were nonwhite immigrants), such an action would "raise many questions and would require a careful study of the situation." Collier used such complexities and his preoccupation with implementing the Indian New Deal among already recognized tribes to justify his statement that he did "not feel that we should with our limited funds undertake such an investigation."[82]

While the Yaquis received no benefits from Collier's Indian New Deal, they did receive marginal benefits from other New Deal programs. Relief funds did make their way into Guadalupe and surrounding communities. Ruby Wood found conditions in Guadalupe to be "terrible" when she arrived in the early 1930s to be a social worker. She wrote, "There wasn't any relief or any welfare or anything and a lot of those people were just freezing to death." In 1934, however, Wood began to work as an adult education teacher as a part of the Emergency Education Program funded through the Federal Emergency Education Act. As a teacher and a volunteer worker at the clinic, she taught classes in health, sanitation, and homemaking and made regular visits to Guadalupe homes. Many Yaquis began to receive direct relief from the government, while others worked for the CCC.[83]

Without federal tribal recognition, however, the Yaqui villages and barrios, unlike the villages of the Tohono O'odham, continued to develop without an overarching tribal structure or reservation. In the postwar era each community maintained its own distinct nexus of social, political, and economic relationships. Guadalupe remained a primarily agricultural village of farmworkers and irrigators, with relatively little interaction with Anglos other than their employers. Pascuans, on the other hand, because of their proximity to Tucson and the University of Arizona, engaged in a wider range of economic activities and developed a closer connection to nearby Anglos, including anthropologists such as Ed Spicer and institutions such as the Tucson Chamber of Commerce, which continued to refer to the Yaquis as an "Indian tribe." Spicer played an important role in recording Yaqui traditions, writing down their history and generating autobiographies, life histories, and ethnographies that reinforced the notion in the Anglo mind that the Yaquis were an Indian tribe. Decades later, his histories would serve as evidence when the Yaquis once again sought tribal recognition by the federal government.[84]

The Pascuans' relationship with Spicer and with other Anglos who viewed the Yaquis as a tribe would, in time, influence their sense of themselves as a people. Thus, it is not surprising that it would be Pascuans who would once again seek federal recognition as a tribe in the early 1960s with the help of a group of Anglo Tucson residents. In contrast, many of the Yaquis who had been raised in Guadalupe, and who therefore had fewer daily interactions with Anglos and more with Mexican Americans, would question whether they wished to be classed as American Indians. Some like Pablo Gonzalez shed their identities as Yaquis altogether, while most held onto a distinct identity that did not easily conform to imposed ethno-racial categories such as Indian and Mexican. Yaquis thus remained border citizens, living on the margins of both the ethno-racial and geopolitical boundaries of the U.S. nation-state.

In south-central Arizona, the most immediately pertinent impact of the New Deal was to expand Indian participation in, and dependency on, wage labor. Despite the reforms of the 1930s, in economic terms the emergency relief programs and labor recruitment practices of the New Deal represented continuity with rather than a change from earlier policies. By the time the Indian New Deal began to be replaced by new programs to terminate and relocate tribes after World War II, more Indians in south-central Arizona than ever would work for wages. Unfortunately, this economic integration was not matched by new political or civil rights. Into the postwar era, Arizona Indians could not vote. With the new policies of termination and relocation after the war, pressures against political sovereignty also would be greater than they had been since the early twentieth century. In this context, ironically, the new tribes and tribal councils that had begun largely as federal impositions would increasingly become vehicles to obtain a greater degree of economic, cultural, and political autonomy.

Over the longer term, then, another effect of the Indian New Deal was to create clearer divisions between indigenous groups, which were designated by reservations and tribes and not just by historical ethnic affiliation, and to demarcate more clearly divisions between Indians and ethnic Mexicans. Thus, Akimel O'odham (Pimas) and Tohono O'odham, who were closely related by culture and language, now had separate tribal councils and membership roles, encouraging further ethnic differentiation between the two peoples. Those Tohono O'odham who still lived in Mexico were alienated from those in the United States more than ever, since they could not elect representatives to the tribal council or benefit from financial resources through the tribe. In this way the international border took on a new significance, threatening to disrupt transnational ties of kinship and culture. The Pimas and Maricopas, who shared two reservations (at Salt River and Gila River), were now united under their own reservation-wide governments, providing a new institutional basis to work together as collective entities—although in both cases they decided to refer to themselves as communities rather than as tribes. Over the course of the next several decades, these new institutional divisions would have a very real impact on the way these groups defined themselves, and on the ways they negotiated with the federal government for resources, cultural autonomy, and their rights as U.S. citizens.

▼ ▼ ▼ ▼ ▼ ▼ ▼ ▼ ▼ ▼ ▼ ▼ ▼ ▼ ▼ ▼ ▼

CHAPTER 6

SHADOWS IN THE SUN BELT

Phoenix Mayor Samuel Mardian Jr. testified before the U.S. Commission on Civil Rights in 1962 that ethnic minorities in Phoenix faced little or no discriminatory treatment. "Indians are not discriminated against in employment, services, or housing," he said, and offered an even more sanguine assessment of Mexican-American prospects: "These people hold high positions in the city government, in industry, and in the professions." To prove the point he noted that one Mexican American held a seat on the Phoenix City Council and that others had recently been elected to the state legislature. Only when discussing the status of the growing population of blacks did Mardian admit to a few lingering problems, noting that certain private businesses avoided hiring them and that "the purchase of homes by Negroes in areas previously all-white meets with resistance." Still, he claimed that "Negroes have made great progress toward complete integration."[1]

These advancements, Mardian concluded, resulted largely from the Anglo community's generosity and civil stewardship, which precluded any need for the federal government to intercede. He maintained that Anglos in Phoenix were imbued with "Yankee self-confidence, southern hospitality, western friendliness, and Midwestern conservatism." It was these traits, inherited from Anglo "pioneers" and settlers from elsewhere in the United States, that defined the essence of citizenship in Arizona and that made federal intervention in civil rights unnecessary. "Minority groups," he declared, "would accomplish more on a voluntary basis than by looking to legal remedies."[2]

Shortly after Mardian's testimony, Herbert Ely, president of the Phoenix Council of Civil Unity, directly challenged his claims. Ely criticized the assertion that a spirit of civility had led Anglos to graciously dismantle discriminatory policies. To the contrary, a series of court cases and protests had forced the desegregation of schools, housing, swimming pools, and other public facilities. Moreover, many employers still would not voluntarily hire "a member of a minority group—a Negro and, in many instances, a Spanish-American." Residential segregation remained rampant and racial discrimination persisted in many forms. "In conclusion, I think it is an illusion to suggest that Phoenix has progressed in the field of civil rights and human relations because, or in spite, of the fact that there have been laws. The antithesis of this statement is closer to the truth."[3]

As this chapter will show, Ely's analysis was indeed more accurate than Mardian's, which was a defensive attempt to keep the federal government out of local civil rights affairs, much like the claims made by local officials in the South as a response to the civil rights movement.[4] But in the twenty years after World War II, ethnic Mexicans, indigenous people, and other subordinated ethno-racial groups found that they could not wait patiently on the sidelines for the cities, the state, or even the federal government to pass ordinances and laws ending segregation and discrimination. These groups faced not only a continuing system of discrimination and segregation but also an array of new challenges, as the region entered a phase of rapid economic, political, and cultural change. For Indians, blacks, and ethnic Mexicans alike, urbanization and mechanization rapidly undermined the pattern of seasonal farmwork that had sustained their communities for decades. Some were able to find jobs in the new manufacturing sector, but discriminatory hiring and promotion were still widespread. At the same time, large-scale recruitment of Mexican braceros—yet another example of the state's shaping of the regional political economy—reinscribed the notion that so-called stoop labor was a job for an "alien" Mexican race. This raised new barriers for Mexican Americans who hoped to be accepted as white or, at least, as patriotic citizens.[5]

From the mid-1940s to the early 1960s, Mexican Americans, Indians, and blacks began to organize in new ways to achieve equal citizenship and chip away at the racialized class structure. Yet, the interests of these groups often differed, and at times they worked at cross-purposes. Mexican Americans who fought to end segregation and gain full citizenship sometimes reinforced racial boundaries between themselves and the regional black and indigenous populations, both of whom the government had officially designated as nonwhite. Indigenous and black activists of the era also tended to focus on integration, but generally without challenging the Anglo-defined cultural foundation of citizenship. Indeed, the myth that true Arizona citizens were those descended from Anglo pioneers—white citizens who had wrested the territory from their Mexican and Indian predecessors—would survive this era largely intact.

RACE AND THE (SUB)URBAN POLITICAL ECONOMY

World War II's impact on the Southwest was dramatic, spurring rapid growth in population, urbanization, and economic change that led contemporary boosters to call the region the Sun Belt to distinguish it from the so-called Rust Belt in the upper Midwest.[6] In the decade after the war, most of Arizona's population would settle primarily in the urban or suburban centers. By 1950 two-thirds of the population lived in metropolitan Tucson and Phoenix. The largest and most influential city in Arizona, and perhaps even in the desert Southwest as a whole, was Phoenix. Its total population soared from 65,414 in 1940 to 439,170 in 1960—growth of 670 percent over two decades. Its surrounding satellite cities of Glendale, Tempe, and Mesa also grew so substantially that by 1970 the population of Maricopa County approached one million.[7]

Phoenix boosters outdid promoters of other cities in the desert Southwest in their drive to attract industry and people in the years following the war, and thus to reshape the state's political economy. Sun Belt cities vied with each other for contracts with the federal government and competed to attract new companies by changing tax structures, passing antilabor laws, and stressing their balmy climate. Phoenix took the lead over El Paso through its aggressive reforms of tax and labor laws. Companies specializing in light, high-tech industries, such as Motorola, General Electric, and Sperry Rand, moved to Arizona after 1946 because the state's right-to-work law severely restricted the power of the unions. These companies helped to triple employment in the manufacturing sector and to stimulate a demographic shift from rural areas to the cities.[8]

As the population of Phoenix grew, thousands of acres of farmland disappeared under new suburban subdivisions, and the agricultural industry employed a declining percentage of the region's total labor force. Before the war Phoenix covered 9.6 square miles and was surrounded by thousands of acres of irrigated farmland. Two decades later, through annexation and real estate development, it had expanded to 187.4 square miles of the Salt River valley. In 1955 agriculture lost its place to manufacturing as the city's most important employer. In the 1970s suburban development removed ten thousand acres from agricultural production every year, so that by 1980 agriculture slipped to third place, behind manufacturing and tourism.[9]

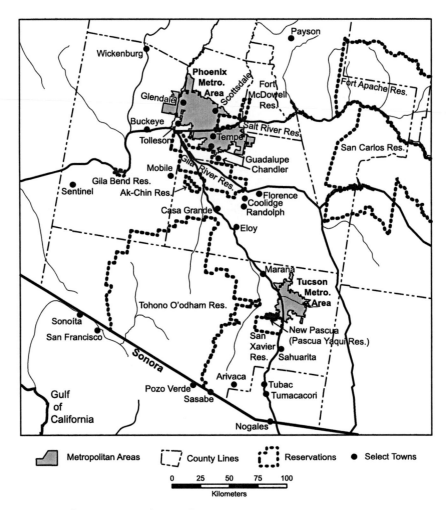

Map 6.1. Urban Areas in South-Central Arizona, ca. 1990

For Arizona's ethnic Mexican, indigenous, and African-American populations, the effects of this economic boom were mixed. World War II veterans were in the best position to benefit from the booming economy. Status as a veteran could often make the difference for applicants looking for
steady, unionized jobs. Joe Torres, for example, who had been an unskilled
worker before the war, found a job with Arizona Public Service, a local util-
ity that had long had a reputation for discrimination against non-Anglos.
For the first time, Torres also became a member of a union affiliated with
the American Federation of Labor (AFL). As he recalled, "When I came

back, my father-in-law got me in the union right away, 'cause you know every veteran had five points to begin with on any job application." The GI Bill helped hundreds of Mexican Americans in Arizona obtain educations and find better-paying jobs. Torres suggested that the GI Bill was "the most important part of our history." Adam Díaz, a local activist turned politician, recalled that "many of our youngsters went into the service, and came out, had GI rights, and that helped a lot. And they took advantage of it, because they went to school, and they were able to go all the way through college and do quite well." Ironically, Torres himself was unable to finish his course in electronics because he had to go back to work to support his family. Many other veterans no doubt discovered that free college tuition was not enough to overcome other obstacles to education and upward mobility.[10]

Many failed to enjoy the fruits of the boom. Low wages, unemployment, and poor living conditions continued to plague the barrios, reservations, and towns. By 1970 in Phoenix and Tucson, about 20 percent of all Hispanics, 30 percent of all Indians, and well over 30 percent of all blacks lived below the poverty line, compared with only 10 percent of the Anglo population. Non-Anglos remained mostly segregated into distinct residential areas. In Maricopa County, endless new suburban subdivisions expanded into the desert and into farming areas, but south Phoenix, where most of the non-Anglo population was concentrated, languished. The population of blacks in Phoenix grew from 4,263 in 1940 to 20,919 in 1960—making up over half of the total population of blacks in Arizona. In the early 1960s, according to a study by the Phoenix Urban League, 97 percent of all blacks in the city lived south of Van Buren Street, in the "worst housing areas in the city."[11]

Federal, state, and municipal policies had long encouraged residential segregation. In 1924 the Phoenix Real Estate Board ordered all realtors to refrain from "introducing into a neighborhood members of any race or nationality, or any individuals detrimental to property values in that neighborhood."[12] In 1938 the Federal Housing Authority (FHA) reinforced such restrictions by developing an underwriter's manual encouraging builders to segregate non-Anglo residents. The manual remained in effect into the 1960s. An investigation by the Phoenix Urban League found that between 1938 and 1960 three builders had constructed thirty-one thousand homes in northern Phoenix, all with "FHA commitments, or savings and loan associations that had Federal insurance." According to Lincoln Ragsdale, a member of the NAACP and the Urban League, "Not one of these new houses . . . [had] been sold to a Negro when new."[13]

Government officials promoted residential segregation in even more directly ways. The Phoenix Housing Authority was created in April 1939 to provide cheaper public housing under federal directives and financing. In 1941 it constructed three racially segregated housing projects: the Frank Luke project for Anglos, the Marcos de Niza project for ethnic Mexicans, and the Mathew Henson Homes project for blacks. Others followed. It was not until November 1955 that the U.S. Supreme Court condemned the construction of segregated public housing. By then Arizona's postwar urban boom had already followed a pattern of strict residential segregation.[14] In 1962, seven years after the Supreme Court decision, Lincoln Ragsdale noted that none of these projects had been truly desegregated. Of seven such projects, "Two of the projects are all-Negro; one project happens to be all white, and in three of them, one has one Negro, another has two Negroes, and a third has three Negroes."[15]

Tucson, which did not grow nearly as fast as Phoenix, faced similar problems. The Southern Pacific Railroad, which bisected the city diagonally from the northwest to the southeast, continued to separate the city's residents according to race. Mexican Americans, Indians, and other non-Anglo groups remained concentrated in the southern and western portions of the city, while Anglos generally lived to the north and the east.[16] A study done in the early 1970s by the University of Arizona found that the Tucson barrios suffered from poor housing and a lack of economic opportunity. According to the report, household heads in 19 percent of ethnic Mexican homes were unemployed. Those who had jobs worked mostly in "some type of labor, i.e., construction work, gardening, operatives, semiskilled work, and other jobs which occur outside the district." The report also noted that between 1960 and 1970 a growing percentage of barrio residents no longer owned their own homes, increasingly renting from absentee owners.[17]

Public facilities in south-central Arizona also remained segregated well into the 1950s. Lincoln Ragsdale remembered that "Phoenix was just like Mississippi. People were just as bigoted. They had segregation. They had signs in many places, 'Mexicans and Negroes not welcome.'" As with the FHA housing projects, segregation was not simply a binary phenomenon in which Anglos were segregated from all nonwhites. Instead, ethnic Mexicans, Indians, and blacks faced different forms of segregation. For a 1941 "kiddies picnic," for example, the city of Phoenix set aside three separate days and two separate parks for its white, ethnic Mexican, and black populations. There was no separate day for Indians, probably because the city did not think enough Indians lived in Phoenix to warrant it. According to the *Arizona Republic*, Riverside Park was reserved for "white kiddies" on Monday afternoon and on "Tuesday the colored children will gather for frolic at

Eastlake Park while the Mexican kiddies will have their picnic Wednesday at the same park."[18] Joe Torres recalled that similar, tripartite segregation policies were common at the swimming pools and local theaters. At the Orpheum Theatre in downtown Phoenix, for example, Mexican Americans were relegated to the balcony, while blacks could enter only on Thursdays. At the Riverside swimming pool, Torres recalled, blacks were excluded altogether, while ethnic Mexicans could use the pool on Sunday only.[19]

The forms of segregation faced by different ethno-racial groups also varied in the schools. Black students, whom government agencies clearly defined as a distinct race, had been entirely restricted from white schools and other public facilities since the first decade of the century.[20] The experience of ethnic Mexicans was somewhat different. In some cases, particularly in rural areas, Mexican Americans attended completely separate schools. In others they attended the same schools as Anglo students but faced discrimination and segregation within the schools and classrooms. Torres recalled that in Phoenix "they either put us way in the back of the class, or way in the front of the class . . . right in front of the teacher. There was a lot of segregation."[21]

Some Mexican-American students found that, unlike blacks and Indians, they could pass as white. Josie Ortega Sánchez, who grew up in Barrio al Altito in Tempe, recalled that when the children at her school had a day off to go on a picnic "the teacher gathered all the Mexican kids and told us that we could join the picnic, but . . . we weren't allowed to go swimming at the old Tempe Swimming Pool." However, one girl was exempted from the restriction because, according to Sánchez, "she was very, very light-complected and her hair was kind of blondish, reddish-blonde—he told her that she could go swimming if she wanted to, but the rest of us, because we were dark-skinned, we couldn't." Although Mexican Americans with light skin could sometimes duck the segregation policies, discrimination at an institutional level persisted, except when Mexican-American activists brought the issue before the courts.[22]

Urban Arizona's conservative political culture limited the ability of Mexican Americans, Indians, and blacks to challenge such discrimination. Phoenix, with at-large elections and a council-manager charter, was similar to other Sun Belt cities. Phoenix politicians claimed that its system was more progressive and efficient because it dispensed with the corruption of machine party politics in the eastern and midwestern United States. But this efficiency came at the expense of the rights of large sectors of the population. As a historian has suggested, "The chief beneficiaries of this government were the upper-income groups in the city, the great majority of them Anglo. Led by businessmen and professionals who lived in the wealthier sections of the city, the reformers advocated 'true' commission–city manager government, featuring fiscal conservatism, the ideals of individualism, and the goal of 'taking politics out of city hall.'"[23]

In the thirty years after the war, a group of elites known as the Phoenix Forty largely controlled both urban and state politics. Among this group, which dominated the Charter Government Committee, were newspaper mogul Eugene Pulliam, real estate developer Del Webb, and the Goldwater brothers, Barry and Robert. This unelected committee was such a potent force in local politics that between 1950 and 1975 every mayoral candidate that it endorsed won election and only two city council members were elected without its endorsement. This elite also greatly influenced state politics, rivaling an older mining and agricultural oligarchy. Members of the committee controlled the major newspapers and offered patronage to major Phoenix corporations. They helped send John Rhodes to Congress as their first Republican representative and elect Paul Fannin governor three times and U.S. senator in 1964. They propelled Barry Goldwater, who began his political career on the Phoenix City Council before becoming a U.S. senator in 1952, to a national campaign for president.[24]

Restrictions on the political participation of non-Anglos allowed conservative Anglo elites from Phoenix to dominate state politics. Blacks, Mexican Americans, and Indians alike continued to face major voting obstacles in the postwar era. Indians, whom the Arizona courts still defined as "under guardianship" until 1948, could not register to vote in Arizona elections. Arizona's literacy test undermined the political power of other minority populations, remaining on the books until 1972, seven years after Congress passed the Voting Rights Act.[25] Such laws were actively exploited to curtail the Mexican-American and African-American vote. In fact, according to many witnesses, a group of young Republican lawyers who functioned under the name Operation Eagle Eye in the early 1960s systematically visited the polls in south Phoenix to intimidate nonwhite voters. One of the primary leaders of the operation purportedly was Phoenix lawyer and future Supreme Court Chief Justice William Rehnquist.[26] This kind of intimidation, combined with Arizona's literacy test and poll tax, were quite effective in disenfranchising much of the non-Anglo population.

RACE AND LABOR IN AGRICULTURE AND MINING

Because ethnic Mexican and indigenous veterans continued to face job discrimination in Arizona's segregated cities, many had little choice but to return to their old jobs in mining and agriculture after the war. Those mines that had closed in the early years of the Depression recovered dramatically early in the war when the War Department signed a contract with Phelps Dodge to supply it with forty-five thousand tons of copper ore per day.[27] The new demand for mine workers, coupled with discriminatory hiring policies in the cities, encouraged non-Anglos to move back to the mining towns. Carlos Contreras recalled being "a ship fitter in the Navy, and when I got out I couldn't comprehend why I couldn't get a job here in Phoenix. . . . I was so dumb about everything that I didn't really realize they didn't want me! I finally had to leave Phoenix to get a job. I was married with one child and unemployed. I got one at Ajo, Arizona, at the Phelps Dodge mines."[28]

Ethnic Mexicans, Indians, and, increasingly, blacks made up the majority of the state's agricultural workforce. Thousands of Mexicans were imported through the Bracero Program. After the war, grower associations such as the Arizona Cotton Growers Association and the Salt River Valley Water Users' Association pleaded with the government to extend the program into the postwar period.[29] Responding to such lobbying efforts, the federal government did extend it into the 1960s.[30]

The Bracero Program restricted Mexican nationals to manual labor, thus helping to reestablish a racialized class system in the fields. Richard H. Salter, the chief of Arizona's Farm Placement Bureau, made this explicit when defending the program before the U.S. Commission on Civil Rights in 1962. As he put it, "These Mexican workers are prohibited from working on machines or operating machinery. They are to be used only for stoop labor, or seasonal activities."[31] Ironically, the program seemed to stimulate undocumented immigration rather than to curtail it. In response the Arizona press often published alarmist articles about an invasion of "wetbacks" who were streaming over the border. Periodically, such as in 1954 under Operation Wetback, the INS deported thousands of Mexican workers even as growers continued to import braceros seasonally.[32]

Growers also recruited Indians from northern Arizona. The BIA had attempted to recruit Apaches, Navajos, and Hopis early in the century but had been unable to attract more than a few. The superintendent of the San Carlos reservation had explained in 1914 that the Apaches were unwilling to work alongside Pimas because "they have a natural antipathy to the Pima Indians, and do not like to work with them."[33] In the 1920s another BIA official explained to Commissioner Charles Burke that despite concerted efforts by cotton growers, only nineteen Hopis and seven Navajos had been enticed to the fields.[34] The cotton growers responded by encouraging the BIA to refine its system of recruitment and transportation. They claimed that such a program would expose the Indians to "civilized surroundings" and "modern methods of industry," and provide "the rudiments of a common school education."[35] Still, before World War II, only the Yavapai from north-central Arizona worked in significant numbers, perhaps about one hundred, in the southern half of the state.[36]

During and after the war, hundreds of Navajos finally began to work in the fields of south-central Arizona. John Jacobs, a spokesman for the Arizona Vegetable Growers, imported between 140 and 250 Navajo workers every year beginning in 1942, the same year that the Bracero Program began. Other vegetable growers followed suit. Navajos generally worked from November to June, living in small frame houses they built themselves. Others were recruited during and after the war to work in the Morenci mine where, according to the director of the state employment service, "Indian labor practically saved the mine from closing." In 1948 BIA officials met with growers to stabilize and standardize the practice of recruiting Navajos as a part of its relocation program. BIA officials hoped to find a way to employ Navajos and Hopis year-round, rather than only from November to June.[37]

Their efforts ultimately failed. Instead, Navajo families joined the migrant labor stream, moving yearly from northern Arizona into the fields, much as Mexican braceros from the south were doing. A spokesman for the cotton growers explained in 1948 that while an additional fifteen thousand workers were required during the cotton and lettuce harvest from October through December, year-round farmworkers simply were not needed. "By the end of January we have no further interest in them," he said.[38] By 1962 Navajos worked mostly in seasonal jobs, moving back and forth from the reservation as their labor was needed. As John Jacobs put it, "Many of them take back rather substantial savings as they return to the reservation for the summer months, which they prefer doing, as many have small farms, herds of goats, sheep, and other livestock, as well as other summer work on the reservation."[39]

Indians from south-central Arizona also worked in the fields in greater numbers than ever. A special report of the U.S. census in 1953 indicates that of 11,176 Tohono O'odham living in Pima, Maricopa, and Pinal counties, 6,399 lived outside the reservations for at least part of the year. Up to two thousand Tohono O'odham lived in Tucson and Ajo, while the remainder lived at least part time in rural towns and labor camps and depended either upon seasonal agricultural work or, increasingly, on more permanent agricultural work near the reservation. A researcher estimated in 1950 that half of all wages earned by the Tohono O'odham came from off-reservation cotton harvesting.[40]

The federal government's postwar "relocation" and "termination" programs attempted to coerce Indians to take up more permanent jobs off the reservation. The relocation program was in part a response to legitimate concerns about poor health conditions on the reservations and to the continuing problem of families taking their children out of the schools so that they could earn extra income as farmworkers. More broadly, though, relocation was a step toward termination. Secretary of the Interior J. C. Krug made this clear when he stated that the objective of the 1949 Papago Development Program was "their integration into the social, economic and political life of the Nation and the termination of federal supervision and control special to Indians." Much as in the late nineteenth and early twentieth centuries, termination defined national belonging in monolithic terms. To achieve equality and integration, Indians would have to take up permanent jobs off the reservation. Management of reservation lands would eventually pass from tribal councils to corporations "owned by all of the enrolled members and created to manage the property of those members held in common."[41]

Ultimately, none of the tribes in south-central Arizona was terminated, and plans for relocating hundreds of families to cities like Los Angeles and Chicago were undermined, in part, by the availability of jobs near the reservations.[42] The demand for seasonal cotton pickers within Arizona reached an all-time high in 1953 when about one million acres were under irrigation in the state. Most Indians chose to work in adjacent farms or in nearby urban centers like Tucson and Phoenix. The Arizona Commission of Indian Affairs explained in 1956 that the "trend toward industrialized farming in Arizona's irrigated areas . . . has meant a source of seasonal employment, which has been utilized by thousands of Pimas, Papagos, and Navajos in recent years." The commission noted its frustration that agricultural work made it extremely difficult to encourage the Tohono O'odham and other groups to accept "permanent Indian settlement off the reservation."[43]

While seasonal agricultural work permitted south-central Arizona's indigenous population to maintain close ties to the reservations, it remained a precarious and unhealthy way to earn a living. Such jobs were highly exploitative and underpaid, and conditions in the labor camps ranged from substandard to miserable with only a few exceptions. It was estimated in 1950 that 95 percent of the housing in south-central Arizona's labor camps would not pass the state's labor code but that none of the growers "would ever be convicted by a jury of his peers—for the peers in this area are all just as guilty." While regulations demanded that parents and children be provided their own rooms, most families lived in tiny one-room cabins that lacked water, furnishings, electricity, or gas and had substandard floors or no floors at all. The camps provided "almost no provision for laundering or bathing," so the residents generally used the same outdoor hydrants from which they obtained their drinking water.[44]

Perhaps the most poignant personal story illustrating the continuing plight of Arizona's indigenous farmworkers is that of Ira Hayes, a Pima World War II veteran. Hayes won a Congressional Medal of Honor during the war, and his participation in the raising of the flag on Mount Suribachi during the battle of Iwo Jima was captured forever by a famous photograph and a seventy-five-foot bronze statue in Washington, D.C. After the war Hayes eventually made his way back to the Gila River reservation, where he had few options but to take up work as a cotton picker. Like thousands of other Pimas and Maricopas with no access to sufficient water or capital to develop their allotments, Hayes and his family worked on neighboring industrial farms for about three dollars per day. During a radio interview in Chicago, he revealed his frustration. "I was out in Arizona for eight years and nobody paid any attention to me," he explained. "They might ask me what I think of the way they treat Indians out here, compared to how we are treated in Chicago. I'd tell them the truth and Arizona would not like it." In 1955, not long after the interview, Hayes died of alcoholism.[45]

Just days after his funeral, Harold Fey, the editor of the *Christian Century*, reported that his death was the result not simply of alcohol but of environmental degradation and exploitation. On a visit he made to the Hayes home on the Gila reservation, Fey found "a typical Indian house, made of wood posts and mud bricks, 25 or 30 feet square." He found few Indians actively farming. "Although the soil was said to be fertile, the surroundings of the Hayes' home presented a picture of dust and desolation, since no water was available for irrigation. After seeing this place, it was easier to understand why Ira Hayes drank his way to oblivion and death; why alcoholism is a major affliction to a frustrated and discouraged people." Fey was particularly struck by the contrast between the reservation and nearby industrial farms. "A few miles away water runs in the irrigation ditches and the desert produces cotton, barley, wheat and alfalfa, to say nothing of citrus fruit." The agricultural boom brought little benefit to the reservation, except through low wages earned by Pima and Maricopa families.[46]

A new threat developed in the mid-1960s when the mechanization of cotton-picking dramatically lowered the demand for seasonal farmworkers in Arizona. During the first half of the decade, machines rapidly replaced human pickers in the cotton fields. In the mid-1950s the total demand for farm labor more than doubled between the off-season and the harvest between October through early January, when some forty-eight

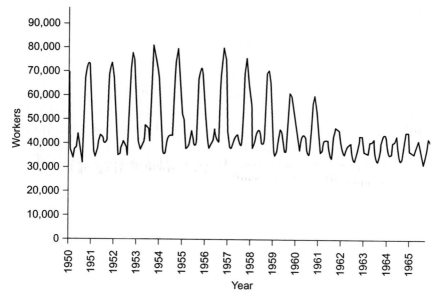

Figure 6.1. Seasonal Farm Labor Demand in Arizona, 1950–1965. Source: Arizona State Employment Service, *Agricultural Employment in Arizona since 1950* (Phoenix, 1968), 9–132.

thousand pickers joined the forty thousand or so year-round workers. By 1963, however, Arizona's cotton growers required only fifty-three hundred additional workers for the harvest. Mechanization flattened the seasonal cycle so that no more than thirty thousand to forty thousand farmworkers were needed throughout the year (Figure 6.1).[47] Lee Athmer of the Arizona Farm Bureau noted this trend in 1962: "In Pinal County, there were 19,000 migrant workers at the peak of the growing season ten years ago. . . . This past growing season there were no more than 1,000 migrant workers in Pinal County at any time."[48] Seasonal farmworkers had to seek new ways to earn income (see Chapter 8).

The much lower demand for seasonal labor played a critical role in ending the Bracero Program in 1964. Nationally, both nativist Anglos and diverse Mexican-American organizations such as the League of United Latin American Citizens (LULAC), the GI Forum, and the National Farm Labor Union led the charge to end the program. In California, Ernesto Galarza, Dolores Huerta, and César Chávez argued that braceros lowered the wages of citizen workers while undermining efforts to unionize. Nationally, LULAC and the GI Forum, which did not promote union organizing, at least agreed with labor activists that braceros lowered the wages and living standards of U.S. citizens.[49]

Mexican Americans, labor activists, and politicians in Arizona raised similar concerns.[50] Manuel Peña Jr., a former migrant worker, testified before the Civil Rights Commission in 1962 that "there has never been a genuine shortage of U.S.-born farmworkers, except during World War II." He requested that the program be terminated immediately: "It is ironic that the agreement between the United States and Mexico is careful to state that the employer shall not practice social or economic discrimination in condition of employment against the imported worker, and at the same time is responsible for the economic discrimination against the U.S.-born farmworker." In 1964 such calls to end the program, combined with the mechanization of agriculture and the resulting decrease in demand for seasonal farm labor, led to its being canceled.[51]

Peña's comments revealed both dissatisfaction with the Bracero Program and tensions between Mexican-American citizens and Mexican nationals. Many Mexican Americans who expressed similar sentiments were not simply worried about wages and worker protections. They also feared that Mexican immigrants threatened to reinforce the racial stereotype of the Mexican peon. Ironically, critiques such as Peña's would help to reify the notion that Mexicans had no just claims to civil rights or federal protections. Such tensions would emerge frequently throughout the postwar era, undermining the ability of Mexican Americans to speak with a unified voice.[52]

POSTWAR STRUGGLES FOR EQUALITY AND FULL LEGAL CITIZENSHIP

In the fifteen years after World War II, activists in south-central Arizona would make important gains in civil and workers' rights without fundamentally redefining the culture or meaning of citizenship. In the legal arena especially, postwar activists made substantial progress despite entrenched opposition by Anglo politicians who touted a supposedly voluntary civil stewardship while upholding the existing racial order. At times, Mexican Americans, Indians, African Americans, and progressive or leftist Anglos worked together, forming new interethnic coalitions. At other times, however, these groups manipulated rather than challenged the racially exclusive national ideology of citizenship to their own advantage. As a result the postwar struggles for equality often manifested themselves as interethnic and intraethnic struggles over identity.

One of the first and most effective postwar movements for racial and economic equality emerged in the mining towns. Mexican and indigenous miners and their families continued to face discriminatory treatment after the war, and they once again turned to labor unions to challenge such treatment. Máximo Alonzo recalled that when he first began working in Miami, the racially ordered wage system was alive and well, and public facilities remained staunchly segregated. As a result, when Mine-Mill labor organizers appeared, Alonzo was eager to join. "The bosses were mean then," he recalled. "They treated us Mexican people like we were nothing. . . . The white man would get three or four dollars a day, but us Mexicans, us bunch of people, only $2.75—that was it. Until the unions came in here, and then we stuck it to them."[53] Enrique Pastor, who also worked in Miami, agreed: "There were no rights or anything. We had none. When the gringo boss came along, you literally bowed down to him. That's the way it was. Until we got our union in the early '40s."[54]

While it has become commonplace to credit returning veterans for the revitalization of Arizona's mining unions, the unions began to make a comeback well before the United States entered World War II. This time they were aided by New Deal legislation such as the Wagner Act, which allowed workers to elect labor unions with a majority vote and to collectively bargain with their employers.[55] Still, the National Labor Relations Board (NLRB) was slow to act, and only under persistent pressure by the unions did it serve the interests of Arizona's workers. Workers began to apply such pressure in 1935, shortly after the passage of the Wagner Act, when Mine-Mill broke from the AFL to join the newly formed Congress of Industrial Organizations (CIO). The CIO and Mine-Mill were determined to organize skilled and unskilled workers alike, regardless of race or ethnicity.[56]

Soon thereafter, union organizers began to enlist workers in Bisbee, the site of the infamous deportation of twelve hundred workers twenty years earlier. Workers affiliated with Mine-Mill went on strike in June 1935 and remained on the picket lines for the next two months. Phelps Dodge retaliated by firing thirty-eight strikers, but the union, which had little other recourse in 1917, quickly responded by filing a complaint before the NLRB. It took five years for the board to decide that Phelps Dodge had engaged in unfair labor practices. Then it demanded that the company stop interfering with the Mine-Mill local, dismantle the company union, reinstate employees who had been fired, and reimburse them for lost wages. When the company refused, the case went before the U.S. Supreme Court. In its 1941 decision, the Court agreed with the NLRB, declaring that Phelps Dodge had acted "against the whole idea of the legitimacy of organization." The decision armed the union to expand its efforts into mining towns throughout the region.[57]

Much as in the 1910s, attitudes among most middle-class Mexican

Americans toward Mine-Mill ranged from lukewarm to hostile. In 1937 an editorial in *El Tucsonense* accused John L. Lewis, the head of the CIO, of being "drunk with power," and it labeled both the tactics and the industrial unionist ideology of the CIO "Communist." While the editors acknowledged that ethnic Mexican miners faced exploitation and discrimination, the only solution they offered was for them to sit down with the companies as "collaborators in the same work." [58]

Still, the union began to achieve piecemeal victories in the early 1940s, before war veterans made their way back to the mines. In 1942 the NLRB ordered that elections take place in Globe-Miami so that workers could choose, by majority vote, whether they wished to be affiliated with the AFL or Mine-Mill. In May 1943, with both Mexican-American and Anglo support, Mine-Mill won the majority of votes in the district. Soon thereafter, the workers won an increase in pay of twenty-six cents per shift and paid, one-week vacations. [59] That same year, ethnic Mexicans at Clifton-Morenci formed their own Mine-Mill local, while in other mining and smelter towns, including Bisbee, Ajo, and Douglas, both AFL craft unionists and Mine-Mill workers fought successfully for higher wages. [60]

By 1945, returning veterans found a revitalized labor movement well under way. Many felt empowered by their war experiences, and they asserted that their patriotic efforts overseas had earned them the right to first-class citizenship. Ed Montoya, a miner at Clifton-Morenci, was one of them. He remembers how "I would say to myself here after I came back, in 1946, 'Hey! Somebody's been lying to me all these years. How come I went in as a private and I came out as a leader? If that can happen in the army, why can't it happen in the smelter?'" [61] Such reasoning proved effective. As Mexican-American miners organized in places like Ray, Clifton-Morenci, Ajo, and Miami, a 1946 editorial in the *Arizona Labor Journal* entitled "Dark Men Fighting for White Liberties" asked, "If a man is good enough to fight a war, is he good enough to participate in the opportunities of peace? . . . It will be left to our hearts and spirits to allow the blacks and yellows to be included within the realm of the white man's privileges." From that perspective, veteran status, regardless of one's race, should guarantee full equality and national belonging. [62]

The patriotic rhetoric of Mexican-American workers did not always serve the interests of other ethnic Mexicans. During the strikes in 1946, Mexican-American union members sometimes emphasized their status as American citizens at the expense of Mexican nationals who also worked in the industry. The *Arizona Labor Journal* reported that Mexican-American veterans in the smelters at Douglas, directly adjacent to the Mexican town

of Agua Prieta, "claim that they are being given the run-around by local employers in that the residents of Agua Prieta are given preference
for jobs. . . . The returned soldiers are very bitter about the alleged discrimination against them." Mexican-American workers criticized the INS for
permitting Mexican nationals to work with six-month visas. According to
the article, the union members "allege that the Mexican workers receive
all the benefits which their organizations have obtained but share none of
the burdens of maintaining the unions." These concerns would be repeated
in future years, when some Mexican-American unionists and civil rights
activists would lay part of the blame for their own subordinate status on
Mexican nationals.[63]

Still, with Anglo support, Mexican-American miners and a smaller
number of indigenous miners in places such as Ajo made great strides in
1946. Between late March and July, workers throughout Arizona, from all
ethnic backgrounds, struck for higher wages. The Mine-Mill local at Clifton-Morenci, for example, known locally as the Mexican union, demanded
equal wages and health benefits regardless of race. After holding out for 107
days, the union won an agreement with Phelps Dodge, ending the racially
ordered wage system at least in its most blatant manifestation. Mexican-
American workers successfully made use of their veteran status to convince enough Anglo workers of their worthiness for equal treatment, and
as a result they won a substantial victory.[64]

The 1946 strikes were pivotal in Arizona labor history, but opposing
forces blunted their impact. Unionized mine workers faced entrenched opposition from the mining companies, the Arizona Farm Bureau, and government officials. In the midst of the 1946 victories, the state legislature passed
a right-to-work law, which permitted nonunionized members to work in
unionized mines and allowed unions from outside Arizona to challenge
the authority of other democratically elected unions. Effective unionization and collective bargaining became more difficult. In response ASFL
organizers put aside their resentment toward the CIO-affiliated Mine-Mill
to contest the measure. They described it as a "nefarious scheme" supported by "sweat shop employers" against "all liberty-loving citizens" and
lobbied intensely to defeat it. In the end the bill passed over the protests of
the unions. Just when the union movement was at its peak, it suffered one
of its greatest blows.[65]

With the new law in place, relatively conservative craft unions successfully challenged the hegemony of Mine-Mill and weakened its ability to
bargain collectively. Enrique Pastor of Miami said that "we [Mine-Mill]
were raided by a number of unions. The Steelworkers wanted to come in

and take over. . . . We were branded as a Communist union."[66] The anti-Communist tenor of the early cold war, combined with the right-to-work law and the appearance of competing unions, persuaded many workers to turn away from Mine-Mill. The pressure on the ethnic Mexican community to do so was particularly intense, because expressions of patriotism and national loyalty just after the war had served as a weapon to achieve economic equality. Any hint of socialist sympathies could be perceived as the gravest treachery and would threaten the gains ethnic Mexicans had made since the war. According to Máximo Alonzo of Miami, "We started with an organization here, the CIO . . . but then we found out that they were affiliated with Communistas *y todo eso* [Communists and all that], so we kicked them out. We got rid of them and we got another union."[67]

Although the postwar labor movement had dismantled the racially ordered wage system in its most blatant manifestation, non-Anglo miners continued to face social segregation and less formal, discriminatory hiring practices. Carlos Contreras, who worked at the Ajo mines in the late 1940s, recalled that "there weren't any Mexican foremen or Mexican supervisors. I was put on the railroad crew. Four Mexicans and two Indians—no Anglo of any sort, except the foreman." Peter Blaine, the former chairman of the Papago tribal council, has described his four years as a worker in Ajo in the early 1950s. He was repeatedly denied a promotion as a driller, while a white man he knew "never started at the bottom. He was a driller right away."[68] Throughout the 1950s the unions continued to struggle for higher wages, better working conditions, and an end to other forms of discrimination. Segregation in the mining towns, however, remained common. The labor movement was unable to end such persistent discrimination.[69]

Indian veterans took on leadership roles in their communities like those assumed by Mexican-American veterans, but they had less influence in the unions largely because of their smaller numbers and their being relegated to often temporary, low-wage jobs. Instead, they focused on sovereignty and full political rights. Nationally, war veterans dominated the National Congress of American Indians (NCAI), established during a pan-Indian conference in Denver in November 1944. Veterans who led the organization "brought with them new skills, a broadened experience of the non-Indian world, a growing disposition to act on a supra-tribal basis, an impatience with the poverty and powerlessness of the reservations, and an eagerness for action." Most relevant for this study was the NCAI's campaign to end Indian voting restrictions in New Mexico and Arizona.[70]

In Arizona, veteran Frank Harrison, a Yavapai, brought the voting issue before the NCAI after the Maricopa County recorder refused to register him for the upcoming election. When he attempted to file suit, the Maricopa County Superior Court refused to hear the case. Two NCAI lawyers, James E. Curry and Felix Cohen, appealed the case to the Arizona Supreme Court. Cohen and Curry argued that because Harrison had served in the military and because he paid taxes and owned property, "some of which" was "located at various times outside the boundaries of said Fort McDowell Indian reservation," the constitutional clause restricting the right of persons under guardianship to vote did not apply. Had the court decided the case on this basis alone, it would have done little for Indians who did not own property and still lived on the reservations.[71]

The court made a much broader ruling in 1948. Justice Udall went beyond the argument that veteran status, property holdings, or payment of taxes were essential prerequisites for the right to vote. Instead, he condemned the court's previous interpretations of the guardianship clause as a "tortuous construction by the judicial branch" and proclaimed that because the government had recognized American Indians as citizens in 1924, the guardianship clause could no longer be applied to them.[72] More than one hundred years after the Treaty of Guadalupe Hidalgo, Arizona Indians had finally gained the right to vote.

Mexican Americans and blacks faced somewhat different forms of discrimination from both Indians (e.g., they were not so explicitly barred from voting) and from each other, and thus the immediate goals of their postwar struggles varied. The NAACP, the Alianza Hispano-Americana, and Phoenix's chapter of LULAC, founded in 1941, were integrationist. In protesting segregation they stressed their patriotism and loyalty to the United States and did not raise questions about generally accepted cultural prerequisites for citizenship. Most Mexican Americans in these organizations did not, for example, assert their right to speak Spanish rather than English nor did they resist the notion that they should assimilate into Anglo-American society. In Phoenix, the Alianza's Committee for Better Americanism (CBA) encouraged ethnic Mexicans to become better Americans, to prove that they were worthy to be equal citizens. Some Mexican Americans also continued to argue that their whiteness entitled them to equal treatment—an argument that held little promise for blacks and Indians.[73]

Even before the war ended, a small number of Mexican Americans managed to enter politics by tying their fates to the Democratic Party and winning elections to city councils and the state legislature. In Phoenix the Latin American Club, founded in 1932 by Southern Pacific Railroad worker Luis Cordova, spearheaded a drive to elect a Mexican American to the legislature. Adam Díaz, who was an early member of the club and of the Alianza, recalled that he and other members walked door-to-door to register voters and that they lobbied the legislature for, in his words, "a little more recognition. . . . We were very anxious to uplift our people and point out to the authorities that they were capable of doing other than just digging ditches." The club managed to register enough voters in 1941, and to appeal to the patronage of the Democratic Party, to elect James Carreon as the first Mexican American to serve in the state legislature. Carreon subsequently fought for federal guarantees for fair employment in war industries and to improve relations with Mexico through the Office of the Coordinator of Inter-American Affairs.[74]

Adam Díaz also benefited from voter registration and the patronage of the Democratic Party. Phoenix businessman George Luhrs had hired Díaz in the mid-1920s to work as an elevator operator for his new skyscraper in downtown Phoenix. While working at the Luhrs building, Díaz made, in his words, "marvelous connections with some great lawyers, and many fine businesspeople." Among them was the future Democratic governor, Sidney Osborn, who lived on the fourth floor. Eventually, Díaz became superintendent of properties owned by Luhrs. Osborn and other Democrats encouraged Díaz and the Latin American Club to register voters, recognizing that Mexican Americans usually voted Democratic. After World War II, when the Republican Party increasingly dominated Arizona politics, Democratic patronage of Mexican Americans became even more important. In 1948 Díaz became the first Mexican American to be elected to the Phoenix City Council. After four years he was appointed vice-mayor, and he personally recommended Val Cordova, the son of the founder of the Latin American Club, to take his place on the council. While this was a real achievement, the council seat remained essentially a token position that was used to back up Anglo claims that Mexican Americans were making progress in Arizona.[75]

Indeed, the few electoral seats that Mexican Americans won served not only their own interests but the interests of both Republican and Democratic Anglos as well. Recall that Phoenix Mayor Samuel Mardian defended the city's civil rights record before the U.S. Commission on Civil Rights in 1962 by pointing out that there were Mexican Americans on the city council and state legislature. Frederic Marquardt, the editor of the conservative *Arizona Republic*, offered a similar defense. "There are many Americans of Mexican extraction in our legislature," he said. "There is one on our city council." Their presence in government positions proved, in his view, that "there is no discrimination in elected public office" and thus that federal intervention in the realm of civil rights was unnecessary.[76]

As they began to achieve some limited political victories, many middle-class Mexican Americans in organizations such as the Latin American Club distanced themselves from Mexican immigrants, blacks, and Indians. As the Latin American Club registered Mexican-American voters in 1935, club leaders sent a resolution to the city of Phoenix requesting that Southside Park, which was in an ethnic Mexican neighborhood near Second Avenue and Grant Street, be made off-limits to blacks.[77] Members of the club, like those in LULAC and in *mutualistas* such as the Alianza Hispano-Americana, generally opposed industrial unionism. They did little to help Mexican nationals beyond encouraging education, naturalization, and self-improvement. Instead, they focused on enhancing the image and political clout of American citizens of Mexican descent. Adam Díaz later declared that "Mexico is just sending hordes of people over here . . . all at the expense of the local taxpayer. . . . I think Mexico should try to do a little bit better, help their own."[78]

In the 1950s a new organization called Vesta aimed to change the public image of those it called Spanish Americans. Eugene Marín, a Phoenix teacher and World War II veteran, founded Vesta with a group of professionals and business leaders in 1954. Their avoidance of Mexican as a term was a strategy designed to distance the Mexican-American community from newer immigrants, and to claim whiteness. According to Marín, the purpose of the club was to encourage "individual effort of self-improvement" and to "change the image, in the public eye, of the Spanish-speaking citizen." The biggest problem facing "Spanish Americans" in Marín's view was the lack of "educational achievement" and the lack of an able leadership. "For generations," he explained in 1962, "these people have been subjected to this conditioning process of unacceptability, insecurity, and semi-citizenship status." Vesta accepted only college students and graduates as members, and it held banquets and benefit dances to raise money for scholarships. Its motto, Progress through Education, summed up its ideology. Vesta did not directly challenge discrimination or segregation in the courts or through voter registration, placing most of the onus instead on Mexican Americans to become better citizens.[79]

Some Mexican-American organizations were less conciliatory in their ideology and became decidedly more assertive in the postwar era. In the early 1950s the Alianza Hispano-Americana extended its campaign to achieve first-class citizenship directly into the political and legal realm, organizing voter registration drives and challenging segregation in schools and other public facilities. Many returning veterans joined this struggle, refusing to settle back into their prewar status as second-class citizens. As one explained, "Fighting for your country doesn't give you the feeling of a second-class citizen. It really gives you the feeling that you did as much as the next guy did, so this is as much your country as it is anybody else's." Working through the Committee for Better Americanism (CBA), the Alianza hoped to educate Mexican Americans to be become better citizens, while dismantling the most egregious legal obstacles to equal citizenship.[80]

The Alianza's and CBA's earliest postwar desegregation case occurred in rural Tolleson in western Maricopa County. The effort began through a grassroots movement within Tolleson to desegregate the elementary school. In 1947–1948, Manuel Peña, who had grown up in the town before being drafted into the army, led a group of community members to organize a voter registration drive. After registering 750 voters, Peña helped to form the Comité Movimiento Unido Mexicano Contra La Discriminación (the Committee of the United Mexican Movement against Discrimination). Its use of Spanish in its name was a decided turn away from the embrace of English made by many other organizations of the era, such as Vesta, the CBA, or LULAC, and was a sign of things to come. The committee contacted the head lawyer for the Alianza, Ralph Estrada, and wrote a letter to the school superintendent demanding that the school be desegregated. On May 5, after the superintendent refused, they filed a class action suit in federal district court.[81]

The Alianza's lawyers based their initial case in *Gonzales et al. v. Sheeley* on the equal protection clause of the Fourteenth Amendment. Ralph Estrada cited a number of precedents involving both ethnic Mexican and black students in California and Texas. Among them was *Mendez v. Westminster*, in which a federal judge in California had determined that segregation against Mexican Americans was unconstitutional in part because it instilled a sense of psychological inferiority. Alianza lawyers also cited *Sweatt v. Painter*, in which a black law student at the University of Texas had successfully sued the university to demand equal accommodations. The Tolleson petitioners pointed out that in the Sweatt case "much less substantial inequities of accommodations were ruled in violation of the Fourteenth Amendment to the Constitution." They had little trouble proving that the school facilities in Tolleson were physically unequal. The Anglo school had a modern gym, benches and trees, a playground with swings and slides, and a cooling system while the Mexican school was a much smaller building constructed of "chicken wire and stucco" with no gym, no play equipment, and no shades or screens.[82]

In the midst of the court proceedings, Alianza lawyers wavered in their commitment to a racially inclusive argument. When the respondents argued that segregation in Arizona was legal, pointing to two Phoenix statutes permitting and/or requiring the segregation of African Americans, Alianza lawyers fell back on the strategic argument that Mexican Americans were white. They suggested that because the statutes singled out blacks they were not meant to apply to children of Mexican descent, who were of the "Caucasoid" race. The respondents attempted to refute this argument by pointing to a previous case, *Pass v. State*, in which the Supreme Court had concluded that "Mexican-Americans are not necessarily of the same race as the Anglo-Americans insofar as it is common knowledge . . . that there exist varying degrees of Indian blood in the so-called Mexican-Americans of the Southwest." The petitioners, however, convinced the court that while *Pass v. State* may have raised questions about the purity of Mexican-American whiteness, this was not sufficient grounds to segregate them. In the words of the court, "While *Pass v. State* may have decided that Mexican Americans are not necessarily of the same race as Anglo-Americans, it does not decide that Mexican Americans are of African descent." This argument, had it been the sole basis for the court's decision, would have implicitly confirmed the segregation of blacks and Indians, whom the U.S. government considered nonwhite.[83]

In the end Judge Dave Ling based his decision on the petitioners' original argument, finding that the very act of separating certain students based upon their ethnic or racial status served as a mark of inferiority, much as in *Mendez v. Westminster*. He declared that "the methods of segregation prevalent in the respondent school district foster antagonisms in the children and suggest inferiority among them where none exists." This argument, of course, would successfully be used again in future cases, including *Brown v. Board of Education* less than two years later. Ling also deflated the argument that ethnic Mexican children could be segregated because they spoke Spanish. While temporary separation for pedagogical reasons might be appropriate, language differences could not justify "general and continuous segregation in separate schools of children of Mexican ancestry from the rest of the elementary school population."[84]

In May 1951, following the success of the Tolleson case, leaders from the Alianza joined with members from the Texas-based G.I. Forum and LULAC and the California-based Community Service Organization to form the interstate American Council of Spanish-Speaking Organizations. The purpose of the organization was "to eliminate public school and housing segregation, to increase participation in juries and public offices, and to end discrimination in employment." In Arizona, Gregorio García from Tucson and Ralph Estrada from Phoenix encouraged the Alianza to adopt more assertive, confrontational tactics. In addition to the Tolleson case, they helped to file appeals for convicted Mexican-American prisoners and threatened to bring legal action against segregated public facilities throughout Arizona.[85]

African-American lawyers simultaneously initiated a number of suits against segregation. The obstacles to their struggle were more clear-cut, since the federal government clearly viewed blacks as nonwhite and because a number of laws in Arizona had explicitly made the segregation of blacks legal. In 1947 black leaders joined with progressive Anglos in Phoenix to form the Greater Phoenix Council for Civic Unity (GPCCU) to eliminate "discrimination in Phoenix and surrounding communities, and to cooperate with local, state, and national groups working toward the same ends." In 1951, through persistent lobbying, they persuaded Arizona's legislature to pass a statute permitting Arizona's school boards to desegregate their schools on a voluntarily basis. While some schools desegregated in response to the statute, many others—including schools in Tolleson and Phoenix—volunteered not to act. This fact clearly contradicts the Phoenix mayor's 1962 claims that the city had desegregated its schools without the interference of the courts or that, as he put it, "minority groups would accomplish more on a voluntary basis than by looking to legal remedies."[86]

After the failure of the Phoenix schools to act, activists from the NAACP and GPCCU jointly filed a suit in Arizona Superior Court to force the admission of three black students from the segregated Carver High School into white high schools in the Phoenix Union district. Local black leaders, such as Lincoln and Eleanor Ragsdale, and Arizona's only two black legislators, Hayzel B. Daniels and Carl Sims, cooperated with Anglo lawyers such as William P. Mahony Jr. to lead the effort. Justice Fred C. Struckmeyer heard the case in the Maricopa County Superior Court. The lawyers for the Phoenix case again crossed racial boundaries by citing a number of California precedents involving Mexican-American students, including *Mendez v. Westminster*. Whether these cases could become the basis for a challenge to the segregation of black children remained an open question.[87]

Struckmeyer ruled that state laws permitting segregation on a voluntary basis were an unconstitutional delegation of power to school boards. His decision ridiculed the doctrine of separate but equal by pointing out that it could be used to justify the segregation of any group of people, not just those deemed to be members of another race. "If such unlimited and unrestricted power can be exercised on the basis of ancestry," he declared, "it can be exercised on such a purely whimsical basis as the color of hair, eyes, or for any other reason as pure fancy might dictate."[88]

The Tolleson and Phoenix Union decisions rendered the Mexican-American legal strategy of claiming whiteness obsolete and opened the way for a new level of cooperation between African-American and Mexican-American leaders. As a symbol of this new willingness to cooperate, in 1954 the Alianza inducted jazz trumpeter Louis Armstrong while he was visiting Tucson on a national tour. Previously, blacks had not been permitted to become members. The next year, Ralph Estrada announced the establishment of the Alianza civil rights department to be directed by Ralph Guzman in East Los Angeles. Alianza lawyers filed suits in Miami, Douglas, and Glendale in Arizona. In 1954, for example, they sued the town of Winslow for excluding Mexican Americans, Indians, and blacks from local swimming pools. The following year, Winslow officials recognized that the tide had turned against segregation, and with no legal basis to defend their segregation policy they settled out of court.[89]

A series of class-action suits in the 1940s and 1950s had successfully torn down the explicit legal foundation for racial segregation in Arizona. By the end of the decade, however, the struggle for inclusion seemed to have taken civil rights activists as far as they could go. Soon, a younger group of activists would point out that while many legal obstacles to full equality had been overturned, whiteness remained the standard for full citizenship and belonging at a cultural and social level. Even if equality were to be achieved, it would not be enough to tear down legal barriers to opportunity. Instead, the very definition of what it meant to be an American citizen would have to be changed.

CHAPTER 7

THE CHICANO MOVEMENT
AND CULTURAL CITIZENSHIP

At the end of World War II, Mario Suárez returned from serving in the U.S. Navy to find that the barrios of Tucson where he had been born and raised had barely changed. In a short story he wrote in 1947, Suárez compared the El Hoyo barrio to *capirotada*, a traditional Mexican dish made with a base of "old, new, stale, and hard bread." One could add any number of ingredients, including "raisins, olives, onions, tomatoes, peanuts, cheese, and general leftovers," and then season it with "salt, sugar, pepper, and sometimes chili or tomato sauce." The dish would be topped off with tequila or sherry and baked so that the ingredients melted together. Each family made the meal in its own way, varying the recipe from day to day. "While in general appearance it does not differ much from one home to another, it tastes different everywhere. Nevertheless it is still *capirotada*. And so it is with El Hoyo's Chicanos." Explaining the metaphor, he said, "While many seem to the undiscerning eye to be alike, it is only because collectively they are referred to as Chicanos. But like *capirotada*, fixed in a thousand ways and served on a thousand tables, which can only be evaluated by individual taste, the Chicanos must be so distinguished."[1]

Suárez, the son of immigrants from the Mexican border states of Sonora and Chihuahua, is recognized as the first writer to use Chicano in a published work to refer to ethnic Mexicans. Mexican Americans themselves had generally used the term in a derogatory manner to refer to the poorest class of ethnic Mexican workers. Suárez used it in a new way to challenge stereotypes and celebrate the diversity of the ethnic Mexican community. He implicitly criticized the romantic image of so-called Spanish Americans promoted both by Arizona boosters and by certain Mexican Americans themselves, writing that "it is doubtful that the Chicanos live in El Hoyo because of its scenic beauty." Finally, he suggested that loyalty to the United States did not require that Chicanos abandon their reverence for Mexico. "On Mexican Independence Day," he explained, "more than one flag is sworn allegiance to."[2]

His stories about Chicanos were a tribute to the border culture of south-central Arizona. In the decades that followed, ethnic Mexicans began to build upon this cultural identity as a source of pride and strength. For many, U.S. citizenship no longer required the rejection of one's cultural or ancestral connections, whether or not they referred to themselves as Chicanos. Activists in the 1960s and '70s generally moved away from the integrationist politics of the 1940s and '50s, having come to resent the notion that full political participation required the adoption of Anglo standards of national belonging. Instead, they promoted cultural pride and used more confrontational tactics to achieve their goals.

The Chicano and farmworker movements in Arizona, which were closely related, were not simply imported from other states, as some scholars have suggested or implied.[3] Arizona's Chicano movement was distinct from those in other communities such as Los Angeles, south Texas, and Denver in its relative absence of separatist sentiment and its deep connections to the state's history of labor activism in the mining towns.[4] One of the few scholars of Arizona's Chicano movement has characterized its goals as "militant integrationism" rather than nationalism.[5] Arizona activists, however, did not attempt to integrate simply through militant means nor, conversely, to form a separate community or nation. Instead they tried to change the very culture and meaning of American citizenship by celebrating their distinct language and cultural heritage while simultaneously demanding full membership in the body politic.

Borrowing from William V. Flores and Renato Rosaldo's idea that cultural citizenship may be defined as a "process that involves claiming membership in, and remaking, America," this chapter examines how Chicano activists in Arizona went beyond a struggle for legal inclusion to engage in a cultural and political struggle for dignity, identity, "belonging, entitlement, and influence." Arizona presents an interesting case study because of its large indigenous population. The Chicano emphasis on indigenous rather than Spanish roots had the potential to provide an impetus for Chicano-Indian cooperation. Arizona thus tested whether the Chicano movement's ideology of indigenismo could provide a foundation for true interethnic coalition building (discussed here and in Chapter 8).[6]

ORIGINS

Arizona's Chicano movement—more accurately, its array of intercon-
nected movements—emerged gradually through a dialogue between old
and new activists from Arizona and other southwestern states. It was
rooted, in part, in the state's long tradition of labor activism in the mining
towns. Arizona activists also retained a central focus on citizenship rather
than separation, though they attempted to revise what it meant to be a full
member of the body politic.

In the mid-1950s old forms of collective action began to evolve through
new interstate connections. In 1956 César Chávez and Fred Ross, who were
members of California's Community Service Organization (CSO), were in
Phoenix to organize barrio residents and register voters. Chávez had been
born in Arizona and so was familiar with the plight of Mexican Americans
and farmworkers in the state. Ross, too, was familiar with Arizona, since
he had worked there in the 1930s with the Farm Security Administration.
Once in Phoenix, Ross and Chávez located Manuel Peña, one of the community's most respected leaders, who had helped to desegregate schools
in Tolleson a few years earlier. Peña became head of the state's first CSO
branch.[7]

The CSO built upon older forms of activism such as voter registration
and citizenship training, while using new, more intimate and versatile
strategies that, in their ideal form, allowed local communities to define
their own needs and agendas. In certain respects CSO leaders echoed the
rhetoric of earlier organizations such as LULAC because of their focus on
voting and citizenship training. A CSO pamphlet that asked "What makes
a nation indivisible?" answered thus: "Citizenship, with its assurance of
protection of home and family when it assures justice and a voice in the
government." The CSO also moved away from earlier, assimilationist mod-
els of organizing. Whereas Vesta and LULAC had focused almost entirely
on the concerns of U.S. citizens, the CSO actively recruited immigrants.
It also defended the interests of Mexican nationals by contesting, for example, the mass deportations during Operation Wetback in 1954. Finally,
it conducted citizenship and health training in Spanish as well as English
and encouraged local communities to identify the issues most important
to them, rather than imposing a top-down agenda.[8]

CSO activists from California provided crucial training for future leaders
of Arizona's farmworker and Chicano movements. As Manuel Peña remembered, with the help of Chávez and Ross he and the Phoenix CSO initiated "projects for learning English, becoming citizens, improving neigh-

borhoods, and registering to vote." Between September 12 and the closing of voter registration for November elections on October 1, 1956, they signed up 1,556 voters in Phoenix barrios. They also held a series of house meetings to discuss the CSO and to determine which issues Arizona's ethnic Mexicans felt were most important. Soon, CSO chapters emerged throughout south-central Arizona, in Tempe, Mesa, and in the rural towns of Casa Grande, Chandler, Coolidge, and Glendale.[9]

The Yaqui/Mexican-American town of Guadalupe serves as a good example of how CSO-style politics functioned and how CSO activists attempted to keep local needs and goals at the forefront. In 1960 Guadalupe was typical of other rural, farm-worker communities in south-central Arizona. It lacked basic services and infrastructure, had no sewer system, paved streets, stop signs, or garbage pickup, and a single county sheriff's car serviced the community of about five thousand.[10] As an unincorporated town, it had no access to state or federal aid for cities, to state or federal revenue-sharing funds, or to state sales and gasoline taxes.[11] By the mid-1960s, according to one researcher, seventy-nine Yaqui families, along with thirty-three families of varying indigenous origins (mostly O'odham), lived on the original 40-acre site that had been placed in trust for the Yaquis in 1914. About ten Mexican-American families also lived on what had become known as the forty acres, but most lived either in the newer neighborhoods on the town's outskirts or in the 92-acre Biehn colony, still held in trust by the Presbyterian Church. Mexican Americans made up about two-thirds of the local population.[12]

The Catholic and Presbyterian churches, which had long served as important meeting places for Yaquis, O'odham, and ethnic Mexicans, were catalysts for interethnic coalition building. In June 1960 Father Fidelis Kuban, a member of the progressive Arizona Council of Churches' Migrant Ministry, invited Lauro García, a student at Arizona State University, to move to Guadalupe to teach catechism classes and to help organize community members to address problems related to poverty, unemployment, and a lack of health care.[13] García helped establish the Guadalupe Health Council shortly after his arrival. Members of the council cleaned and painted the local health clinic and lobbied the county to double the number of monthly clinics to two. Soon they expanded their activities into politics. In 1962 there were only 180 registered voters in Guadalupe partly because of the state's literacy test and the absence of a local polling place. The health council gathered enough signatures to create a new Guadalupe precinct, dedicated in June of that year.[14]

As the health council began to have more influence in the community, the minister at the local Presbyterian church contacted Fred Ross in order to enhance existing organizing efforts. When Ross arrived in Guadalupe in April 1964, he located community leaders associated with the health council and the Young Christian Workers, including Lauro García. He arranged a series of house meetings so residents could voice their opinions on community problems.[15]

Women were instrumental in these early efforts. They played a central role as hosts of the house meetings, bringing their experience as homemakers and community caretakers to politics, while bringing politics into their homes. Esther Cota recalled that she and other women associated with the Young Christian Workers helped compile a list of grievances related to the safety of their homes and their neighborhoods. Women also worked alongside men as voter registrars, increasing the number of voters to 715 from 180. Ross accompanied Lauro García to visit a county supervisor to explain how many voters had registered. As a result of that meeting, according to García, Guadalupe soon received funding for a resident deputy sheriff, and the county began to install pavement and stop signs on the main roads. The health council then changed its name to the Guadalupe Organization (GO) to reflect its increasingly broad political and economic goals.[16] Guadalupe thus served as a small but important example of interethnic, grass-roots organizing between Yaquis and ethnic Mexicans.

The CSO was not alone in inspiring grassroots activism in Arizona. The American Coordinating Council on Political Education (ACCPE) also grew out of a combination of homegrown and out-of-state influences. It began as a local branch of the interstate Political Association of Spanish-Speaking Organizations (PASO) founded in Victoria, Texas, in 1961. In Texas, PASO paid the poll taxes of Mexican Americans, registered voters, and worked with the Democratic Party to campaign for Mexican-American candidates. José Angel Gutiérrez, who would eventually become the leader of the Raza Unida Party in Texas, has suggested that PASO's efforts in the summer of 1962 represented "the beginnings of Chicano power." As a young man not yet of voting age, Gutiérrez was drawn to PASO because it "stated up front that the group was political," because its name expressed pride in the Spanish language, and especially because "they spoke of gringo injustice and implored us as Chicanos to do something about it."[17]

PASO took on a more moderate form in Arizona. Hoping to extend its influence beyond Texas, it held its first interstate meeting in Phoenix in 1961, inviting leaders from the city's Vesta organization, the Alianza Hispano Americana, and local chapters of LULAC and the CSO. Carlos McCormick of the Alianza became the executive secretary of PASO, and

Eugene Marín became one of four local vice presidents. Marín and others instilled Arizona's branch with a different agenda and ideology than the Texas branch had, reflecting their belief in self-improvement and accommodation—ideals that Marín had first promoted through Vesta. Arizona organizers soon decided to change the name of their local chapter to the American Coordinating Council on Political Education, in part because they did not agree with the priority PASO placed on preserving the Spanish language and engaging in confrontational politics. Marín became the ACCPE's president. Speaking to the U.S. Civil Rights Commission in 1962, he described the council's strategy as a "program of intense political education" intended to "give these citizens broader perspective and higher aspirations to compete in all of the fields of endeavor in our country."[18]

Arizona's ACCPE thus turned away from PASO's emphasis on reinforcing Chicano culture and language. Its leaders endorsed political candidates, just as PASO did in Texas. Marín, however, felt that Mexican Americans had to change themselves more than Arizona's political culture. In the process, he argued, they would improve the public image of Hispanics and earn acceptance as equal U.S. citizens. He declared, "Neither Phoenix, nor this Nation, can any longer afford the luxury of second-class citizenship. Our survival as a free society is being tested on this very point." To emphasize the importance of citizenship training, the ACCPE adopted the slogan Helping to Make Citizens Citizens.[19]

For a brief period, the ACCPE was successful in helping elect Mexican-American candidates. Tapping into existing networks such as Vesta, the Alianza Hispano-Americana, Viva Kennedy clubs, and labor unions, the ACCPE expanded to about twenty-five hundred members in ten different chapters throughout the state. Marín personally traveled from town to town to help establish many of these locals, having come to the conclusion that Mexican Americans were "being used" by both the Democratic and Republican parties. Still, rather than form an independent party, the ACCPE worked to influence the two-party system from within.[20]

Chapters of the ACCPE evolved into unique variations depending upon the cultures of local communities. In the mining town of Miami, for example, union members worked with the nascent local chapter of the ACCPE to run a slate of Mexican-American candidates to the town council. The new chapter became an amalgamation of the ACCPE and of preexisting networks associated with the mining unions. Immediately before the ACCPE arrived in the community, a police officer had beaten a Mexican-American resident. As Otto Santa Anna, a member of the Teamsters Union, later explained, "Police brutality, intimidation, and violations of one's civil rights was the order of the day in 1962. . . . The beating this man took was the last straw." Because of a history of intimidation and voting restrictions, Santa Anna found that "we first had to convince the Hispanic that the right to register to vote was guaranteed by the U.S. Constitution. Many knew this, though they also knew that opposition to local authority mean[t] walking in fear of verbal or physical retaliation." They managed to register 1,056 voters, and then ran a slate of six candidates, among whom were Santa Anna and the local union president. The ACCPE slate won three of seven seats on the council.[21]

By the mid-1960s, however, more and more Mexican Americans were voicing their dissatisfaction with the assimilation strategies of the ACCPE and similar organizations. In the same year as the Miami election, a radio broadcaster in Phoenix, Grace Gil Olivarez, criticized ACCPE President Eugene Marín while testifying beside him before the Civil Rights Commission. Olivarez felt that Marín's self-identification as Spanish American was a rejection of his Mexican heritage. In fact, she placed much of the blame for the continuing poverty and discrimination of the working class on middle-class Mexican Americans such as Marín. As she put it, "Personally, I feel that the Mexican Americans are to blame—that group of the Mexican Americans that has acquired a professional or semiprofessional status; that group that resents being called the Mexican American and claims they are Spanish American, Spanish-speaking, or of Spanish origin; that group that takes pride in saying that neither they nor their children speak Spanish, and are quick to admit this because they are ashamed of their heritage."[22]

Her comments reflected the opinions of a growing number of young Chicanas/os in the 1960s. Many felt that Mexican Americans who deemphasized their Mexican heritage and refused to speak Spanish implicitly accepted Mexicans' lower status. As Olivarez put it, "By admitting that they do not speak Spanish they are admitting that being a Mexican is the equivalent of being inferior." To the contrary, she asserted, the protection of Mexican culture was critical to the struggle for equality. Mexican Americans, she argued, should fight to preserve their "very rich culture," rather than leave it behind in their struggle for full citizenship. "A failure to do so," she concluded, is "harmful to this Nation or, should I say, 'our' Nation because, regardless of how anyone feels about us, we are American citizens."[23]

Ironically, even Olivarez partly based her claim for being fully American on her whiteness. As she said, "I sure hope this small group of prejudiced Anglos learn[s] to know us, and start[s] out by finding out what race we belong to. We happen to belong to the white race; yet we find people talking about Orientals, Negroes, whites, and Mexican Americans as if we were a race all by ourselves." She did not mention Arizona's indigenous population alongside these other racialized groups, perhaps because she feared reminding the commission of the Indian ancestry of most ethnic Mexicans. Not until later in the decade would a new group of young activists dispense altogether with this equation of whiteness with citizenship.[24]

Because the ACCPE and the CSO remained focused on citizenship, job training, and voter registration, many people who had begun their activist careers within these organizations grew frustrated with them and began to branch off to organize in other ways. The founder of Phoenix's CSO chapter, Manuel Peña, followed in the footsteps of Fred Ross and César Chávez in California and abandoned the organization in 1963. Peña, like Chávez, felt that the CSO did not adequately address class issues such as wages, working conditions, and the right to bargain collectively. In the months that followed, he attempted to organize a farmworkers union in Maricopa County. Soon, however, he wrote to Chávez that after signing up 212 members, some of his union officers had undermined the effort through poor management. Frustrated, he turned to other issues in 1964, saying that "there just does not seem to be enough hours in the day to work at it."[25]

Others took up union organizing in the years that followed. In 1965 the Migrant Ministry of the Arizona Council of Churches spearheaded a new labor organization from which a more effective unionization drive would emerge. That year Rev. Jim Lundgren of the Migrant Ministry applied for a grant from the Labor Department to establish the Migrant Opportunity Program (MOP). The federal government prohibited MOP leaders from union organizing as long as they received funding from the Office of Economic Opportunity (OEO). Instead, they provided adult education and job training to help farmworkers adapt to the changing economy and were soon operating in Maricopa, Pima, Pinal, Cochise, and Navajo counties. In May, MOP organized a training session in Tolleson at which Fred Ross and César Chávez were the featured speakers. They brought with them an ideology that challenged the limited role the program was permitted to take in offering aid to farmworkers.[26]

While the Migrant Opportunity Program steered clear of direct union organizing, it provided early experiences for women and men who would become leaders in Arizona's interrelated United Farm Workers (UFW) and Chicano movements. Carolina Hernández and Gustavo Gutiérrez attended the early sessions with Ross and Chávez and helped form the Stanfield labor organization, which provided basic services to farmworkers. In 1965

Gutiérrez made several trips to California where he observed the early stages of the famous Delano strike and participated in the 1966 Easter march to Sacramento. The march, with its combined symbolism of labor protest, folk Catholicism, and political empowerment, had a profound effect on him. After returning to Arizona, he continued to correspond with Chávez. His experience with the UFW made him grow increasingly frustrated with the federal guidelines that did not allow the Migrant Opportunity Program to organize a union.[27]

Gutiérrez and a number of other Arizona activists soon formed their own union. Working from Tolleson and utilizing CSO tactics, they held house meetings and walked door-to-door in rural neighborhoods and labor camps. Because Chávez and other UFW activists in California were absorbed with the five-year strike in Delano, they provided little direct help to Arizona's organizers before 1969. They did, however, enlist activists such as Gutiérrez to participate in the nationwide boycott against grapes in Arizona stores which, in turn, inspired a growing number of Arizonans to become activists. The boycott and picketing also fostered new connections between rural and urban activists who were concerned with poor housing, education, political representation, and urban poverty.[28]

By 1968 a diverse network of Mexican-American leaders in Arizona formed a rough consensus that political inclusion, economic opportunity, and cultural pride were equally important, interrelated goals. Mexican Americans from around the state, including Lauro García of the Guadalupe Organization and Gustavo Guttiérrez of the UFW, among others, gathered for a meeting in Phoenix in January which they called the "Statewide Consultation on Mexican-American Concerns." Attendees agreed upon a list of fifteen needs. They prefaced the list by saying that "the entire community, especially Anglo culture, needs to understand the background, history, and culture of Mexican Americans, and to accept the culture and language, to the extent of becoming bi-lingual." To achieve this goal, they pledged to promote an "improved self-image by Mexican Americans, lifting up cultural heritage to discover better self-cultural identity." The statement suggested not only that ethnic Mexicans should preserve their own culture but that all citizens should work toward bilingualism and multiculturalism. Mexican Americans were now demanding that long-held cultural prerequisites for full citizenship be changed.[29]

The attendees went further, listing a number of very specific goals. To "overcome Anglo and English language bias" they vowed to revise laws such as the Arizona literacy test (which remained on the books despite the 1965 Voting Rights Act) and a state law that prohibited bilingual education. With the help of external pressure from the federal government after the passage of the Bilingual Education Act, they paved the way for the first bilingual education pilot program at Phoenix Union High School in the fall of 1968. They also hoped to reform the Wagner Act to protect agricultural workers, while encouraging the development of new institutions to provide better job training and placement services. Finally, they called for better "indigenous leadership" by local Mexican Americans, cooperation among various Chicano institutions, "greater concern for youth," counseling in Spanish for those seeking public services, and comprehensive health care for the poor.[30]

There were, however, cracks in the consensus. One of the most forceful critiques came from a member of Phoenix's LULAC chapter. Narcisa Espinoza criticized the patriarchal rhetoric of male activists at the conference, the relegation of women to the background in Mexican-American organizations, and the absence of specific references to women's concerns in the list of needs. According to the conference minutes, only she broached the subject of women's roles. As she put it, "Since so much of this reference has been made to the machismo I have not heard very much about the *madrecita* [a term of endearment for a mother]. After all, is this a forgotten role?" When she asked, "Can a woman become a leader?" there was no response from the mostly male participants, as recorded in the minutes of the meeting. The silence reflected a broader failure around the Southwest to acknowledge the distinct problems women experienced, and to permit women to speak out publicly for the Chicano movement.[31]

Silence also greeted the possibility of reaching out to other ethnic groups. Only briefly did conference attendees mention the possibility of interethnic mobilization, but when they did the discussion was infused with a contradictory spirit of resentment toward ethno-racial groups perceived to be favored by federal agencies. Polo M. Rivera at first seemed to offer a foundation for interethnic coalition building when he declared that the basic needs of Mexican Americans were "in reality no different than the Negro or the Indian or any other disadvantaged group." Rivera followed this up, however, by declaring that "war on poverty" programs were "biased toward Negroes" and were designed "to cater to and pacify" them. Mexican Americans, he argued, did not need to be pacified, as blacks perhaps did: "I can take you into neighborhoods in Phoenix and have you talk to people and they will tell you, 'We do not want to get involved in riots; we are proud; we have a heritage; we fight for our freedom, we came here as settlers and explorers, we did not come here as slaves.'" Rivera thus echoed the political rhetoric common to Arizona's Anglos that made one's ancestors' status as settlers or explorers a prerequisite for full citizenship, relegating those of presumably less noble or indigenous origins to second-class status. The comments did not bode well for interethnic coalition building.[32]

Other disagreements emerged when many of the same activists converged for a second consultation six months later. During that meeting some attendees, including Lauro García, emphasized the importance of collective grassroots activism, while others, such as Eugene Marín, continued to stress education and self-improvement. Marín also raised concerns that identity politics might lead to the creation of "an apartheid system by ourselves and for ourselves." Gustavo Gutiérrez of the UFW once again made a call for labor activism, and he was the only member of the conference to question the Vietnam War publicly. He also felt that education was important, but unlike Marín he argued that the educational system itself had to be seriously reformed to better serve a diverse society.[33]

Finally there was disagreement about political party affiliation. Some members sympathized with efforts in South Texas to create a third party called El Partido de La Raza Unida (Party of the United People/Race). Most, however, rejected the idea. Rev. Trinidad Salazar, for example, suggested that "if this movement, La Raza Unida, is going to become a political movement, well it is death because immediately there will be division. . . . So La Raza Unida will become La Raza Desunida (disunited people/race)." Most attendees expressed loyalty to the Democratic Party, although Marín, who would eventually declare himself a Republican, complained that many Democratic leaders "used the vote of the Mexican American as if they were a bunch of sheep." At one level, then, the conference showed that much work had to be done to reach agreement over the direction of Chicano activism. And yet, from another angle, the meeting evinced a new vitality of debate among Mexican Americans—a debate that would spawn more assertive grassroots activism in the years to come.[34]

THE STUDENT MOVEMENT AND CHICANOS POR LA CAUSA

The years 1967–1969 were pivotal to Arizona's Chicano movement. In 1967 students at the University of Arizona formed the Mexican American Student Association; the next year, a group of Chicano students at Arizona State University formed the Mexican American Student Organization (MASO). Not long thereafter, activists from college campuses, the United Farm Workers, and Phoenix barrios began to meet in south Phoenix homes, forming the core of a new organization called Chicanos por La Causa (CPLC). Among the participants were Gustavo Gutiérrez of the

UFW, Richard Zazueta of MOP, Lauro García of the Guadalupe Organization, and Alfredo Gutiérrez and Manuel Marín of MASO.[35] These organizations would serve as the heart of the regional Chicano movement for the next several years. They would adopt new, often confrontational tactics to achieve their goals, while proclaiming more clearly than ever that cultural difference could serve as the basis for, rather than an obstacle to, full and equal citizenship.

The rise of these groups corresponded with the increasing urbanization of Arizona's Chicano population. By 1970 fully 81 percent of Arizona's Mexican Americans lived in cities, closely corresponding to the 82 percent of the Anglo population who did and far greater than the 29.6 percent of Indians who lived in cities. (In considering why Chicanos and Indians tended not to organize together, this demographic disparity is important.) Urbanization resulted in new opportunities in work and education. Mexican-American men in cities became twice as likely to work as professionals (from 3.5 percent to 7.5 percent) and were nearly three times as likely to have clerical jobs (3.7 percent to 9.1 percent). Women experienced similar changes in employment, surpassing men in acquiring professional jobs, largely as teachers. Male urban professionals and clerical workers earned a median income of $8,559 and $7,516 respectively, significantly higher than the average of $3,413 in rural areas and $4,766 in the mining towns.[36]

Beyond seeking more skilled and better-paying jobs in Phoenix, Tucson, and their satellite towns, many young people moved to the cities to attend universities and community colleges. In general, education levels among urban Chicanos substantially surpassed those in rural towns and farm areas. Chicanos in the cities completed, on average, 9.7 years of formal education, one year more than those in smaller towns and three years more than those who lived and worked on the regional farms. The differences for women were not as great but were still significant. Urban Chicanas attended school on average for 8.8 years in the city, as opposed to 7.9 in regional farming areas. More dramatically, Mexican Americans in urban areas (Phoenix and Tucson) were twice as likely to attend college than were those in rural areas.[37]

Maricopa was Arizona's most populous county, and by 1970 it had the largest ethnic Mexican population (140,607) in the state, surpassing the combined populations of ethnic Mexicans in the three other counties in south-central Arizona—Pima (82,667), Pinal (24,813), and Santa Cruz (10,792). Phoenix was both an agricultural center and an urban metropolis, and thus the ideal arena in which to examine the connections between the urban and rural movements and to explore how the diversity of the

Mexican-American population impacted the cultural and civil rights struggles of the era.[38]

Young men and women from the mining towns had much to offer their urban counterparts in Phoenix, particularly as union organizers. Alfredo Gutiérrez, for example, frequently attended union meetings with his father while growing up in Miami before he moved to Tempe to attend Arizona State. He recalled that "there weren't classes in union organizing, there wasn't indoctrination, but the whole town was an organizational tool." Growing up in a mining town helped to prepare him to become a campus activist. "You understand at a very young age why you were striking, why you didn't cross the picket line," he said. Other Chicanos, including Geneva Duarte Escovedo and Manuel Marín, also credited their experiences in the mining towns for their early education as activists. Joe Eddie López, a Phoenix native who would work closely with these newcomers from the mining towns, felt that "*los mineros* became among the articulate leaders" of the Chicano movement. "It was destined to happen," he explained, "but how long it would have evolved . . . it may have been a lot longer in coming."[39]

Chicano students at Arizona State were also influenced by activists in Tucson and from outside the state. In 1967 Sal Baldenegro led Chicanos at the University of Arizona to form the Mexican American Student Association. Baldenegro had lived in Los Angeles while attending El Camino College; he had returned to Tucson with a commitment to start an organization similar to those he had observed in California. Soon thereafter, in 1968, Alfredo Gutiérrez helped to organize the Mexican American Student Organization (MASO) at Arizona State.[40] Among the other early leaders were Arturo Rosales, an Arizona native and veteran who already had experience with the UFW, and Ed Pastor, who like Gutiérrez had grown up in the mining town of Miami. Gutiérrez later estimated that 90 percent of Arizona State students who initially decided to form the chapter of MASO "were from mining towns." Pastor remembered that their familiarity with labor unions allowed them to feel "very comfortable with the idea when people were talking about organizing at ASU."[41]

Not surprisingly, students from the mining towns initially focused their attention on labor. On November 20, 1968, MASO members wrote a formal letter of grievance to the administration at Arizona State, asking for a cancellation of its contract with Phoenix Linen and Towel Supply because of its pattern of subjecting ethnic Mexicans to "racial discrimination, substandard wages and inferior working conditions." The students pointed out that while 83 percent of those working for the company were Chicanos, "in the past 36 years one Chicano has been promoted to a supervisory position." MASO worked alongside other campus organizations, including a local chapter of the Young Socialist Alliance (YSA), an offshoot of Students for a Democratic Society, to form the Student Coalition for Justice. The coalition jointly collected about five thousand signatures in support of their cause and then led three hundred students in a march on the administration building to meet with President G. Homer Durham. A week after a two-day sit-in, officials from the university declared that they would not renew the contract the following year. The apparent success of the protest rapidly raised MASO's stature in the eyes of many students.[42]

Soon, MASO extended its activism beyond campus boundaries into Phoenix and the rural areas of Maricopa and Pinal counties. Alfredo Gutiérrez helped to organize urban laundry workers in Phoenix, and he and other student activists worked closely with UFW organizers such as Gustavo Gutiérrez. The students helped to set up pickets in front of Phoenix stores that sold Delano grapes.[43] The MASO newsletter often put farm labor issues at the top of its agenda. As one issue put it, "MASO has . . . pledged itself to continue helping the *Huelga* [the strike] in any way that it can and has recently cooperated with the newly formed Phoenix-Tempe chapter of the Friends of the Farmworkers organization. This organization is dedicated to helping with the picketing of stores and raising money for food for the striking laborers." Their participation in the boycott persuaded the Arizona State Food Service to stop purchasing grapes.[44]

Even as they helped to organize workers on campus and off, many MASO members expressed discomfort with the socialist and/or nationalist leanings of other campus organizations like Young Socialist Alliance (YSA) and Chicano student organizations in other states. Alfredo Gutiérrez, the primary founder of MASO, distanced himself from the rhetoric of more radical activists. In 1968, before MASO was formally established, Gutiérrez had invited San Francisco activist Armando Valdez to visit the campus and encourage Chicanos to become politically active. While Gutiérrez credited Valdez for helping to spur the movement, he later admitted, "I just couldn't relate completely to his notion that Ho Chi Minh was a figure that we should emulate." Arturo Rosales also recalled that many members were uncomfortable with nationalism and Marxism. As a result, in late November, only weeks after the victory over the linen contract, MASO voted 42–3 to dissociate from the YSA by dissolving the Student Coalition for Justice. Nevertheless, most members took from YSA a dedication to democratic principles and decentralization of leadership, and members of the two groups often found themselves participating together in future protests—especially as part of the movement against the Vietnam War.[45]

MASO activists asserted pride in Chicano culture, but for the most part they did so without invoking separatist language. Their central concerns remained racial inequities in the workplace, ASU's poor record of admitting Chicano students, obstacles to political participation, and cultural pride.[46] They arranged a Chicano cultural week and pressured the university to establish a Chicano studies program. Even when discussing cultural issues, however, most MASO leaders emphasized the need to change mainstream institutions to be more inclusive and pluralistic, rather than demanding the formation of a separate Chicano nation. As Arturo Rosales explained to a student journalist in 1968, "Through the Chicano studies program, the Chicano people themselves can become aware of their own position and achieve cultural pride, which has been robbed by a society where, if you are a Chicano, you are inferior." When Arizona State refused to establish such a program, students grew less patient and more aggressive in their rhetoric. In 1970 a student activist suggested in an interview with the campus newspaper that "for years society neglected and raped our culture. . . . This university has not allowed the barrio people and the Chicano students here to initiate or have any input into university programs."[47]

MASO's goals were reformist rather than revolutionary, even if its tactics, including marches, protests, and sit-ins, were often provocative and confrontational. Still, it differed from earlier Mexican-American activism in Arizona with its greater emphasis on labor rights and culture. One MASO student conference featured workshops that encouraged the support of the grape boycott by harnessing what it called student power potential. Two faculty members from the Spanish Department spoke about preserving the cultural heritage of Chicano students, while Noel Stowe, a professor of Latin American history, spoke in favor of a Chicano studies program. Lauro García closed the meeting by discussing community organizing tactics among Yaquis and ethnic Mexicans in Guadalupe, elaborating on the strategies of earlier organizations like the CSO. García encouraged the students to follow similar tactics in the barrios.[48]

In late 1968 and early 1969 as some organizers graduated, several Arizona State students and alumni decided to branch off from MASO in order to focus on issues of discrimination off-campus, and they soon began to work with activists in south Phoenix to form the core of Chicanos por La Causa. By April 1968, Joe Eddie López, a steamfitter and member of Phoenix's construction workers union, Local 469, emerged as one of the primary leaders of the new organization. A diverse group of activists attended the early meetings. Participants elected Rosie López and Gustavo Gutiérrez president and vice president, respectively, of the executive committee.[49] An early CPLC proposal criticized the top-down approach of existing OEO programs and argued that "to be effective, efforts must come from within the barrios." Women and men alike played important roles in the CPLC, but as with many other Chicano organizations, it was the men who held the most visible positions as leaders and spokesmen. As Rosie López, who was married to Joe Eddie López, recalled, "We [women] did a lot of the work, we did the cooking and the calling. We did the mobilizing and the guys, once everybody was in place, the guys would get up there and speak."[50]

Labor rights and urban living conditions occupied most of CPLC's attention in its early months, reflecting the experiences of its members.[51] Soon, however, a crisis at Phoenix Union High School turned attention toward the issue of education in inner-city schools. In August and September a series of fights broke out between black and Chicano students at Phoenix Union (Anglos were a minority at the school). Members of the downtown and south Phoenix Mexican-American community met to discuss the issue, and CPLC took the lead in urging the school administration to resolve the problems that had led to the conflicts. When the administration did little, CPLC helped to organize a protest march on September 15. The march, involving about three hundred protesters, began at the Santa Rita Center, the home office of the CPLC, and ended at the Phoenix Municipal Building.[52]

The protesters presented a list of nine demands to city officials. First, they asked for more security guards at the high school, "with equal representation from the Chicano community," and that any student who infringed on the rights of other students be "promptly dealt with." The other demands, however, focused on broad concerns related to general inequities in the school system and stressed the need to reform the curriculum to address cultural concerns. Although the high school had recently instituted a small, pilot bilingual education program according to the 1968 Bilingual Education Act, CPLC members felt much more had to be done. They demanded that the school hire more Chicano counselors and teachers (only one of eighteen counselors was Chicano) and that Chicano teachers be hired to teach in the Minority Studies Program. They created their own citizen's curriculum committee to press for the implementation of the program. They also demanded that no student be faced with recrimination for participating in "Chicano leadership and social awareness." They viewed all of these steps as part of a larger goal to ensure that Chicano students and parents be recognized as "first-class citizens."[53]

School officials fanned the flames of discontent with their lackluster and at times racist responses. Certain administrators explicitly blamed the problems Mexican Americans faced in the schools on the students and their families. A 1962 report by the superintendent of Phoenix Elementary School, District One, had listed four problems faced by "minority children." These included their "cultural handicaps," their propensity for speaking Spanish, the "tendency of minorities to concentrate in their own separate residential areas," and the "failure of minority groups to recognize the importance of education." None of the issues placed any of the blame on institutional segregation or on the schools themselves, creating little impetus for reform.[54] Seven years later, as CPLC protested against Phoenix Union High School, little had changed. One month after the September march, Donald Covey, a consultant to the social studies program, echoed the earlier assessment that Chicanos had failed themselves: "Being oriented by passion and subjectivity, the Spanish-speaking person lacks continuity and perseverance in attaining the same goals as the man of action symbolized by the Anglo-American."[55]

Phoenix Union Principal Robert Dye dragged his feet in response to most of the demands by parents and students. Beyond agreeing not to punish students who had engaged in the protests, Dye addressed only the issue of campus security by saying, "If it's security they want, it's security they'll get." The mainstream press did not help matters, blaming the protests on "racial strife" and reinforcing the widespread belief that the real problem was the tendency of Chicanos and blacks toward irrationality and violence.[56] A flurry of newspaper editorials criticized the activists for engaging in uncivil protest. The *Phoenix Gazette,* for example, commented, "Demands which approach the force of ultimatums—the non-negotiable demand, for example—are avoided by wise and sober men for the reason that when the answer is no, there is nothing left but to fight or run."[57]

The response by school administrators energized parents and students to demand reformation of the school district from the inside out. Chicano students and community leaders organized a parent-student boycott committee and carried out a series of new protests and walkouts. They complained of "rotten curriculum, incompetent administration, and a lack of community involvement in policymaking decisions."[58] School administrators met on several occasions with representatives of the boycott committee, forming a citizens advisory committee to analyze problems. Once again, however, the only real solution administrators offered was to increase security. In response, Joe Eddie López ran in the 1970 election for the school board; he was defeated.[59]

The Phoenix Union boycott propelled the CPLC into the center of Arizona's developing Chicano movement. CPLC opened its doors to all members of the ethnic Mexican community, rarely engaging in the kind of separatist rhetoric that was common in organizations like the Crusade for Justice in Denver or the Centro de Acción Social Autónomo in Los Angeles. Rather than criticize those who refused to identify as Chicanos, CPLC leaders welcomed them, declaring that "Chicanos, La Raza [Unida], Mexican Americans, the Spanish-speaking—these are the people of Chicanos por La Causa." By 1970, having gained federal tax-exempt status and financial support from the Southwest Council of La Raza, they developed separate branches to engage in barrio planning, housing improvements, economic development, and education. They also actively supported Chicano-owned businesses.[60] To keep in touch with residents of the barrios, they held regular, CSO-style house meetings. They worked with the Department of Housing and Urban Development to provide more low-income housing and organized conferences to "help Chicano families better manage their financial and personal commitments in order to be able to buy their own home." Their economic development division provided advice to develop a "sound economic base" for the Chicano community, conducting market surveys, feasibility studies, and financing assistance among other services.[61]

CPLC also initiated a variety of cultural programs. Its leaders were highly critical of mainstream, Anglo-dominated political culture and were "dedicated to supporting the Chicano community in its struggle to bring about systematic change in those institutions which continue to oppress Chicanos."[62] Indeed, its programs were designed not only to educate Chicanos to become good citizens but also to change the very meaning of citizenship and national belonging. The Barrio Youth Project, for example, which was started in October 1969, worked to "develop and implement creative and educational programs for and by barrio youth," and to promote youth services and seminars. Alfredo Gutiérrez initially directed the program. Influenced by California's farmworker and student movements, the youth project also helped youth write and perform their own brief *actos* (skits), including "satirical attacks on those institutions which have oppressed the Chicano community," and reenactments of events important "to the Chicano culture and heritage."[63]

In October 1970, a year after the first protests at Phoenix Union, CPLC boycotted the school, condemning the lack of sufficient action by officials. This time the boycott committee demanded that Superintendent Seymour and Principal Dye resign. Half of the twenty-five hundred students at the school stayed home during the peak days of the boycott in October. Joe Eddie López warned that Chicanos would pull their students out permanently and establish their own schools if the administration failed to address their demands, and Alfredo Gutiérrez suggested that they would begin a recall of the school board. The CPLC received the endorsement of about one hundred teachers belonging to the Arizona Association of Mexican-American Educators and enjoyed direct encouragement by Chicano leaders from around the Southwest. At the height of the boycott, Corky González of Denver's Crusade for Justice visited Phoenix to lend his support, and members of the Teatro Popular from UCLA read poetry and performed satirical skits.[64]

Some school officials grudgingly acknowledged the need for reform. School board member Don Jackson cited the success of the pilot bilingual education program: while the average Chicano dropout rate for the district was about 20 percent, only 1 percent of the one hundred Chicanos enrolled in the bilingual program had dropped out during the previous year. Others, however, pointed out that bilingual education was not the only solution. At the height of the boycott, on October 16, Mexican-American educators held a bilingual education awareness institute in Phoenix in which Thomas Carter, a resident scholar at the U.S. Civil Rights Commission, gave a speech entitled "Way Beyond Bilingual Education." He called it a "feeble first step," stressing that the entire curriculum needed to be changed. "Any history that omits a realistic portrayal of the Mexican-American and Spanish involvement in past and present society is not only false but dangerous," he explained. He then offered his own definition of American citizenship, suggesting that those who participated in boycotts, sit-down strikes, and marches were "citizens in the best democratic tradition of the United States and Mexico." The comment earned loud applause from conference attendees.[65]

The boycott lasted officially until November 2, at which time school officials agreed to cooperate in a study to be conducted by members of the parent-student boycott committee. In response CPLC leaders backed away from the demand that the school superintendent resign.[66] A new committee conducted an investigation of the school, and it issued its report in May 1971. The report emphasized the familiar theme that the schools "are unresponsive to the needs of these citizens," and it offered thirty-seven specific recommendations. Among them were that counseling should be improved; students should no longer be tracked into vocational programs; security and other staff should reflect the "ethnic patterns of student population"; all written reports from school officials should be available in Spanish as well as English; teachers and staff should attend workshops on inner-city life; and the school should maintain an active dialogue with the community it served. When school administrators accepted the recommendations, at least in principle, CPLC activists agreed to stop engaging in mass protests. While it was unclear precisely when and how the recommendations would be implemented, CPLC had taken a step toward asserting its own definition of citizenship: it should be active, vigilant, participatory, and culturally inclusive.[67]

As CPLC pursued its agenda in the barrios, MASO evolved as well. In March 1971 MASO changed its name to reflect its new affiliation with California's Movimiento Estudiantil de Chicanos de Aztlán (MEChA). A trip to a Chicano student conference in Long Beach, California, in the summer of 1970 inspired the change. As Jerry Pastor, the co-chair of the new MEChA branch at Arizona State, recalled, "That summer we went to Long Beach and that is where we heard about MEChA. We wanted to connect somewhere because the isolation was difficult here on campus. We felt we were vulnerable, we were recognized in our classroom as activists, and felt that our degrees could be held back." As one scholar has put it, the students who attended the meeting "were captivated by the reappropriation of Spanish, the defiant anti-assimilationist stance and the urgent need to gain political control of the barrio."[68]

At Arizona State the MEChA chapter soon began to publish a newsletter, *Voz de Aztlán*, which rejected the relatively moderate language of MASO and CPLC by directly invoking the rhetoric of Chicano nationalism. The first issue explained the significance of Aztlán, a mythical place of origin to the north of the Aztec empire in central Mexico. For Chicanos, the Plan Espiritual de Aztlán (spiritual plan of Aztlán), which had first been adopted in March 1969 during the Chicano Liberation Youth Conference in Denver, represented a unification of identity and a common connection to the Aztec past (real and imagined) and to the indigenous roots of Chicanos in the Southwest. The article explained that Chicano nationalism was a "prerequisite to assert our proper role on our communities and be given the respect we deserve." The newsletter criticized the reformist politics of other organizations, and a poem entitled "Tío Tomas" (involving Spanish wordplay on the African-American stereotype of the Uncle Tom) accused those who called themselves Mexican Americans of bowing to Anglo authority.[69] In the second issue, Ruben Salazar, a well-known journalist in Los Angeles, wrote that "a Chicano is a Mexican-American with a non-Anglo image of himself. He resents being told Columbus discovered America when the Chicanos' ancestors, the Mayans and the Aztecs, founded highly sophisticated civilizations centuries before Spain financed the Italian explorer's trip to the new world."[70]

While MEChA activists ideologically embraced their indigenous heritage (*indigenismo*), it is important to note that they emphasized mostly the Aztec antecedents to Chicano culture rather than connections to the tens of thousands of Indians, among them Yaquis, Tohono O'odham, Pimas, and Maricopas, who lived in contemporary Arizona. As Salazar's article suggests, the Aztecs were an alluring symbol largely because they represented the historical presence of a powerful, "highly sophisticated civilization" before Europeans arrived in the Americas. Somewhat paradoxically, this brand of indigenismo drew upon a rather narrow, ethnocentric definition of civilization characterized by urbanization, centralization, hierarchical government, and empire. This ideology attracted little direct interest from the mostly rural indigenous population of Arizona.[71] With the exception of some small, local movements, such as in South Tucson and Guadalupe, Chicanos and Indians maintained mostly separate institutions and focused on divergent goals. This separation reflected the limitations of Chicano indigenismo, the demographic differences of the indigenous and Chicano populations (mostly rural/mostly urban), and the distinct location of each group in the regional political economy (see Chapter 8). Chicanos, then, even while embracing their indigenous past, held onto their ethnic distinction from Indians in the present.

This separation occasionally expressed itself as outright resentment. In October 1974, for example, MEChA at Arizona State sent a letter to the administration protesting that Indians were being treated more favorably than Chicanos on campus. They complained of "preferential treatment of one minority over the other," citing the fact that the Native American Club had its own operational center for which it paid no rent, and that the university financed a coordinator to deal with Indian but not with Chicano issues. MEChA's goal was reasonable enough: to establish benefits similar to those that Indian students received. In doing so, however, it painted itself as a competitor to (rather than a collaborator with) Native students, and it adopted a rhetorical opposition to racial preferences that potentially played into the hands of those who were against affirmative action and other progressive policies. On occasion, Chicanos and Indians on campus worked together, and in the 1990s, they would form what they referred to as the Xicano indigenous movement to put the ideology of indigenismo into direct practice. But for the most part, the ideological and institutional gulf between the two remained profound.[72]

At the same time, MEChA's sometimes hostile critiques of "hyphenated Americans" alienated longtime Mexican-American activists who might otherwise have provided more support. Eugene Marín, for example, who served as ASU's director of financial aid beginning in 1972, had always supported a moderate-to-conservative agenda in which education and self-help would lead to first-class citizenship, but he also remained open to new, progressive strategies of coalition building. As he put it, "Perhaps the time is right when the blacks, the Indians, the Mexican Americans as minorities are going to get together politically." He pointed out that while the ideology of Chicano nationalism might successfully raise the consciousness of students and inspire organizing, it failed to provide an ideological foundation for a broad-based coalition for change.[73]

Still, the rhetorical turn in *Voz de Aztlán* should not be accepted at face value as the voice of the majority of MEChA students at Arizona State. In fact, MEChA leaders continued to adopt an agenda similar to that of their predecessors at MASO—one that focused primarily on eliminating obstacles to equal employment, the education of Chicano youth, and ethnic pride and union organizing.[74] In 1972, for example, after the university administration refused to rectify inequities in the employment of Chicanos in the housing administration, between eighty and one hundred students protested during the inauguration of the new university president, John Schwada. They demanded, as MASO had, an end to discriminatory hiring practices along with a commitment to recruit more Chicano students, to establish a Chicano studies program, and to dismiss plans to raise admission standards. Some members of the YSA and the Student Koalition of Indian Natives (SKIN) showed up for the protest, but the latter steered clear of MEChA activists. One Indian graduate student who attended the protest told a reporter for the campus newspaper, "We don't mix with socialists or Chicanos. We're Indians and we've got our own problems." Indeed, the SKIN students were there to assert a separate and distinct agenda, including a Native American equal opportunity program and improvements to the existing Native American studies program.[75]

MEChA continued to engage in confrontational tactics into the mid-1970s, but the results of its activism were mixed. In March 1973 MEChA filed a complaint against Arizona State University before the Equal Employment Opportunity Commission (EEOC) for perpetuating a "pattern of discrimination" against Chicano employees. They followed this in 1975 with a complaint before the Office for Civil Rights of the U.S. Department of Health, Education, and Welfare and with a suit against ASU in federal district court to force it to follow its affirmative action program and initiate an aggressive recruitment policy.[76] In May the EEOC determined that the university "had engaged in a pattern of discrimination based on national origin against Chicanos or Mexican Americans." Because of the added pressure, President Schwada agreed, in principle, to enhance recruitment of Chicanos, and he began a search for a new, full-time affirmative action officer (it had been only a part-time position).[77] While Schwada permitted MEChA members to make recommendations for the position, however, he ultimately ignored them, hiring the assistant of the former part-time affirmative action officer over their vehement objections. It would take another five years for the university to institutionalize a Minority Student Recruitment and Retention Program.[78]

MEChA also continued to press for a Chicano studies program. The group succeeded in encouraging faculty to offer new Chicano studies courses and successfully pushed for the establishment of a Chicano section of ASU's Hayden Library. Not until 1995, however, would ASU establish its own Department of Chicana and Chicano Studies. Meantime, MEChA continued to work in cooperation with the CPLC and the United Farm Workers to fight for worker rights and equality off campus.[79]

One scholar has argued that Chicanos at ASU were moderate in their goals, compared with many student activists in California: "They were driven by practical concerns of political empowerment and economic advancement. Although some MEChA students employed revolutionary rhetoric to articulate their views, their goals at best reflected a militant integrationist perspective." This view needs revision because the integration was to occur on Chicano rather than Anglo terms. Chicano students refused to shed their culture, language, and identity in the struggle to achieve first-class citizenship and economic advancement. In effect, they demanded that the prerequisites and culture of citizenship be changed. This position was significantly different from that of earlier Mexican-American organizations, but it was not a complete reversal.[80]

THE UFW, ELECTORAL POLITICS, AND DECLINE

The United Farm Workers was more active in 1972 than at any other time in Arizona history, and yet that year also marked the beginning of its decline. In a battle over a new antilabor bill, the plight of Chicanos in the state was briefly cast into the national spotlight, bringing César Chávez, Dolores Huerta, and other well-known activists to Arizona to combat the measure. In the years that followed, the more radical rhetoric of the grassroots Chicano movement would subside, but in the process some of the more moderate goals and aspirations of the Chicano and farmworker movements would be achieved.

Arizona's legislature passed the antiunion Agricultural Employment Relations Act (HR 2134) with bipartisan support in May 1972. The law allowed courts to issue ten-day restraining orders to halt work stoppages during harvests, forbade workers to strike without first voting by secret ballot under the observance of a board appointed by the governor, prohibited unions from recruiting in the fields, limited primary boycotts to single growers, and outlawed secondary boycotts. It established criminal penalties for those who violated its provisions. Some of these were later altered by the courts (allowing, for example, a small number of picketers to engage in secondary boycotts) but for the most part, the law put up an enormous barrier against union organizing. Secondary boycotts and strikes during harvest season, when workers had the most collective bargaining power, had been the UFW's most powerful weapons in California. Without such weapons the union would be hobbled.[81]

Arizona's farmworkers and their supporters refused to accept defeat. Local activists associated with the UFW, CPLC, and MEChA worked directly with national leaders such as Chávez and Huerta to organize a large-scale protest against the new law and to support a drive to recall Governor Jack Williams. Opponents of the law targeted Williams in large part because of the unorthodox manner in which he signed the bill. He had ordered the Highway Patrol to deliver the bill to him within two hours after it was passed. This violated the custom of waiting at least one day to allow the attorney general to review new legislation. In protest, Chávez began what he called a fast of love. As he later explained, "We didn't want to keep fighting similar bills in other states. So we thought if we recalled this governor, got him voted out of office, the others would get a little religion." He also hoped to revitalize the farmworker struggle in the state. Chávez recalled that "in Arizona, the people were beaten. You could see the difference. Every time we talked about fighting the law, people would say, 'no se puede, no se puede'—it's not possible. It can't be done." To combat the growing pessimism, Dolores Huerta coined the phrase Sí, se puede (Yes, we can), which became the UFW's rallying cry.[82]

The recall campaign ultimately failed, but it raised the political consciousness of many Arizonans. The three-and-a-half-week fast by Chávez ended on June 4 after his doctors discovered that he had an erratic heartbeat. Arizona activists, however, continued to collect signatures and register voters. Chávez and other UFW organizers toured the state, "visiting Chicanos, Indians, farmworkers" and walking door-to-door "in the old CSO method." Eventually, they gathered 168,000 signatures. The state attorney general declared sixty thousand of those signatures invalid, but months later a federal court ruled that they were legal. Unfortunately, as Chávez recalled, "by that time it was too close to the general election to make a special recall election worthwhile."[83] Many activists continued to defy the new antilabor law. In October 1973, for example, over 125 workers from the UFW picketed Safeway stores in Phoenix, ignoring a court injunction. Many wore gags around their mouths to protest the injunction, which limited the number of picketers in front of any one store to fifteen and made it illegal to ask patrons to shop elsewhere.[84]

While the recall effort failed, it would provide long-term leverage in lobbying efforts and help elect a significant number of Mexican Americans into political office. Leaders of the campaign registered thousands of voters. One of its directors in Pima County claims to have registered close to one hundred thousand voters. While it is impossible to verify exactly how many new voters were registered as a direct result of the campaign, a comparison of overall registration numbers before and after 1972 provides some insight. Between 1970 and 1974, according to the secretary of state, the number of registered Arizona voters increased from 618,411 to 890,794. Certainly, this increase was not solely due to the registration drive, but evidence suggests that the campaign had played a meaningful role.[85]

It is important to acknowledge that injunctions and antilabor legislation were not the only threats to the union. The growers' practice of recruiting undocumented immigrants also interfered with organizing efforts. One source estimates that Arizona growers hired up to one hundred thousand Mexican nationals over the course of the decade. Most new immigrants had scant knowledge of the UFW, and after having traveled hundreds of miles to help provide for their families in Mexico, or having brought their families with them, they were not inclined to rock the boat. Still, some did join; among them was Demetrio Díaz. According to Díaz, a man named Alberto recruited him in his hometown, Cuamil, Michoacán, to work in the Arizona fields. Díaz borrowed fifteen hundred pesos from his grandfather, part of which he paid to a coyote who brought him and about twenty other men across the border to Casa Grande, Arizona. From there, labor recruiters from Arrowhead Ranch near Phoenix paid, in Díaz's words, "$80 per worker to several contractors who drive workers from a pick-up point in Casa Grande to the ranch"—a story that was confirmed by at least two other Mexican workers. Upon reaching the ranch, undocumented workers labored for "ten hours a day, six days a week" with wages averaging $30–$60 per week.[86]

Díaz was one of about two hundred Mexicans hired to break a UFW strike at Arrowhead Ranch in 1974. The day after Díaz arrived, the foreman ordered him and the others to work. When he protested that his feet were swollen and he was tired from the trip, the foreman responded that he would contact *la migra* (the INS) and have him shipped back to Mexico.

Díaz would hear many such threats in subsequent weeks. "The boss does all the work with illegals," he explained. "He never hires any others because we can't do anything to him. He kept us against our will. There's not one of us who doesn't have debts to the contractors." Debt, the fear of retribution and deportation, and the need to support their families kept most Mexican nationals from protesting. Díaz, who joined the UFW, was an exception.[87]

Thousands of Mexican-American farmworkers refused to join the UFW for reasons ranging from fear of retribution to the need to provide for their families. Manuel and Eva Acuña—a married couple who worked near Casa Grande—explained that while they had little respect for the growers and foremen, they chose to protest with their feet rather than join the union. Eva explained that her husband "never put up with a foreman, you know, trying to tell him this or that. So we moved a lot." Manuel took pride in his ability to provide for his family, boasting that he could pick a thousand pounds of cotton and earn thirty dollars per day. While Eva was more open to the UFW, she consented to her husband's wishes not to join. As she explained it, "I thought a lot of [César] Chávez, but my husband and I don't see the same things. . . . People would say that he was leading the migrant workers. He was fighting for 'em, you know, going through a lot. . . . But people didn't see it that way. In Chandler they kicked him out of there. They told him they were making good money."[88]

These stories demonstrate that antilabor laws and injunctions were not solely responsible for the relatively weak presence of the UFW in Arizona. The ethnic Mexican working class was diverse, consisting of new and old immigrants and of American citizens with varying ideologies. Mexican nationals were often preoccupied with maintaining a basic level of subsistence. Many held onto the hope that they could find their way out of farmwork altogether or return to their families in Mexico rather than expend their energies collectively protesting. Nevertheless, state organizers carried on the struggle throughout the 1970s with varying degrees of success. They continued to boycott California grapes and wines, and in 1977 they attempted to revitalize the farmworker movement through the formation of the Maricopa County Organizing Project followed by the Arizona Farm Workers Union (AFW) in 1978. These organizations led a few successful strikes but soon faced court injunctions and arrests for misdemeanor charges ranging from trespassing to disturbing the peace. The AFW signed contracts for approximately fifteen hundred workers by the end of the decade, but that number was too small to have much of an impact.[89]

Still, union organizing, especially the 1972 recall, left a lasting legacy on voter registration and electoral politics. The Chicano and farmworker movements created a new voting bloc of Mexican Americans and trained a new cadre of elected leaders. In 1965 only six Mexican Americans had run successfully to become state senators. After 1972, however, Chicano activists benefited greatly from the registration of thousands of new voters. In the years of the recall effort, MASO founder Alfredo Gutiérrez won election to the state senate, and Joe Eddie López, the former CPLC chairman, successfully ran for the Maricopa County Board of Supervisors. In 1991 he would become a state representative and in 1996 would be elected a state senator. Jerry Pastor also eventually ran successfully to become a state senator, and Manuel Marín, a state representative. In 1976 Ed Pastor, another member of CPLC, was elected to the Maricopa County Board of Supervisors. He would serve three terms before running successfully for U.S. Congress in 1991.[90] As early as 1974 there were eleven Mexican Americans in the state senate.[91]

The success of Democratic Chicano candidates helped to undermine the development of La Raza Unida Party in Arizona, but it did have a significant, albeit short-lived, presence in Tucson. Activists Sal Baldenegro, Raúl Grijalva, and Lupe Castillo, among others, believed that the Democrats there were insensitive to Chicano issues. Because Tucson had an Anglo majority and citywide voting, Raza Unida had few illusions about winning elections. As Grijalva put it, "We decided to go into elective politics more in the sense of an educational tool rather than an opportunity for winning." The Tucson activists formed a branch of Raza Unida in February 1971, and for the next three years they worked to influence the political process there. According to one of its national leaders, José Angel Gutiérrez, some Tohono O'odham in Tucson supported the party, but the extent of their involvement is unclear. Their platform included progressive measures such as national health care, community control of local institutions, and a federally guaranteed income. It also stressed the importance of bilingual and bicultural education and the formation of Chicano studies programs.[92]

Most Tucson Latinos supported the Democrats rather than Raza Unida. In a run for the city council in 1971, Baldenegro received 5,862 votes, losing by a wide margin to another Mexican American, Ruben Romero, who ran as a Democrat. The following year, Raúl Grijalva unsuccessfully ran for the Tucson school board. In 1974 he ran again as a Democrat for the same position and won, having abandoned Raza Unida because he felt that most Chicanas/os viewed it as too radical. Raza Unida made one more unsuccessful bid in electoral politics, this time in the municipality of South

Tucson. Even with the town's Chicano, Yaqui, and O'odham majority, however, it failed to garner any victories and dissolved after 1974. The party did leave behind a legacy of social services, including the Centro Aztlán, which provided a bilingual preschool, counseling, and other community services.[93]

Historian Armando Navarro offers a sanguine assessment of Raza Unida, suggesting that "as a result of its work, changes occurred that enhanced the Mexicano's struggle for political empowerment." It is important to note, however, that the Democratic Party, the CPLC, and the UFW proved to be more successful springboards into electoral politics.[94] Of those who had been involved in Raza Unida, only Raúl Grijalva had a significant career as a politician and then only after he became a Democrat. In 2002 Grijalva would be elected as an Arizona representative to the U.S. Congress.[95]

Chicano politicians who had emerged as leaders during the grassroots movement generally continued to support its goals. As a U.S. congressman, Ed Pastor persistently supported affirmative action, higher funding for public education, the preservation of social security, and the expansion of funding for other social services. He worked to expand the issuance of visas to immigrant workers and to permit undocumented workers to apply for citizenship or legal residency. He strongly opposed Arizona's antibilingual education initiative, Proposition 203, declaring, "I think it is an extension of an English-only movement by Anglos somehow afraid that Americans are going to lose part of their culture." In 2002 his voting record earned him a rating of 93 percent from the American Civil Liberties Union, and 0 percent from the Federation for American Immigration Reform (FAIR), an organization that has sought to intensify border security and to stop undocumented immigration.[96] Grijalva took comparable stands on immigration, labor, taxation, and social services. He received a rating of 0 percent from FAIR, and 100 percent from the Leadership Conference on Civil Rights.[97]

Not all Mexican-American politicians, however, so consistently supported progressive policies. In 1974 Raúl Castro was elected the first Mexican-American governor of Arizona. Castro was an immigrant, having been born in Cananea, Sonora, before moving with his parents to Douglas in 1916 where he worked in the copper smelters. In 1939 he earned a bachelor's degree from Arizona State Teachers College, and over the next three decades he worked in various public positions—as an official in the U.S. Foreign Service, as a judge in Agua Prieta, Sonora, as Pima County attorney, and as ambassador to El Salvador and Bolivia. He first ran for governor as a Democrat against Republican Jack Williams in 1970 but lost the election with 49.1 percent of the vote. Four years later he ran again, this time benefiting directly from the UFW's 1972 voter registration drive. He ran as a moderate, declaring support for bilingual education and desegregation while maintaining a probusiness stance. By doing so he gained the support of the majority of the Latino and Native American vote (90 percent of the Mexican-American vote) and a significant percentage of the Anglo vote. Castro frequently capitalized on his image as an immigrant Horatio Alger. He explained in a 1977 speech before the Arizona Mexican-American Political Conference, "I never have believed that I have been excluded from anything I wanted to work hard enough to achieve simply because of my ethnic heritage. We cannot expect the door to opportunity to open automatically for us. We must try and try again to gain success."[98]

As governor, Castro supported certain measures deemed important by Chicano activists, but his moderate stance turned off many movement leaders. In 1975 he pleased his Mexican-American supporters by signing an executive order creating an affirmative action task force. He also served as a co-chair at a 1975 conference in Washington, D.C., that created the National Hispanic Caucus, which demanded a larger voice in drafting the Democratic platform for the 1976 election and which helped organize a national drive to register Hispanic voters. Castro gave a speech in which he declared that "we have no other way but to unite and demand our rights . . . Somos del mismo barro—we are of the same clay."[99]

Yet he did little to support the interests of labor. Instead, he ardently enforced the Agricultural Employment Relations Act and thus helped to undermine the UFW—the very organization that had helped to elect him. His actions were condemned by some Chicano activists. UFW leader Gustavo Gutiérrez suggested that he was a poor choice for governor and a Republican in ideology. Chicano activist-scholar Rodolfo Acuña suggests that Castro's tenure illustrates that "just getting people elected was not enough," because he "spent most of his time supporting the state's right-to-work law and placating Arizona's conservatives." Ultimately, Castro served only for two years, resigning in 1977 when President Jimmy Carter appointed him as the new ambassador to Argentina.[100]

In his recent book on the Chicano movement in Los Angeles, Ernesto Chávez answers the question "Why are we not marching like in the '70s?" He suggests that "the end of that dramatic era did not mean the death of ethnic Mexican reform efforts. Rather, the emphasis shifted, as it had on earlier occasions, to electoral politics." Chávez also contends that historians should view the Chicano movement not as a radical break with the past or a pinnacle of Mexican-American activism, but rather as "part of a continuum." Its legacy, he argues, was to propel greater numbers of Mexican Americans into political office, although "in being transformed into purely electoral efforts, the grassroots elements and the ability to truly redefine the American political landscape—to bring about days of revolution—[have] disappeared."[101]

A similar argument could be made about Arizona's Chicano movement with some important revisions. There, too, one of the legacies of the movement was in electoral politics. But the movement also left a legacy at an institutional and cultural level. CPLC, for example, remains an important institution to this day, providing financial services to Mexican-American businesses and economic and social services to thousands. The movement significantly altered the state's public culture. Schools became more sensitive to the cultural differences of non-Anglo students, and bilingual education became standard, at least until recently. Chicano studies programs eventually flourished at the two largest state universities. The movement led to the publication of numerous works on Chicano culture, history, and literature, and to a muralist movement that, as anthropologist Carlos Vélez-Ibáñez says, served as a symbolic "reclamation of space and place" in Arizona's urban areas.[102] Most broadly, the very idea that diversity rather than cultural homogeneity is a goal worth achieving, however contested and incomplete, was a significant change from the common wisdom that cultural homogeneity was required for the nation to function.

Nevertheless, Arizona's movement had important shortcomings. It failed to guarantee the rights of workers to bargain collectively. There is no greater symbol of this defeat than the 1972 Agricultural Employment Relations Act. While respect for a culturally diverse body politic had become more common (if not hegemonic), a substantial proportion of Arizona's population apparently had no tolerance for another vision of citizenship—one in which citizens could struggle as a group to fight not only for their civil rights but also for their collective rights as workers.

It is also important to acknowledge the movement's own internal contradictions. Too often did the complex and fluid vision of a mestizo identity articulated in the story by Mario Suárez about El Hoyo become simplified in the hands of Chicano activists in the 1960s and '70s. In 1947 Suárez used his *capirotada* metaphor to emphasize diversity while simultaneously celebrating certain common cultural characteristics and interests. The Chicano movement, however, sometimes fell back on static definitions of identity, demanding conformity to a certain ideal of what a Chicano should look and act like and undermining the possibility of coalition building with other ethnic groups.[103] It is ironic that, although many Chicano activists celebrated their own indigenous roots, most had little to say about the needs and interests of the state's contemporary indigenous population (the Guadalupe Organization and La Raza Unida being rare exceptions).

CHAPTER 8

VILLAGES, TRIBES, AND NATIONS

An editorial in the *Arizona Daily Star* in 1960 proved that old notions about Indians being incapable of full and equal citizenship were alive and well. Pointing to factionalism on the Tohono O'odham reservations, the writer suggested that Anglo-Arizonans, "who have had the job of working with warring Indian Tribes and more recently working with the reservation Indians, should have some idea of what a task it is to change primitive people into modern citizens." The editorial ignored the considerable factionalism among non-Indians and the fact that recent tensions on the reservations were largely the outgrowth of new and unfamiliar political structures that conflicted with older standards of village autonomy and government by consensus. It continued, "In one hundred years we have been barely able to advance these people to any point beyond tribal self-government."[1]

Enos Francisco, the Tohono O'odham tribal chairman, responded to the editorial by turning its argument on its head. He suggested that it was modern white citizens who had trouble understanding anything beyond their own, shortsighted standards of government and citizenship. "Your editorial," he wrote, "implies that consistent, intelligent efforts have been made over the past century to help Indians achieve a position of social and economic independence and to assume the responsibilities of full citizenship. Anyone with even a slight knowledge of Indian affairs knows how far this is from the truth." The politics of the Anglo majority from his perspective were at least as contentious and even less comprehensible, he went on. "It can be said more accurately that Indians, and particularly those in Arizona who have had the job of trying to work with warring white groups, and more recently working with the tribes of administrative whites, should have some idea of what a task it is to change modern citizens into understandable people."[2] His willingness to challenge Anglo standards of citizenship evinced the growing political assertiveness of the Papago Tribal Council from the 1950s through the 1970s.

This chapter will examine how south-central Arizona's Indian population struggled to adapt to the rapidly changing political economy of postwar Arizona and how new cultural expressions and institutions simultaneously altered indigenous notions of identity, sovereignty, citizenship, and national belonging. The focus here is on the Tohono O'odham and the Yaquis because they historically transcended the territorial border between Mexico and the United States and the ethnic border separating Mexican and Indian identities.

The development of the Papago Tribal Council, and of the notion of Tohono O'odham nationhood, must be understood within the broader context of a changing regional economy and the rapid evolution of federal policy, from the Indian New Deal to termination and to self-determination. Tohono O'odham villages lost much of their autonomy during this period in part because reservation farming, small-scale ranching, and seasonal farmwork all declined and because the Arizona economy shifted toward new high-tech and service industries. As a result, thousands of O'odham lived off the reservations for extended periods. Some grew alienated from both the villages and the tribe. For others, however, the elected tribal and district councils became the best means to assert authority over their own cultural, political, and economic concerns, however imperfectly such institutions fit their traditional political culture.[3]

Meanwhile, Yaquis debated whether to seek federal acknowledgement as an American Indian tribe. This debate coincided with and was influenced by the Chicano movement, and it occurred in the context of new federal policies that offered greater sovereignty and resources to Indians. For many Yaquis, recognition as American Indians would ensure more control over politics, economics, and culture while securing their status as full American citizens—an ironic reversal from an era in which tribal membership disqualified Indians from equal citizenship. Others, however, chose to embrace their Mexican heritage as an assertion of ethnic pride and a rejection of the perceived dependency of Indians on the nation-state. An analysis of this debate reveals much about how race, political economy, and evolving definitions of citizenship affected identity formation within Arizona's intercultural borderland.[4]

CONSOLIDATING THE TOHONO O'ODHAM NATION

In the years after World War II, rapid changes in south-central Arizona's economy, ecology, demography, and in its political environment forced the Tohono O'odham to adapt in new and often dramatic ways. Federal policy reforms that moved from termination in the 1940s to 1960s to self-determination in the 1970s helped to expand the relevance and power of the tribal and district councils. At the same time, the tribal council demanded a higher level of authority over its own political economy and cultural affairs, including the power to grant or to cancel leases, to secure water rights and compensation for lost lands, and to protect the sacredness of their land and culture. While the council's frequent deviations from Tohono O'odham tradition bred rancorous debate, the slow and contested development of tribal government permitted the O'odham to change the institution of the tribe and to alter substantially their relationship to the U.S. nation-state. The result would be a new conception of Tohono O'odham nationhood—one that would eventually challenge the territorial boundaries of the United States.

Especially significant for the Tohono O'odham in the postwar years was the rapid decline of subsistence agriculture and cattle ranching on the reservations. At the beginning of World War II, O'odham farmers cultivated 12,900 acres on the reservations, and about 80 percent of all reservation families farmed for subsistence and/or for the market. In the decade that followed, however, a severe drought, erosion, and depletion of groundwater combined with the lure of wage work to lead many O'odham to abandon farming. By 1950 the Tohono O'odham cultivated only 1,252 acres of reservation land, a drop of 90 percent in a single decade. The cattle industry also suffered in these years, although not to the same extent. In 1940 there were twenty-seven thousand cattle on the reservations. Overgrazing, drought, and disease so seriously impeded the livelihoods of O'odham ranchers that by 1949 only 8,858 cattle were divided among 6,873 individuals. The further development of *charcos* helped the industry so that by 1960 there were fifteen thousand cattle. Yet fewer than 5 percent of families, most of whom were located in the southeastern sections of the reservation, owned over 80 percent of the livestock. This evolving class division would have important implications for the tribe.[5]

Some Tohono O'odham blamed the decline of reservation farming on the abandonment of the Himdag—the collective body of traditions that had sustained the O'odham for centuries. In the latter 1960s an O'odham tractor operator who lived permanently off-reservation felt that the problem arose, at least in part, from the failure to practice the *nawait* ceremony. As he explained, "That's why they had those wine feasts back then; I guess they worked because they used to have more rains then and more farming than they do now. There is nothing but cholla, cactus, and bones over there now."[6] Peter Blaine, a former tribal chairman, suggested that the availability of leasing income and an erosion of traditional values had led to the decline of farming. As he put it in the latter 1970s, "No, the lack of water is not the reason the people don't farm at San Xavier anymore. The young people today don't do anything at San Xavier because of that mine that opened on the south part of the reservation. That's where they get their money. From royalties! The heck with the fields."[7]

Others rejected the notion that a return to tradition would resolve the crisis. They looked to the tribal and district councils to protect O'odham interests. However, the expansion of the councils' influence over the lives of individual O'odham was often highly contested. Just after the war ended, the Papago Tribal Council functioned largely at the behest of the Bureau of Indian Affairs and other government agencies. In 1949, responding to the decline of farming and ranching, the council worked with BIA officials to put together a Papago Development Program. Federal officials largely dictated the details of the plan, which called for the improvement of reservation resources, termination of tribal status, and relocation of at least half the O'odham off the reservations, where they might obtain full-time jobs. Management of reservation land would pass from the tribal council to a "board of directors of a corporation owned by all of the enrolled members and created to manage the property of those members held in common." Responsibility for law and order would be turned over to the state and the counties.[8]

During the next decade the relocation program sparked contentious debate. Many O'odham leaders viewed the program (and rightly so) as part of a broader plan to terminate trust status. They sought to expand economic opportunities on or near the reservations. Tribal Chairman Mark Manuel suggested that seasonal work on nearby farms allowed O'odham working off the reservation to "go back to take part in things on the reservation, which is really the Papagos' home." Indeed, the seasonality of farmwork allowed many O'odham to make frequent visits to their villages for fiestas, baptisms, funerals, and other events.[9] Archie Hendricks, the tribal council representative from the Chukut Kuk district, attended a meeting in 1960 of the National Congress of American Indians (NCAI), which was taking a stand against termination. Reporting back to the tribal council, Hendricks explained that the meeting made it clear to him that relocation was simply one element of a plan to end tribal sovereignty. "If work could be found on the reservations," he argued, "young people wouldn't have to go off the reservation to work."[10]

Some tribal leaders felt that the practice of moving on and off the reservations to work complicated tribal government. Chester Higman, the tribal legal counsel, recognized this when he visited Santa Rosa with Mark Manuel to discuss a proposed tribal resolution in 1958. As he explained in his journal, "We drove fourteen miles to Santa Rosa village to the trading post there, only to find that the chairman had gone to Casa Grande, and were told the vice-chairman had left for the cotton fields to work." According to his account, only three people remained in town. He found a similar situation at Chuichu. "It is very hard to get them together, and especially at this time of the year, when so many Papagos are picking cotton."[11] Due both to the persistence of this seasonal pattern and to a distrust of the notion of tribal governance, only certain districts and towns participated fully in tribal politics. The most densely populated southeastern districts of the Sells reservation and of San Xavier dominated tribal leadership. Residents of those districts earned a disproportionate share of income through livestock and leasing, which allowed them to live more permanently on the reservations and participate more steadily in tribal affairs.[12]

Tribal leaders struggled to enhance their authority and gain control over reservation resources. In 1951 the tribal council initiated a campaign to obtain full mineral rights on the reservations, characterizing the move as a means to combat relocation and achieve greater autonomy. Non-Indian miners had patented 3,590 acres of O'odham land, and claims on 35,653 additional acres were pending. Some tribal leaders protested that the reservation was being invaded by prospectors.[13] In 1955 these leaders persuaded Democratic Congressman Morris Udall to present a bill before Congress that would grant the Tohono O'odham ownership of the reservations' subsurface minerals.[14] Because such an arrangement had become standard throughout the country, the bill faced little opposition in Congress, and President Eisenhower signed it into law. Tribal members could now earn income by charging fees for leasing permits and by collecting royalties, and/or by working for wages for the companies who leased reservation lands.[15]

While Mark Manuel praised the legislation as a restoration of tribal autonomy, leasing brought underlying tensions over an evolving tribal political culture to the surface. In 1957 the tribe granted the first major lease to the American Smelting and Refining Company (Asarco) on the San Xavier reservation. Because San Xavier had been allotted, the leasing process was complicated, requiring a majority of heirs to agree to a common set of terms. The process ran counter to an older political culture in which the O'odham made decisions that affected the entire community by consensus.[16] In the end a majority of allottees approved the lease, leaving those in the minority with little recourse. Asarco agreed to pay over $1 million immediately as well as royalties while operations continued. Collectively, the tribe received only $24,000. The remainder was divided between individuals and families in increments ranging from 30 cents to $30,000: some through lump payments, others through yearly annuities.[17]

Leasing tied the interests of some O'odham to the tribe more than ever. James McCarthy's family provides a good example. In the 1930s and '40s, the McCarthys, like hundreds of other O'odham families, depended upon seasonal and temporary wage jobs to survive. In the 1950s, however, James obtained a permanent job in Tucson, and he settled with his wife, Emilia, and their sons at San Xavier. Soon thereafter, the district council chair called a meeting to talk about a company that wanted to mine copper on the reservation. According to James, "Those of us who owned land southwest of the San Xavier Mission were asked to lease our land. My two brothers and I agreed to the lease. Later we were told that we had some money waiting for us at the Papago headquarters in Sells." With the new income, McCarthy was able to quit his job and build a new house for his family. Jobs as construction workers that his two sons found at the new mine allowed them to remain on the reservation.[18]

James, who had paid little attention to tribal politics before, became increasingly familiar with the tribe because of his leasing arrangement and because the endless movement that had characterized his life was over. As he recalled, "Once we had settled in our new home, I had more time to visit and know our people. I was surprised when one day in the 1960s I was asked to be on the District Council. . . . I served three times—I became a veteran councilman." McCarthy's role as a lease shareholder and his growing familiarity with the community tied his fate more closely than ever to the tribe and gave him a new reason to be closely engaged in tribal affairs.[19]

Ironically, even those who opposed such leases often became more engaged with the district and tribal councils. Some complained that the land was worth much more than the tribal and the BIA officials had paid for it. Alonso Flores, who leased some of his land at San Xavier to Asarco, recalled, "I don't see why the agency . . . made it so cheap the way they leased this out. . . . And I didn't like it when I first heard about it." Flores began attending district council meetings, voicing his concerns to his cousin, councilman Harry Throssel. He also tried to rally the community not to cave in to low prices negotiated by BIA officials. While he resented the presumptuousness of the council to act without consensus, the district's control over leases prompted him to participate in district and tribal politics. Such was the irony of the new tribal institutions. Those who were interested in local concerns had little choice but to engage with the councils, even if that engagement was sparked by fundamental differences. Over time the legitimacy of the councils as the proper venue for political debate would be enhanced.[20]

Leasing also sparked new debates over the balance of power between and the distribution of wealth among individuals, villages, districts, and the tribe. While to outside observers these negotiations seemed like petty intratribal bickering, they really involved negotiating a new balance of power within the context of a dramatically new political structure and new disparities in wealth between districts and individuals. At San Xavier, leasing exacerbated existing class divisions between O'odham allottees with large shares and those with none. Moreover, some district leaders viewed the tribe's authority to grant leases as an infringement upon their right to manage their own affairs and to profit from their own enterprises. In 1960 the district councils of mineral-rich sectors of the reservations fought to keep the profits from their own leases. Conversely, leaders from those districts with few or no leases hoped that profits would go to the tribe as a whole. Eventually, a compromise was reached in which half of all rents would go to the districts in which they were collected and half would go to the tribe. The idea that resources from one district belonged to the entire tribe was novel for the Tohono O'odham, marking a decided shift in the balance of power from the villages to the tribe.[21]

The authority of the district and tribal councils expanded further in 1964 with President Lyndon Johnson's Great Society programs. As more O'odham obtained jobs or received financial support through tribal and federal programs, tribal institutions became increasingly relevant. Under a former tribal chairman, Thomas Segundo, the tribe organized a community action program committee, which directed the formation of a tribal work experience program, a Head Start program, and established reservation housing and community centers. Funding for many of the new programs did not come through the BIA but went directly to the tribe. The programs also provided educational and work opportunities, accelerating a pattern toward centralization into larger towns and increasing the power of the tribal council vis-à-vis both the villages and the BIA. By the late 1960s, as much as 67 percent of average annual income on the reservations was derived from federal and tribal sources.[22]

As the tribe's administrative hub, Sells became a center of politics, social services, employment, and a range of social activities. By 1966, as more
Tohono O'odham moved in from smaller villages, the population grew to
eight hundred. The BIA and the public health service in Sells ranked first
and second in providing the most jobs on the reservation, while the Papago
Tribe itself ranked fourth, and the community action program, sixth.[23]
Tribal and federal institutions also expanded their presence in a few other
key communities, such as Topawa, Santa Rosa, Chuichu, and Pisinemo,
which became secondary administrative and commercial centers. In these
towns O'odham had access to, or worked for, schools, welfare administration and public health, postal, and other services. These connections tied
the interests of growing numbers of O'odham directly to the tribe.[24]

One of the most important effects of increased funding for social services was that more women were brought into public affairs and, eventually, into tribal politics. Ethnographer Päivi Hoikkala has studied this
trend at the Salt River Pima and Maricopa Community near Phoenix, noting that "Salt River residents readily accepted women's involvement in
community action programs as an extension of their roles of mother and
wife." On the Tohono O'odham reservations, many women worked for the
BIA, for various War on Poverty programs, in the schools, and in other
social services by the mid-1960s. They extended their roles as caretakers
of their families into the public sphere. On the Sells reservation, for example, Alberta Flannery and Mary Bliss, sisters who grew up near Sells,
were among the first women to receive bachelor's degrees and to enroll in
graduate school. Bliss attended college in the early 1970s with government
funding, and in 1974 she went to work at the Arizona Department of Economic Security. Flannery earned a degree in secondary education from the
University of Arizona in 1976 and then went to work as the coordinator of
the Indian education program for the Tucson Unified School District. Both
women earned master's degrees in 1981, after which Bliss declared that she
hoped to use her education to ensure that "the tribe could develop its own
social services program outside the BIA."[25]

Some of these women eventually expanded their roles into politics. By
1983 four women served on the twenty-two-member tribal council, and
for the first time two women ran for the positions of chair and vice-chair.
Vivian Juan entered college in the late 1970s to earn a degree in political
science and secondary education which, she explained upon graduation in
1981, she hoped to use "to help out in tribal politics." A little over two
decades later, Juan would become the first woman to be elected as chair
of the Tohono O'odham nation with an impressive 59 percent of the vote.

Her election was a strong indication of how substantially women's roles in O'odham society were changing as the influence of the tribe grew.[26]

Even as the authority of tribal institutions increased, thousands of O'odham moved outside the reservations for longer periods of time, thus farther away from their reach. As the availability of seasonal labor declined in the early 1960s, hundreds obtained more permanent, off-reservation jobs as irrigators and tractor drivers, while others moved to the cities or mining towns. A 1968 study found that 38 percent of O'odham had moved away from the reservation entirely. This figure can be misleading, however, since only 10 percent of the permanent emigrants moved to distant cities like Los Angeles or Chicago. Most moved to rural towns or urban centers near the reservations from which they could make frequent visits.[27]

In 1969 ethnographer Jack Waddell noted that some off-reservation settlements had become full-fledged "Indian villages" because "they have maintained some of the traditional features of the village organization and have also incorporated organization features that characterize the political influence of the Bureau of Indian Affairs on the reservation." On the larger, rural settlements of this kind, adult men often worked either permanently or part time on various farms, while women usually cared for the homes and sometimes worked seasonally to help increase family income. While the homes of nuclear families predominated, they were generally arranged into extended-family clusters. Ethnographer Bernard Fontana has noted that, throughout the 1970s, Florence Indian village, Gila Bend, Darby Well, and Bates Well near Ajo continued to choose their own headmen and village councilmen. By 1974 the Florence settlement became so well established that the federal government recognized it as a 20-acre reservation, permitting federal funds to be used for Indian housing, health, and other services, and allowing residents to elect their own tribal representatives.[28]

Life was significantly different in the mining town of Ajo than in the rural areas, but the O'odham there still found ways to maintain a strong sense of ethnic community, and to involve themselves increasingly in tribal affairs. For decades, Ajo had been among the largest O'odham population centers on or off the reservation. While new technologies and new and more permanent housing meant less need for migration back and forth to the reservation, most people retained their connections through frequent visits. Moreover, the high concentration of O'odham living at Ajo precluded assimilation. The O'odham had their own church at Ajo Indian Village. In 1961 they also organized themselves as a new district, and residents soon elected their own district council and a representative onto the tribal council. One Ajo man who was elected to the council continued to organize a yearly feast of the Sacred Heart on the reservation, drawing people from several villages every year. His complex connections to a variety of political and cultural institutions illustrate how permanent off-reservation residence did not necessarily sever connections to the reservations or interest in tribal affairs.[29]

By the late 1960s the largest single Tohono O'odham community on or off the reservation was in Tucson. According to Waddell, many O'odham, particularly those in South Tucson, lived in "urban family clusters" and retained "somewhat permanent relationships with a larger urban [O'odham] community" so that their cultural identification was "still largely Papago." Of course, some lived outside recognizably O'odham neighborhoods altogether. Some individuals had largely detached themselves from "extensive kinship involvement," and it was this group that most frequently suffered from alcoholism and poverty. Others continued to live with families in suburban O'odham households. The suburban O'odham—some eighteen households—tended to be members either of the middle class or of the skilled working class (primarily through electrical and mechanical occupations). This group also formed a kind of "intelligentsia" with "administrative concern over the low status of many Tucson Papagos and with continuing involvement through kinship ties." Anthony Cypriano (a pseudonym), for example, worked actively with the Tucson Indian Center and with the urban schools and church where O'odham attended.[30]

One of the most visible differences between urban and rural communities was the gendered division of labor. In Tucson hundreds of women worked for wages, particularly in domestic labor. In the late 1960s, fully 50.7 percent of Tohono O'odham women in Tucson were employed, while in all of the other towns and villages only 18.7 percent had wage or salary jobs. Tucson women also had a lower fertility rate and a slightly higher level of formal education than their rural counterparts. The lower fertility rate was at least partly attributable to the fact that 14.4 percent more women than men lived in Tucson. Moreover, many of these women were single and had not yet started families.[31]

This brief overview of Tohono O'odham communities in villages, towns, and urban neighborhoods demonstrates that the population was diversifying and adapting to local circumstances. Some of the more intimate connections from the old villages and *rancherías* had been lost, but in their absence tribal institutions protected O'odham communities and created an emerging sense of peoplehood. This could be true even for those who disliked the often contentious majoritarian politics of the councils. In sum the very idea of a collective entity or imagined community known as the

Papago Tribe became a catalyst for cultural self-identification and for communication of that identity to non-Indians.

The power of the tribal council continued to grow in the 1970s in part because of critical transformations in federal policy. In January 1975 Congress passed the Indian Self-Determination and Education Assistance Act. It was intended to "respond to the strong expression of the Indian people for self-determination by assuring maximum Indian participation in the direction of educational as well as other federal services to Indian communities." Congress created a review commission to analyze the impact of the new federal policy. In a 1977 report the commission reaffirmed that the Indian population had "a relationship recognized in the law of this Nation as that of domestic, dependent sovereign." Directly repudiating the language of termination, it suggested that the relationship has "at sometimes in the past been honored but more frequently violated and at times even terminated."[32]

With this federal affirmation of Indian self-determination, the Papago Tribal Council had a new weapon in its struggle for sovereignty and for land and water rights—a battle that, in turn, would increase its visibility, relevance, and legitimacy. The first issue to come to the fore was compensation for lost lands. All O'odham shared an interest in financial compensation for lost territory. The federal government had established the Indian Claims Commission (ICC) in 1946 to resolve outstanding land disputes through cash payments. Not an altruistic measure, this was a means to lay territorial conflicts to rest so termination and relocation could move forward.[33] The Papago Tribal Council filed a petition in 1951, but the commission waited until 1964 to hear the case and until 1976 to make a monetary award available. During the hearings, reports by ethnographers Ruth Underhill, Robert Hackenberg, Bernard Fontana, and William Kelly, among others, documented "aboriginal land use and occupancy," population figures, and cultural continuity over centuries.[34]

In the end the ICC found that non-Indian settlers had divested the Tohono O'odham of millions of acres between the Altar valley in Sonora and the Gila River in Arizona. It also recognized that the arid western region between Ajo and the Atlas-Gila Mountains "was occupied to a sufficient extent by Papago Indians to support a finding of aboriginal title." Finally, it found that the O'odham had undisputed historical claim to the Santa Cruz valley, including the sites of Tubac and Tucson. In 1970 the ICC awarded $26 million for the loss of six million acres based on 1916 land values. This amount could not have compensated the O'odham for the livelihoods and income they might have derived from the territory. Still, it meant a symbolic recognition that their traditional homeland was much larger than the contemporary reservations and that the United States had, in the words of the ICC ruling, "fail[ed] in its duty to its Papago Indian wards" to protect them from the "steady encroachment and aggression of the non-Indian settlers."[35]

While the ICC intended to preclude future litigation over land, in a broader sense the thousand pages of detailed evidence produced during the procedures publicly and legally acknowledged the O'odham's deep cultural and historical connection to the region. In the future the tribe would use this as state-sanctioned evidence for the expansion of its autonomy and self-determination and to attempt to purchase certain lands that had been lost.[36] This had hardly been the intention of the ICC. Still, the documents produced in the case became yet another building block in the construction of the Tohono O'odham nation. A collective, tribal identity was evolving not simply through the internal teachings from one generation to the next, but as a dialectic between the Tohono O'odham, government officials, Anglo scholars, and the public at large.

The monetary award created new dilemmas. Who would be eligible to receive payments? Should individuals who had never enrolled in the tribe be included? Should the money go to the tribe as a collective body, to the districts, or to individuals? The council worked with the BIA office in Phoenix to develop a plan. The 1970 settlement stipulated that at least 20 percent of the money be used for tribal programs. In two public hearings in November 1981, O'odham opinions varied widely. Some, especially older members, felt that the other 80 percent should be distributed evenly to individuals. One said, "I am old and tired, and soon I will go to my rest. . . . Give me some of my fortune now. I won't have it when I go to heaven." His opinion reflected both a personal interest in receiving the money before he died and the traditional ethic that no single tribal entity should make decisions for individual members.[37]

Others had developed more trust in the tribal council and felt that the money could be used more wisely and efficiently if it remained in a lump sum for capital improvements, health, education, social services, and other investments. Nick Francisco of Sil Nakya believed that if the money was distributed in per capita checks, individuals would likely "use it all at once and be poor again." Hilda Manuel, a tribal court judge at Sells, felt that the tribe should use the money to buy back some of its traditional lands. In one of the more provocative comments at the meeting, she called the settlement "blood money" rather than a just compensation for the homeland. "We lost aboriginal rights," she said, "and here we are willing to accept payment, forgetting the people who died for it, forgetting the people who are unborn. Invest it for land. Don't just get a check in the mail for $1,500 and spend it."[38]

Significantly, while the debate was often rancorous, few would challenge the tribal council's final decision. Ultimately, the council voted unanimously, reflecting a long tradition of government by consensus. Half the money would go to the tribe as a collective entity and half would be distributed in per capita payments. All members who had enrolled in the tribe between 1937 and 1940 (when the tribe was first established) were automatically eligible, as were their descendants. In addition, anyone with 50 percent O'odham "blood quantum" who had not yet enrolled could do so within 180 days to receive payments. By January 1983, with accrued interest, the amount to be distributed was close to $44 million, leaving $23 million to be distributed in individual payments. The disbursements inspired some O'odham to enroll as tribal members for the first time.[39]

Meanwhile, the Papago Tribal Council turned to what was among the most complicated and contentious issues in south-central Arizona—water. In 1975 the tribe filed suit against the City of Tucson for depleting underground water sources. At the same time, the Tohono O'odham worked together with Pimas, Maricopas, Yavapais, and with pantribal organizations such as the National Congress of American Indians and the Association on American Indian Affairs. In October, representatives and lawyers for the tribes appeared before the Senate Interior Committee to secure enough water to promote economic self-reliance. When Arizona's two Republican senators, Barry Goldwater and Paul Fannin (the ranking Republican on the Interior committee), refused to support the effort, tribal officials enlisted the help of Massachusetts Senator Edward Kennedy. Kennedy introduced Senate Bill 3298 in April 1976, dubbing it the Central Arizona Indian Tribal Water Rights Settlement Bill. It called upon Congress to account for "the failures of the federal government to protect water supplies of the Central Arizona Tribes and the ongoing deprivation of water use which these tribes have suffered."[40]

Opponents and proponents alike framed the debate as being over citizenship rights as well as water. Senator Goldwater, in a statement that seemed to imply that Indians were something other than full American citizens, declared, "The water rights legislation, offered in the name of justice for the Indians, would dispossess thousands of American citizens who have contributed their capital, their labor, and lifetimes of effort to developing agricultural operations."[41] Conversely, Gerald Anton, president of the Salt River Pima-Maricopa Indian Community, in a letter that appeared in the *New*

York Times, wisely portrayed the issue not as an ethnic conflict but as an economic struggle between indigenous citizens and corporate interests. As he put it, "While it has impoverished the tribes, Interior has been generous in bestowing Indian water on powerful commercial interests. Some large corporate farms irrigated by federal reclamation projects use more surface water than all the twenty-seven hundred Salt River Pima-Maricopas or the eighteen thousand Papago." As a result, he said, "Now we must depend on welfare to buy the very provisions that we once produced abundantly ourselves." He pleaded with his "fellow Americans" to acknowledge that the Indians had a "constitutionally protected right to petition for redress of grievances." With a return of their water rights, he suggested, Indians could secure their status as independent, self-reliant citizens.[42]

Ultimately, Senators Goldwater and Fannin helped to kill the bill, but the defeat proved to be a new beginning rather than an end to a protracted battle. In the years that followed, the water struggle would be decided in piecemeal court decisions and legislation rather than as a single, comprehensive law. The earliest two settlements impacted the Tohono O'odham. In 1978 Congress passed the Ak-Chin Act, from which the mixed Pima/Tohono O'odham community on the small, 20,000-acre Ak-Chin reservation would receive 85,000 acre-feet of water annually from the Central Arizona Project. The settlement was important because it represented an admission by the federal government that it had failed to meet its trust responsibility. On the other hand, it protected non-Indian water users from future litigation.[43] The second settlement guaranteed water for the San Xavier reservation and the Shuk Toak district of the Sells reservation. The Southern Arizona Water Rights Settlement Act passed both houses of Congress in 1982, allocating 76,000 acre-feet of water per year from a combination of groundwater, Tucson effluent, and Central Arizona Project water. Overall, San Xavier and Shuk Toak would receive 66,000 acre-feet of water annually.[44]

The Tohono O'odham disagreed sharply about what to do with the water once it became available. (As it turned out, it would be decades before any water reached the reservations.) The tribal council voted 10–1 to approve a plan to allow a California company to lease both land and water at San Xavier and build a development large enough to house over one hundred thousand people. Before the plan could move forward, however, the majority of allottees would have to accept it.[45] The ensuing debate once again raised fundamental questions about Tohono O'odham sovereignty and identity. Opponents organized as a group called the Defenders of O'odham Land Rights and argued that the lease would "destro[y] our tribal sovereignty." In an advertisement in the tribal newspaper, the *Papago Runner,* they declared that "land, water, sovereignty, and tribal jurisdiction is [sic] much more important to us as a people—*as an Indian Nation*—because without a land base, a place to call home, we have nothing and begin to lose our identity as Papagos" (emphasis added).[46] Others rejected what they felt was a simplistic equation of land with Tohono O'odham identity. Alonso Flores, an allottee who approved the lease, argued, "No matter where I sit I'm still Papago. They've been brainwashed to think that possessing land makes you who you are."[47]

The details of this ongoing dispute, which lasted into the latter 1980s, are outside of the temporal scope of this book, but it is important to note that after several years the tribal council reversed its earlier decision and ended further consideration of the lease. As explained by ethnographer Thomas McGuire, who consulted with the tribe as it debated its options, the decision had somewhat contradictory implications for sovereignty. In asserting its authority to cut off the debate, the tribal council turned further away from its tradition of leaving local decisions up to local communities and districts, though its decision did protect the interests of those allottees who felt the lease would erode tribal sovereignty. Somewhat paradoxically, then, the tribal council infringed upon one tradition—that of local autonomy—while indirectly upholding a tradition of consensus by preventing one group from imposing its will on another.[48]

By the late 1970s the power of the tribal council had grown sufficiently to permit it to flex its muscles in an unprecedented manner—to look beyond the confines of the U.S. territorial border to address the fate of those O'odham who still lived in Mexico. Figures on how many were there vary widely. In 1979 the Instituto Nacional Indigenista (INI, or National Indigenous Institute) counted only two hundred Sonoran "Papagos." This was undoubtedly an underestimate, since those with marginal ties to the traditional communities or who temporarily lived outside of those communities were likely excluded. In fact, census takers in 1979 noted that an unknown number of Mexican O'odham were staying in Arizona, where they worked in rural areas surrounding the Sells reservation. Very recent estimates are much higher, suggesting that as many as fourteen hundred Tohono O'odham live in Mexico today.[49]

Mexican and U.S. O'odham maintained close connections in a number of ways, cross-border ritual events among them. Many hundreds of Arizona O'odham continued to travel to Magdalena, Sonora, in October to celebrate the feast day of St. Francis.[50] Others crossed to participate in a harvest ceremony called the *wi:gita* at Quitovac in late July or early August. The

Quitovac ceremony combined elements of the *nawait*, or wine feast, making it quite distinct from the *wi:gita* in Arizona near Santa Rosa, where the *nawait* and *wi:gita* were held separately in late July and November, respectively.[51] Fontana describes the Quitovac ritual, as he witnessed it in 1980, as "a religious dance drama . . . a prayer for abundant rain, good crops, lush desert growth, health, and long life for the members of each family." For those Arizona O'odham who participated, it remained an important link to O'odham culture, to Sonoran desert ecology, and to their relatives in Mexico.[52]

Many Mexican O'odham periodically loaded up their trucks with produce from their farms and with lard, cheese, and tequila and traveled to the border to sell them to O'odham in the United States. For those on the U.S. side who lived in small villages far from Sells or Tucson, it was often easiest to obtain such items at the border. This was especially true for those who wished to purchase liquor, which remained illegal on the Sells reservation. Meetings to sell or trade such goods often became transnational fiestas in which participants listened to *conjunto* and country music.[53]

Mexican O'odham continued to cross the border to find work, visit U.S. hospitals, and send their children to U.S. schools. While it is impossible to quantify how many crossed for such purposes, anecdotal evidence suggests it was commonly done. Ana Antone, who was born in 1949 in Pozo Verde, Sonora, recalls that when she was a child she "lived south of the imaginary line and went to school in San Miguel on my Nations' lands to the north. . . . The imaginary line was already there and it was always open, but the difference was there was not a Border Patrol. We used to freely come and go." Dolores López, who was born near Caborca, Sonora, has a similar recollection of her parents moving periodically across the border to Ajo, where her father worked in the mines. In 1947 she moved to Eloy to work in the fields and care for the children of some of her relatives. Not until the 1980s did she find that she was no longer able to cross freely because policing of the border increased.[54]

In the 1970s the O'odham in Mexico faced a wide range of problems, and they turned to the Papago Tribe in Arizona for help. They complained principally about encroachments by Mexican landholders. The INI had established an office called the Residencia Papago in 1975 to begin to address O'odham concerns, but Mexican O'odham complained that it was not doing nearly enough to protect them from these encroachments. The Mexican government officially recognized O'odham communal landholdings of several thousand acres only at Pozo Verde. Encroachments remained a problem, however, especially for those who continued to move seasonally between villages, across the border, or between their farming villages and large, ethnically mixed towns such as Caborca. In their absence much of their land had been sold to private ranchers.[55]

Francisco Valenzuela was among those who complained about Mexico's failure to recognize O'odham land rights. Valenzuela's wheat field was near Plenty Coyotes village, directly adjacent to the border. He had been raised in Sonora, but like many Mexican O'odham his family had never received a deed to their land. They lived part of the year on their farm and part of it near a well, miles from Plenty Coyotes. One year, while he was away from the fields, the Mexican government sold some of his land, along with that of many other O'odham nearby, to a wealthy, absentee rancher. Valenzuela then joined a group of O'odham who took their case to the Mexican government and to the tribal council in the United States. The Mexican government responded by setting aside a little over fifty thousand acres as communal land at San Francisquito and El Carrizalito, a gesture that was small and inadequate.[56]

After considerable coaxing by Mexican O'odham, on May 16, 1979, the Papago Tribal Council in the United States passed three resolutions addressing their concerns. The first, Resolution 43-79, declared that the Treaty of Guadalupe Hidalgo and the Gadsden Purchase had unjustly divided Tohono O'odham lands "without consultation with or consent of the indigenous Papago population." These treaties, the resolution said, "separated the Papago people residing in Mexico and the United States from the lands in the other country which constitute Papago sanctuaries and traditional sites of Papago folklore, custom, tradition, rite and religion." The resolution demanded that either "the lands within Sonora, Mexico . . . be ceded or transferred to the United States of America in trust for the Papago Nation as a whole, or be set aside and reserved for, and be made part of the Papago Tribe of Mexico." The council also asserted that the O'odham should "have free access across the international Border and freedom to worship through ceremonials and traditional rites at all Papago sanctuaries and religious sites."[57]

The tribal council passed two other related resolutions. Resolution 44-79 criticized Mexico for depriving the Sonoran O'odham of their "lands and resources, including water and wells." It requested that officials of the United States, Mexico, and the United Nations "investigate the continuing encroachments against the lands and resources of the Papago Indian population in the State of Sonora." Finally, with Resolution 45-79, the council requested that Sonoran O'odham be recognized as full members of the Papago tribe and thus be entitled to federal resources and a portion of the $26 million judgment.[58]

This was only the opening salvo in an ongoing struggle by the leaders of the Tohono O'odham Nation to challenge the legitimacy of the U.S.-Mexican border, at least as the border applied to them. Mexican O'odham engaged in dramatic protests, including the occupation of the INI offices in Caborca.[59] Forty-four Mexican O'odham wrote an open letter in 1990 addressed to "Our Blood Brothers of the United States." In it, they declared that "as O'odham we are one people" and complained that the INI office in northern Sonora had been "weak, under funded, and mostly working with ranchers and dope traffickers to taking more O'odham land." They asked the U.S. tribe for assistance in securing their "traditions, culture, language and sacred sites."[60] In response the tribe, which had renamed itself officially the Tohono O'odham Nation, presented several bills before Congress designed to allow Mexican O'odham to join the tribal rolls, receive financial, educational, and health services from the United States, and ensure the rights of their people to cross the border freely. The first, introduced in 1987, was withdrawn before it reached Congress, and the most recent bill, introduced in 2003, died in committee. Nevertheless, this ongoing campaign reveals that, while the direction that the Tohono O'odham Nation will take in the future remains contested, growing numbers of O'odham see themselves first and foremost as citizens of their own nation, transcending the boundaries of either Mexico or the United States.[61]

The roots of this sentiment can be traced to the emergence between 1910 and 1937 of panvillage tribal institutions and, ironically, to policies initiated by the U.S. government. These tribal institutions gained strength in the 1960s and '70s as village autonomy was undermined through economic change, and as new U.S. laws guaranteed a greater degree of Indian sovereignty. In defining themselves as a nation rather than as a tribe, in rejecting the imposed "Papago" for the indigenous "Tohono O'odham," and in demanding recognition and protection of their transnational homeland, the Tohono O'odham have built upon a tribal/national identity that developed in a dialectical relationship with U.S. institutions and Anglo preconceptions to assert their sovereignty beyond the confines of the cultural, political, and territorial boundaries of the United States.

THE POLITICS OF YAQUI ETHNICITY

While the Tohono O'odham were debating the implications of tribal authority, Yaquis in Arizona endured without similar tribal institutions. Instead, Yaqui settlements in Pascua, New Pascua, Guadalupe, and Barrio Libre, among other settlements, maintained their own community networks and institutions with relatively tenuous connections between them.

Only in the 1960s did Yaquis from the Pascua barrio, in Tucson, begin a sustained campaign to persuade the U.S. government to acknowledge them as a tribe. In so doing, they challenged the racialized ethnic boundary between "Indian" and "Mexican" status.

Many Yaquis did not identify themselves as American Indians, having developed close ties to ethnic Mexicans who lived and worked alongside them in labor camps, rural settlements, and urban barrios. An increasing number no longer spoke Yaqui. At the same time, many Anglos refused to see the Yaquis as Indians. Rancher Turney Smith was among them, saying in 1964 that the Pascua Yaquis were "not Indians in the proper sense of the word" because they were "a mixture of several breeds." Still, as discussed in the Introduction, with the help of Congressman Udall, Pascua Yaquis successfully pressed the government in 1965 to grant them a 202-acre plot of federal trust land near the San Xavier reservation, which they called New Pascua. Yet, while Congress referred to the Yaquis as Indians, it refused to endorse the idea that their Indianness entitled them to federal resources. This ambiguity virtually guaranteed that the debate about the status of the Yaquis would continue.

Yaquis constantly had to reckon with the preconceptions of Anglos who viewed them either as American Indians, thus expecting them to act accordingly, or who assumed that they were not Indians at all because they had come from Mexico and shared many traditions with Mexicans. Sometimes Yaquis directly challenged such perceptions; at other times they strategically deployed them as a political tool. It is therefore not surprising that the campaign for federal recognition started in Pascua and New Pascua. Both communities were more ethnically homogeneous than most other Yaqui settlements. Moreover, Anglos in Tucson had long referred to the Pascua Yaquis as an "Indian tribe," had acknowledged certain leaders as "chiefs," and had even tried to gain federal recognition of the Yaquis as Indians in the 1930s.

For the New Pascuans, federal recognition would provide several advantages. Arizona's recent shift from an economy based upon extractive industries to one based upon service and light manufacturing industries undermined one of the most important sources of income for the Pascua Yaquis—seasonal farm labor. Moreover, New Pascua was plagued by a lack of social services and infrastructure, and because it was on nontaxable federal trust land the county would not pay for improvements. While the Office of Economic Opportunity (OEO) initially funded housing construction, this was cut off in the early 1970s.[62] In its place the town received funds from the Office of Native American Programs of the Department of Health, Education, and Welfare, but nothing through the BIA.[63] Federal recognition would provide both access to new resources and a new tool to protect the cultural autonomy of Yaqui settlements.

New Pascuans faced opposition to their campaign for federal acknowledgement from Anglos and Yaquis alike. A Protestant missionary complained in a letter to the head of the OEO that New Pascua was a scheme conjured up by anthropologists to satisfy their research agendas. As he put it, such an experiment "may be fine from the viewpoint of the anthropologist or may even boost the Tucson tourist trade to establish a 'museum of Yaqui culture' just southwest of the city. But how does this help a backward ethnic group which needs to be brought up to par with this generation rather than be pushed back into the past to satisfy someone's greedy self-interest?" The missionary also complained that Anselmo Valencia, who had initiated the effort to establish New Pascua, did not intend to allow the Presbyterians to build a church there. Even anthropologist Edward Spicer did not entirely trust Valencia, suspecting him of desiring power as a "caudillo." Meanwhile, the majority of Pascuans, some of whom were Presbyterians, refused to move to New Pascua, remaining in what became known as Old Pascua, where their families had lived for generations.[64]

New Pascuans also had a difficult time persuading Yaquis from other communities, such as Guadalupe, to support their cause. Many Guadalupanos identified closely with the ethnic Mexicans in their community and did not think of themselves as American Indians. Yaquis and ethnic Mexicans in Guadalupe traditionally attended the same churches, worked and lived together, and formed close ties of *compadrazgo* through baptisms, marriages, and other ritual events.[65] The two groups continued to intermarry and have children so that by the mid-1960s Anglos like teacher Ruby Wood felt that "with the people, Mexican and Yaqui, [you] can hardly tell the difference now."[66]

Wood's suggestion that there was little difference between Yaquis and ethnic Mexicans in Guadalupe was overstated. Yaquis continued to practice distinct rituals that highlighted their difference from neighboring ethnic Mexicans. Yaqui ceremonies held during Easter remained, in the words of an observer in the early 1960s, "extremely critical to the differentiation" between the two groups. Mexican Americans were excluded from membership in the ceremonial sodalities, although some participated in a supportive role as *compadres* and *comadres*.[67] At times, tensions surfaced. Some Guadalupe Yaquis recalled Mexican Americans throwing rocks at the *chapayekas*—one of the important sodalities (ritual organizations) that participated in the Lenten and Easter ceremonies.[68]

Tensions between Yaquis and Mexican Americans also reflected class differences. Of those Guadalupanos who were employed, Yaquis among them worked as unskilled farmworkers in much greater numbers than did Hispanics. A 1969 study indicated that the latter generally lived in "well kept, moderately priced homes" and were "ashamed of the poverty which [was] found on the forty acres."[69] A decade later, according to the federal census, 26.27 percent of Guadalupe Indians still worked as farm laborers, while 17.75 percent of those of Hispanic origin did so.[70] Guadalupe Yaquis recalled that Mexican Americans often referred to them as "dirty Indian," "hillbilly," and "junkhouse."[71] According to Ruby Wood, some Yaquis felt uncomfortable attending the Catholic Church because "there are quite a few Mexicans that dress real nice and have good jobs and all, and they'd say, 'Who wants to sit by a dirty Yaqui?'"[72] Such labels had a profound impact on Yaqui identity and self-perception. As Alberto Tavena said, "When I was growing up, I was raised by my grandmother who was a Mayo. I didn't know I was a Yaqui until I went to school and the kids called me a 'dirty Yaqui.'"[73]

Ethnic tensions of this sort led to deep resentment. These resentments surfaced in the early 1960s when the Catholic Church and the Guadalupe Organization (GO) attempted to buy the plaza at the center of the original forty-acre townsite, where the Yaqui Easter ceremonies were performed to make improvements to the plaza and the church. They also encouraged Yaquis to purchase their home lots. Some Yaquis viewed the action as a direct threat by the ethnic Mexican community. Benito Quijada turned directly to the federal government for help, writing to President John F. Kennedy, "We are being harassed by the Mexicans and ignored by the authorities. . . . We have always, since 1910 lived as a Yaqui Tribe, believing this land was set aside for the Yaqui refugees from Mexico, through the good works of farmers, priests, and Carl Hayden." To Quijada, the forty acres symbolized a compact between the Yaquis and the United States—a pact that guaranteed both the Yaquis' membership within and their distinct cultural and legal relationship to the U.S. nation. In the end the Guadalupe Organization and the Catholic Church withdrew their proposal to acquire the plaza, although many Yaquis did acquire their land as private property in subsequent years.[74]

Tensions between Yaqui and ethnic Mexican Guadalupanos, however, were mitigated. Shared seasonal fiestas, religious celebrations, intermarriage, and *compadrazgo* worked to break down ethnic animosities. GO also fostered cooperation between some Yaquis and ethnic Mexicans. Gabriel Alvarez, a Yaqui who married a Mexican-American woman, felt that GO was critical in bridging the gap between the two groups. Describing it as "the most important organization" in Guadalupe's postwar history, he felt that GO "somehow made us pull together and unite together, not only Yaquis but Mexican Americans. . . . Got us together to try and accomplish a certain goal and we were able to accomplish it."[75]

Many Guadalupe Yaquis therefore shunned the efforts in New Pascua to seek federal recognition as a tribe. "I was one of those who thought," Gabe Alvarez said, "I don't want to become part of the U.S. Tribe. . . . I saw myself as like a Mexican tribe, and I felt that I didn't fit into that category. . . . I'm not an American, I'm a Mexican." Although he was objecting to being pigeonholed as an American Indian, his comments conformed to traditional ethno-racial and national boundaries in another way. Because he was of Mexican ancestry, he felt that he was "not an American," despite having been born in the United States. Thus, he reinforced one ethno-racial boundary while questioning another.[76]

While New Pascuans sought federal acknowledgment as a tribe, Guadalupanos cooperated across ethnic lines to promote their interests. In 1965 GO's role in Guadalupe expanded after receiving a $500,000 OEO grant. GO then became the state's first community action program.[77] With the funds, GO developed Neighborhood Youth and Head Start programs and initiated an adult education and rehabilitation program through which 114 members earned high school equivalency diplomas. It also provided vocational training in basic plumbing, electrical work, and carpentry and established a credit union.[78]

GO consciously tapped into the Chicano movement's rhetoric and the imagery of *indigenismo* to build interethnic support for the organization. The cover of one of its pamphlets featured the image of a Yaqui deer dancer superimposed on the Aztec calendar. The image served as a reminder of the two groups' shared indigenous heritage. The pamphlet declared that GO's primary purpose was "to keep and further develop the identity of Guadalupe as a community due to its unique Mexican Yaqui culture and its rich heritage." GO thus represented a rare instance when *indigenismo* in Arizona helped to provide a unifying ideology, however imperfect, for interethnic cooperation.[79]

In the 1970s GO's impact spread beyond Guadalupe. In 1971 Socorro Hernandez de Bernasconi, a Guadalupe school counselor, protested to officials of the Tempe Elementary School District that they had disproportionately placed ethnic Mexican and Indian children in special education classes. Ethnic Mexicans and Yaquis made up 67 percent of the students in such classes—a number that was vastly out of sync with their total enrollment of 17 percent. When Hernandez asked Guadalupe's public school, the Frank School, to offer multilingual testing, it refused.[80] Hernandez then enlisted the help of GO, which filed a class-action lawsuit against the school district. In 1972 the district court ruled in favor of Hernandez, mandating that all schools test in students' primary language. Soon thereafter, all but one of the children named as petitioners in the suit were moved to regular classes. GO was legitimately able to boast that it had scored a major victory for "all bilingual children in the State of Arizona, be they Pima Indians, Papagos, Filipinos, Yaquis or Mexicans."[81]

This achievement was followed by a substantial setback—a setback that explicitly revealed the deep connection drawn by the federal courts between a homogeneous education and the stability of the nation. Shortly after the first legal victory, GO filed another, more ambitious class-action suit on behalf of all 12,280 students of the Tempe Elementary School District to demand not only testing in multiple languages but a pluralistic approach to education throughout the curriculum. GO called for a multicultural education that reflected the "particular history of the parents of each child attending the school."[82] But in 1978, after an appeal, the Ninth Circuit Court ruled against GO. "Our analysis," the court explained, "returns us to the foundations of organized society as manifested by the nation-state. We commence by recognizing that the existence of the nation-state rests ultimately on the consent of its people." Clearly, however, not everyone's consent was required. "Linguistic and cultural diversity within the nation-state," the court continued, "whatever may be its advantages from time to time, can restrict the scope of the fundamental compact. Diversity limits unity [and Tempe's decision] to provide a predominantly mono-cultural and mono-lingual educational system was a rational response to a quintessentially 'legitimate' state interest."[83]

The court thus asserted, in no uncertain terms, that state and school officials had a responsibility to encourage a monolithic ideal of cultural citizenship and collective national identity. The decision, which English-only advocates often cite as a major victory in their struggle against bilingual education, was an important and symbolic statement on the relationship between culture, language, citizenship, and the nation. In suggesting that cultural diversity could threaten the state's interest to promote a "mono-cultural" national identity, the court, in effect, acknowledged that the residents of Guadalupe, in their fight to preserve their cultural heritage, were engaged in a struggle to reformulate the boundaries of the nation itself. The decision demonstrated just how difficult that struggle could be.[84]

Guadalupanos, however, did not wait passively for the courts to reform the school system. While the second suit was tied up in the courts, GO opened an alternative private school. This action was prompted, in part, by the busing program that began in 1973. Buses transported Anglo students from Tempe into Guadalupe, and Mexican and Indian students from Guadalupe to six different schools in Tempe. Parents in Guadalupe were concerned about discrimination in the Tempe schools, about the distance their children had to travel to attend them, and about a curriculum and faculty that did not reflect the town's history, culture, and ethnic makeup. As an alternative, the new private school, named *I'tom escuela* (our school, in Yaqui and Spanish), offered classes for students from kindergarten through sixth grade. Two hundred enrolled. The curriculum served as a model of the intercultural education that Guadalupanos hoped to spread into the public school system. Teachers emphasized Mexican and Yaqui history and culture in addition to U.S. history, reading, writing, and arithmetic. The school also required every student—Anglo, Mexican, and Yaqui alike—to speak English and Spanish on alternate days and to take lessons in the Yaqui language twice a week.[85]

In the mid-1970s GO spearheaded a drive to incorporate Guadalupe as an independent municipality, arguing that the move would empower the community to protect its culture and interests. Some Guadalupanos feared that Tempe planned to annex the town and turn it into an industrial park; others feared higher tax rates and stricter housing codes.[86] GO responded by drawing up its own master plan, suggesting that incorporation would preserve the town's distinct Yaqui and Mexican heritage.[87]

Once again, not all Guadalupanos were in agreement. While GO leaders tried to reach out to the Yaqui community, many Yaquis still distrusted its motives. A few felt that ethnic Mexicans in GO were simply using them as a means to obtain federal funds, capitalizing on the federal government's relatively favorable policies toward Indians in the 1970s.[88] Other Yaquis and Mexican Americans expressed concern that the town did not have the resources or the political know-how to maintain its own streets, its own police force, and all of the other elements of self-government that would be necessary. Still, when the issue came to a vote, 295 Guadalupanos voted yes and 216 voted no. Jimmy Molina, a Yaqui, became the first mayor.[89]

In the years following incorporation, Guadalupe continued to experience a period of cultural revitalization. In 1976 local educators initiated the Yaqui Project with a special $25,000 grant from the Department of Health, Education and Welfare. With these funds six former Head Start teachers began to teach Yaqui history and to develop a Yaqui vocabulary list so that traditional stories could be written down. The funds also helped residents to begin to reconnect, in a small way, with Yaquis who still lived in Sonora. A community service director took a trip to Mexico to obtain "native toys, tools, art objects, kitchen utensils and artifacts used by Yaqui medicine men for use in the classroom." About one hundred children took part in the program that year.[90] Such programs helped to renew awareness of Yaqui history and culture and instilled a sense of dignity among many town residents. Guadalupanos thus felt a growing sense of pride in their heritage. As Jimmy Molina later said, "It wasn't cool to be a Yaqui when I was growing up, but now it's the 'in' thing to be a Yaqui."[91]

The new town council also used its power to defend the town's culture from exploitation by outside observers. A city ordinance outlawed photography and note taking during Holy Week. The ordinance imposed a $300 fine or six months in jail for breaking the new law. One resident praised the ordinance for distinguishing Guadalupe from New Pascua, where the Yaquis printed brochures and constructed bleachers for observers of the Easter ceremonies and had allowed a photographer to take pictures for a feature in *Arizona Highways*.[92]

While Guadalupe entered a period of revitalization, New Pascua struggled merely to survive; as a result, residents intensified their campaign for federal recognition as an Indian tribe. Conditions for such a strategy were more favorable in the mid-1970s than they had been in the early 1960s. In 1965 when New Pascua had been established, termination was still the guiding policy of the U.S. government. After the passage of the 1975 Self-Determination Act, however, conditions changed substantially. That year, New Pascuans began to send letters to Congressman Udall to help them seek tribal status.[93] Federal officials, however, were ambivalent. George Castile, who worked with the OEO in New Pascua at the time, recalled, "The OEO was as perplexed as everyone else regarding the Yaqui's status: Were they Chicanos or Indians or what?"[94]

Udall introduced the matter of tribal recognition to Congress in 1975, but the bill faced opposition from many fronts.[95] Among those opposed were some of Arizona's other tribes, in part because they were concerned about competition for resources but also because they hoped to maintain cultural boundaries between those who should be considered Indians and those who should not. Such concerns were sometimes expressed in racial and nativist terms. The chair of the Colorado River Indian Tribes suggested that federal funds were already stretched thin and that because the Yaquis were "outcasts from Mexico," they should not be eligible for recognition. White Mountain and San Carlos Apaches also opposed the bill, and some tribes purportedly referred to the Yaquis as "a bunch of Mexicans, a bunch of wetbacks."[96] The Arizona Inter-Tribal Council brought the issue before the Arizona Commission of Indian Affairs, raising concerns about a non-indigenous people receiving recognition as a tribe. Anselmo Valencia appeared before the commission to plead his case and said, "I am sorry if we have taken from one of the other Arizona Indian tribes, but we do need this help."[97]

Many Yaquis also continued to oppose the quest for federal acknowledgement as a tribe. Ramon Jaurique from Old Pascua feared that the Yaquis might lose their individual rights if they became federal "wards."[98] Opposition was especially strong in Guadalupe—a problem that was exacerbated when Anselmo Valencia, in a 1975 meeting before the Inter-Tribal Council, presumptuously claimed that "the Guadalupe people are not happy here [in Guadalupe]; they want to move to Tucson to live with us."[99] This merely fed the fears of Guadalupanos that they might be forced to move without their consent. One Guadalupe woman recalled that some members of the community "were telling my [mother] . . . that they were going to take her land away and put her on the reservation."[100]

Despite such opposition, and urged on by Valencia and other New Pascuans, Udall repeatedly brought the issue before Congress. The new requests came at a propitious time, since South Dakota Senator James Abourezk was simultaneously introducing new procedures for acknowledging unrecognized tribes. Abourezk was the chairman of the American Indian Policy Review Commission, which had been established in 1975 when the Self-Determination Act became law. As the commission worked on the new procedures, Udall introduced another bill, House Resolution 6612, in April 1977, providing for the extension of federal benefits and services to the Pascua Yaqui Indians of Arizona. Arizona Senator Dennis DeConcini and Senator Abourezk introduced a companion bill in the Senate.[101]

Over the next year and a half, as Congress debated the new bills, the federal government made several important decisions that signaled growing support for Indian self-determination. On May 17 the commission issued its final report, declaring that the status of Indian tribes as "domestic, dependent sovereigns" should be "nurtured and cherished by this Nation." Then, in August 1978 Congress issued a broad policy statement protecting American Indian religious freedom. Most importantly for the Pascua Yaquis, in October the Bureau of Indian Affairs issued new "procedures for establishing that an American Indian group exists as an Indian tribe." While the procedures were "intended to cover only those American Indian groups indigenous to the continental United States," the definition of *indigenous* was left rather ambiguous. Indians would be recognized if they could establish that they had "been identified from historical times until the present on a substantially continuous basis, as 'American Indian,' or 'aboriginal.'" Evidence for such status could include federal and/or state documents, "repeated identification as an Indian entity in newspapers and books," and/or works by "anthropologists, historians, or other scholars."[102]

The fate of the Yaquis was decided a month before the government adopted these new procedures, but the fact that Congress was deliberating over the problems and that Abourezk himself introduced the Yaqui bill suggests that the deliberations influenced the decision. During Senate hearings there was much discussion about what it meant to be Indian in the United States. Abourezk opened the proceedings by declaring that the "Yaqui people have lived in areas including what is now the southwestern United States and northern Mexico since time immemorial." Senator DeConcini, who could not attend the hearings, issued a prepared statement that anticipated the language of the soon-to-be released federal acknowledgement procedures. In his words, "The Yaqui Indians . . . have been identified by every recognized authority as being a major and unique American Indian tribe." He also made the highly questionable declaration that the Yaquis had lived in "what we call the Southwest, including the area of the Gadsden Purchase, from time immemorial." More plausibly, he wrote about their "pride and strength of culture, language, and character that has carried these people through much adversity."[103]

During the hearings, Anselmo Valencia made the New Pascuan case directly before the Senate. Turning rancher Turney Smith's rhetoric on its head, he argued that "The Yaquis are Indians in every sense of the word. We have our own language, our own culture, such as the Pascola Dancing, the deer dancing, and the coyote dancing. These dances are Indian in origin." He then reviewed the history of oppression that the Yaquis had faced in their long struggle to survive. "The Catholic faith and the various governments under which the Yaquis have had to suffer have tried for centuries to undermine our 'Yaquiness,' but after four hundred years they have not succeeded." Rather than claim that the Yaquis had lived in territory now controlled by the United States since "time immemorial," he made the more likely suggestion that "Yaqui Indians are, and have been, from the southwest since before the establishment of international boundaries which divide this continent."[104]

In the end the hearings convinced Congress that the Yaquis were, indeed, American Indians, and it passed Public Law 95-375 to that effect on September 18, 1978. The act rescinded the language of the 1965 act that had withheld federal resources or privileges reserved for American Indians from the Yaquis. Instead, the new legislation stated that the Yaquis were to be eligible "for services and assistance provided to Indians *because of their status as Indians* by or through any department, agency, or instrumentality of the United States" (emphasis added).[105]

Ethnographer George Castile has suggested that a critical reason Congress granted federal recognition to the Yaquis was the unproven yet oft-repeated idea that the Yaquis were descendants of the Toltecs, and the far-fetched suggestion that Toltecs had once lived in territory that was now the Southwest. Indeed, Senators Abourezk and DeConcini both made such claims during the hearings.[106] It is important to note, however, that even if it influenced the Senate's decision, BIA federal acknowledgment guidelines did not make such a claim imperative. The new legislation required that a tribe had existed from a "historical time." It was undeniable that the Yaquis had been living in the United States at least since the late nineteenth century, which was certainly a historical time. Moreover, throughout the century, anthropologists like Edward Spicer had referred to the Yaquis as an Indian tribe.[107]

While it is interesting to consider the role that purported Toltec ancestry played in congressional hearings over federal recognition, the debate over the Yaquis' status in the United States raises deeper questions. What did it mean to be defined as indigenous in a nation whose territorial boundaries had been firmly established only in 1854, not long before thousands of Yaquis began crossing from Sonora into Arizona? It must be remembered that U.S. influence had never stopped at the territorial border. The presence of U.S. investors in northern Sonora and the support of the U.S. government for the Díaz regime had played a significant role in dislodging thousands of Yaquis from Sonora in the first place. Did the United States then not bear some of the responsibility for rectifying such historical injustices?

Debates over the status of the Yaquis shed light on the ways in which Americans of various ethnic backgrounds have insisted that people be defined into readily understandable ethno-racial categories, and how that insistence has affected the ethnic identity of indigenous peoples. It was incomprehensible to many outside observers that the Yaquis could be both Mexican and Indian or, more to the point, that they are something altogether different. To Anglos such as Turney Smith, the liminality of the Yaquis, in cultural and national terms, made them "not citizens of any country," even though legally they had been recognized as U.S. citizens for many decades. Other Indian tribes, too, insisted on maintaining solid boundaries around Indian status, declaring at various times that the Yaquis were "wetbacks" or Mexican outcasts and not like them. And then there were Yaquis themselves, such as Gabe Alvarez who asked how he could be a Native American when his ancestors originated in Mexico and when he listened to Mexican music and ate Mexican food.

All of these groups, and not just Anglos, frequently resorted to simple ethno-racial categories—categories that had helped to define the social and cultural fabric of the nation by defining how different groups fit, or did not fit, into that fabric. The Yaquis threatened to disrupt that comprehensible world because they challenged by their very existence the cultural and racial borders that helped to define the limits of citizenship and the boundaries of the nation. Congress, by defining the Yaquis as Indians, moved toward putting such debates to rest, substantially clarifying the place of the Yaquis within the nation.

On one hand, in 1978 the Pascua Yaquis successfully redefined what an American Indian could be, since they were, after all, descendants of immigrants. But on the other, their success depended in part upon their willingness to accept aspects of an externally derived, essentialist conception of Indianness. The Pascua Yaqui Association was replaced by the Pascua Yaqui Tribe, and New Pascua became an Indian reservation. Membership was now based on genetics; the tribal rolls were open only to people of one-quarter "Yaqui blood." [108] Never before had the Yaquis had a permanent tribal government, and never before had the proportion of one's blood determined whether or not one was a Yaqui. One's kinship relationships, cultural practices, and any number of other factors were more important. In fact, some Yaquis, especially those in Guadalupe where intermarriage was common, continued to fight against the high level of blood quantum necessary for membership, pushing for a decrease to one-eighth. [109]

Yaqui tribal recognition affected Yaqui culture and identity in other ways as well. The new tribal government in Pascua provided the opportunity for women to obtain leadership positions that had not existed before. Historically, only men served as headmen, *gobernadores*, or members of village councils. Now, like the Tohono O'odham, Yaqui women expanded their public roles into the world of electoral politics. Octaviana Salazar, for example, who was the first Yaqui from Guadalupe to earn a PhD, eventually became the first Guadalupano, and one of the first women, to serve on the Pascua Yaqui Tribal Council. For two months she also served as interim chair of the Pascua Yaqui Tribe. [110] More recently, in June 2004, Herminia Frías was the first woman in the tribe's history to be elected chair. Her election demonstrates how a new institution, the Yaqui Tribal Council, over time has altered the gender standards of political authority within Yaqui culture.[111] As Barbara Valencia, who served as vice mayor of Guadalupe, put it in 1995, "We're a totally macho culture, but we're trying to change that too. This is a new Yaqui here."[112]

Perhaps it was the Guadalupe Yaquis who succeeded best in transcending imposed, static, ethno-racial boundaries. A homegrown social movement, influenced by the Chicano movement, built upon the community's own evolving interethnic heritage to assert a new political identity—one that embraced cultural *mestizaje* as a basis of empowerment rather than as a sign of racial impurity. GO's emphasis on the town's mixed Mexican Indian culture as a basis for political empowerment demonstrates that Guadalupanos rejected the equation of whiteness with first-class citizenship without embracing other static terms that would pigeonhole them into an externally defined place within the nation.[113] And yet, as this book has attempted to demonstrate, judging the authenticity of ethnic identities is an ill-advised pursuit. It can distract scholars from the task of taking existing identities seriously and understanding what they mean to the people who live them, while interrogating how and why they emerged, adapted, and/or disappeared over time.

CONCLUSION

Borders Old and New

Vivian Juan-Saunders and Herminia Frías, chairwomen of the Tohono O'odham and Yaqui nations in Arizona, traveled to Sarmiento, Mexico, in November 2004 to participate in the Ninth Annual Assembly of Indigenous Women. There they met up with O'odham and Yaquis from Mexico, along with other indigenous peoples from Arizona, California, Sonora, and Sinaloa, to discuss their future. The meeting was remarkable in a number of ways. First, that both leaders were there to represent their respective indigenous nations reveals how much their political cultures had changed since the nineteenth century, when individual villages were considered autonomous and the idea of a national or tribal leadership elected by a majority was unheard of. Second, the election of women by the Yaqui and Tohono O'odham nations to the highest positions of political power revealed a dramatic cultural shift from a time when all-male village councils made decisions by consensus. Finally, the meetings symbolized an extension of a pan-Indian notion of sovereignty that was no longer confined within the borders of the United States.[1]

On the other hand, one might see the meeting as a sign of the loss of tradition and cultural integrity, and of unresolved contradictions. The very idea that Juan-Saunders and Frías could claim to speak for the O'odham and Yaqui nations was evidence of a decline in village autonomy. This concept of O'odham and Yaqui nationhood was one among many ways in which indigenous culture in Arizona's borderlands had changed. Thousands of Yaquis and Tohono O'odham no longer spoke their native languages. The adoption of majoritarian democracy countered a history of government by consensus. The creation of the Yaqui and Tohono O'odham nations has appeared to confirm rather than challenge the idea that the world is organized into discrete ethnic groups or nations with impermeable boundaries.

Indeed, as old borders eroded, new ones emerged. This was true not just metaphorically but also in very concrete terms. Chairwoman Juan-Saunders proclaimed that "it is critical that all recognized members of the Tohono O'odham Nation maintain the right to cross the border to see families and friends, to receive services and to participate in religious ceremonies and other events." At the same time, she initially condoned the construction of a fence through traditional O'odham lands along the Sonora border in order to stop, in her words, the "approximately fifteen hundred undocumented immigrants and smugglers [who] cross through the Tohono O'odham Nation daily."[2] The Tohono O'odham thus simultaneously raised the radical prospect of delegitimizing the international border for themselves while reinforcing it for others. Some Yaquis and O'odham worked through the Indigenous Alliance Without Borders (led by Jose Matus, a Yaqui Indian) and the O'odham Voice Against the Wall to challenge the effort.[3] They eventually convinced her to change her position.

The idea that there are inalienable differences and boundaries between ethnic groups and nations remains largely intact. Yet, this is not simply the natural order of things; it is the product of history. Ever since the Treaty of Guadalupe Hidalgo and the Gadsden Purchase, government officials and economic elites had worked to classify and rank Arizona's regional population according to its economic value and suitability for American citizenship. In the borderlands, race served to reconcile contradictions between a high demand for labor, regardless of ethnicity or national origin, and cultural demands to foster national homogeneity. Racial classification worked to promote, if not a monocultural nation, at least the homogeneity of the citizenry by withholding full citizenship rights from those deemed worthy to work but unworthy to be full members of the U.S. body politic.

Over the course of one hundred years, restrictions on voting, segregation statutes, miscegenation laws, federal Indian policies, and anti-immigration measures ranked and classified the regional population into specific, ethno-racial categories. But in the fluid space of the borderlands in the nineteenth and early twentieth centuries, identification as Indian or Mexican had often occurred on a continuum rather than in binary terms. This was also true for Anglos or whites, since Italians, Greeks, Spaniards, and Poles, among others, had not been fully accepted as white at the turn of the century. Over time, most of these groups managed to secure social acceptance into the circle of whiteness. By midcentury, Mexican, Anglo, or Indian had become more strictly bounded ethno-racial categories, with much less room for in-betweens.

Throughout this period, the region's immigrant, Mexican-American, and indigenous populations fought to maintain their cultural integrity and define their own relationship to the U.S. nation-state. For decades, Tohono O'odham, Pimas, and Maricopas retained relatively autonomous cultural spaces by farming, raising cattle, and periodically moving between their reservation villages and Anglo-owned farms, ranches, and mines. In the 1930s the Indian New Deal accelerated the process of economic change on and off the reservations and laid the groundwork for tribal councils to supersede village-level government. After World War II, as commercial agriculture became fully mechanized and Arizona shifted to a service and manufacturing economy, seasonal migration from villages and *rancherías* into temporary wage jobs became much less tenable. These changes encouraged indigenous people to embrace new tribal or national identities in order to preserve their cultural heritage and assert their economic and political rights.

At the same time, ethnic Mexicans developed a number of sometimes contradictory tactics such as demanding acceptance as white American citizens; joining *mutualistas* for economic security, to protect their Mexican heritage, and to claim American citizenship; or forming labor unions to challenge the racially ordered class system. In the early 1960s ethnic Mexicans associated with the Chicano movement began to assert their indigenous and mestizo heritage, rather than their whiteness, as a basis for political empowerment. Still, as this book has suggested, even those who identified as Chicanos tended to trace this indigenous heritage to the hierarchical civilization of the Aztecs rather than link themselves to the indigenous population in south-central Arizona with whom they worked, lived, and intermarried. In that sense they conformed to dominant conceptions of what constituted civilization and what did not.

The liminal ethno-racial status of the Yaquis lasted perhaps the longest. Yaquis challenged the racial categories of Indian and Mexican by preserving a highly Hispanicized indigenous culture and forming close ties with ethnic Mexicans. In the 1960s some Yaquis embraced their cultural *mestizaje* as the basis for an interethnic movement for economic and political rights, while others sought federal recognition as a tribe. The quest for federal recognition implied a degree of acceptance of dominant American definitions of how Indians should behave, how the boundaries of Indian identity should be defined, and what the relationship of Indians to the U.S. nation-state should be. It also, however, provided a new tool to secure resources and exercise political sovereignty and cultural self-determination.

Indeed, by the end of the 1970s both Indians and ethnic Mexicans in Arizona's borderlands had substantially redefined their relationships to the U.S. nation in ways that countered the historical intentions of Anglo policymakers. Through assertions of Chicano cultural citizenship and semiautonomous, indigenous nationhood, these movements defied the dominant Anglo majority's claims of authority to define the contours and boundaries of the nation, even as they borrowed from traditional Anglo-American notions of citizenship and nationhood. It should not be surprising that, after a century and a half of interethnic interaction in the U.S. Southwest, such politicized forms of ethnic identity both confronted and reflected dominant definitions of national belonging. Such is the nature of resistant adaptation in the era of nation-states.

In recent years these groups have faced new challenges, as some Americans have attempted to shore up the boundaries of citizenship and the nation. An early example of this reaction occurred in Guadalupe in response to a local suit in the mid-1970s to institute multilingual and multicultural education in Tempe schools. The rhetoric of the federal court's 1978 ruling against the suit—that it was supposedly a legitimate state interest "to provide a predominantly mono-cultural and mono-lingual educational system"—would be repeated over and over again in coming decades as English-only advocates sought to end bilingual education.[4] Twenty-two years later, the campaign culminated in Arizona with Proposition 203, which was overwhelmingly approved by voters in November 2000. It requires Arizona's public schools to dismantle bilingual education, replacing it with English-immersion programs. Combined with a similar bill passed in California, the victory reassured English-only advocates from Texas to Massachusetts that they were not fighting in vain.[5]

Even more recently, concerns over protecting cultural and territorial national borders, and the boundaries of citizenship, reemerged in passionate regional and national debate. In November 2004, the Arizona Taxpayer and Citizenship Protection Act, Proposition 200, was approved by 56 percent of Arizona voters. The proposition begins with a declaration that illegal immigration "contradicts federal immigration policy, undermines the security of our borders and *demeans the value of citizenship*" (emphasis added). The measure mandates that at the polls every voter produce either a driver's license or two other forms of identification to prove their U.S. citizenship. It also directs each "agency of the state" to verify the identity and citizenship of applicants for public benefits and requires all state employees to report any applicant who is suspected of violating immigration laws. Any who fail to comply with the law could be charged with a Class II misdemeanor. In May 2006 a coalition of Arizonans challenged the law in federal court but the challenge failed, and the law was implemented in the November midterm elections.[6]

Meanwhile, the U.S. House passed HR 4437 in 2005. If approved by the Senate, the bill would have enhanced border protection through new technologies, more personnel, and hundreds of miles of new fencing. It would have made criminals of undocumented immigrants—and anyone who aids or abets such immigrants—subjecting them to mandatory minimum sentences. It would expand the power of government agencies to carry through deportations and would have given the attorney general discretionary authority to deport immigrants based on immoral character. It would have enacted new penalties and enforcement measures against employers who fail to make a concerted effort to find and report undocumented job applicants. Finally, border security officials would work with tribal governments, particularly with the Tohono O'odham, to secure their reservations against illegal border crossing.[7]

The passage of HR 4437 spawned protests throughout the nation, including a march by as many as two hundred thousand people in downtown Phoenix in April 2006, the largest demonstration in Arizona history. Protest organizers and politicians such as Steve Gallardo, an Arizona congressman, focused on the need to challenge recent restrictionist immigration bills and state resolutions and for Latinos to register to vote to make their voices heard. Meanwhile, watching from the sidelines, a Republican state senator told a reporter that the government must crack down on illegal immigration and the production of counterfeit immigration papers. "Who knows which documents are real and which are not real?" she asked. "They look real. They're very well done." The statement only confirmed many of the Latino protesters' worst fears. After all, if one can never tell whether immigration and citizenship papers are real, all Latinos are suspect.[8]

The symbolism of the march was revealing. Demonstrators carried signs reading *Somos America* (We Are America) and U.S. flags, heeding the advice of organizers who hoped to undercut critics of earlier protests in which some participants had waved Mexican flags. The tactic resembled historical strategies by Mexican-American activists in groups like LULAC and Arizona's ACCPE who strove for equality by asserting their patriotism. On the other hand, the fact that Latino citizens and foreign nationals protested together suggests an emerging solidarity across lines of national citizenship. Moreover, the slogan *Somos America* sent the message that even non-English speakers could be equal citizens—a clear challenge to those who advocated a monolingual and monocultural citizenry in the United States.

As some observers have pointed out, the protests were also about labor rights. A large percentage of the protesters were noncitizen workers who came to the United States either to send wages back to their home countries or to settle permanently, and legally, in the United States. The demonstrators were aware that the federal government was once again considering a guest worker program since it had become front-page news throughout the country. The proverbial devil, however, was in the details. Would a new guest worker program provide immigrants with a path to citizenship, or at least legalization? Would it establish protections for foreign nationals from exploitative employers? Or would it look much like the old Bracero Program, which had permitted only temporary admittance without a path to permanent residence, thus implicitly reinforcing the notion that Latinos were good enough to be workers but not to be citizens? The protesting immigrants put themselves at risk by publicly demanding, at a minimum, that noncitizen workers have dignity, respect, and the tools to defend themselves from exploitation and discrimination.[9]

Recent challenges to current immigration and border enforcement proposals have crossed ethnic lines. In the past several years, Chicano activists-turned-politicians in Arizona have taken up the cause of the Tohono O'odham to recognize their right to a homeland that transcends the U.S.-Mexico border. In June 2001 Representative Ed Pastor, a member of Chicanos por La Causa in the 1970s, introduced the Tohono O'odham citizenship bill in the U.S. House to grant members of the Tohono O'odham nation citizenship regardless of their residence in Mexico or the United States. Representative Frank Pallone Jr. introduced a second bill which declared, "Notwithstanding the Immigration and Nationality Act, all members of the Tohono O'odham Nation of Arizona shall be entitled to pass and repass freely the borders of the United States." To support the bills, a delegation from the Tohono O'odham nation traveled to Washington, D.C. Henry Ramón, the vice-chair of the nation, demanded that "the federal government needs to right a wrong committed in 1853, when our traditional lands were divided between Mexico and the United States."[10]

When the bills stalled in the Republican-led Congress, another long-standing Chicano activist, Raúl Grijalva, introduced a new bill in February 2003. Grijalva had been among the primary organizers in South Tucson in the 1970s of the Raza Unida Party, which had support from some local Tohono O'odham residents. Like the earlier bills, HR 731 would make all members of the Tohono O'odham nation U.S. citizens, and make tribal membership credentials the legal equivalent of a U.S. birth certificate. Unfortunately, the bill never made it to the floor for a vote.[11]

As these recent events suggest, rigid ethnic and national boundaries in Arizona and the United States—as elsewhere around the globe—remain highly contested to this day. Will the struggles of workers and the transnational nature of capital soften national borders, as some have suggested? Or will recent concerns over border security and immigration shore up national boundaries and lead to a new era of restrictive nationalism?[12] Will Yaquis, Tohono O'odham, ethnic Mexicans, and others cross ethno-racial boundaries (such as in the case of the recent Tohono O'odham citizenship bills) to form new coalitions that challenge exploitation and discrimination and secure political and economic rights? It remains to be seen. As always, we stand at a historic crossroads.

NOTES

ARCHIVE ABBREVIATIONS

AHST   Arizona Historical Society Museum and Archives, Tempe
POHP   Phoenix Oral History Project
AHF   Arizona Historical Foundation Archives, Arizona State University, Tempe
    ACGAR   Arizona Cotton Growers Association Records
ASMT   The Arizona State Museum, Tucson
    DAIOH   Doris Duke American Indian Oral History Project
AZSPC   Arizona Statehood Proposal Collection 1901–1910, Special Collections, Northern Arizona University, Flagstaff
BIA-RG75   Records of the Bureau of Indian Affairs, National Archives, Laguna Niguel, California
BLAC   The Benson Latin American Collection, University of Texas, Austin
BOHP   Barrios Oral History Project, Tempe Historical Museum, Tempe, Arizona
GTH   Guadalupe Town Hall, news clippings binder, Guadalupe, Arizona
OFJC   *Native Americans and the New Deal: The Office Files of John Collier, 1933–1945*, microfilm (Bethesda, MD: University Publications of America, 1993)
OLGC   Our Lady of Guadalupe Church, Guadalupe History File, Arizona
SCASU   Special Collections, Hayden Reading Room, Arizona State University, Tempe
    CHASU   Chicano collection
        MSS-150   MASO/MECHA records 1968–1999
        MSS-168   *Cuentos y Memorias:* Mexican Americans in Miami, AZ, Oral History Collection

MSS-130 Rose Marie and Joe Eddie López Papers, 1968–1988

P-CB-BIO Manuel "Lito" Peña Papers

CH-MSS Carl Hayden Papers

RW-MSS Ruby Olive Haigler Wood Papers 1903–1965

SCUA Special Collections, University of Arizona, Tucson

BO-MSS Bonaventure Oblasser Papers

U-MSS Morris Udall Papers

H-MSS Chester Higman Papers

SRPA Salt River Project Archives, Tempe, Arizona

VGLSC Special Collections, Venito García Library, Sells, Tohono O'odham Reservation, Arizona

INTRODUCTION

1. Quoted is Edward Spicer from George P. Castile, "Yaquis, Edward H. Spicer, and Federal Indian Policy: From Immigrants to Native Americans," *Journal of the Southwest* 44 (Winter 2002): 295, 383–436.

2. Pascua Yaqui Association, *Articles of Incorporation*, May 13, 1963, SCUA, U-MSS, box 165, folder 14. See also Edward Spicer, *The Yaquis: A Cultural History* (Tucson: University of Arizona Press, 1980), 256; Castile, "Yaquis," 395.

3. Painter discusses the founding of PAC in a letter to Udall, February 22, 1963, SCUA, U-MSS, box 165, folder 14.

4. Valencia to Udall, n.d., SCUA, U-MSS, box 165, folder 14. See also Mark E. Miller, "The Yaquis Become American Indians: The Process of Federal Tribal Recognition," *The Journal of Arizona History* 35 (Summer 1994): 183–204, 186–187.

5. Udall to Wayne N. Aspinall, chairman, Committee on Interior and Insular Affairs, May 14, 1963, SCUA, U-MSS, box 165, folder 14; *Providing for the Conveyance of Certain Land of the United States to the Pascua Yaqui Association Inc.*, HR 1530, 88th Cong., 2d sess., in SCUA, U-MSS, box 165, folder 14.

6. For historical surveys of the Yaquis in Sonora, see Spicer, *The Yaquis*; Evelyn Hu-DeHart, *Missionaries, Miners, and Indians: Spanish Contact with the Yaqui Nation of Northwestern New Spain, 1533–1820* (Tucson: University of Arizona Press, 1981); Hu-DeHart, *Yaqui Resistance and Survival: The Struggle for Land and Autonomy, 1821–1910* (Madison: University of Wisconsin Press, 1984).

7. Turney Smith to Udall, August 11, 1964, and Udall to Smith, August 13, 1964, both in SCUA, U-MSS, box 165, folder 14. Other letters opposing the bill for a variety of reasons include the Reverend John Swank to Udall, August 5, 1964, the Revs. Bruce Garrison and John Swank to Udall, February 20, 1964, and Joseph Cesare, September 12, 1964, all in U-MSS.

8. Quoted are Barbara Valencia and Tomasa Carpio, from an interview by the author, Phoenix, October 19, 1994. This section is also drawn from Gabriel and Francis Alvarez, author's interview, Guadalupe, April 26, 1995, and from Chris Hernandez, my interview, Tempe, April 4, 1995.

9. Author's interview.

10. *An Act to Provide for the Conveyance of Certain Land of the United States to the Pascua Yaqui Association Inc.*, Private Law 88-359, 88th Cong., 2d sess. (October 9, 1964).

11. See David Gutiérrez, *Walls and Mirrors: Mexican Americans, Mexican Immigrants, and the Politics of Ethnicity* (Berkeley: University of California Press, 1995); Neil Foley, *The White Scourge: Mexicans, Blacks, and Poor Whites in Texas Cotton Culture* (Berkeley: University of California Press, 1997); Cynthia Radding, *Wandering Peoples: Colonialism, Ethnic Spaces, and Ecological Frontiers in Northwestern Mexico, 1700–1850* (Durham: Duke University Press, 1997); Alexandra Harmon, *Indians in the Making: Ethnic Relations and Indian Identities Around Puget Sound* (Berkeley: University of California Press, 1998); Linda Gordon, *The Great Arizona Orphan Abduction* (Cambridge: Harvard University Press, 1999); Samuel Truett and Elliott Young, eds., *Continental Crossroads: Remapping U.S.-Mexico Borderlands History* (Durham: Duke University Press, 2004); and Andrés Reséndez, *Changing National Identities at the Frontier: Texas and New Mexico, 1800–1850* (Cambridge, UK: Cambridge University Press, 2005).

12. Truett and Young, *Continental Crossroads*, 12.

13. The concept of resistant adaptation is discussed by Steve J. Stern in "New Approaches to the Study of Peasant Rebellion and Consciousness: Implications of the Andean Experience," in *Resistance, Rebellion, and Consciousness in the Andean Peasant World, 18th to 20th Centuries*, ed. Steve J. Stern (Madison: University of Wisconsin Press, 1987), 7, and by Radding, *Wandering Peoples*, 16, 249.

14. Michael Omi and Howard Winant, *Racial Formation in the United States: From the 1960s to the 1990s*, 2nd ed. (New York: Routledge, 1994), 54; Stuart Hall, "Gramsci's Relevance for the Study of Race and Ethnicity," in *Stuart Hall: Critical Dialogues in Cultural Studies*, ed. David Morley and Kuan-Hsing Chen (New York: Routledge, 1996), 431.

15. James Clifford, *The Predicament of Culture* (Cambridge: Harvard University Press, 1988), 339–344; Jean and John Comaroff, *Ethnography and the Historical Imagination* (Boulder: Westview, 1992), 54, 60.

16. Thomas E. Sheridan, *Arizona: A History* (Tucson: University of Arizona Press, 1995), 161–186, 233. See also James Byrkit, *Forging the Copper Collar: Arizona's Labor-Management War of 1901–1921* (Tucson: University of Arizona Press, 1982); Philip Mellinger, *Race and Labor in Western Copper: The Fight for Equality, 1896–1918* (Tucson: University of Arizona Press, 1995); Gordon, *Orphan Abduction*, 20–33, 44–64.

17. Harland Padfield and William E. Martin, *Farmers, Workers, and Machines: Technological and Social Change in Farm Industries of Arizona* (Tucson: University of Arizona Press, 1965), 85; Donald Worster, *Rivers of Empire: Water, Aridity, and the Growth of the American West* (New York: Pantheon, 1985), 172–182.

18. James C. Marr, "The Use and Duty of Water in the Salt River Valley," *Agricultural Experiment Station Bulletin 120* (University of Arizona, College of

Agriculture, 1927), 70–88; Padfield and Martin, *Farmers, Workers, and Machines,* 85; Sheridan, *Arizona,* 213.

19. Sen. Carl Hayden, *A History of the Pima Indians and the San Carlos Irrigation Project* (Washington, DC: U.S. Government Printing Office, 1965).

20. See also Thomas M. Wilson and Hastings Donnan, "Nation, State and Identity at International Borders," in *Border Identities: Nation and State at International Frontiers,* ed. Wilson and Donnan (New York: Cambridge University Press, 1998), 1–30; David Thelen, "Rethinking History and the Nation-State: Mexico and the United States" and David G. Gutíerrez, "Migration, Emergent Ethnicity, and the 'Third Space': The Shifting Politics of Nationalism in Greater Mexico," both in *Journal of American History* 86 (September 1999): 439–517. For a similar perspective in an entirely different context, see Renato Rosaldo, ed., *Cultural Citizenship in Island Southeast Asia: Nation and Belonging in the Hinterlands* (Berkeley: University of California Press, 2003), 2–3.

21. Wilson and Donnan, *Border Identities,* 7–11. See also Alendro Lugo, "Reflections on Border Theory," in *Border Theory: The Limits of Cultural Politics,* ed. Scott Michaelsen and David E. Johnson (Minneapolis: University of Minnesota Press, 1997).

22. Benedict Anderson, *Imagined Communities: Reflections on the Origin and Spread of Nationalism* (London: Verso, 1991).

23. The Indian Citizenship Act is reprinted in full in Francis Paul Prucha, ed., *Documents of United States Indian Policy,* 2nd ed. (Lincoln: University of Nebraska Press, 1990), 218.

24. Alden Stevens, "Voice of the Native," *New York Times Magazine,* November 2, 1952, 65; Arizona Constitution (1912), art. V, sec. 2.

25. Renato Rosaldo and William V. Flores, "Identity, Conflict, and Evolving Latino Communities: Cultural Citizenship in San Jose, California," in *Latino Cultural Citizenship: Claiming Identity, Space, and Rights,* ed. William V. Flores and Rina Benmayor (Boston: Beacon, 1997), 57–60. See also Aihwa Ong, "Cultural Citizenship as Subject Making: Immigrants Negotiate Racial and Cultural Boundaries in the United States," 263–264; Richard Delgado, "Citizenship," 247–252; and Renato Rosaldo, "Cultural Citizenship, Inequality, and Multiculturalism," 253–261, all in *Race, Identity, and Citizenship: A Reader,* ed. Rodolfo F. Mirón and Jonathan Xavier Inda (Malden, MA: Blackwell, 1999).

26. Anthropologist Michael Kearney has succinctly characterized this conundrum in his discussion of twentieth-century California by suggesting that "foreign labor [is] desired, but the persons in whom it is embodied are not desired." Kearney, "Transnationalism in California and Mexico at the End of Empire," in Wilson and Donnan, *Border Identities,* 125. See also Lisa Lowe, *Immigrant Acts: On Asian American Cultural Politics* (Durham: Duke University Press, 1996), 13.

27. On the law of 1917 and exemptions for immigrants from the Americas, see Marc Reisler, *By the Sweat of Their Brow: Mexican Immigrant Labor in the United States: 1900–1940* (Westport, CT: Greenwood, 1976), 24–25, 27, 40–41, 56, 199. Also

see Reisler, 58–59, on the Immigration Act of 1924 and exemptions for immigrants from the Americas; Roger Daniels, *Coming to America: A History of Immigration and Ethnicity in American Life* (New York: Harper Perennial, 1990), 265, 282–284, 292–294.

28. On Americanization programs and Mexican immigrants, see Gilbert González, *Culture of Empire: American Writers, Mexico, and Mexican Immigrants, 1880–1930* (Austin: University of Texas Press, 2004), 71–102. On Los Angeles specifically, see George Sánchez, *Becoming Mexican American: Ethnicity, Culture and Identity in Chicano Los Angeles, 1900–1945* (Oxford, UK: Oxford University Press, 1993), 87–107.

29. On the Tohono O'odham challenge to the legitimacy of the international border, see Guadalupe Castillo and Margo Cowan, eds., *It Is Not Our Fault: The Case for Amending Present Nationality Law to Make All Members of the Tohono O'odham Nation United States Citizens, Now and Forever* (Sells, AZ, 2001).

30. On the permeability and historically contingent definition of whiteness, see Noel Ignatiev, *How the Irish Became White* (New York: Routledge, 1995); David Roediger, *The Wages of Whiteness: Race and the Making of the American Working Class* (London: Verso, 1999); and Matthew Frye Jacobson, *Whiteness of a Different Color: European Immigrants and the Alchemy of Race* (Cambridge: Harvard University Press, 1998). On whiteness in the Southwest, see Foley, *White Scourge*, and Gordon, *Orphan Abduction*, 101–104, 166, 205, 223–226, 242, 311.

31. On the struggle by Mexican Americans to define themselves as white, see Neil Foley, "Becoming Hispanic: Mexican Americans and the Faustian Pact with Whiteness," *Reflexiones 1997: New Directions in Mexican American Studies*, ed. Neil Foley (Austin, TX, 1998), 53–70. For an insightful discussion of the divisions and commonalities between Mexican nationals and Mexican Americans in Texas and California, see Gutiérrez, *Walls and Mirrors*, passim.

I

1. A note on my use of *empire*. In many respects the relationship between Arizona and the nation-state was imperial in the classic sense. Euro-Americans moved into the territory to extract the region's resources by exploiting the labor of the resident indigenous and ethnic Mexican populations. These native populations would find themselves relegated to being noncitizens or second-class citizens well into the twentieth century. In fact, many officials in the federal government hoped to maintain Arizona as a territory indefinitely, explicitly comparing it to overseas colonial possessions. Still, most Americans agreed that Arizona would eventually become a state, with all of the rights of representation. In that sense it may be more accurate to call Arizona an internal colony, defined here as "a colony of the United States within its borders." See Gordon, *Orphan Abduction*, 179–180. See also Mario Barrera, *Race and Class in the Southwest* (Notre Dame: University of Notre Dame Press, 1979); Tomás Almaguer, *Racial Fault Lines: The Historical Origins of White*

Supremacy in California (Berkeley: University of California Press, 1994); and David Montejano, *Anglos and Mexicans in the Making of Texas, 1836–1986* (Austin: University of Texas Press, 1987).

2. Throughout this book I use Bureau of Indian Affairs to refer to the federal bureaucracy that has been called, at various times, the Indian Bureau, the Indian Office, the Indian Service, and the Indian Desk.

3. Jay Wagoner, *Arizona Territory, 1863–1912: A Political History* (Tucson: University of Arizona Press, 1970), 14; Sylvester Mowry, "The Geography and Resources of Arizona and Sonora" (address before the American Geographical and Statistical Society, San Francisco, 1863), BLAC.

4. Anderson, *Imagined Communities,* 165–166.

5. James C. Scott, *Seeing Like a State: How Certain Schemes to Improve the Human Condition Have Failed* (New Haven: Yale University Press, 1998).

6. Mowry, "Geography and Resources," 14–16.

7. Ibid.

8. Wagoner, *Arizona Territory,* 14.

9. Mowry, "Geography and Resources," 94.

10. Ronald Takaki, *Iron Cages: Race and Culture in Nineteenth-Century America* (New York: Knopf, 1979), 163; Rodolfo Acuña, *Occupied America: A History of Chicanos,* 3rd ed. (New York: Harper Collins, 1988), 90.

11. Mowry, "Geography and Resources," 15.

12. Thomas E. Sheridan, *Los Tucsonenses: The Mexican Community in Tucson: 1854–1941* (Tucson: University of Arizona Press, 1986), 42.

13. Manuel Servín, "The Role of Mexican-Americans in the Development of Early Arizona," in *An Awakened Minority: The Mexican Americans,* 2nd ed., ed. Manuel Servín (Beverly Hills: Glencoe, 1974), 30.

14. On the complex relationships between various indigenous and colonial powers in the Spanish and Mexican borderlands, see in order of publication Edward Spicer, *Cycles of Conquest: The Impact of Spain, Mexico, and the United States on the Indians of the Southwest, 1533–1960* (Tucson: University of Arizona, 1962); Elizabeth A. H. John, *Storms Brewed in Other Men's Worlds: The Confrontation of Indians, Spanish, and French in the Southwest, 1540–1795* (Norman: University of Oklahoma Press, 1975); David J. Weber, *The Spanish Frontier in North America* (New Haven: Yale University Press, 1992); and James F. Brooks, *Captives and Cousins: Slavery, Kinship, and Community in the Southwest Borderlands* (Chapel Hill: University of North Carolina Press, 1992).

15. Robert C. West, *Sonora: Its Geographical Personality* (Austin: University of Texas Press, 1993), 9. West quotes Forest Shreve and I. L. Wiggins, *Vegetation and Flora of the Sonoran Desert* (Stanford, CA: Stanford University Press, 1964), 25.

16. West, *Sonora,* 3–9.

17. West, *Sonora,* 12–14.

18. Spicer, *Cycles of Conquest,* 86; Joel Shertzer, "Genetic Classification of the Languages of the Americas," in *America in 1492,* ed. Alvin M. Josephy Jr. (New York: Knopf, 1992), 447; Alice B. Kehoe, *North American Indians: A Comprehen-*

sive Account, 2nd ed. (Englewood Cliffs, NJ: Prentice Hall, 1992), 114–116; Paul E. Ezell, "History of the Pima," in *Handbook of North American Indians,* vol. 10, ed. Alfonso Ortiz (Washington, DC: Smithsonian Institution, 1983).

19. Ruth Murray Underhill, *Social Organization of the Papago Indians* (New York: AMS, 1969), 78–83.

20. Peter Macmillian Booth, "Creation of a Nation: The Development of the Tohono O'odham Political Culture: 1900–1937" (PhD diss., Purdue University, 2000), 45–52.

21. Ezell, "History of the Pima," 151; Henry F. Manuel, Juliann Ramón, and Bernard L. Fontana, "Dressing for the Window: Papago Indians and Economic Development," in *American Indian Economic Development,* ed. Sam Stanley (The Hague: Mouton, 1978), 521–522.

22. Manuel, Ramón, and Fontana, "Dressing," 519–522; Booth, "Creation of a Nation," 68–77.

23. Manuel, Ramón, and Fontana, "Dressing," 519–522; Booth, "Creation of a Nation," 68–77.

24. Paul H. Ezell, "The Maricopas: An Identification from Documentary Sources," *Anthropological Papers of the University of Arizona* 6 (1963): 1–20 (hereafter cited as *APUA*); Spicer, *Cycles of Conquest,* 262–263; Henry O. Harwell and Marsha C. S. Kelly, "Maricopa," in Ortiz, *Handbook,* 10, 71–85, 73; Frank Russell, *The Pima Indians* (Tucson: University of Arizona Press, 1975), 215.

25. Spicer, *Cycles of Conquest,* 93–99, 103; Ignaz Pfefferkorn, *Sonora: A Description of the Province,* trans. Theodore E. Treutlein (Tucson: University of Arizona Press, 1989), 239–244. See also Radding, *Wandering Peoples.*

26. Hu-DeHart, *Missionaries,* 11–13.

27. Spicer, *Cycles of Conquest,* 374–375.

28. Hu-Dehart, *Missionaries,* 40–60, 6.

29. Spicer, *The Yaquis,* 5–16. Hu-DeHart, *Missionaries,* 58–90; Hu-DeHart, *Yaqui Resistance and Survival,* 20, 51–55.

30. Martha Menchaca, *Recovering History, Constructing Race: The Indian, Black, and White Roots of Mexican Americans* (Austin: University of Texas Press, 2001), 191–194; Henry F. Dobyns, *Spanish Colonial Tucson: A Demographic History* (Tucson: University of Arizona Press, 1976).

31. Francisco Neblina to Fray José Mar a Pérez, February 28, 1835; Antonio Urrea to the Ayuntamiento of Altar, March 4, 1835, trans. Kieran McCarty, in Kieran McCarty, *A Frontier Documentary: Sonora and Tucson, 1821–1848* (Tucson: University of Arizona Press, 1997), 26–28, 48–49; James Officer, *Hispanic Arizona* (Tucson: University of Arizona Press, 1987), 86–88, 130–133, 153–154; David J. Weber, *The Mexican Frontier, 1821–1846: The American Southwest Under Mexico* (Albuquerque: University of New Mexico Press, 1983), 11.

32. Miguel Tinker Salas, *In the Shadow of the Eagles: Sonora and the Transformation of the Border during the Porfiriato* (Berkeley: University of California Press, 1997), 26–27.

33. Jack O. Waddell, "Papago Indians at Work," *APUA* 12 (1969): 71.

34. Edward F. Ronstadt, ed., *Borderman: Memoirs of Federico José María Ronstadt* (Tucson: University of Arizona Press, 2003); Sheridan, *Arizona*, 6; Sheridan, *Tucsonenses*, 42–51; Servín, "Role of Mexican-Americans," 30.

35. Gordon, *Orphan Abduction*, 29.

36. Evelyn Nakano Glenn, *Unequal Freedom: How Race and Gender Shaped American Citizenship and Labor* (Cambridge: Harvard University Press, 2002), 68–69.

37. Joseph Park, "The History of Mexican Labor in Arizona during the Territorial Period" (master's thesis, University of Arizona, 1961), 46–50.

38. John Hall, quoted in Tinker Salas, *Shadow of the Eagles*, 89.

39. Park, "History of Mexican Labor," 46–61; Tinker Salas, *Shadow of the Eagles*, 90–91. The quotation is from Park, "History of Mexican Labor," 52.

40. Glenn, *Unequal Freedom*, 68–69.

41. Bernard Fontana, *Of Earth and Little Rain: The Papago Indians* (Tucson: University of Arizona Press, 1989), 73; Park, "History of Mexican Labor," 79.

42. Sheridan, *Arizona*, 116; Park, "History of Mexican Labor," 191; Gordon, *Orphan Abduction*, 29.

43. Josiah Heyman, *Life and Labor on the Border: Working People of Northeastern Sonora, Mexico, 1886–1986* (Tucson: University of Arizona Press, 1991), 20, 24; Fernando Lozano Ascencio, ed., *Sonorenses en Arizona: Proceso de formación de una región binacional* (Hermosillo, Mexico: Universidad de Sonora, 1997), 24–27. See also George F. Leaming, *Labor and Copper in Arizona* (Tucson: University of Arizona College of Business, 1973), 1–16.

44. Servín, "Role of Mexican Americans," 30; Sheridan, *Tucsonenses*, 42–51; Ronstadt, *Borderman*.

45. Tinker Salas, *Shadow of the Eagles*, 225; Park, "History of Mexican Labor," 192–206.

46. Mario T. García, *Desert Immigrants: The Mexicans of El Paso, 1880–1920* (New Haven: Yale University Press, 1981), 13, 17, 33–64; Gunther Peck, *Reinventing Free Labor: Padrones and Immigrant Workers in the North American West, 1880–1930* (Cambridge, UK: Cambridge University Press, 2000) 5, 40, 69–75, 195.

47. *Arizona Daily Citizen*, December 27, 1890, as quoted by Park, "History of Mexican Labor," 207.

48. Ninety-six percent of the Canadian-born, 95 percent percent of the English-born, 97 percent percent of the Irish-born, and 96 percent of German-born earned a minimum of $3.50 per day. Senate Commission on Immigration, *Immigrant Labor in Mining, Smelting, and Refining Industry*, 61st Cong., 2d sess., 1911, 129–132. See also James R. Kluger, *The Clifton-Morenci Strike: Labor Difficulty in Arizona, 1915–16* (Tucson: University of Arizona Press, 1970), 23.

49. Senate Immigration Commission, *Immigrant Labor in Mining*, 129–132.

50. Ibid., 192–193.

51. Tinker Salas, *Shadow of the Eagles*, 133–134.

52. *Fourteenth Census of the United States 1920, Population Schedules, Pima*

County, Arizona; "1200 Men on Strike at Ajo," *Arizona Labor Journal,* December 1, 1916, 1.

53. On competing government bureaucracies and water reclamation, see Donald J. Pisani, *Water and American Government: The Reclamation Bureau, National Water Policy, and the West, 1902–1935* (Berkeley: University of California Press, 2002).

54. Manuel, Ramón, and Fontana, "Dressing for the Window," 523.

55. Edward Soza, "Mexican Homesteaders in the San Pedro Valley under the Homestead Act of 1862: 1870–1908," unpublished paper, BLAC.

56. Eva Antonia Wilbur-Cruce, *A Beautiful, Cruel Country* (Tucson: University of Arizona Press, 1987), 102.

57. Soza, "Mexican Homesteaders," 13–15.

58. Hu-Dehart, *Yaqui Resistance,* 66, 94–115; Clifton B. Kroeber, *Man, Land, and Water: Mexico's Farmlands Irrigation Policies 1885–1911* (Berkeley: University of California Press, 1983), 144.

59. Hu-DeHart, *Yaqui Resistance,* 94–115, 176; Kroeber, *Man, Land, and Water,* 144–148; Spicer, *The Yaquis,* 149; West, *Sonora,* 98–103.

60. Hu-DeHart, *Yaqui Resistance,* 94–115, 176; Kroeber, *Man, Land, and Water,* 144–148; Spicer, *The Yaquis,* 149; West, *Sonora,* 98–103.

61. Booth, "Creation," 81–85.

62. Booth, "Creation," 80–81; Robert Hackenberg, "Pima and Papago Land Use," in Ortiz, *Handbook,* 10, 172–173; Robert Hackenberg, "Aboriginal Land Use and Occupancy," in Horr, *Papago Indians I* (New York: Garland, 1974), 305–308; Winston P. Erickson, *Sharing the Desert: The Tohono O'odham in History* (Tucson: University of Arizona Press, 1994), 91–94.

63. Booth, "Creation," 85–91.

64. Geoffrey P. Mawn, "Promoters, Speculators, and the Selection of the Phoenix Townsite," *Arizona and the West* 19 (Fall 1997): 208–214.

65. Bradford Luckingham, *Phoenix: The History of a Southwestern Metropolis* (Tucson: University of Arizona Press, 1989), 15, 20–21, 28–29; Sheridan, *Arizona,* 200.

66. House Committee on Expenditures in Interior Dept., *Report in the Matter of the Investigation of the Salt and Gila Rivers—Reservations and Reclamation Service,* 62nd Cong., 3d sess., H. Doc. 1506, 239–323 (hereafter cited as House, *Investigation of the Salt and Gila Rivers*). See also Earl Zarbin, "Dr. A. J. Chandler, Practitioner in Land Fraud," *Journal of Arizona History* 36 (Summer 1995): 173–188 (hereafter cited as *JAZH*).

67. Sheridan, *Arizona,* 97–98.

68. Mowry, "Geography and Resources," 15.

69. *A History of the Pima Indians and the San Carlos Irrigation Project,* 89th Cong., 1st sess., S. Doc. 11, 48, 51, 55.

70. Quotation is from Joseph Barlow Lippincott's testimony in House, *Investigation of the Salt and Gila Rivers,* 70. See also David H. DeJong, "See the New

Country: The Removal Controversy and Pima-Maricopa Water Rights, 1869–1879," *JAZH* 33 (Winter 1992): 367, 372; Henry Dobyns, "Who Killed the Gila?" *JAZH* 19 (Spring 1978): 17–30; and Senate, *A History of the Pima Indians*, 59–75.

71. DeJong, "See the New Country," 372–373.

72. DeJong, "See the New Country," 384–391; Robert A. Hackenberg, "Pima and Papago Ecological Adaptations," in Ortiz, *Handbook*, 173.

73. Karen Smith, "The Campaign for Water in Central Arizona, 1890–1903," *Arizona and the West* 23 (Summer 1981): 127–148, 133; House, *Conserving the Rights of the Pima Indians: Arizona: Letters and Petitions*, 62nd Cong., 2d sess., 1912, H. Doc. 521, 4–9 (hereafter cited as U.S. Congress, House, *Conserving the Rights*); Pisani, *Water and American Government*, 181–182.

74. Padfield and Martin, *Farmers, Workers, and Machines*, 85.

75. Marr, "The Use and Duty of Water," AESB 120, 70–88; Padfield and Martin, *Farmers, Workers, and Machines*, 85; Sheridan, *Arizona*, 213.

76. Antonio Córdova, interview by Patricia Preciado Martin, in Patricia Preciado Martin and Louis Carlos Bernal, *Images and Conversations: Mexican Americans Recall a Southwestern Past* (Tucson: University of Arizona Press, 1996), 21; Herminia Córdova, interview by Martin and Bernal, *Images and Conversations*, 25.

77. Howard R. Lamar, *The Far Southwest: 1846–1912: A Territorial History* (New Haven: Yale University Press, 1966), 422–425.

78. A recent book that makes a similar point about the Southeast, Southwest, and Hawaii is Glenn, *Unequal Freedom*.

79. See a fairly detailed discussion of Arizona's quest for statehood in Lamar, *Far Southwest*, 478–485. Harrison is quoted on 480.

80. "For Statehood: The Views of Secretary Trott of the Democratic Committee," *Arizona Republican*, October 9, 1901, 7 (hereafter cited as *ARN*). The "full enfranchisement" and "territorial vassalage" quotes are from "The Question of Statehood," *ARN*, September 20, 1901, 2.

81. The resolution is reprinted in "From Glimmer to Glitter," *Arizona Republican*, October 27, 1901, 3 (hereafter cited as *AR*).

82. Smith's statements before Congress appear in "Statehood Now Up to Senate," *Arizona Democrat*, May 10, 1902, 1 (hereafter cited as *AD*). See also, "To Work for Statehood," *AD*, May 10, 1902, 5.

83. *The Daily Enterprise* is quoted by David R. Berman, *Reformers, Corporations, and the Electorate: An Analysis of Arizona's Age of Reform* (Niwot, CO: University Press of Colorado, 1992), 54. Sloan is quoted by Servín, "Role of Mexican-Americans," 39.

84. Mary Melcher, "Blacks and Whites Together: Interracial Leadership in the Phoenix Civil Rights Movement," *Journal of Arizona History* 32 (Summer 1991): 196–197.

85. "Beveridge Is Holding the Omnibus Bill," *AD*, May 29, 1902, 1; "Will Continue to Work for Statehood," *AD*, June 6, 1902, 5; "Sidetracked the Statehood Measure: Republicans Have Refused to Consider the Bill," *AD*, June 15, 1902, 1.

86. Beveridge's "March of the Flag" is reproduced in Elliott J. Gorn, Randy Roberts, Terry D. Bilhartz, eds., *Constructing the American Past: A Source Book of a People's History*, 4th ed. (New York: Longman, 2002), 84–86.

87. Quotations are from "Quay Defies the Senate," *AD*, December 12, 1902, 1. See also, in *AD:* "Statehood in the Balance," December 4, 1902, 1; "Statehood a Catspaw," December, 5, 1902, 1; "Traitors to Statehood," December 6, 1902, 1; "Beveridge a Malingerer," December 7, 1902, 1; also see, "The Statehood Bill First in the Senate," *ARN*, December 4, 1902; "State of Oklahoma Alone Recommended," *The Weekly Arizona Republican*, December 4, 1902, 1.

88. "New Scheme for Division," *AD*, February 11, 1902, 5; "Hon. Smith Asks for Advice, *AD*, February 5, 1903, 1; Lamar, *Far Southwest*, 488, 494–495.

89. "Hon. Smith Asks for Advice," *AD*, February 5, 1903, 1.

90. "Quay Defies the Senate," *AD*, December 12, 1902, 1.

91. "Report of Governor of Arizona to the Secretary of the Interior," AZSPC, folder 3.

92. *Protest Against Union of Arizona with New Mexico*, 59th Cong, 1st sess., S. Doc. 216, 1906, 1, 4, 16, AZSPC.

93. Lamar, *Far Southwest*, 496–498.

94. Michael E. Parrish, *Mexican Workers, Progressives, and Copper: The Failure of Industrial Democracy in Arizona during the Wilson Years* (San Diego: University of California Press, 1979), 5, 6, 20.

95. On whiteness in Arizona's mining towns, see Gordon, *Orphan Abduction*.

96. Quotations are from Berman, *Arizona's Age of Reform*. 81. See also Mellinger, *Race and Labor*, 84–86.

97. Arizona Constitution (1912), art. 5, sec. 2; Alden Stevens, "Voice of the Native," *New York Times Magazine*, November 2, 1952, 65; Henry Christman, "Southwestern Indians Win the Vote," *The American Indian* 4, no. 4, 1948.

98. Berman, *Arizona's Age of Reform*, 92. On Cochise County, see Katherine A. Benton, "What About Women in the White Man's Camp?: Gender, Nation, and the Redefinition of Race in Cochise County, Arizona, 1853–1941" (PhD diss., University of Wisconsin-Madison, 2002), 123.

2

1. See Frederick E. Hoxie, *A Final Promise: The Campaign to Assimilate the Indians, 1880–1920*, 2nd ed. (Lincoln: University of Nebraska Press, 2001); and Alice Littlefield, "Learning to Labor: Native American Education in the United States, 1880–1930," in *The Political Economy of North American Indians*, ed. John H. More (Norman: University of Oklahoma Press, 1993), 43–58.

2. Robert F. Berkhofer Jr. discusses the paradox of viewing Indians as inherently noble and independent, while simultaneously demanding that they be "reformed according to White criteria and their labor, lands, and souls put to 'higher uses' in line with White Goals." Berkhofer, *The White Man's Indian: Images of the*

American Indian from Columbus to the Present (New York: Vintage, 1979), 114. See also Hoxie, *A Final Promise*, xii–xiii, xix.

3. Harmon, *Indians in the Making*, 60.

4. Frederick Cooper, Thomas C. Holt, Rebecca J. Scott, *Beyond Slavery: Explorations of Race, Labor, and Citizenship in Postemancipation Societies* (Chapel Hill: University of North Carolina Press, 2000), 29–30. For an example within the Southwest of a similar pattern of circular migration, see Sarah Deutsch, *No Separate Refuge: Culture, Class, and Gender on an Anglo-Hispanic Frontier in the American Southwest, 1880–1940* (New York: Oxford University Press, 1987).

5. *General Allotment Act* (Dawes Act), February 8, 1887, in Francis Paul Prucha, *Documents of the United States Indian Policy*, 2nd ed., (Lincoln: University of Nebraska Press), 171–174; Harmon, *Indians in the Making*, 138.

6. Hackenberg, "Pima and Papago Land Use," 172–173; Hackenberg, "Aboriginal Land Use," 305–308; Erickson, *Sharing the Desert*, 91–94; Thomas R. McGuire, "Operations on the Concept of Sovereignty: A Case Study of Indian Decision-Making," *Urban Anthropology* 17 (1988): 75–86, 78; Fontana, *Of Earth and Little Rain*, 78.

7. Robert A. Trennert Jr., *The Phoenix Indian School: Forced Assimilation in Arizona, 1891–1935* (Norman: University of Oklahoma Press, 1988), 3–11, 13–14, 39, 52; Spicer, *Cycles of Conquest*, 149; Fontana, *Of Earth and Little Rain*, 75–76; David Rich Lewis, *Neither Wolf nor Dog: American Indians, Environment, and Agrarian Change* (New York: Oxford University Press, 1994), 143; Alonso Flores, interview by Timothy Dunnigan, June 1969, DAIOH. Flores was one of dozens of Tohono O'odham sent to Chilocco. He lived there about three decades before returning to Arizona.

8. Trennert, *Phoenix Indian School*, 12–56. Quotes from 21 and 29.

9. Janette Woodruff, as told to Cecil Dryden in Jannette Woodruff and Cecil Dryden, *Indian Oasis* (Caldwell, ID: Caxton, 1939), 228, 241–247. On the establishment of a field matron office in Tucson, see Minnie Estabrook to H. J. McQuigg, November 16, 1914, and E. B. Meritt to McQuigg, n.d., both in BIA-RG75, box 189, folder "Field matron's correspondence, Minnie M. Estabrook, 1914–1916."

10. Trennert, *Phoenix Indian School*, 31.

11. Ibid., 12–56, 70. Quotations from 21, 29, and 35.

12. Hoxie, *A Final Promise*, 168; Francis Leupp, "Annual Report of the Commissioner of Indian Affairs," September 30, 1905, in Prucha, *Documents*, 204–206.

13. Leupp, "Annual Report, 1905," 206.

14. Hoxie, *A Final Promise*, 165, 220; Harmon, *Indians in the Making*, 162.

15. W. H. Code's letter presenting this plan can be found in House, *Conserving the Rights*, 24. See also *Investigation of the Salt and Gila Rivers*, 62d Cong., 3d sess., H. Doc. 1506, 23–32; and David DeJong, "A Scheme to Rob Them of Their Land," *Journal of Arizona History* 44 (Summer 2003): 99–132, 100.

16. 19 Indian Claims Comm. 394, September 10, 1968, "Findings of Fact"

in David Agee Horr, *Papago Indians III* (New York: Garland, 1974), 229–257; Hackenberg, "Pima and Papago Land Use," 172–173; Hackenberg, "Aboriginal Land Use and Occupancy," in Horr, *Papago Indians III,* 305–308; Erickson, *Sharing the Desert,* 91–94; McGuire, "Operations on the Concept of Sovereignty," 75–86, 78; Fontana, *Of Earth and Little Rain,* 78.

17. Trennert, *Phoenix Indian School,* 52; Fontana, *Of Earth and Little Rain,* 75–76; Lewis, *Neither Wolf nor Dog,* 143.

18. Cato Sells to Frank Thackery, February 6, 1914, SCUA, BO-MSS, box 1, folder "1916."

19. Cato Sells to Charles Coe, February 6, 1914, BIA-RG75, box "Pima, Thackery," folder F-73.

20. McQuigg to commissioner of Indian Affairs, July 19, 1913, BIA-RG75, box 189, folder "Reports of Mrs. Lydia A Gibbs."

21. Woodruff, *Indian Oasis,* 229.

22. On the tendency to view Indians as naturally pure, see Philip J. Deloria, *Playing Indian* (New Haven: Yale University Press, 1998), 95–128, 103.

23. Woodruff, *Indian Oasis,* 269. A similar story about a "half-breed Mexican" was related by Superintendent McQuigg to Frank Thackery, September 16, 1913, BIA-RG75, box 189, folder "Reports of Mrs. Lydia A Gibbs."

24. Thackery to Cato Sells, May 26, 1916, BIA-RG75, box 27, folder F-106.

25. Santeo to Thackery, August 18, September 18, September 25, 1913, BIA-RG75, box "Pima, Thackery," folder F-73.

26. Bonaventure Oblasser to Novatus Benzing, October 29, 1925, SCUA, BO-MSS, box 2, folder 5. Much of this section originally appeared in Eric V. Meeks, "The Tohono O'odham, Wage Labor, and Resistant Adaptation, 1900–1930," *Western Historical Quarterly* 34 (Winter 2003): 468–489.

27. Ruth M. Underhill, "Reasons for the Choice of Santa Rosa as an Area of Investigation," 18 March 1942, OFJC, reel #11; Ruth M. Underhill, *Papago Woman* (Prospect Heights, IL: Waveland, 1979), 4.

28. For similar perspectives on the history of Indians, wage labor, and economic change, see Robert B. Campbell, "Newlands, Old Lands: Native American Labor, Agrarian Ideology, and the Progressive-Era State in the Making of the Newlands Reclamation Project, 1902–1926," *Pacific Historical Review* 71 (May 2002): 203–238; Harmon, *Indians in the Making;* Brian Hosmer and Colleen O'Neill, eds., *Native Pathways: American Indian Culture and Economic Development in the Twentieth Century* (Boulder: University Press of Colorado, 2004); Brian Hosmer, *American Indians in the Marketplace: Persistence and Innovation among the Menominees and Metlakatlans, 1870–1920* (Lawrence: University Press of Kansas, 1999); Rolf Knight, *Indians At Work: An Informal History of Native Indian Labour in British Columbia, 1858–1930* (Vancouver: New Star Books, 1978); Alice Littlefield and Martha C. Knack, *Native Americans and Wage Labor: Ethnohistorical Perspectives* (Norman: University of Oklahoma Press, 1996); Colleen O'Neill, "Navajo Workers and White Man's Ways: Negotiating the World of Wage Labor, 1930–1972" (PhD diss., Rutgers,

1997); Colleen O'Neill, "The 'Making' of the Navajo Worker: Navajo Households, the Bureau of Indian Affairs, and Off-Reservation Wage Work, 1948–1960," *New Mexico Historical Review* 74 (October 1999): 375–403.

29. Radding, *Wandering Peoples*, 154–161.

30. Flores, interview with Dunnigan.

31. Park, "History of Mexican Labor," 79.

32. Wilbur-Cruce, *A Beautiful, Cruel Country*, 28, 208, 123; Underhill, *Papago Woman*, 68.

33. Manuel, Ramón, and Fontana, "Dressing for the Window," 519; Erickson, *Sharing the Desert*, 69; Gwyneth H. Xavier, "The Cattle Industry of the Southern Papago Districts," in Horr, *Papago Indians I*, 298–301; Booth, "Creation of a Nation," 88–95.

34. Booth, "Creation of a Nation," 107–112.

35. 19 Indian Claims Comm. 394, September 10, 1968, "Findings of Fact," 417–418; Lewis, *Neither Wolf nor Dog*, 143; Booth, "Creation of a Nation," 119–120.

36. Hackenberg, "Pima and Papago Land Use," 172–173; Hackenberg, "Aboriginal Land Use and Occupancy," in Horr, *Papago Indians III*, 305–308; McGuire, "Operations on the Concept of Sovereignty," 75–86, 78; Fontana, *Of Earth and Little Rain*, 78.

37. Committee of Eight to Cato Sells, August 18, 1915, BIA-RG75, box 12, folder "Land-Report on new reservation"; Booth, "Creation of a Nation," 132–133.

38. Committee of Eight to Cato Sells, August 18, 1915, BIA-RG75, box 12, folder "Land-Report on new reservation"; Booth, "Creation of a Nation," 132–133.

39. Erickson, *Sharing the Desert*, 107; *Tucson Daily Citizen*, n.d., in BIA-RG75, box 12, folder "New Papago Indian Reservation Complaints and Investigation"; Executive order by Woodrow Wilson, SCASU, CH-MSS, box 624, folder 6; Carl Hayden to Andrew Martin, March 11, 1916 and Paul Hobby to Carl Hayden, January 12, 1917, CH-MSS, box 624, folder 6.

40. Thackery to Oblasser, May 12, 1916, SCASU, BO-MSS, box 1, folder 1916. See also Thackery to Sells, January 1, 1916, BIA-RG75, box 27, folder F-106.

41. Buchitt to Hayden, July 19, 1916, SCASU, CH-MSS, box 624, folder 6.

42. See John Thursdell to Frank Thackery, BIA-RG75, box 27, folder F103; P. A. Tardy to Bonaventure Oblasser, June 15, 1916, SCASU, BO-MSS, box 1, folder 1916; Booth, "Creation of a Nation," 150–152.

43. Lewis, *Neither Wolf nor Dog*, 147–151.

44. Ibid., 149–151; William S. King and Delmos J. Jones, "Papago Population Studies," in Horr, *Papago Indians II*, 269–274; Booth, "Creation of a Nation," 215. On the *nawait* ceremony and other rituals, see Ruth Underhill and others, *Rainhouse and Ocean: Speeches for the Papago Year* (Tucson: University of Arizona Press, 1997).

45. Santeo to Thackery, August 18, September 18, September 25, 1913, BIA-RG75, box "Pima, Thackery," folder F-73. See also W. H. Knox to Walter Swingle, November 26, 1913, BIA-RG75, box "Pima, Thackery," folder F-73.

46. Castillo and Cowan, eds., *It Is Not Our Fault*, 18, 19, 30.

47. Rosamund B. Spicer, "People on the Desert," in *The Desert People,* ed. Rosamund B. Spicer (Chicago: University of Chicago Press, 1949), 48–49; Underhill, *Social Organization,* 206–207; Ochoa interview, DAIOH.

48. James McCarthy, *A Papago Traveler: The Memories of James McCarthy,* ed. John G. Westover (Tucson: University of Arizona Press), 106–107, 117.

49. In BIA-RG75: Janette Woodruff Weekly Reports, November 18, 1916, box 190, folder "Field matron Janette Woodruff, 1915–1918"; Superintendent [McQuigg] to E. E. Newton, May 15, 1913, box 189, folder "Field matron's correspondence, Lydia Gibbs."

50. Elia Chico, interviewer unknown, January 1, 1969, in DAIOH.

51. In BIA-RG75: "Annual Report as Field Matron," July 1, 1918, box 190, folder "Field Matron Janette Woodruff, 1915–1918"; Woodruff Weekly Report, October 9, 1926, box 191, folder "Field Matron weekly reports, Janette Woodruff, 1925–1926"; C. Hauke to Henry McQuigg, June 21, 1913, box 189, folder "Field matron's correspondence, Lydia Gibbs."

52. Ochoa interview; Frances Manuel and Deborah Neff, *Desert Indian Woman: Stories and Dreams* (Tucson: University of Arizona Press, 2001), 53.

53. Woodruff and Dryden, *Indian Oasis,* 246; Woodruff Weekly Report, November 21, 1925, BIA-RG75, box 191, folder "Field matron weekly reports, Janette Woodruff, 1925–1926."

54. Quotation is from a field matron weekly report dated December 7, 1929. See also reports from December 3 and 4, 1929, box 190, folder "052.1 G&S statistical rpts: 1928–1931" in BIA-RG75.

55. Woodruff to Sells, 31 January and 1 March 1917, BIA-RG75, box 190, folder "Field matron Janette Woodruff, 1915–1918."

56. *Fourteenth Census of the United States 1920, Population Schedules, Pima County, Arizona;* Waddell, "Papago Indians at Work," *APUA,* 53–54.

57. McCarthy, *Papago Traveler,* 117; Peter Blaine and Michael S. Adams, *Papagos and Politics* (Tucson: Arizona Historical Society, 1981), 118–119.

58. In *Arizona Labor Journal:* "1200 Men," December 1, 1916, 1; "End of the Strike," July 15, 1915, 2; "Strike Ended," July 15, 1915, 1; H. C. Brown, "Ajo Strike Reviewed," December 15, 1916; "N.C. Employees Walk Out," November 25, 1916, 1; "The Strike," December 9, 1916, 1. See also Mike Curley to Rev. T. Wand, November 30, 1916, SCUA, BO-MSS, box 1, folder 1916; and Parrish, *Mexican Workers,* 13–14.

59. George Webb, *A Pima Remembers* (Tucson: University of Arizona Press, 1965), 122–124.

60. Anna Moore Shaw, *A Pima Past* (Tucson: University of Arizona Press, 1994) 77–80; Hackenberg, "Pima and Papago Ecological Adaptations," 161–177, 173.

61. Webb, *A Pima Remembers,* 122–124.

62. Shaw, *A Pima Past,* 216.

63. Chief Antonio Azul to F. E. Leupp, March 1, 1906, and Azul to Leupp, July 30, 1906, both reproduced in House, *Investigation of the Salt and Gila Rivers,* 151–153.

64. Ibid.

65. Valentine's letter is reproduced in House, *Conserving the Rights*, 19–21.

66. House, *Conserving the Rights*, 4–11. On Lee's findings, see DeJong, "A Scheme to Rob Them," 107.

67. Geological survey on the San Carlos reservoir, in House, *Investigation of the Salt and Gila Rivers*, 61.

68. House, *Conserving the Rights*, 4–11.

69. David H. DeJong, "An Equal Chance? The Pima Indians and the 1916 Florence-Casa Grande Irrigation Project," *Journal of Arizona History* 45 (Spring 2004): 75–96.

70. Brosius's letter is reproduced in House, *Conserving the Rights*, 9. See also Carl Hayden's report in Senate, *A History of the Pima Indians*, 59–75; and DeJong, "An Equal Chance," 66–67.

71. The quotation is from DeJong, "An Equal Chance," 74. See also DeJong, "A Scheme to Rob Them," 118–121; and Shelly C. Dudley, "Pima Indians, Water Rights, and the Federal Government: *U.S. v. Gila Valley Irrigation District*" (master's thesis, Arizona State University, 1996), 22–25.

72. DeJong, "A Scheme to Rob Them," 122–127.

73. Ibid.

74. Records of the Pima agricultural and market activities in the 1910s and '20s can be found in BIA-RG75: box 18, folder "1, 1–75"; box "Pima, Thackery, F73-F103," folder "supervisors and inspectors"; box "old subject, 1918–1926," folders "industries: cotton," "industries: stats," "industries: statistics," and "industrial survey." For more general agricultural statistics, see Hackenberg, "Pima and Papago Ecological Adaptations," 174.

75. "Statement of Hon. Carl Hayden, A Representative in Congress from the State of Arizona," CH-MSS, box 653, folder 15, 262.

76. Duclos to commissioner of Indian Affairs, January 12, 1926, BIA-RG75, box "old subject, 1918–1926," folder "industrial survey"; Charles Burke to W. H. Knox, June 19, 1922, and Burke to Duclos, June 22, 1922, both in BIA-RG75, box "old subject, 1918–1926," folder "employment of Indians: 1919–1925."

77. Burke to Knox, June 19, 1922, and Burke to Duclos, June 22, 1922, both in BIA-RG75, box "old subject, 1918–1926," folder "employment of Indians: 1919–1925."

78. Duclos to Burke, April 19, 1923, BIA-RG75, box "old subject, 1918–1926," folder "employment of Indians: 1919–1925."

79. Hoxie, *A Final Promise*, 236–238; "The Indian Citizenship Act," in Prucha, ed., *Documents*, 218; Alden Stevens, "Voice of the Native," *New York Times Magazine*, November 2, 1952, 65; Henry Christman, "Southwestern Indians Win the Vote," *The American Indian* 4, no. 4, 1948; Arizona Constitution (1912), art. V, sec. 2.

3

1. Rosalio Moisés, Jane Holden Kelley, and William Curry Holden, *A Yaqui Life: The Personal Chronicle of a Yaqui Indian* (Lincoln: University of Nebraska

Press, 1971), 1–15. Quotations from 1, 13, and 15. Antonia Valenzuela's life history is related by Jane Holden Kelley in *Yaqui Women: Contemporary Life Histories* (Lincoln: University of Nebraska Press, 1978), 198–203.

2. Moisés, *A Yaqui Life*, 15–35; Kelley, *Yaqui Women*, 204–208.

3. Moisés, *A Yaqui Life*, 36–130; Kelley, *Yaqui Women*, 208–212.

4. Moisés, *A Yaqui Life*, 129; Kelley, *Yaqui Women*, 213–219.

5. For a fairly recent example of the push-pull model, see Daniels, *Coming to America*. For a series of essays that attempt to revise this model by focusing on global transformations, comparative perspectives, and a critique of American exceptionalism, see Virginia Yans-McLaughlin, ed., *Immigration Reconsidered: History, Sociology, and Politics* (New York: Oxford University Press, 1990).

6. Gutiérrez, "Migration, Emergent Ethnicity, and the 'Third Space,'" *Journal of American History*, 487.

7. See Gutiérrez, *Walls and Mirrors*, 69.

8. Ascencio, *Sonorenses en Arizona*, 13.

9. Ascencio, *Sonorenses en Arizona*, 21–23; García, *Desert Immigrants*, 13, 17, 33–64; Peck, *Reinventing Free Labor*, 5, 40, 69–75, 195; Senate, *Reports of the Immigration Commission*, "Japanese and Other Immigrant Races in the Pacific Coast and Rocky Mountain States," 61st Cong., 2d sess., 1911, 12–14.

10. University of Virginia Geospatial and Statistical Data Center, http://fisher.lib.virginia.edu/census/ [August 2004]; Senate, *Reports of the Immigration Commission*, 12–14.

11. Heyman, *Life and Labor on the Border*, 63.

12. The Kibby quote is from Gordon, *Orphan Abduction*, 48. Lawrence A. Cardoso estimates that 65–70 percent of all Mexican nationals in the United States in the 1920s were young men. See Cardoso, *Mexican Emigration to the United States, 1897–1931* (Tucson: University of Arizona Press, 1980), 82.

13. Heymen, *Life and Labor on the Border*, 93–97.

14. These quotations are from excerpts of oral histories from Castillo and Cowan, eds., *It Is Not Our Fault*, 52, 84.

15. Gordon, *Orphan Abduction*, 59–60.

16. Sheridan, *Los Tucsonenses*, 79–84, 165–187.

17. Sheridan, *Los Tucsonenses*, 77, 166.

18. Federico Ronstadt's unedited and unpublished memoir can be found in the Ronstadt family archives, SCUA, or at http://www.library.arizona.edu/images/ronstadt/borderman/bmepilog.html. For a published and edited version, see Ronstadt, *Borderman*. Quotations in this paragraph are on 31 and 35, respectively.

19. Ibid., 69.

20. Herbert B. Peterson, "Twentieth-Century Search for Cíbola," in Servín, *An Awakened Minority*, 116–117; and Reisler, *By the Sweat of Their Brow*, 24–37.

21. John H. Bratton, "Long Staple Cotton Monopoly Threatens the Small Farmer," *Arizona Labor Journal*, Sept. 24, 1920, 1. On the emergence in the nineteenth century of an ideology that citizenship was based on one's labor not one's property, see David Montgomery, *Citizen Worker: The Experience of Workers in the*

United States with Democracy and the Free Market during the Nineteenth Century (Cambridge, UK: Cambridge University Press, 1993). For discussions of how this process was related to race, see Roediger, *Wages of Whiteness*, and Glenn, *Unequal Freedom.*

22. On the implications of this debate for Mexican Americans, see Gutiérrez, *Walls and Mirrors*, 46

23. Carl Hayden, "Restriction of Immigration" (speech by Hon. Carl Hayden of Arizona in the U.S. House, February 4, 1915) SCASU, CH-MSS, box 653, folder 16, 6.

24. Carl Hayden, "Statement of Hon. Carl Hayden," SCASU, CH-MSS, box 653, folder 15, 262, 275.

25. Statistics on Mexican nationals are from the University of Virginia Geospatial and Statistical Data Center http://fisher.lib.virginia.edu/census/. See also Peterson, "Twentieth-Century Search for Cíbola," 116–117; and Reisler, *By the Sweat of their Brow*, 24–37. On segregation in south Phoenix, see Shirley J. Roberts, "Minority-Group Poverty in Phoenix: A Socio-Economic Survey," *Journal of Arizona History* 14 (Winter 1973): 347–353.

26. Lucius Zittier to M. Katherine Drexel, January 28, 1908, and Zittier, "Memorandum *In Re Guadalupe Townsite:* Legal process of establishing Yaqui settlement," n.d., both in OLGC; Leah Glaser, "Working for Community: The Yaqui Indians at the Salt River Project," *Journal of Arizona History* 37 (Winter 1996): 339.

27. Glaser, "Working for Community," 341–343; Howard Ruppers, "Yaqui" in *The 'Current' News*, February 1957, 2–4, SRPA.

28. Spicer, *The Yaquis*, 237; Spicer, *People of Pascua*, ed. Kathleen M. Sands and Rosamund B. Spicer (Tucson: University of Arizona Press, 1988), 35–36.

29. Sheridan, *Los Tucsonenses.*

30. See Booth, "Creation of a Nation"; Henry Dobyns, *The Papago People* (Phoenix: Indian Tribal Series, 1972); Erickson, *Sharing the Desert*; Spicer, *The Yaquis*; Spicer, *Pascua: A Yaqui Village* (Chicago: University of Chicago Press, 1940). On Arizona, two exceptions to this rule are Harry T. Getty, *Interethnic Relationships in the Community of Tucson* (New York: Arno, 1976); and James S. Griffith, *A Shared Space: Folklife in the Arizona-Sonora Borderlands* (Logan: Utah State University Press, 1995).

31. Jeré Franco, "Unlawful Love: A History of Arizona's Miscegenation Law," *Journal of Arizona History* 27 (Winter 1986): 377–390. See also Peggy Pascoe, "Miscegenation Law, Court Cases, and Ideologies of 'Race' in Twentieth-Century America," in *Sex, Love, Race: Crossing Boundaries in North American History*, ed. Martha Hodes (New York: New York University Press, 1999), 464–490.

32. Pascoe, *Miscegenation Law*, 464–469.

33. Franco, *Unlawful Love*, 283–284.

34. Sheridan, *Los Tucsonenses*, 149.

35. Benton, "What about Women," 41.

36. Benton, "What about Women," 45–56. See also Al Hurtado, *Intimate Frontiers: Sex, Gender, and Culture in Old California* (Albuquerque: University of

New Mexico Press, 1999); and Deena J. González, *Refusing the Favor: The Spanish-Mexican Women of Santa Fe, 1820–1880* (Oxford: Oxford University Press, 1999).

37. Sheridan, *Los Tucsonenses*, 149.

38. Benton, "What about Women," 269–272. Quotation from 271.

39. Field matron report, January 25, 1930, BIA-RG75, box 190, folder "052.1 G&S statistical reports."

40. Andrés Reséndez, "Genetics, Culture, and the Vagaries of Mestizaje among Indians, Europeans, and Africans in Greater Mexico," (paper presented at the Rocky Mountain Council for Latin American Studies, Tucson, April 1, 2005).

41. Superintendent McQuigg to commissioner of Indian Affairs, September 13, 1913, BIA-RG75, box 189, folder "Field matron reports: 1912–1913."

42. Woodruff Weekly Report, September 10, 1927, BIA-RG75, box 191, folder "Field matron's weekly report: Janette Woodruff, 1927–1929."

43. Spicer, *People of Pascua*, 81–96.

44. Carlos Vélez-Ibáñez, *Border Visions: Mexican Cultures of the Southwest United States* (Tucson: University of Arizona Press, 1996), 316.

45. Kelley, *Yaqui Women*, 111.

46. On the Yaquis, see Spicer, *People of Pascua*, 83–86. On the O'odham, see Elisabeth J. Tooker, "Papagos in Tucson: An Introduction to Their History, Community Life, and Acculturation" (master's thesis, University of Arizona, 1952), 47; Griffith, *A Shared Space*, 45; and Lolita Ochoa, interview by Timothy Dunnigan, August 5, 1969, ASMT, DAIOH.

47. McCarthy, *A Papago Traveler*, 24–25; Ochoa interview.

48. Tooker, *Papagos in Tucson*, 19–20.

49. Father Nicholas, untitled, July 25, 1914, SCUA BO-MSS, box 1, folder 4.

50. Tooker, *Papagos in Tucson*, 27, 82–83.

51. The most detailed published account of the Yaqui ceremonies and of other important traditions is offered by Muriel Thayer Painter, *With Good Heart: Yaqui Beliefs and Ceremonies in Pascua Village*, ed. Edward H. Spicer and Wilma Kaemlein (Tucson: University of Arizona Press, 1986). See also Spicer, *The Yaquis*, 59–118. I observed the Pascua ceremonies several times in Guadalupe in the 1990s.

52. Antonio Córdova, interview by Patricia Preciado Martin, in Bernal and Bernal, *Images and Conversations*, 13–21, 13; and Jacinta Jacobo Carranza, interview by Patricia Preciado Martin in Bernal and Bernal, *Images and Conversations*, 59–67.

53. Griffith, *A Shared Space*, 36; Weber, *The Spanish Frontier*, 242; Spicer, *Cycles of Conquest*, 139.

54. Woodruff and Dryden, *Indian Oasis*, 282; Dobyns, *The Papago People*, 67; "Esperan a Los Yaquis de Arizona en Magdalena," *El Tucsonense*, September 21, 1937. The article claims that thousands of Yaquis and over eight hundred Tohono O'odham traveled to the festival annually in automobile caravans.

55. Wilbur-Cruce, *A Beautiful, Cruel Country*, 59.

56. Alberto Alvaro Ríos, *Capirotada: A Nogales Memoir* (Albuquerque: University of New Mexico Press, 1999), 77. For other examples of Mexicans and Yaquis

attending the festival, see Jane Holden Kelley, *Yaqui Women*, 111; and Castillo and Cowan, *It Is Not Our Fault*, 30.

57. L. Frye to Thackery, September 5, 1913; Thackery to Dr. L. H. Richards, n.d.; Richards to Thackery, September 12, 1913, all in BIA-RG75, box 18, folder 71-76-162.

58. Weekly report, April 30, 1919, BIA-RG75, box 191, folder "Field matron correspondence, Janette Woodruff, 1919–1920."

59. Dobyns, *The Papago People*, 67.

60. Such gendered divisions of labor are apparent in many memoirs and life histories from south-central Arizona. See, for example, Manuel Gamio, *The Mexican Immigrant* (New York: Arno Press, 1969); Bernal and Bernal, *Images and Conversations*; Patricia Preciado Martin, *Songs My Mother Sang to Me: An Oral History of Mexican American Women* (Tucson: University of Arizona Press, 1992); McCarthy, *A Papago Traveler*; Refugio Savala, *Autobiography of a Yaqui Poet*, ed. Kathleen Sands (Tucson: University of Arizona Press, 1980); Webb, *A Pima Remembers*; Moisés, *A Yaqui Life*; Blaine and Adams, *Papagos and Politics*; and Kelley, *Yaqui Women*.

61. Heyman, *Life and Labor on the Border*, 93–97.

62. Benton, "What about Women," 95–105. Quotation from 98.

63. Savala, *Autobiography*, 18–20, 33. Quotation on 18.

64. Sheridan, *Los Tucsonenses*, 142.

65. See Janette Woodruff's reports from 15, 20 September; 4, 18 October; 6, 27 December 1924; 3 January; 18, 25 April; 30 May 1925; 2 January; 24 April; 19 September; and 2 October 1926, all in BIA-RG75, box 191, folder "Field matron weekly reports, Janette Woodruff, 1925–1926." Quotation from 9 October 1926.

66. Spicer, *Pascua*, 29.

67. *Fourteenth Census of the United States 1920*, 97–100.

68. Vicki L. Ruiz, *From out of the Shadows: Mexican Women in Twentieth-Century America* (New York: Oxford University Press, 1998), 63. For a discussion of chaperoning, see 51–71.

69. Estrada is quoted by Vicki Ruiz in *From out of the Shadows*, 59.

70. Livia León Montiel, interview by Patricia Preciado Martin, in Martin, *Songs My Mother Sang*, 20.

71. *Fourteenth Census of the United States, 1920*, 46–49.

72. Spicer, *People of Pascua*, 34–37. On Yaqui women, see Spicer, *Pascua*, 30, 34; and Kelley, *Yaqui Women*, 32.

73. Kelley, *Yaqui Women*, 120.

74. Ibid., 220–221.

75. Tooker, "Papagos in Tucson," 8.

76. Woodruff weekly report, November 18, 1916, BIA-RG75, box 190, folder "Field matron Janette Woodruff, 1915–1918."

77. Getty, *Interethnic Relationships*, 122–124.

78. On Mexican-American attitudes toward immigrants in Texas and California, see Gutiérrez, *Walls and Mirrors*, passim.

79. Sheridan, *Los Tucsonenses*, 89–93, 115–126. The last Mexican American to be elected to the territorial legislature (1905) was Alfred Ruiz. Servín, "Role of Mexican Americans," 30.

80. Sheridan, *Los Tucsonenses*, 110–112, 168–169, 180.

81. James D. McBride, "The Liga Protectora Latina: A Mexican-American Benevolent Society in Arizona," *Journal of the West* 14 (October 1975): 82–90, 84.

82. Peterson, "Twentieth-Century Search for Cíbola," 117.

83. Barry Edward Lamb, "The Making of a Chicano Civil Rights Activist: Ralph Estrada of Arizona," (master's thesis, Arizona State University, 1988), 44–48.

84. Peterson, "Twentieth-Century Search for Cíbola," 118; Lamb, "The Making of a Chicano Civil Rights Activist," 48–50. For a comparative discussion of labor contractors, or *padrones*, in three immigrant communities, see Peck, *Reinventing Free Labor*.

85. Peterson, "Twentieth-Century Search for Cíbola," 118; McBride, "The Liga Protectora Latina," 88–89.

86. Adam Díaz, interview by Karin Ullmann, April 16, 1976, AHST, POHP; Bradford Luckingham, *Minorities in Phoenix*, (Tucson: University of Arizona Press, 1995), 34–36; Mary Ruth Titcomb, "Americanization and Mexicans in the Southwest: A History of Phoenix's Friendly House, 1920–1983" (master's thesis, University of California, Santa Barbara, 1984), 38–40.

87. Carlos Morales, interview in Gamio, *The Mexican Immigrant* (New York: Arno Press, 1969), 11–13.

4

1. "Johnson Introduces New Immigration Bill," *Arizona Labor Journal*, July 5, 1930, 4 (hereafter cited as *ALJ*).

2. On Spanish, Slavic, and Italian immigrants and whiteness, see Gordon, *Orphan Abduction*, 101–104, 166, 205, 223–226, 242, 311; and Benton, "What About Women," passim.

3. On the migration of farmworkers from the south-central plains states into Arizona, see Marsha L Weisiger, *Land of Plenty: Oklahomans in the Cotton Fields of Arizona, 1933–1942* (Norman: University of Oklahoma Press, 1995). On migrant workers in Texas, see Foley, *White Scourge*.

4. Ignatiev, *How the Irish became White*; Roediger, *Wages of Whiteness*; Gordon, *Orphan Abduction*.

5. Foley, *White Scourge*, 167, 183–201.

6. Gordon, *Orphan Abduction*, 101–102.

7. Berman, *Reformers, Corporations, and the Electorate*, 59.

8. James R. Kluger, *The Clifton-Morenci Strike: Labor Difficulty in Arizona, 1915–1916* (Tucson: University of Arizona Press, 1970), 50.

9. Benton, "What About Women," 134.

10. Senate, *Reports of the Immigration Commission*, "Immigrant Labor in Mining, Smelting, and Refining Industry," 61st Cong., 2d sess., 1911, 129–132.

11. Benton, "What about Women," 139, 225–227.

12. Quotations are from, respectively, Berman, *Arizona's Age of Reform*, 61, and Gordon, *Orphan Abduction*, 224. See Gordon 209–243 for a summary of the strike.

13. Gordon, *Orphan Abduction*, 220–240; Mellinger, *Race and Labor*, 60–67.

14. Gordon, *Orphan Abduction*, 205, 209.

15. Parrish, *Mexican Workers, Progressives, and Copper*, 13–14; Mellinger, *Race and Labor*, 76–78, 88–90; Benton, "What about Women," 218.

16. "Company Gunmen in Ray Streets," *ALJ*, July 1, 1915, 1, 4; Andrés E. Jiménez Montoya, *Political Domination in the Labor Market: Racial Division in the Arizona Copper Industry* (Berkeley: University of California Chicano Studies Library Publications, 1977); Phillip Mellinger, "'The Men Have Become Organizers': Labor Conflict and Unionization in the Mexican Mining Communities of Arizona, 1900–1915," *Western Historical Quarterly* 23 (1993): 322–347, 338; Mellinger, *Race and Labor*, 138–139. See also Leaming, *Labor and Copper*.

17. Enrique Pastor, interview by Rita Magdaleno, September 1, 1995, CHASU, MSS-168, box 1, folder 17, 13.

18. "Company Gunmen in Ray Streets," *ALJ*, July 1, 1915, 1, 4; Mellinger, *Race and Labor*, 146–149.

19. Mellinger accepts, without comment, reports from the *Daily Silver Belt* and *Miners' Magazine* that the Ray strike began when a group of "Mexican revolutionary agitators" met to help Mexico fight against the United States and then decided instead to strike. No other evidence, other than a couple of mainstream press accounts, supports the claim that the strikers were racially or nationally motivated revolutionaries. See Mellinger, *Race and Labor*, 145–146, 157. Historians have also raised doubts about whether the Plan of San Diego had much of an impact outside south Texas. See especially Alan Knight, *The Mexican Revolution*, vol. 2, *Counter Revolution and Reconstruction* (Lincoln: University of Nebraska Press, 1986), 344; Don M. Coerver and Linda B. Hall, *Texas and the Mexican Revolution: A Study in State and National Border Policy, 1910–1920* (San Antonio, TX: Trinity University Press, 1984), 87; Acuña, *Occupied America: A History of Chicanos*, 3rd ed. (New York: Harper-Collins, 1988), 161–162.

20. Quotations are from "Company Gunmen in Ray Streets," *ALJ*, July 1, 1915, 1; "Ray Miners Secure W.F.M. Charter," *ALJ*, July 8, 1915. For a general description of the changing nature of the ASFL and WFM's leadership, see Mellinger, *Race and Labor*, 164–165.

21. Quotations are from "Ray Miners Secure W.F.M. Charter," *ALJ*, July 8, 1915, and "Company Gunmen in Ray Streets," *ALJ*, July 1, 1915, 1.

22. "The End of the Strike," *ALJ*, July 15, 1915, 2; "Strike Ended," *ALJ*, July 15, 1915, 1.

23. Mellinger, "Men Have Become Organizers," 342.

24. Kluger, *The Clifton-Morenci Strike*, 70; Byrkit, *Forging the Copper Collar*, 61.

25. Parrish, *Mexican Workers*, 13–14; Mellinger, *Race and Labor*, 174–176.

26. Sheridan, *Los Tucsonenses*, 110–112, 168–169, 180.

27. McBride, "The Liga Protectora Latina," 82–90.

28. "1200 Men on Strike at Ajo," *ALJ*, 1 December 1916, 1; H. C. Brown, "Ajo Strike Reviewed Day by Day," *ALJ*, 15 December 1916; "N.C. Employees Walk Out," *Ajo Copper News*, 25 November 1916, 1 (hereafter cited as *ACN*); "The Strike," *ACN*, 9 December 1916, 1.

29. Mike Curley to Rev. T. Wand, November 30, 1916, BO-MSS, box 1, folder 1916; "1200 Men," *ALJ*, 1.

30. In *ALJ*: J. L. Donnelly, "Raise Funds Now," 22 December 1916, 1; Ed Miller, "Sheriff Forbes Arrests Women," 22 December 1916, 1; Arthur T. Thatcher, "Timely Review of the Ajo Strike," 29 December 1916, 2; "Ajo Strike is Still On," 29 December 1916; "Funds Needed For Men in Tucson Jail," 2 February 1917, 1; "Ajo Strikers Still in Tucson Jail," 9 February 1917, 1. In *ACN:* "Troops Here," 23 December 1916, 1; Editorial, 23 December 1916, 1.

31. "Strike Called Off by Western Federation," *ALJ*, January 20, 1917, 1. See also, "Ajo Strike Called Off by Unions," *ALJ*, January 26, 1916, 1, which admitted that the strike was a failure. An analysis of the strike was also printed in Spanish in "*La Huelga de El Ajo,*" *ALJ*, January 26, 1917, 3.

32. The warning appeared in bold on the front page of *ACN* on December 30, 1916.

33. Editorial, *ACN*, March 10, 1917, 2.

34. Editorial, *ACN*, July 6, 1917, 1.

35. McBride, "Liga Protectora Latina," 85–86; "Company Gunmen in Ray Streets," *ALJ*, 1.

36. Sheridan, *Arizona*, 180–183, 215–216. The most detailed accounts of the events leading up to the Bisbee deportation can be found in Byrkit, *Forging the Copper Collar*, 97–215, and Benton, "What about Women," 397–404.

37. Benton, "What about Women," especially 434. For a different perspective on gender and the Bisbee strike, focusing on women and domesticity, see Colleen O'Neill, "Domesticity Deployed: Gender, Race, and the Construction of Class Struggle in the Bisbee Deportation," *Labor History* 34 (Spring/Summer 1993): 256–273.

38. Benton, "What about Women," 481–493; Byrkit, *Forging the Copper Collar*, 97–215.

39. Mellinger, *Race and Labor*, 194–203.

40. Parrish, *Mexican Workers*, 3, 44–47.

41. Carlos Contreras, "Carlos Contreras" (unpublished autobiographical paper, 1972), SCASU, CHASU, 3.

42. Pastor interview, CHASU, MSS-168; Alonzo interview, MSS-168.

43. "State Federation Is Investigating Status of Imported Mexican Labor," *ALJ*, February 6, 1920, 1, 3; "Report of Investigation Forced by the Federation," *ALJ*, August 6, 1920, 1.

44. "Better to Return to Alfalfa," *ALJ*, May 14, 1920, 1. The ASFL's reports helped to spark an investigation by the Los Angeles Mexican consul, who helped

to negotiate a wage increase from three to four cents per pound. See Peterson, "Twentieth-Century Search for Cíbola," 120–128.

45. French to Wilson, 3 February 1920, reprinted in *ALJ*, 6 Feb 1920, 3; "Federal Labor Union Chartered," *ALJ*, 21 May 1920, 1; "State Federation Is Investigating," *ALJ*, 6 February 1920, 1, 3.

46. In *ALJ*: "Illegal Deportations Common," 25 June 1920, 1; "Deported Mexican Left Family Behind," 23 July 1920, 1; "Mexicans Held in Depot Two Days," 9 December 1920, 1; "A Means to an End," 25 November 1920, 4; "Sanchez Reported Released," *ALJ*, 3 February 1921, 4.

47. Peterson, "Twentieth-Century Search for Cibola," 122–124.

48. John H. Bratton, "Long Staple Cotton Monopoly Threatens Small Farmer," *ALJ*, 24 September 1920, 1.

49. Sheridan, *Arizona*, 216. In September and October 1926, unable to find a sufficient number of resident laborers to pick cotton, the ACGA hoped to recruit twelve hundred Puerto Ricans. The plan quickly turned sour, however, as most of the recruits refused to work under the substandard conditions in the Salt River valley. See ACGA "Report of the Porto Rican Situation," SCASU, CH-MSS, box 638, folder 1; and "The Porto Rican Labor Bubble," *The Associated Arizona Producer*, October 15, 1926, 6.

50. The aggregate economic figures are from Sheridan, *Arizona*, 253. Picking rates are from Weisiger, *Land of Plenty*, 47.

51. The letter from J. H. Francis to Albert Johnson and the telegram from Globe-Miami both appeared in *ALJ*, 1 March 1930, 1. The white citizen-worker quote is from "Johnson Introduces New Immigration Bill," *ALJ*, July 5, 1930, 4.

52. "Glamour of Mexico Deceives Pilgrims," *ALJ*, March 1, 1930, 3.

53. "Restriction of Immigration": Speech of Hon. Carl Hayden of Arizona in the U.S. House, February 4, 1915, SCASU, CH-MSS, box 653, folder 16, 6; "Statement of Hon. Carl Hayden," CH-MSS, box 653, folder 15, 262, 275; "Hayden Opposes Harris Bill," *ALJ*, April 26, 1930, 1, 4; "Senator Hayden Seeks Deportation of Aliens," *ALJ*, December 20, 1930, 4.

54. Abraham Hoffman, *Unwanted Mexican Americans in the Great Depression: Repatriation Pressures, 1929–1939* (Tucson: University of Arizona Press, 1974), 30–41.

55. Maximo Alonzo, interview by Rita Magdaleno, March 18, 1995, MSS-168, box 1, folder 9, 4–5.

56. Paul S. Taylor, "Mexican Labor in the United States: Migration Statistics," *University of California Publications in Economics*, vol. 3 (Berkeley: University of California Press, 1934).

57. Muñoz is quoted by Raymond Johnson Flores, "The Socio-Economic Status Trends of the Mexican People Residing in Arizona" (master's thesis, Arizona State University, 1951), 10–11.

58. In *El Tucsonense* (hereafter cited as *TUC*): "*Extranjeros de Arizona*," November 12, 1937, 2; "*Cruel, brutal, insocial y anti-cristiana*," November 23, 1937, 1; "*Los no ciudadanos*," December 7, 1937, 2.

59. Gutiérrez, *Walls and Mirrors*, 6, 56–65.

60. Getty, "Interethnic Relationships," 32–35. On the Mexican-American strategy of claiming whiteness as the foundation for full citizenship, see Foley, "Becoming Hispanic," 53–70.

61. Adam Díaz, interview by Karin Ullmann, April 16, 1976, AHST, POHP. See also Luckingham, *Minorities in Phoenix*, 48–49.

62. "*Club hispano-americano independiente de la municipalidad de Sur Tucson,*" *TUC*, February 12, 1937, 3; "*Votaron ayer por la incorporacion de Sur Tucson,*" *TUC*, August 11, 1936; Robert Roth, "Life was slower back then," *El Independiente*, May 7, 1976, 1; "South Tucson is Voting On Incorporation," *Tucson Daily Citizen*, August 10, 1936, 1; "South Tucson Municipality Gets Underway," *Tucson Daily Citizen*, August 12, 1936, 12.

63. "*Candidatos de nuestra raza en Sur Tucson,*" *TUC*, March 5, 1937, 1; "*Hispano-Americanos ganan en Sur Tucson,*" *TUC*, April 13, 1937, 1; "*En Sur Tucson, en elección de ayer sorpresa,*" *TUC*, May 25, 1937, 1.

64. Díaz interview; Luckingham, *Minorities in Phoenix*, 34–36; Titcomb, "Americanization and Mexicans," 38–40.

65. Titcomb, "Americanization and Mexicans," 42–43; Luckingham, *Minorities in Phoenix*, 35, 36, 45; Sheridan, *Los Tucsonenses*, 210–211.

66. Weisiger, *Land of Plenty*.

67. Malcolm Brown and Orin Cassmore, *Migratory Cotton Pickers in Arizona* (Washington, DC, 1939), 67–68.

68. Philip Greisinger and George W. Barr, *Agricultural Land Ownership and Operating Tenures in Casa Grande Valley*, Agricultural Experiment Station Bulletin 175 (Tucson, 1941), 281, 284–288. For aggregate Pinal County and Arizona figures, see Sheridan, *Arizona*, 219, 255. See also E. D. Tetreau, *Arizona Farm Leases*, Agricultural Experiment Station Bulletin 179 (Tucson, 1942).

69. Tetreau, *Arizona's Farm Laborers*, 334; Varden Fuller and E. D. Tetreau, *Volume and Characteristics of Migration to Arizona, 1930–1939*, Agricultural Experiment Station Bulletin 176 (Tucson, 1941), 300. On black migrant workers in Arizona, see Geta LeSeur, *Not All Okies Are White: The Lives of Black Cotton Pickers in Arizona* (Columbia: University of Missouri Press, 2000).

70. Foley argues that the decline of tenant farming "eroded their status from semi-independent white tenant farmers to semi-white farm workers." Foley, *White Scourge*, 167.

71. Brown and Cassmore, *Migratory Cotton Pickers*, 7–8.

72. Emmett McLoughlin, *People's Padre: An Autobiography* (Boston: Beacon, 1954), 40–41.

73. University of Virginia Geospatial and Statistical Data Center, http://fisher.lib.virginia.edu/census/.

74. LeSeur, *Not All Okies Are White*, 24–29. On the relationship between blacks and Indians, see LeSeur's interviews with Myrtle and Jeff Jordan, 72–93.

75. Weisiger, *Land of Plenty*, 143.

76. The radio address is reprinted in full in the *ALJ*, December 14, 1939, 4.

77. Weisiger, *Land of Plenty*, 145.

78. Edward Hooper, interview by Marsha Weisiger, transcript, May 30, 1992, Oklahoma-Arizona Migration Project (OAMP), AHST.

79. From AHST: Dennis Kirkland, interview by Marsha Weisiger, May 20, 1992, OAMP; Sam Cambron, interview by Marsha Weisiger, May 21, 1992, OAMP.

80. Stuart Jamieson, *Labor Unionism in American Agriculture* (New York: Arno, 1976), 199; Dewey Phares and Jewel Phares, interview by Marsha Weisiger, May 27, 1992, OAMP.

81. In *ALJ*: "Vegetable Men Form Union," December 16, 1933, 1; "Chester Installs New Union," December 30, 1933, 1; Eli Follett, "From Vegetable Packers," February 24, 1934, 3. Also see Jamieson, *Labor Unionism*, 198. The ambiguity of the NRA's definition of "agricultural labor" is discussed by Cindy Hahamovich, *The Fruits of Their Labor: Atlantic Coast Farmworkers and the Making of Migrant Poverty, 1870–1945* (Chapel Hill: University of North Carolina Press, 1997), 146–147.

82. Jamieson, *Labor Unionism*, 196–197; Weisiger, *Land of Plenty*, 47.

83. In *ALJ*: "Coolidge Farmers Refuse Arbitration," August 30, 1934, 1; "Doane Deplores Coolidge Valley Relief Agencies," September 13, 1934, 1; "Casa Grande Farm Workers' Union Formed," November 15, 1934, 1. See also, Jamieson, *Labor Unionism*, 197, and Weisiger, *Land of Plenty*, 47.

84. In *ALJ*: "Slaves Were Fed," 24 March 1938, 2; "Government Adds to Unemployment," 21 April 1938, 1; "Who Are the Associated Farmers?," 14 December 1939, 4; "Senate Committee Probes 'Farmers'," 1 February 1940, 1; also see, Ammon Hennacy, *Two Agitators: Peter Maurin-Ammon Hennacy*, Catholic Worker group pamphlet (October 1959), 24, 28, 32. See also Jamieson, *Labor Unionism*, 201–202; Weisiger, *Land of Plenty*, 80–81.

85. In BIA-RG75 see weekly field matron reports for 3 January 1931, 16 and 24 February 1931; 21 and 28 March 1931, 19 June 1931, in box 190, folder "052.1 G&S statistical reports: field nurses and matrons monthly reports—1928–1931."

86. Getty, "Interethnic Relationships," 40–45.

87. According to the 1930 census, there were 30,679 "native white persons" in Pima County and 21,699 persons of "other races." Of the latter most were of Mexican and Indian descent (blacks were separated into their own category). See the online census reports at University of Virginia Geospatial and Statistical Data Center, http://fisher.lib.virginia.edu/census/.

88. Peter MacMillian Booth, "Cactizonians: The Civilian Conservation Corps in Pima County, 1933–1942," *Journal of Arizona History* 32 (Autumn, 1991): 294–297.

89. Weisiger, *Land of Plenty*, 108–111, 136. For examples of FSA discouragement of union organization, see *Desert Sentinel* "Editorial," January 28, 1941, 3; "Editorial," February 3, 1941, 2; "Off the Manager's Desk," October 6, 1941, 2. On the goals of the FSA camps, see Hahamovich, *Fruits of Their Labor*, 156.

90. In OAMP: Phares interview; Cambron interview; Murrell Harrisk, interview by Marsha Weisiger, May 23, 1992.

91. In OAMP: Kirkland interview; Phares interview; Harrisk interview.

92. Edward Banfield, *Government Project* (Glencoe, IL: Free Press, 1951), 147–156; 151, 153; Hooper interview, OAMP.

93. Banfield, *Government Project*, 155–156, 186–188, 217.

94. Ibid.

95. The Agua Fria camp paper, *The Desert Sentinel*, listed the names of heads of new families in every edition. The first appearance in several years of a few Hispanic names was in the February 24, 1941, issue 2. Among thirty-five new families, eight had Hispanic names.

96. Lee and Flora Davis, interview by Marsha Weisiger, May 19, 1992, OAMP.

5

1. Blaine and Adams, *Papagos and Politics*, 9–28.

2. Ibid., 38, 40, 46, 68, 91.

3. Ibid., 17.

4. The Indian Reorganization Act is reproduced in Prucha, *Documents*, 222–225.

5. For a discussion of the impact of the IRA on Indian identity and sociopolitical organization, see Stephen Cornell, *Return of the Native: American Indian Political Resurgence* (New York: Oxford University Press, 1988), 71–105 (quotation from 96); Graham Taylor, *The New Deal and American Indian Tribalism: The Administration of the Indian Reorganization Act, 1934–1945* (Lincoln: University of Nebraska Press, 1980); and James S. Olson and Raymond Wilson, *Native Americans in the Twentieth Century* (Chicago: University of Chicago Press, 1986), 107–128.

6. John Collier, "This is Just By Way of Getting Ourselves Located," *Indians at Work*, August 15, 1933, 1–2 (hereafter cited as *IAW*). Also in *IAW*: Collier's opening statement, September 1, 1933, 1; "Employment Under the Civil Works Administration," December 1, 1933, 5–6; "The Anniversary of Indian Emergency Conservation Work," May 15, 1934, 7–10; "To the Aid of Indian Artists," January 1, 1934, 32–33; James D. Young, "The Revival and Development of Indian Arts and Crafts," April 1, 1940, 27, 29–35.

7. In addition to the February report, other field matron reports from 1931 expose this crisis. In particular, see reports from 3 January, 16 February, 24 February, 21 March, 28 March, 19 June, BIA-RG75, box 190, folder "052.1 G&S statistical reports: field nurses and matrons monthly reports—1928–1931."

8. Agnes Vavages to Gracie Taylor, March 9, 1933, and Taylor to Vavages, March 27, 1933, BIA-RG75, box 147, folder "Senior placement matron Gracie Taylor: 1929–1934." On unemployment in Phoenix, see Trennert, *Phoenix Indian School*, 203–204.

9. There are hundreds of work relief applications in BIA-RG75, box 144, folder 2: "Indian employment files of the community worker, Doris L. Weston."

10. While the majority of the workers were Tohono O'odham, the Indian crews on the Sells reservation also included men from the Yuma, Cherokee, Pima, and Mari-

copa tribes; see "The Indian Emergency Conservation Work Program in Figures,"
IAW, September 1, 1933, 10–14; Harris H. Roberts, Walter C. Coe, and Claude C.
Cornwall, "Remaking a Reservation Range—IECW—Part I," *IAW*, December 1,
1934, 18–24, and "Remaking a Reservation Range—IECW—Part II," *IAW*, December 15, 1934, 8–14; Erik Allstrom, "In Papago Land," *IAW*, April 1, 1939, 11. On
Harwood Hall, see Booth, "Cactizonians," 310.

11. Senate, *A History of the Pima Indians and the San Carlos Irrigation Project*,
89th Cong., 1st sess., S. Doc. 11, 58–59; Dudley, "Pima Indians," 30, 75–76. Patton
quoted on 100.

12. Hackenberg, "Pima and Papago Ecological Adaptations," 174–175. For a detailed account of the drawn-out litigation over the San Carlos Project, see Dudley,
"Pima Indians," 31–106. See also "Recommended Settlement," *IAW*, August 1, 1934,
25.

13. A. H. Kneale, "Irrigation of Pima Lands," *IAW*, May 1, 1935, 35–37.

14. "The Public Works Grant for Indian Irrigation," *IAW*, September 15, 1933, 34;
C. C. Wright, "Marketing Alfalfa and Other Forage Crops," *IAW*, December 15, 1935,
37–41, 37; Hackenberg, "Pima and Papago Ecological Adaptations," 175; Greisinger
and Barr, *Agricultural Land Ownership*, University of Arizona Agricultural Experiment Station Bulletin 175 (1941), 281, 286–287 (hereafter cited as *AESB*).

15. C. J. Moody, "The San Carlos Irrigation Project," *IAW*, February 1, 1934, 29;
A. E. Robinson, "Irrigation of Pima Lands," *IAW*, April 15, 1936, 5–8.

16. A. H. Kneale, "Irrigation of Pima Lands," *IAW*, May 1, 1935, 35–37;
Hackenberg, "Pima and Papago Ecological Adaptations," 175. See also in the *Tucson
Daily Citizen* for 1937: "Pima Indians Object to Paying for Water," April 2; "Collier
to Pay Visit to Pima Tribes," May 18; "John Collier Explains Plan to Help Indians,"
May 22; "Pima Indians Refuse to Pay Water Charge," May 24.

17. C. C. Wright, "Marketing Alfalfa," *IAW*, December 15, 1935, 37–41. On the
Navajo sheep reduction program, see Richard White, *Roots of Dependency: Subsistence, Environment, and Social Change among the Choctaws, Pawnees, and Navajos* (Lincoln: University of Nebraska Press, 1983), 248–249, 252–315.

18. Trennert, *Phoenix Indian School*, 143.

19. Wright, "Marketing Alfalfa"; Erik W. Allstrom, "Water, Alfalfa, and Cattle,"
IAW, November 1, 1938, 14–15. Figures on average amounts of irrigated acreage from
C. H. Southworth, acting director of irrigation, memorandum for the commissioner,
February 6, 1941, OFJC, reel 16.

20. Nathan Allen, "The Akimel O'othom: Pima People," in *Native Peoples of
the Southwest: Negotiating Land, Water, and Ethnicities*, ed. Laurie Weinstein
(Westport, CT: Bergin & Garvey, 2001), 89–98, 95.

21. "Corporate Charter of the Gila River Pima-Maricopa Indian Community,"
1936, BIA-RG75, box 194, folder "Charter of incorporation"; Ralph A. Barnes, "The
Indians Claims Commission," in Horr, *Papago Indians I*, 13–16; Spicer, *Cycles of
Conquest*, 151.

22. Tetreau, "Arizona's Farm Laborers," *AESB* 163 (1939): 226–330.

23. Blaine and Adams, *Papagos and Politics*, 73–74.

24. Geta LaSeur's interview with Myrtle Jordon is found in LaSeur, *Not All Okies Are White*, 72–85. Quotation from 75.

25. "Tribal Leaders Voice their Opinion," *IAW*, September 15, 1933, 28; Lewis, *Neither Wolf nor Dog*, 154.

26. Rosamund Spicer, "People on the Desert" in *The Desert People*, 104–105. See also Erickson, *Sharing the Desert*, 100–101, 130–131.

27. Lewis, *Neither Wolf nor Dog*, 162; Booth, "Creation of a Nation," 229–237.

28. In SCUA, BO-MSS: Juan Joaquín, head of the League of Papago Chiefs, to Charles Burke, November 16, 1928, box 3, folder 1928; Papago Chiefs and Oblasser to Burke, March 16, 1929; Chairman, Papago Chiefs to Burke, June 5, 1929, box 3, folder 1929; Oblasser to H. Hammond, March 26, 1930; Oblasser to Sen. Henry Ashurst, May 13, 1930; Oblasser to Elliot, November 16, 1930, box 3, folder, 1929.

29. Quotation is from a letter from Joaquín to Burke, November 16, 1928, SCUA, BO-MSS, box 3, folder 1928. On the wine feast, see Bonaventure Oblasser to C. Wayne Clampitt, Commissioner of Indian Affairs, BO-MSS, box 3, folder 1932.

30. Booth, "Creation of a Nation," 323–324.

31. Request for withdrawal by C. J. Rhoads to Secretary of the Interior Ray Lyman Wilbur, October 28, 1932, SCUA, BO-MSS, box 3, folder 1933.

32. In SCUA, BO-MSS: "Resolution Adopted by the Papago Tribal Council," December 2, 1932, box 3, folder "July-Dec"; "Request for withdrawal," n.d., box 3, folder 1933; and Oblasser to Collier, February 13, 1934, box 3, folder "Jan-June." See also Blaine and Adams, *Papagos and Politics*, 50.

33. Blaine and Adams, *Papagos and Politics*, 50; Oblasser to Collier, Februry 13, 1934, BO-MSS, box 3, folder "Jan-June."

34. Blaine and Adams, *Papagos and Politics*, 57–64; Carl Hayden to secretary of the interior, November 30, 1932, BO-MSS, box 3, folder "July-Dec"; Oblasser to Collier, February 13, 1934, box 3, folder "Jan-June."

35. In SCUA, BO-MSS: Oblasser to Collier, February 13, 1934, box 3, folder "Jan-June, 1932"; Collier to Oblasser, July 31, 1934, box 3, folder "July-Dec 1934"; Oblasser to Nathan Margold, U.S. Department of the Interior, September 23, 1934, box 3, folder "July-Dec 1934"; Attorney General Homer Cummings to the secretary of the interior, November 1, 1934, box 3, folder "July-Dec 1934"; Collier to Sup. Theodore Hall, Sells agency, November 8, 1934, box 3, folder "July-Dec 1934"; and see the Indian Reorganization Act, Prucha, *Documents*, 222. See also Blaine and Adams, *Papagos and Politics*, 57–64.

36. Booth, "Creation of a Nation," 355–358.

37. Draft of Public Law 709, SCUA, BO-MSS, folder "1931 (Jan-June)," box 3; Erickson, *Sharing the Desert*, 132–142.

38. "List of ballot boxes, by districts, 1934 ref., showing total vote cast," BIA-RG75, box 197, folder "District List-Totals"; Lewis, *Neither Wolf nor Dog*, 155.

39. Booth, "Creation of a Nation," 385–400.

40. Dobyns, *The Papago People*, 64.

41. Blaine and Adams, *Papagos and Politics*, 69–81.

42. John H. Holst, "The Organization of the Papagos," *IAW*, February 1937, 23–28; Oblasser, "Chief José Anton: Papago Indian Patriot," *IAW*, February 1937; Department of the Interior, Office of Indian Affairs, "Constitution and By-Laws of the Papago Tribe, Arizona," approved January 6, 1937, BIA-RG75, box 194, folder "Charter of incorporation"; Erickson, *Sharing the Desert*, 148–149.

43. In BIA-RG75: "Precinct election returns—Referendum on the proposed Papago constitution and by-laws," box 194, folder "Certificates of precinct election returns"; untitled document listing polling locations in each district, box 196, folder "Constitution voting." In OFJC: Ruth Underhill, "Reasons for the choice of Santa Rosa as an area of investigation," March 18, 1942, and Laura Thompson, "Coordinator's report for the research committee on Indian education," March 16, 1942, both on reel 11.

44. John H. Holst, "The Organization of the Papagos," *IAW*, February 1, 1937, 28.

45. Lewis, *Neither Wolf nor Dog*, 155; Wilson, "Papago Has Leadership," *IAW*, June 1939, 8.

46. Wilson, "Papago Has Leadership;" Underhill, "Reasons for the Choice of Santa Rosa;" Rosamund Spicer, "People on the Desert," 48–49; Underhill, *Social Organization*, 206–207.

47. Fontana, *Of Earth and Little Rain*, 85, 90–91.

48. Fontana, *Of Earth and Little Rain*, 89–92. Castillo and Cowan, eds., *It Is Not Our Fault*.

49. Papago Tribal Council, *The Papago Development Program, 1949: Report of the Papago Tribal Council* (Haskell Institute Print Shop, 1949), 31–33, 57, ASU government documents; Henry Dobyns, *Papagos in the Cotton Fields, 1950* (Tucson: University of Arizona Press, 1951), 78.

50. Lucius Zittier to M. Katherine Drexel, November 15, 1910, OLGC.

51. Lucius Zittier, "Memorandum *In re Guadalupe Townsite*," n.d., OLGC.

52. Spicer, *People of Pascua*, 59, 265.

53. Ruby Haigler Wood, interview by Marjorie H. Wilson, August 7, 1968, 34, AHF.

54. Hu-DeHart, *Yaqui Resistance and Survival*, 176.

55. Pablo "Paul" Amado Chavarría, interview by Scott Solliday, April 8, 1993, AHST, POHP, cat. no. 133.

56. Ibid.

57. Ray M. Chavarría, interview by Scott Solliday, August 17, 1993, AHST, POHP, cat. no. OH-136.

58. Ray Chavarría interview; Paul Chavarría interview.

59. Spicer, *People of Pascua*, 265–266.

60. Zittier, "Memorandum"; and Zittier to Drexel, January 28, 1908, OLGC.

61. Spicer, *People of Pascua*, 37.

62. Howard Ruppers, "Yaqui," *The 'Current' News*, February 1957, 2–4.

63. Glaser, "Working for Community," 341.

64. Thamar Richey, a teacher at the Pascua Elementary School, recounts the founding of Pascua in a letter to Carl Hayden on February 23, 1937, SCASU, CH-MSS. See also Spicer, *People of Pascua*, 46–49, 178; George Pierre Castile, "Yaquis, Edward Spicer, and Federal Indian Policy: From Immigrants to Native Americans," *Journal of the Southwest* 44 (Winter 2002): 383–435, 391.

65. Savala, *Autobiography of a Yaqui Poet*, 37, 43, 45.

66. Spicer, *People of Pascua*, 61–68.

67. Earl Harrington, Bureau of Land Management, to Carl Hayden, October 24, 1955, SCASU, CH-MSS, box 203, folder 15; Frank and Esther Cota, author's interview, May 21, 1995, Guadalupe.

68. Ann Ramenofsky, "The Rise of Guadalupe Yaqui Factions from Legal Claims to Plaza Land" (master's thesis, Arizona State University, 1968), 11.

69. Rita Morales, "News from the Scottsdale Camp," *The 'Current' News*, May 13, 1946.

70. Leah Glaser, "The Story of Guadalupe: The Survival and Preservation of a Yaqui Community" (master's thesis, Arizona State University, 1996), 42–52; Wood interview, 21–22.

71. Thamar Richey to Carl Hayden, February 23, 1937, SCASU, CH-MSS. See also Spicer, *People of Pascua*, 46–49, 178.

72. Spicer, *People of Pascua*, 166–167, 178.

73. Glaser, "Story of Guadalupe," 46–47, 341.

74. Edward J. Shaughnessy to Carl Hayden, March 25, 1937, SCASU, CH-MSS, box 625, folder 24.

75. Shaughnessy to Hayden, March 25, 1937, SCASU, CH-MSS, box 625, folder 24; "Arizona Yaqui May Return to Homeland," *Arizona Republican*, February 25, 1937, 1; Cordell Hull to Carl Hayden, March 16, 1937, SCASU, CH-MSS, box 625, folder 24; "*Contra regreso de los Yaquis de Tucson a Sonora*," *TUC*, April 6, 1937, 1 (author's translation); Castile, "Yaquis," 388.

76. Moisés, *A Yaqui Life*, 121–133.

77. Collier is quoted by Castile, "Yaquis," 389.

78. Hayden to "My dear Jack," December 15, 1936, SCASU, CH-MSS, box 625, folder 24.

79. In SCASU, CH-MSS, box 625, folder 24 (for 1937): Houghteling to secretary of state, December 8; Shaughnessy to Carl Hayden, May 1.

80. In SCASU, CH-MSS, box 625, folder 24 (for 1937): Thamar Richey to Hayden, February 3; Will W. Alexander, Resettlement Administration, to Hayden, March 17; Hayden to Thamar Richey, March 22.

81. In SCASU, CH-MSS, box 625, folder 24 (for 1937): Mrs. J. R. Fitzgerald to Hayden, November 4; Fitzgerald to Hayden, November 7.

82. John Collier to Hayden, December 6, 1937, SCASU, CH-MSS, box 625, folder 24.

83. Wood interview. See also the handwritten manuscript by Ruby Wood, 1965, and her special teaching permit issued by Emergency Educational Programs of

Arizona, Federal Emergency Relief Administration, September 15, 1934, RW-MSS, SCASU.

84. The earliest of these publications was *Pascua. The Yaquis: A History* followed; his *People of Pascua* would be published posthumously. He also helped to edit and/or produce a number of autobiographies and life histories in the bibliography.

6

1. U.S. Commission on Civil Rights, "Statement for the Record of the Honorable Samuel Mardian Jr.," *Hearings Before the U.S. Commission on Civil Rights,* Phoenix, February 3, 1962, 13–16 (hereafter cited as *1962 Hearings*).

2. Ibid., 8–10, 15–16.

3. "Statement of Herbert Ely," *1962 Hearings,* 132–134.

4. See William H. Chafe, *Civilities and Civil Rights: Greensboro, North Carolina, and the Black Struggle for Freedom* (New York: Oxford University Press, 1980).

5. For an analysis of a similar situation in Texas and California, see Gutiérrez, *Walls and Mirrors.*

6. On the rise of the Sun Belt cities, see Carl Abbott, *The Metropolitan Frontier: Cities in the Modern American West* (Tucson: University of Arizona Press, 1993); Bradford Luckingham, *The Urban Southwest: A Profile History of Albuquerque, El Paso, Phoenix, and Tucson* (El Paso: Texas Western Press, 1985); and Gerald Nash, *The American West Transformed: The Impact of the Second World War* (Bloomington: Indiana University Press, 1985).

7. Luckingham, *Phoenix,* 136–159, 195–196; Sheridan, *Arizona,* 276–278.

8. Luckingham, *Urban Southwest,* 83.

9. Luckingham, *Phoenix,* 159–164, 188.

10. Joe Torres, interview by Mary Melcher, June 3, 1999 and Adam Díaz, interview by Karin Ullmann, April 16, 1976, in AHST, POHP.

11. Joyotpaul Chaudhri, *Urban Indians of Arizona: Phoenix, Tucson, and Flagstaff* (Tucson: University of Arizona Press, 1974), 65; John E. Crow, *Mexican Americans in Contemporary Arizona: A Social and Demographic View* (San Francisco: R&E Research Associates, 1975), 63. Also see *1962 Hearings,* "Testimony of Charles Harlins," 44, "Statement for the Record by Charles F. Harlins," 61, and "Statement for the Record by Lincoln Ragsdale," 63–64.

12. Mathew Whitaker, "Creative Conflict: Lincoln and Eleanor Ragsdale, Collaboration, and Community Activism in Phoenix, 1953–1965," *Western Historical Quarterly* 34 (Summer 2003): 165–190, 169; and Michael J. Kotlanger, "Phoenix, Arizona, 1920–1940" (PhD diss., Arizona State University, 1983), 445–446.

13. "Testimony of Lincoln J. Ragsdale," *1962 Hearings,* 47.

14. "Testimony of Roy B. Yanez," *1962 Hearings,* 34–40.

15. "Testimony of Lincoln J. Ragsdale," *1962 Hearings,* 48.

16. Sheridan, *Los Tucsonenses,* 329–245.

17. Dennis Bell, *Barrio Historico, Tucson* (Tucson: College of Architecture, University of Arizona, 1972), 1, 53, 68–69.

18. Luckingham, *Minorities,* 158–159.

19. Torres interview.

20. Berman, *Reformers,* 54. Berman cites *The Daily Enterprise,* July 3, 1900, 2.

21. Torres interview.

22. Josie Ortega Sánchez, interview by Richard Nearing, June 23, 1992, Tempe, BOHP.

23. Luckingham, *Urban Southwest,* 88; Abbott, *Metropolitan Frontier,* 101.

24. Sheridan, *Arizona,* 320–321.

25. *Harrison v. Laveen,* 196 P.2d 456 (Arizona Supreme Court, 1948); Alden Stevens, "Voice of the Native" *New York Times Magazine,* November 2, 1952, 65; Henry Christman, "Southwestern Indians Win the Vote," *The American Indian* 4, no. 4 (1948): 6–10; Luckingham, *Minorities,* 48–49, 160, 168.

26. According to several witnesses, including activist and poll watcher Manuel Peña and the director of the local NAACP, Rev. George Brooks, Rehnquist personally intimidated voters at polls in black and ethnic Mexican neighborhoods. See Senate Committee on the Judiciary, "Statement of Manuel Pena," 96th Cong., 2d sess., 1065–1078. See also Dave Wagner, "Rehnquist Tactics in '62 Vote Were Probed," *Arizona Republic,* January 10, 1999, and "Rehnquist's Circle," *Arizona Republic,* December 26, 2000, clippings in CHASU, P-CB-BIO. On Brooks's accusations against Rehnquist, see Luckingham, *Minorities,* 48–49, 160, 168.

27. "Los Mineros," an episode in *The American Experience,* PBS, 1991; Sheridan, *Arizona,* 278.

28. Carlos Contreras, "Carlos Contreras: 1972," SCASU, CHASU, cat. no. MM CHSM-147, 3.

29. In SCASU, CH-MSS, box 130, folder 19: Keith Taylor, ACGA secretary treasurer, to Carl Hayden, 8 August 1944; Philip Bruton to Hayden, 30 August 1944; I. S. Terrell to Hayden, 24 October 1944; Resolution of the SRVWUA board of governors, 19 October 1945; Lin B. Orme, SRVWUA president, to Hayden, 19 October 1945.

30. In AHF, ACGAR: E. S. McSweeny to William Larson, May 21, 1952; Lease between ACGA and United States of America, January 25, 1952; Maurice J. Tobin, secretary of labor, and Cecil H. Collerette, ACGA president, "Agreement to Secure Performance of Indemnity Agreements," September 16, 1952, all in box 24, folder 2. For a brief overview of the origins of the Bracero Program, see Acuña, *Occupied America,* 3rd ed., 264–265.

31. "Testimony of Richard H. Salter," *1962 Hearings,* 69.

32. "Jails Stuffed as 'Wetbacks' Stream Over Mexico Line," *Arizona Labor Journal,* September 15, 1949, 1 (hereafter cited as *ALJ*). In the *Arizona Daily Star* (1953), see "Flood of 'Wetbacks' Entering U.S." May 10, B5; "Wetbacks Ousted Wholesale," June 12; "6000 Rounded Up in California, Arizona," June 14; "3,261 Wetbacks Deported in 1st Week of Evacuation," June 15; "13,370 Taken in Arizona, California," June 19.

33. In BIA-RG75, box "Pima, Thackery," folder F-73, see Superintendent of San Carlos to Thackery, August 7, 1914, and E. McGray to Thackery, August 15, 1914.

34. W. H. Knox to Burke, June 14, 1922, BIA-RG75, box "Old subject, 1918–1926," folder "Employment of Indians: 1919–1925."

35. Burke to Knox, February 1, 1923, in BIA-RG75, box "Old subject, 1918–1926," folder "Employment of Indians: 1919–1925."

36. Thackery to Joe Taylor, August 4, 1914; Taylor to Thackery, August 14, 1914, in BIA-RG75, box "Pima Thackery F73-F103," folder "F73 Cotton picking 1914–1915." Letters from Yavapais who worked in Salt River valley fields can be found in SCASU, box 3, folders 4 and 5 of the Carlos Montezuma papers.

37. "Minutes of Meeting to Discuss Off-Reservation Employment for Navajo and Hopi Indians," Westward Ho Hotel, Phoenix, Arizona, January 30, 1948, in BIA-RG75, box 109, folder 57363-1948-920, 4.

38. Ibid., 6–7.

39. "Testimony of Mr. John Jacobs," 1962 Hearings, 76–78. See also Chaudhri, Urban Indians, 25; Colleen O'Neill, "The 'Making' of the Navajo Worker: Navajo Households, the Bureau of Indian Affairs, and Off-Reservation Wage Work, 1948–1960," New Mexico Historical Review 74 (October 1999): 375–403.

40. Dobyns, Papagos in the Cotton Fields, 19–20. In SCASU, see Papago Tribal Council, Papago Development Program, 1949, 7, 3–33; and Arizona Commission of Indian Affairs, The Off-Reservation Papagos, Sells, Arizona, December 7, 1957 (Phoenix, 1957), 10–11.

41. Quotations from Tribal council, Papago Development Program, 3, 23–24, 77. On the national job-training and relocation programs, see Donald Fixico, The Urban Indian Experience in America (Albuquerque: University of New Mexico Press, 2000), 13; Elaine M. Neils, Indian Migration and Federal Relocation (Chicago: University of Chicago, Geography Department, 1971).

42. On the intent to relocate O'odham to Los Angeles and Chicago, see Papago Newsletter (PN), December 1953, 6, and Papago Tribal Council, Papago Development Program 24, 77. See also Fixico, Urban Indian Experience, 13.

43. In SCUSA: Arizona Commission of Indian Affairs, Annual Report to the Governor of Arizona for Fiscal Years 1954, 1955, and 1956 (Phoenix, 1956), 3; Robert Hackenberg and C. Roderick Wilson, "Reluctant Emigrants: the Role of Migration in Papago Indian Adaptation," Human Organization 31, 2 (Summer 1972): 173–179.

44. Dobyns, Papagos in the Cotton Fields, 7, 24–78. See also Papago Development Program, 8, 62.

45. In SCUSA: Harold E. Fey, "The Pima's Fight for Water" and "Ira Hayes—Our Accuser," Indian Rights and American Justice (Chicago: Christian Century Foundation, 1955), 8–10.

46. Ibid.

47. In SCUSA: Arizona State Employment Service, Arizona's Agricultural Workers: An Analysis of Arizona's Year-Around and Migratory Agricultural Employment (Phoenix, 1951), 6–10; and Arizona State Employment Service, Agricultural Employ-

ment in Arizona since 1950 (Phoenix, 1968), 50–67; also see Padfield and Martin, *Farmers, Workers and Machines,* 90; Waddell, "Papago Indians at Work," 138–140.

48. Lee Athmer, "So-called Migrant Camp Mislabeled," *Farm Bureau News,* April 5, 1962, 5.

49. Gutiérrez, *Walls and Mirrors,* 127, 154–157.

50. "ALF Union Demands 'Wetbacks' Return," *ALJ,* December 22, 1949, 14. In SCASU, CH-MSS, box 130, folder 19: Governor Sidney Osborn to Carl Hayden, March 18, 1946, and Ann Tinnon, of Local 78, Fresh Fruit and Vegetable Workers Union, to Hayden, November 13, 1946.

51. "Testimony of Manuel Peña Jr.," *1962 Hearings,* 75–76.

52. Gutiérrez, *Walls and Mirrors,* passim.

53. Máximo Alonso, interview by Rita Magdaleno, March 18, 1995, 5, 13, in CHASU, MSS-168, box 1, folder 9.

54. Enrique Pastor, interview by Rita Magdaleno, September 2, 1995, in CHASU, MSS-168, box 1, folder 17, 2.

55. "Los Mineros." This best-known account of Arizona's Mexican-American miners credits returning World War II veterans for the revitalization of the unions without mentioning pro-labor legislation associated with the New Deal.

56. Jonathan Rosenblum, *Copper Crucible: How the Arizona Miners' Strike of 1983 Recast Labor-Management Relations in America* (Ithaca, NY: ILR Press, 1995), 32–37.

57. *Phelps Dodge Corp v. National Labor Relations Board,* 313 U.S. 177 (1941); Marshal A. Oldman, "Phelps-Dodge and Organized Labor in Bisbee and Douglas," *Western Legal History* 5, 1 (1992): 83–95.

58. In *El Tucsonense: "Prejuicio de clases!"* March 12, 1937, 3; "*Batallas entre unionistas*" and "John L. Lewis," April 2, 1937, 2 (author's translation).

59. Enrique Pastor interview, SCASU, CHASU, MSS-168.

60. Rosenblum, *Copper Crucible,* 32–33; Leaming, *Labor and Copper,* 18–19.

61. "Los Mineros."

62. "Dark Men fighting for White Liberties," *ALJ,* May 23, 1946, 4.

63. "Border Towns Harassed by Cheap Labor," *ALJ,* December 12, 1946, 1.

64. Rosenblum, *Copper Crucible,* 33–35.

65. In *ALJ:* "Right to Work?," September 13, 1945, 2; "'Right-to-Starve' Sponsors," May 2, 1946, 4; "The Right to Starve," July 11, 1946, 6.

66. Enrique Pastor interview, 7.

67. Máximo Alonso interview, 7.

68. Contreras, "Carlos Contreras: 1972," 3; Blaine and Adams, *Papagos and Politics,* 118–119; Enrique Pastor interview, 3.

69. See in the *Arizona Daily Star:* "Mine, Mill and Smelter Workers Get Bargaining Rights at Kennecott Plant, Ray," 24 August 1954, 5; "AFL Unions Chosen in Miami Elections," 23 October 1954, 5; "Agreement Halts Miami Strike," 18 November 1954, 5; "Mine, Mill, Smelter Workers accept 5 1/2-cent increase," 16 September 1954, 6; "Mine, Mill and Smelter Workers Declared Bargaining Unit

for Banner Mine," 28 September 1954, 6; "Kennecott Strike Settled," 17 August 1955, 1. For a broad discussion of union activity between 1946 and the mid 1960s, see Rosenblum, *Copper Crucible*, 33–45.

70. Tomas W. Cowger, *The National Congress of American Indians: The Founding Years* (Lincoln: University of Nebraska Press, 1999), 37–38; Cornell, *Return of the Native*, 119–120, 191. Quotation is from Cornell, 191.

71. *Harrison v. Laveen*, 196 P.2d 456 (Arizona Supreme Court 1948); Stevens, "Voice of the Native," 65; Christman, "Southwestern Indians." Quotations from Christman, 8 and 7.

72. Quoted by Christman, "Southwestern Indians," 8. See also "The Courts Affirm Indian Rights," *The American Indian* 4, no. 4 (1948): 1.

73. On the CBA see Lamb, "The Making of a Chicano Civil Rights Activist," 91–115; Luckingham, *Minorities*, 55.

74. Díaz interview, 7, 13; Luckingham, *Minorities*, 46; Juan Gómez-Quiñones, *Chicano Politics: Reality and Promise, 1940–1990* (Albuquerque: University of New Mexico Press, 1990), 35, 48.

75. Díaz interview, 14–15.

76. "Statement of Frederic S. Marquardt," *1962 Hearings*, 135.

77. Luckingham, *Minorities*, 45–46.

78. Díaz interview, 64.

79. Quotations are from "Statement for the Record by Eugene Marín, Teacher and Founder of the Vesta Club," *1962 Hearings*, 94–95. See also Eugene Marín, interview by Socorro Ocano, March 9, 1973, SCASU, CHASU, 2; "Organizations Making News: Vesta Club," *El Coordinador*, September 1962, newspaper clipping, SCASU.

80. Quotation from Luckingham, *Minorities*, 55. See also Lamb, "Making of a Chicano Civil Rights Activist," 91–115.

81. In SCASU, CHASU, P-CB-Bio: Wilfredo J. Peña Jr., "Biography of Manuel 'Lito' Peña," July 31, 2000; Howard Fischer, "Lito Peña," *Business Journal*, September 30, 1991, 14; "Remarks by Senator Peña at the graduation ceremony of the 'Lito' Peña Learning Center," June 11, 1996. Quotation from "Remarks by Senator Peña," 4.

82. *Gonzales et al. v. Sheely*, 96 F.Supp.1004 (1951); Lamb, "Making of a Chicano Civil Rights Activist, 95–104. Quotation from 104.

83. Lamb, "Making of a Chicano Civil Rights Activist," 104–114. Quotations from 104 and 105. See also Kaye Briegel, "Alianza Hispano-Americana and Some Mexican-American Civil Rights Cases in the 1950s," in Servín, *An Awakened Minority: The Mexican-Americans*.

84. *Gonzales et al. v. Sheely*, 96 F.Supp.1004 (1951).

85. Gómez-Quiñones, *Chicano Politics*, 63–65.

86. Whitaker, "Creative Conflict," 168; "Statement for the Record of the Honorable Samuel Mardian," *1962 Hearings*, 7–16; Mary Melcher, "Blacks and Whites Together: Interracial Leadership in the Phoenix Civil Rights Movement," *Journal of Arizona History* 32 (Summer 1991): 198–202.

87. "Local NAACP Plans Suit Against School Boards," *Arizona Sun*, September 14, 1951; Bob Lord, "Court Ruling Outlaws School Segregation," *Phoenix Gazette*, February 10, 1953; Whitaker, "Creative Conflict," 171–172.

88. Whitaker, 171–172. Struckmeyer's decision quoted on 172.

89. Briegel, "Alianza Hispano-Americana," 180–182.

7

1. Mario Suárez, "El Hoyo," in *The Heath Anthology of American Literature*, ed. Paul Lauter, 4th ed. (Boston, 2002), 2:2097–2098. Details about Suárez's life are from Raymund A. Paredes, "Mario Suárez 1925–1998," in *Heath Anthology*, 2:2095–2096.

2. Suárez, "Capirotada," in *Heath Anthology*, 2:2097–2098. On the romantic image of the Spanish past, see Weber, *The Spanish Frontier in North America*, 335–360; Charles Montgomery, *The Spanish Redemption: Heritage, Power, and Loss on New Mexico's Upper Rio Grande* (Berkeley: University of California Press, 2002), passim.

3. For examples of this interpretation, see Jacques E. Levy, *César Chávez: Autobiography of La Causa* (New York: Norton, 1975), 468; Susan Ferriss and Ricardo Sandoval, *The Fight in the Fields: Cesar Chavez and the Farmworkers Movement* (San Diego: Harcourt Brace, 1997), 197–198. Works that include sections on Arizona's Chicano movement include Armando Navarro, *La Raza Unida Party: A Chicano Challenge to the U.S. Two-Party Dictatorship* (Philadelphia: Temple University Press, 2000), 202–218; Arturo Rosales, *Chicano! The History of the Mexican-American Civil Rights Movement*, (Houston: Arte Publico Press), 210–214. See also Maria Eva Valle, "MEChA and the Transformation of Chicano Student Activism: Generational Change, Conflict, and Continuity" (PhD diss., University of California, San Diego); José A. Maldonado, "*¡Si Se Puede!* The Farm Worker Movement in Arizona 1965–1979" (master's thesis, Arizona State University, 1995); Nick Tapia, "Cactus in the Desert: The Chicano Movement in Maricopa County, Arizona 1968–1978" (master's thesis, Arizona State University, 1999); and Patricia A. Adank, "Chicano Activism in Maricopa County—Two Incidents in Retrospect," in *An Awakened Minority: The Mexican-Americans*, ed. Manuel Servín (Beverly Hills, CA: Glencoe, 1974), 246–262. For a broad overview of the United Farm Workers and its impact, see Craig Jenkins, *The Politics of Insurgency: The Farm Worker Movement in the 1960s* (New York: Columbia University Press, 1985).

4. For a broad and mostly celebratory overview of the Chicano movement, see Rosales, *Chicano!* For an overview of the largely youth-driven, nationalist movement, see Carlos Muñoz, *Youth, Identity, Power: The Chicano Movement* (New York: Verso, 1989). For a more critical perspective on the movement, and particularly on the ideology of Chicano nationalism, see Ernesto Chávez, *Mi Raza Primero: Nationalism, Identity, and Insurgency in the Chicano Movement in Los Angeles, 1966–1978* (Berkeley: University of California Press, 2002).

5. Valle, "MEChA and Chicano Student Activism," 131.

6. Rosaldo and Flores, "Identity, Conflict, and Evolving Latino Communities," in *Latino Cultural Citizenship,* ed. William Flores and Rina Benmayor (Boston: Beacon, 1997), 58–59.

7. Donald C. Reitzes and Dietrich C. Reitzes, *The Alinsky Legacy: Alive and Kicking* (Greenwich, CT: JAI Press), 202; Sonny Peña, "On Behalf of the Peña Family" (speech at the Peña Elementary School dedication November 20, 2003), SCASU, CHASU, P-CB-BIO.

8. Gutiérrez, *Walls and Mirrors,* 168–178, CSO quotation from 169–170. See also Chávez, *Mi Raza Primero,* 12–14; Reitzes and Reitzes, *Alinsky Legacy,* 106.

9. In SCASU, CHASU, P-CB-BIO: Fred Ross to Nick Avila, n.d.; César Chávez to Manuel Peña, February 20, 1962. Peña quote from "Remarks by Senator Peña at the graduation ceremony of the 'Lito' Peña Learning Center," June 11, 1996.

10. "Guadalupe Residents Seek Community Improvements," *Arizona Republic,* September 3, 1963 (hereafter cited as *AR*).

11. Raymond Zylla, "Guadalupe: Was Incorporation Best?" SCASU, CHASU, cat. no. ME CHI H-11.

12. Ramenofsky, "The Rise of Guadalupe Yaqui Factions," 10; Earl Harrington, Bureau of Land Management, to Carl Hayden, October 24, 1955, CH-MSS, box 203, folder 15; Cota interview.

13. Lauro García to Father Joe Baur, August 25, 1987, OLGC; "Late Priest's Vision Flowers in Guadalupe," *AR,* July 21, 1982; Lauro García, interview by Ella Varbel, November 19, 1973, CHASU, 16–18; Cota interview; Maldonado, *"¡Si Se Puede!"* 5; "Testimony of Rev. Harold Lundgren," *1962 Hearings,* 72–74.

14. García interview, 15–19; Friends of Guadalupe Organization, "Where Cultures Meet" (Friends of Guadalupe Organization, 1970), CHASU; Noel Osment, "GO Aids Guadalupe," *AR,* November 15, 1964, F8.

15. Reitzes and Reitzes, *Alinsky Legacy,* 206–212; Cota interview; García interview, 19; Noel Osment, "GO Aids Guadalupe," *AR,* F8.

16. Cota interview; Osment, "GO Aids Guadalupe"; García interview, 19.

17. José Angel Gutiérrez, *The Making of a Chicano Militant: Lessons from Cristal* (Madison: University of Wisconsin Press, 1998), 35–40.

18. Eugene Marín, interview by Socorro Ocano, March 9, 1973, CH-ASU; Gómez-Quiñones, *Chicano Politics,* 69–71; Ruth Lamb, *Mexican Americans: Sons of the Southwest* (Claremont, CA: Ocelot Press, 1970), 120–121; "Statement for the Record by Eugene Marín," *1962 Hearings,* 94.

19. "Statement for the Record by Eugene Marín," *1962 Hearings,* 94; Marín interview, 3; ACCPE, "Helping to Make Citizens Citizens," March 24, 1972, CHASU.

20. Marín interview, 8.

21. Otto Santa Anna, "Why Local Politics," September 1983, SCASU, CHASU, P-CB-BIO 2520; Otto Santa Anna, "Autobiography: Otto Santa Anna BSBA," January 18, 1983, CHASU; Gómez-Quiñones, "Chicano Politics," 70. On the Crystal City elections, see Gutiérrez, *Making of a Chicano Militant,* 35–42, and Marc Rodriguez, "A Movement of Young Mexican Americans Seeking Change: Critical Citizenship,

Migration, and the Chicano Movement in Texas and Wisconsin, 1960–1976," *Western Historical Quarterly* 34 (Autumn 2003): 275–300.

22. "Testimony of Grace Gil-Olivarez," *1962 Hearings*, 88.

23. Ibid., 88–90.

24. Ibid., 89–90.

25. In SCASU, CHASU, P-CB-BIO: Chávez to Peña, 1 February 1963; Peña to Chávez, 12 September 1963; Peña to Chávez, 30 January 1964. See also William C. Griffin to John A. Wagner, 23 July 1959.

26. Carlos Gutiérrez, Migrant Opportunity Program, "Partial Record: Arizona Statewide Consultation of Mexican American Concerns," January 13, 1968, 21, CHASU; Maldonado, "*¡Si Se Puede!*" 5–6.

27. Armando Morado, "Gustavo Gutiérrez: Arizona's United Farm Workers' Organizing Committee Organizer, 1965–1973," unpublished paper, May 1974, 2–4, CHASU. The march to Sacramento is discussed in Ferriss and Sandoval, *Fight in the Fields*, 117–123.

28. Maldonado, "*¡Si Se Puede!*" 4–20; Adank, "Chicano Activism," passim; Tapia, "Cactus in the Desert," 23–24.

29. "The Record and Findings of the Arizona Statewide Consultation on Mexican-American Concerns," January 13, 1968, 1, CHASU.

30. Ibid., 1–2.

31. Ibid., 18.

32. Ibid., 6–7.

33. "The Record and Findings of the Second Arizona Consultation on Mexican-Americans," October 30, 1968, CHASU. Marín quote, 18.

34. Ibid. Salazar quote, 14.

35. CPLC minutes, March 2 and 23, 1969, CHASU, MSS-130. See also Tapia, *Cactus in the Desert*, 50.

36. Crow, *Mexican Americans*, 23, 39–49.

37. Ibid., 29, 30.

38. Ibid., 17.

39. Athia L. Hardt, "Mines to Mainstream," *AR*, December 14, 1986, E1, E3; Tapia, "Cactus in the Desert," 13–14.

40. Rosales, *Chicano!* 211–212; Navarro, *Raza Unida*, 204–205.

41. Hardt, "Mines to Mainstream"; Tapia, "Cactus in the Desert," 13–16, 27–28; "Mexican Americans Form First Campus Organization," *State Press*, October 18, 1968, CHASU, MSS-150, box 2, folder 1 (hereafter cited as *SP*).

42. Newspaper clippings (1968) in SCASU, CHASU, MSS-150, box 2, folder 1: "Protestors Storm Durham's Office," *SP*, November 20; "Campus Groups Ask Officials to Break Pact with Linen Firm," *SP*, November 20; "ASU Gathering Asks Towel-Company Boycott," *PG*, November 20; Albert Sitter, "Sit-in at Durham's Office," *AR*, November 21; Sitter, "ASU Pledges Probe of Laundry," *SP*, November 22; "Tentative Settlement Reached in Laundry Dispute," *SP*, November 22; Russ Spavin, "Students Claim Win; ASU To Drop Contract," *Phoenix Gazette*, November 26

(hereafter cited as *PG*). See also, "MASO History," in *MASO Newsletter* 2, May 1970, 1–2, CHASU, MSS-150, box 2, folder 11; Tapia, "Cactus in the Desert," 29–31; and Rosales, *Chicano!* 212.

43. "MASO to Boycott grapes," *SP*, May 9, 1969, CHASU, MSS-150, box 2, folder 3; John Aldape, "El Rancho Market Target of Demonstrations," *SP*, March 19, 1970, MSS-150, box 2, folder 3, 1; "HUELGA-1969," pamphlet, MSS-150, box 2, folder 11; CPLC minutes, March 2, 1969, MSS-130, box 1, folder 6.

44. "MASO History," *MASO Newsletter* 2, May 1970, MSS-150, box 2, folder 11; Tapia, "Cactus in the Desert," 29–34; Adank, "Chicano Activism," 248.

45. Athia Hardt, "MASO Puts an End to Coalition," *SP*, November 26, 1968, 1–2, MSS-150, box 2, folder 1; "Crowds Throng Mall, Halls on Moratorium Day," *SP*, October 16, 1969, MSS-150, box 2, folder 2; Rosales, *Chicano!* 212; Valle, "MEChA," 13.

46. In CHASU, MSS-150, box 2, folder 3: Daniel Ben-Horn, "ASU Minority Recruitment Drive Criticized by MASO," *AR*, August 29, 1970, 25; Albert Sitter, "ASU Policy called Discriminatory," *AR*, October 5, 1970.

47. In CHASU, MSS-150 box 2, folder 3: John Aldape, "Chicano Program Needed," *SP*, December 4, 1968, 1, 5; Jim Spencer, "MASO Members Urge Chicano Studies," *SP*, October 6, 1970, 2.

48. "Mexican American Student Conference," pamphlet in CHASU, MSS-150, box 1, folder 14.

49. CPLC minutes, March 2 and 9, April 13, 1969, MSS-120, box 1, folder 6; CPLC minutes, March 23, 1970, MSS-130, box 20, folder 8; Rosales, *Chicano!* 212–213.

50. CPLC, "A Proposal to Provide Leadership Training and Community Education in Resource Utilization and Development," September 1969, MSS-150, box 20, folder 2; Tapia, "Cactus in the Desert," 53–55.

51. CPLC minutes, March 2, 1969, MSS-130, box 1, folder 6; Tapia, "Cactus in the Desert," 53–55.

52. "Chicanos por la Causa, 1969," MSS-130, box 20, folder 2; "Chicano Action," *Voice of the City*, September 18, 1969, 1 (hereafter cited as *VoC*); Peter B. Mann, "Chicanos March on City Hall," *AR*, September 27, 1969, 25–26, MSS-130, box 3, folder 4.

53. "Chicanos por la Causa, 1969"; CPLC, "Freshman Program: PUHS," n.d., MSS-130, box 2, folder 2; Jack Crowe, "Mexican-Americans March on City Hall," *AR*, September 16, 1969, 17 and 21, and "Chicano Action," *VoC*, n.d., MSS-130, box 3, folder 4. Over a hundred other newspaper clippings on the boycotts and walkouts are in the same folder. On the bilingual education program, see Roger Timberlake, "'Must be Integrated': Chicano Program Hampered," *Scottsdale Daily Progress*, October 14, 1970, MSS-130, box 3, folder 4; CPLC minutes, MSS-130, box 20, folder 8.

54. "Statement for the Record by Loren Vaught Jr.," *1962 Hearings*, 24.

55. Joe Eddie López et al., "Recommendations from a Data Base for Comprehensive Change at Phoenix Union High School," *Educational Services Bulletin* 40 (May 1971): 4, CHASU. Covey's quote is reprinted in "Recommendations."

56. John H. Vesey, "School Moves to Avert Crisis," *PG*, September 17, 1969, MSS-130, box 3, folder 4.

57. "Ultimatums Unwise," *PG*, October 7, 1969, 6. Newspapers would continue to blame the protests on an ambiguously defined "racial strife" into the following year. See editorial cartoon, *PG*, October 19, 1970, MSS-130, box 3, folder 4; Jack Crowe, "Chicanos at PUHS Seek Confrontation on Racial Tensions," *AR*, October 9, 1970, and "Is the *Republic* Trying to Create a Racial Incident?" *VoC*, October 15, 1970.

58. Quotation from López et al., "Recommendations," 4. See also Peter Mann, "Chicanos March on City Hall," *AR*, September 27, 1969, MSS-130, box 3, folder 5.

59. CPLC board of directors minutes, November 1, 1969, MSS-130, box 1, folder 6; "Jose Eddie López for PUHS Board," *VoC*, September 24, 1970, 3, MSS-130, box 3, folder 5. See also Rosales, *Chicano!* 212–213.

60. In CHASU, MSS-130: District director, department of the treasury to Joe Eddie López, December 29, 1970, box 20, folder 4; Juan Alvarez, "Chicanos Por la Causa: Proposal to the Southwest Council of La Raza," box 1, folder 6.

61. In CHASU, MSS-130: Ronnie López to CPLC board of directors, August 17, 1970, box 2, folder 1; Charles García, "Workable Housing Program for the Housing Component of Chicanos Por La Causa" (1971?), box 2, folder 1; "Chicanos por la Causa," undated report (probably 1971), box 1, folder 5.

62. "Chicanos por la Causa," undated report, MSS-130, box 1, folder 5.

63. In MSS-130: Certificate of Incorporation, Barrio Youth Project, April 22, 1970, and "Articles of Incorporation of Barrio Youth Project," box 2, folder 2; "Barrio Youth Project Objectives," box 20, folder 4; CPLC minutes, March 23, 1969, box 3, folder 8; see also CPLC board of directors minutes, October 12, 1969, and December 7, 1968, box 1, folder 6; CPLC special meeting minutes, January 24, 1970, box 20, folder 8.

64. In MSS-130: Ronnie López to CPLC member directors, August 17, 1970, box 2, folder 1; in box 3, folder 4: "Latins Demand Seymour Quit," *PG*, October 9, 1970; Jack Crowe, "Chicanos at PUHS Seek Confrontation on Racial Tensions," *AR*, October 9, 1970; Albert J. Sitter, "Chicanos Call Boycott of PUHS," *PG*, October 10, 1970; "Mexican-American Teachers Vote Support of PUHS Boycott," *VoC*, October 11, 1970; John Vessey, "Phoenix Union Boycott Starts," *PG*, October 12, 1970; Vesey, "PU Boycott Costing Aid," *PG*, October 13, 1970; Vesey, "PUHS May be Closed," *PG*, October 14, 1970, A-1, A-8; "Statement of AMAE on Phoenix Union High School," *VoC*, October 15, 1970.

65. In MSS-130, box 3, folder 4: Connie Koenenn, "Interim PUHS to Open," *AR*, October 15, 1970, 27–28; Bryce McIntyre, "Scholar Lauds Chicanos for Seeking Rights," *AR*, October 17, 1970, 25.

66. In MSS-130, box 3, folder 4: John Vesey, "Investigation Begins on School Procedures," *PG*, November 3, 1970; Vesey, "School Advisory Committee Seen as Boycott Deterrent," *PG*, November 16, 1970.

67. López, Grinder, Clark, "Recommendations," 38–47.

68. John Aldape, "Chicanos United to Form MEChA," *SP*, March 3, 1971, 4,

MSS-150, box 2, folder 4; Valle, "MEChA," 126, 129, 130. On the change from MASA to MEChA at the University of Arizona, see Navarro, *Raza Unida,* 207.

69. In MSS-150, box 3, folder 2: Abelardo B. Delgado, "Today's Lesson, Aztlán," *Voz de Aztlán 1,* March 1, 1972, 4–5; Toni Loroña, "Tio Tomás," *Voz de Aztlán 1,* 5.

70. Rubén Salazar, "Today's Lesson: Who Is a Chicano and What Does a Chicano Want," *Voz de Aztlán 2,* March 14, 1972, 3, MSS-150, box 3, folder 2.

71. Similar criticisms of this form of *indigenismo* have been made before, most notably by feminist scholars such as Gloria Anzaldúa who criticizes it for its glorification of the Aztec's "militaristic, bureaucratic state where male predatory warfare and conquest were based on patrilineal nobility." At the same time, Anzaldúa romanticizes an earlier Aztec past, which she describes as more balanced between the sexes. See Anzaldúa, *Borderlands/La Frontera: The New Mestiza,* 2nd ed. (San Francisco: Aunt Lute Books, 1999), 53–56.

72. Position paper, MEChA executive board, October 2, 1974, MSS-150. On the Xicano indigenous movement in the 1990s, see box 3, folder 13.

73. Marín interview, 1972, 15.

74. In MSS-150: "*La Semana de la Raza,* Nov. 8–12, 1971," box 2, folder 12; "MEChA Dancers Push Chicano Culture," *AR,* May 15, 1971, box 2, folder 4; "MEChA Central, 100-Point Program," May 1971, box 1, folder 4.

75. In MSS-150, box 1, folder 9: Daniel Ortega to Dr. Gayle Shuman, ASU director of housing, 17 March 1972; Gayle Shuman, letter of notice, 6 April 1972; Ronnie L. Martínez to President John W. Schwada, 6 April 1972. In box 2, folder 5: Dan Huff, "Chicanos Charge Bias," *SP,* 9 March 1972; Ronnie Martínez, guest editorial, *SP,* 14 March 1972; Dave Gianelli, "Students Hit Inaugural," *SP,* 14 March 1972; John Beadle, "Indians, Chicanos in Ariz. Action," *The Militant,* 17 April 1972.

76. In MSS-130: Clif Glasgow, "Chicano Group Files Suit," *SP,* 7 March 1973, box 2, folder 4; Ronnie Martínez to Henry Koelbl, ASU director of personnel, 8 March 1973; Bill Ross, "Hiring Policy Defended," *SP,* 8 March 1973, 1; John Banasqewski, "Chicano Claims Hiring Violation," *SP,* 4 May 1973, 1; Bonnie Bartak, "ASU Sued on Charges of Job Bias," box 2, folder 8, Herman Alcantar Jr. to unnamed receiver, 25 March 1975, MSS-150, box 1, folder 10.

77. Valle, "MEChA," 150–158. In MSS-150, box 2, folder 8: Maria Arellano, "Student Organization Continues Actions on Discrimination," July 10, 1975, *SP,* 1; Arellano, "Agreement Reached for Screening Committee Seat," *SP,* July 24, 1975, 1; "Schwada Soon to Appoint Equal Employment Officer," *SP,* November 18, 1975.

78. From *SP* in MSS-150, box 2, folder 9: Bill Judson, "MECHA Charges ASU with Breach of Faith," 30 January 1976, 1–2; Jim Boardman, "Chicanos Force Entry Into Shwada's Office," 3 February 1976, 1–2; "Object of Protest Criticizes MECHA," 3 February 1976, 1; Mike Tulumello, "Protesters May Face Disciplinary Measures," 6 February 1976, 1; "MECHA Leader to Seek Moral Support Resolution," 6 February 1976, 3. See also "Statement by Dr. Eugene A. Marín," 3 June 1981, CHASU.

79. Valle, "MEChA," 151–155; Debbie Salas, UFW, to Herman Alcantar, April 12, 1975, MSS-150, box 1, folder 10.

80. Valle, "MEChA," 142–143; quotation from 131.

81. The bill is quoted by Jordan McKinzie, "Creating New Politics: The Movement to Recall Arizona Governor Jack Williams" (unpublished paper in author's possession, May 2005), 3. See also Maldonado, "¡Si Se Puede!" 97–135; Al Bradshaw Jr., "House Approves Measure to Limit Farm Strikes," *Arizona Daily Star*, May 5, 1972, A1; "Senate Passes Farm-Worker Control Bill," *Arizona Daily Star*, May 11, 1972, B1.

82. Dolores Huerta, author's informal interview, Flagstaff, Arizona, April 6, 2006; Morado, "Gustavo Gutiérrez," 6; Richard Griswold del Castillo and Richard A. García, *César Chávez, A Triumph of Spirit* (Norman: University of Oklahoma Press, 1995), 121; Ferriss and Sandoval, *Fight in the Fields*, 197–198; McKinzie, "Creating New Politics," 10; Barry Kirschner, "Governor Recall Started," *New Times*, May 1972, MSS-150, box 2, folder 5. Chávez quote from Levy, *César Chávez*, 464.

83. Levy, 464–469; Griswold del Castillo and García, *César Chávez*, 121; Ferriss and Sandoval, *Fight in the Fields*, 197–198.

84. "United Farm Workers Defy Injunction Limiting Free Speech," *Voice of the Southwest*, October 25, 1973, MSS-130, box 3, folder 5.

85. Voter figures from McKinzie, "Creating New Politics," 21. See also Ben MacNitt, "How Castro Won: Hard Work, Defections in GOP," *Arizona Daily Star*, November 3, 1971, A1.

86. UFW, "Illegal Alien Farm Labor Activity in California and Arizona" (Keene, CA: United Farm Workers, 1974) in BLAC. See also Demetrio Díaz, "Diary of a Strikebreaker, 1974," in Ferris and Sandoval, *Fight in the Fields*, 118.

87. UFW, "Illegal Alien Farm Labor Activity"; Díaz, "Diary of a Strikebreaker," 118.

88. Interview with Manuel and Eva Acuña by Geta LeSeur in LeSeur, *Not All Okies Are White*, 55–71.

89. Maldonado, "¡Sí, Se Puede!" 97–135; Robert Leon, "Farmworkers Ask Wine Boycott," *SP*, March 28, 1975, MSS-150, box 2, folder 8; UFW, "Illegal Alien Farm Labor Activity."

90. Tapia, "Cactus in the Desert," 72–73, 79–80.

91. Acuña, *Occupied America*, 3rd ed., 418.

92. Navarro, *Raza Unida*, 209; Gutiérrez, *Making of a Chicano Militant*, 217.

93. Elaine Nathanson, "Centro Creates Pride in S. Tucson Youth," *Arizona Daily Star*, November 22, 1971, 4B; Elaine Nathanson, "Twelve Seek South Tucson Council Seats," *Arizona Daily Star*, February 23, 1973, 1; Navarro, *Raza Unida*, 209–218.

94. Navarro, *Raza Unida*, 209–218.

95. See the biography of Raúl Grijalva at http://www.house.gov/grijalva/biography.html (accessed March 2005).

96. Daniel González, "Bilingual Schooling Targeted," *AR*, June 28, 2000.

97. From U.S. Rep. Raúl Grijalva, "Arizona Border Control Plan is Flawed" March 16, 2003, http://www.house.gov/grijalva/press/press_releases/pr_031604.html (ac-

cessed January 2005). Pastor's record available at http://www.issues2000.org/House/Ed_Pastor_HouseMatch.html (accessed January 2005).

98. "Castro—'Success Story,'" *Voice of the City*, October 29, 1970, MSS-130, box 3, folder 5; James Johnson, *Arizona Politicians: The Noble and the Notorious* (Tucson: University of Arizona Press, 2002), 158–167. Quotation is from Raúl Castro, "Keynote Address," Arizona Mexican-American political conference, MSS-130, box 39, folder 9.

99. Bonnie Bartak, "Castro Signs Orders to Prevent Job Bias," *AR*, MSS-150, box 2, folder 8; "Latins Announce Creation of National Hispanic Caucus Affiliated with Democratic Party," *New York Times*, November 3, 1975, 18.

100. Morado, "Gustavo Gutiérrez," 7; Rodolfo Acuña, *Occupied America: A History of Chicanos*, 5th ed. (New York: Pearson, 2004), 359; Robert Lindsey, "Murder Inquiry Dims Arizona Governor's Future," *New York Times*, March 20, 1977, 26.

101. Chávez, *Mi Raza Primero*, 117, 119.

102. Vélez-Ibáñez, *Border Visions*, 255–257, 316.

103. Ernesto Chávez makes a similar point when he refers to "an ideologically bankrupt cultural nationalism," Chávez, *Mi Raza Primero*, 120.

8

1. Enos J. Francisco to *Arizona Daily Star*, September 27, 1960, SCUA, CH-MSS, box 2, folder "Government—tribal council minutes."

2. Ibid.

3. For works that provide historical sketches of the Pagago Tribe during this period, see Erickson, *Sharing the Desert*, 153–166; Dobyns, *Papago People*, 75–103; Fontana, "History of the Papago."

4. Two scholars have written about Yaqui tribal acknowledgment, but both have focused on federal policy and one community, Pascua. See Mark E. Miller, "The Yaquis Become American Indians: The Process of Federal Tribal Recognition," *Journal of Arizona History* 35 (Summer 1994): 183–204; George P. Castile, "Yaquis, Edward H. Spicer, and Federal Indian Policy: From Immigrants to Native Americans," *Journal of the Southwest* 44 (Winter 2002): 383–436. On Guadalupe, see Eric Meeks, "Cross-Ethnic Political Mobilization and Yaqui Identity Formation in Guadalupe, Arizona," *Reflexiones: New Directions in Mexican American Studies* (1997), ed. Neil Foley (Austin, 1998), 77–108.

5. Lewis, *Neither Wolf Nor Dog*, 162–164; Gary Nabhan, *The Desert Smells Like Rain: A Naturalist in Papago Indian Country* (San Francisco: North Point, 1982), 47.

6. Quotation is from Waddell, "Papago Indians at Work," *APUA*, 101. See also Teri Knutson Woods, Karen Blaine, and Lauri Francisco, "O'odham Himdag as a Source of Strength and Wellness Among the Tohono O'odham of Southern Arizona and Northern Sonora, Mexico," *Journal of Sociology and Social Welfare* 29, no. 1 (March 2002): 35–54.

7. Blaine, *Papagos and Politics*, 122–123.

8. The plan called for the relocation of at least four hundred families who would accept "permanent off reservation employment." *Papago Development Program, 1949,* 24, 77. On the national job training and relocation program, see Neils, *Indian Migration,* passim; Fixico, *The Urban Indian Experience,* 13.

9. Dobyns, *Papagos in the Cotton Fields,* 26, 82. See also Arizona Commission of Indian Affairs, *Annual Report to the Governor for Fiscal Years 1954, 1955, and 1956,* 3, SCUSA; Padfield and Martin, *Farmers, Workers, and Machines,* 93–95.

10. Hendricks is quoted in "Minutes of the Papago Council," January 8, 1960, H-MSS, 6. Manuel is quoted in Arizona Commission of Indian Affairs, *Off-Reservation Papagos,* 10–11.

11. Chester Higman's journal, September 17, 1958, H-MSS, box 2, folder "Journal: Feb. 1958–1959."

12. Manuel, Ramón, and Fontana, "Dressing for the Window," 532.

13. *Papago Development Program, 1949,* 73.

14. "Udall Presents Bill to Congress to Give Mineral Right Title," *Arizona Daily Star,* January 21, 1955, A1 (hereafter cited as *ADS*); "Small Mine Owners Meet, Condemn Bill," *ADS,* January 28, 1955, B3.

15. In *ADS:* "Interior Subcommittee Approves Bill," 29 April 1955, 1; "Udall, Goldwater Deny Charge of Politics," 30 April 1955, 2; "Interior Committee Approves Bill," 4 May 1955, 1; "Bill Passes House," 18 May 1955, 2; "Senate Passes Bill," 20 May 1955, 7; "Bill Sent to President," 24 May 1955, 1; "Bill Signed," 28 May 1955, 7; Mark Manuel, "Letter to the editor," 24 June 1955, D8.

16. Thomas R. McGuire, "Operations on the Concept of Sovereignty: A Case Study of Indian Decision-Making," *Urban Anthropology* 17, no. 1 (1988): 75–86, 78.

17. Lewis, *Neither Wolf Nor Dog,* 165; Erickson, *Sharing the Desert,* 161–162.

18. McCarthy, *A Papago Traveler,* 185–188.

19. Ibid., 188–196.

20. Alonso Flores, interview by Timothy Dunnigan, transcript, June 1969, ASMT, DAIOH.

21. In SCUA, H-MSS, box 2, folder "Government—tribal council minutes, 1960": "Minutes of the Papago Council," 6 May 1960, 6; 3 June 1960, 2; 8 July 1960, 4; and 2 September 1960, 4. See also Fontana, "History of the Papago," 147.

22. Human Sciences Research Inc., *A Comprehensive Evaluation of OEO Community Action Programs on Six Selected American Indian Reservations* (McLean, VA: 1966), 136 (hereafter cited as *OEO Study*); Dobyns, *Papago People,* 84–88; Manuel, Ramón, and Fontana, "Dressing for the Window," 529–530, 532–553, 7; Lewis, *Neither Wolf nor Dog,* 166.

23. For employment data on the reservation in 1966, see Papago agency, Sells, "Survey of Income and Employment: Papago Reservation Calendar Year 1966," VGLSC. These rankings from 3, 4, 9, and 10.

24. *OEO Study,* 106; Kerry D. Feldman, "Deviation, Demography, and Development: Differences Between Papago Indian Communities," *Human Organization* 31, no. 2 (Summer 1972): 137–148; Manuel, Ramón, and Fontana, "Dressing for the Window," 534–537.

25. Carol Sowell, "Papago Sisters Break Social Barriers to Earn Master's," *ADS*, May 14, 1981, H8; Pävi H. Hoikkala, "Mothers and Community Builders: Salt River Pima and Maricopa Women in Community Action," in *Negotiators of Change: Historical Perspectives on Native American Women*, ed. Nancy Shoemaker (New York: Routledge, 1995), 49–71, 224.

26. At VGLSC: Ed Severson, "Titles Stirring Cultural Conflict," *ADS*, December 14, 1981; Ernie Heltsley, "2 Women Among 16 Candidates in Contest for Top Papago Posts," *ADS*, April 17, 1983; Stephanie Innes, "O'odham Inauguration: Push for Progress," *ADS*, June 28, 2003, B1, B5; D. A. Barber, "The New Boss," *Tucson Weekly*, December 4, 2003, 17, 20, 21; Lee Allen, "Madam Chairwoman of the Tohono O'odham Nation," *The Desert Leaf*, January 2004. See also Philip Burnhan, "Interview with Tohono O'odham Nation's Vivian Juan-Saunders," November 6, 2003, *Indian Country Today*.

27. See Hackenberg and Wilson, "Reluctant Emigrants," 173–179; Kelly, "The Papago Indians of Arizona: A Population and Economic Study" (Tucson: University of Arizona Bureau of Ethnic Research Report, 1963), 112–118.

28. Waddell, "Papagos at Work," *Anthropological Papers of the University of Arizona*, 30–32 (hereafter cited as *APUA*); Fontana, *Of Earth and Little Rain*, 118.

29. Waddell, "Papagos at Work," *APUA*, 54–58, 108.

30. Ibid., 32–33, 72, 79–80, 110.

31. Ibid., 72, 79; Julie M. Uhlmann, "The Impact of Modernization on Papago Indian Fertility," *Human Organization* 31, no. 2 (Summer 1972): 149–161. See also Hackenberg and Wilson, "Reluctant Emigrants," 177. On the diversification between and within O'odham communities, see Feldman, "Deviation, Demography, and Development," 146.

32. The Self-Determination Act and the review commission's report are partially reproduced in Prucha, *Documents*, 274–277, 281–283. Quotes are from 274, 281–282.

33. Ralph A. Barney, "The Indian Claims Commission," in Horr, *Papago Indians I*, 13–14; Robert A. Hackenberg, "Introduction to the Ethnohistorical Reports on the Land Claims Cases," in Horr, *Papago Indians I*, 17.

34. These reports were eventually compiled and published by Garland Press in three volumes edited by David Horr: *Papago Indians I, Papago Indians II*, and *Papago Indians III*.

35. Indian Claims Commission, "Findings of Fact" and "Opinion of the Commission," 19 ICC 394, September 10, 1968, and "Additional Findings of Fact," 21 ICC 403, October 1, 1969, all in Horr, *Papago Indians III*, 228–271. Quotations from 251 and 253, respectively. See also Dobyns, *Papago People*, 75.

36. The tribe eventually sought to purchase lands lost by the Hia C'ed O'odham in the arid regions west of the Sells reservation. See Donna Jones, "Sand Papagos, A Forgotten Group Work for Recognition and Land," *Papago Runner*, February 9, 1984, 1–2 (hereafter cited as *PR*).

37. In *PR*: "$26 Million Plan is Vague and Two Years Away," 9 November 1979, 1; "$26 Million Procedures," 1 February 1980, 4; "$26 Million Planning Effort Is

Again Dusted Off," 23 January 1981, 1; "Reservation Hearings Set on $26 Million Plan," 10 November 1981, 1, 3. See also "$26 Million from U.S.," *ADS,* 22 May 1976, 1; Jane Kay, "Papagos Seeking a Claim in Future with Land Settlement," *ADS,* 29 November 1981, B2. Quotation from "Papagos Support Plan Splitting $39 Million," *ADS,* 23 November 1981, VGLSC.

38. Kay, "Papagos Seeking a Claim in Future."

39. In *PR:* "$26 Million Plan to Face Interior Consent Or Rejection," 20 January 1982, 1, 8; "Land Judgment Bill Drafted," 9 July 1982, 1; "Land Bill Passage Approaches," 24 November 1982, 1, 4; "Distribution of $22 Million Is Closer With Bill's Passage," 23 December 1982, 1, 8; "Reagan OKs Money Use Bill," 12 January 1983, 1; "Deadline Is Established For Enrollment Applications," 12 February 1983, 1; "Given Up Yet On $26 Million?" 13 April 1983, 1; "Land Judgment Per Capita Checks Get June 16 Target," 9 June 1983, 1; "It Can Be Agitating for Those Awaiting Per Capita Checks," 19 June 1983, 1; "More Tribal Members Should be Receiving $1,000 Judgment Checks," 27 July 1984, 5.

40. Senate, *The Central Arizona Indian Tribal Water Rights Settlement Bill,* 94th Cong., 2d sess., S. Rep. 3298, SCUA, U-MSS, box 588, folder 10. In U-MSS, box 588, folder 9, see Roger Lewis to William Byler, December 3, 1975; Byler to Lewis, December 3, 1975. In U-MSS, box 588, folder 10, see Byler to Lewis, February 6, 1976, and Charles E. Trimble, NCAI executive director, to Chairman Henry M. Jackson, Committee on Interior and Insular Affairs, August 6, 1976.

41. S 14059-60, 94th Cong., 2d sess. (August 10, 1976) in U-MSS, box 599, folder 9.

42. Gerald Anton, "An Arizona Indian Asks Congress to Enact a Water-Rights Bill," *New York Times,* August 5, 1976, U-MSS, box 588, folder 9.

43. Thomas R. McGuire, "Getting to Yes in the New West," in *State and Reservation: New Perspectives on Federal Indian Policy,* ed. George Pierre Castile and Robert L. Bee (Tucson: University of Arizona Press, 1992), 224–246, 232; Sheridan, *Arizona,* 347–348. On the arguments made by the Ak-Chin Indians for a water settlement, see Bill McClellan, "From Mud Huts to Prosperity," *Phoenix Gazette,* February 6, 1976, C1; Jayce Smith to Congressman John Moss, May 24, 1976, U-MSS, box 588, folder 9.

44. Donna Jones, "Reagan OKs Water Bill," *PR,* October 20, 1982, 1, 4; Thomas R. McGuire, "Indian Water Rights Settlements: A Case Study in the Rhetoric of Implementation," *American Indian Culture and Research Journal* 15, no. 2 (1991): 139–169, 141. See also Sheridan, *Arizona,* 347–348.

45. Donna Jones, "Opponents Are Vocal Over Planned Development," *PR,* September 21, 1983, 1. See also Ernie Heltsley, "Land Awaits its Destiny," *ADS,* September 15, 1983, 1A, 2A.

46. "San Xavier Land Dispute Update," *PR,* May 8, 1984, 8. See also Howard Allen and Maggy Zanger, "Welcome to San Xavier: Coming Soon to Your Backyard: A New City of 100,000 People," *Tucson Weekly,* 17–23 April 1985, 4–5; "Living in San Xavier: Questions Abound about Authority, Bureaucracy and the 48-page Lease," *Tucson Weekly,* 24–30 April 1985, 3, 5.

47. Donna Jones, "SX Development Touches People Differently," *PR*, April 26, 1984, 1, 7.

48. McGuire, "Operations on the Concept of Sovereignty," 75–84; McGuire, "Indian Water Rights Settlements," 153–156.

49. Fontana, *Of Earth and Little Rain*, 90–96. The figure 1400 is from Castillo and Cowan, eds., *It Is Not Our Fault*, 10. See also Tom Miller, *On the Border: Portraits of America's Southwestern Frontier* (Tucson: University of Arizona Press, 1981), 178–179.

50. In 1979 journalist Judith Ratliff estimated that forty thousand people from Mexico and the U.S. Southwest visited the Magdalena festival in ten days. Ratliff, "Magdalena Fiesta a Time for Feasting, and for Praying," *ADS*, October 6, 1979, VGLSC.

51. The northern and southern variations of the *wi:gita* are discussed by Underhill and others, *Rainhouse and Ocean*, 83.

52. Fontana, *Of Earth and Little Rain*, 100–101; Alan Weisman and Jay Dusard, *La Frontera: The United States Border with Mexico* (San Diego: Harcourt, Brace, 1984), 149.

53. Weisman, *La Frontera*, 147; Miller, *On the Border*, 179.

54. Castillo and Cowan, eds., *It Is Not Our Fault*. Quotes from the interviews on 62, 65, and 68, respectively.

55. "The Sonoran Papagos Press for Land and Recognition," *PR*, August 31, 1979, 1, 3; Ray Panzarella, "75 Sonoran Papagos Occupying Building in Land Protest," *ADS*, March 14, 1982, A1, A6; Donna Jones, "Battle to Get and Keep Land is Endless for Sonora Papagos" and "Sonoran Papagos Are Fighting to Keep Land," *PR*, June 28, 1984, 1, 8. See also Fontana, *Of Earth and Little Rain*, 83, 93.

56. Gary Nabhan confirmed in a phone conversation with the author on January 21, 2005, that the pseudonym Isidro refers to Francisco Valenzuela, whose story is documented in Weisman's work. Versions of Francisco's story can be found in Nabhan, *The Desert Smells Like Rain*, 67–74; and Weisman, *La Frontera*, 147–149. On García, see Fontana, *Of Earth and Little Rain*, 82, 85, 92, 93, 96. See also "The Sonoran Papagos Press for Land and Recognition," *PR*, August 31, 1979, 1, 3.

57. Tribal resolution 43–79, May 16, 1979, "O'odham in Mexico" file, VGLSC. See also in *PR*: "Tribal Council," 7 June 1979, 5; "Sonoran Papagos Press for Land and Recognition," 31 August 1979, 1; "Sonoran Papagos To Hear Explanation of Resolution," 15 January 1980, 3.

58. Tribal resolutions 44–79 and 45–79, May 16, 1979, "O'odham in Mexico" file, VGLSC. See also "Tribal Council," *PR*, June 7, 1979, 5.

59. "Sonoran Papagos," *PR*, 10 March 1983, 8; Ray Panzarella, "75 Sonoran Papagos Occupying Building in Land Protest," *ADS*, 14 March 1982, A1, A6; Maria Vigil, "Papagos Relinquish Building," *ADC*, 17 March 1982, VGLSC; Tim Steller, "O'odham Group Takes Over Government Office in Sonora," *ADS*, 18 April 1999, B2.

60. "O'odham in Mexico—Open Letter to the Public and to Native Officials, 1990," VGLSC.

61. *Tohono O'odham Citizenship Act of 2001*, HR 2348, 107th Cong., 1st sess.; *A Bill to Clarify the Citizenship Eligibility for Certain Members of the Tohono O'odham Nation of Arizona, and for Other Purposes*, HR 1502 IH, 107th Cong., 1st sess; *Tohono O'odham Citizenship Act of 2003*, HR 731 IH, 108th Cong., 1st sess. The 1987 bill is discussed by Eric Volante, "Proposed Federal Restrictions Spur Withdrawal of O'odham Border Bill," *ADS*, July 14, 1988, in VGLSC, "O'odham borderlands issues" file.

62. "American Yaqui Indians Facing Dilemma," *ADS*, September 26, 1975.

63. Miller, "The Yaquis," 186–187; Castile, "Yaquis," 403.

64. Castile, "Yaquis," 401–403. The second quote is from Garrison and Swank to Udall, February 20, 1964 in U-MSS, box 165, folder 14.

65. Gabriel and Francis Alvarez, interview by author, Guadalupe, Arizona, April 26, 1995; Chris Hernandez, interview by author, Tempe, Arizona, April 4, 1995; Cota interview. See also, for a good description of the role of compadres in the ceremonies, Painter, *With Good Heart*. On Guadalupe specifically see William Simpson, "An Ethnographic Account of Yaqui Guadalupe Compared With the Culture of Poverty" (master's thesis, Arizona State University, 1969), 39.

66. Wood interview, 13.

67. Ramenofsky, "The Rise of Guadalupe Yaqui Factions," 11.

68. Simpson, "An Ethnographic Account," 41; Barbara Valencia and Tomasa Carpio, interview by author, Phoenix, October 19, 1994.

69. Simpson, "An Ethnographic Account," 14–15, 56.

70. *1980 Census: General Social and Economic Characteristics, Arizona*, 4–192.

71. Simpson, "An Ethnographic Account," 41, 56, 57; Valencia and Carpio interview.

72. Wood interview, 23.

73. Cathryn Retzlaff Shaffer, "Preservation of Yaqui Language and Culture in Guadalupe, Arizona" (master's thesis substitute, Arizona State University, 1986), 30, CHASU.

74. Benito M. Quijada to "The President: The White House," August 18, 1962, OLGC. For a more detailed discussion of tensions between Yaquis, Mexican Americans, the Catholic Church, the forty acres, and GO see Meeks, "Cross-Ethnic Political Organization."

75. Alvarez interview.

76. Ibid.

77. "War on Poverty," *AR*, June 18, 1967, GTH.

78. Guadalupe Organization, "Where Cultures Meet: *Donde Nacen Las Culturas*" (Guadalupe, AZ: 1970), 3, CHASU.

79. Guadalupe Organization, *Final Report Covering Technical Assistance Grant From June 15, 1971 to June 14, 1972* (Guadalupe, AZ: 1972), appendix, Guadalupe Public Library.

80. "Tempe Rejects Plan to Hire Only Bilingual Teachers," *Arizona Republic*, December 7, 1972, GTH.

81. Guadalupe Organization, *Final Report*, 10, Guadalupe Public Library.

An outline of the 1971–1972 case can be found in *Bernasconi v. Tempe Elementary School Dist. No. 3*, 548 F.2d 857 (1977), 860. See also, Octaviana Trujillo, "A Tribal Approach to Language and Literacy Development in a Trilingual Setting," *Teaching Indigenous Languages,* ed. Jon Reyhner (Flagstaff: Northern Arizona University, 1997), 10–21; Leticia Hernandez, "Hernandez Family," CHASU; "The Guadalupe Suit," *PG,* August 13, 1971, 1; "News about Education," *GO Newsletter,* May 13, 1972, 3–5; "Tempe Schools to Reform IQ tests," *Arizona Republic,* May 10, 1972, GTH.

82. *Guadalupe Organization, Inc. v. Tempe Elementary School District,* 587 F.2d 1022 (1978), 1025.

83. Ibid., 1027.

84. Ibid.

85. Cathryn R. Shaffer, "Trilingual School Keeps Hanging On," *AR,* October 12, 1983, clipping, GTH.

86. Cota interview.

87. Guadalupe Organization, *Final Report,* appendix.

88. Carpio and Valencia interview.

89. "Guadalupe Council to Ponder Rezoning," *Tempe Daily News,* May 5, 1982, GTH; "Decision May Violate State Open Meet Law," *Tempe Daily News,* August 27, 1977, GTH; Maricopa County, Office of the Clerk, *Adoption of Resolution RE: Incorporation of Town of Guadalupe,* docket 11047, 880–882, February 25, 1975, OLGC.

90. In GTH: "Via Head Start Program: Yaqui Culture Revitalized," *Mesa Tribune,* August 12, 1976, and "Keep Customs Going: Yaquis Working to Preserve Heritage," *Tempe Daily News,* March 4, 1977, 5.

91. Jimmy Molina, interview by author, May 25, 1995, Guadalupe, Arizona.

92. "Yaqui Indian Ceremonies Off Limits: Guadalupe Bans Photos," GTH; Carpio and Valencia interview.

93. Castile, "Yaquis," 403–412; Miller, "The Yaquis," passim.

94. Castile, "Yaquis," 339.

95. *A Bill to Provide for the Extension of Certain Federal Benefits, Services, and Assistance to the Pascua Yaqui Indians of Arizona, and For Other Purposes,* HR 8411, 94th Cong., 1st sess. (8 July 1975), U-MSS, box 165, folder 14; "Udall Bill Would Recognize Yaquis," *ADS,* September 19, 1975, clipping, U-MSS, box 165, folder 14.

96. Castile, "Yaquis," 405–406.

97. Valencia is quoted in Arizona Commission of Indian Affairs, business meeting minutes, June 27, 1975, 9, U-MSS, box 165, folder 14 (hereafter cited as ACIA minutes).

98. "Yaqui Elders Rebel at Becoming 'Wards,'" *TDC,* November 19, 1975, U-MSS, box 165, folder 14.

99. ACIA minutes, 9.

100. Carpio and Valencia interview.

101. *A Bill To Provide for the Extension of Certain Federal Benefits;* Castile, "Yaquis," 405;

102. These documents reproduced in Prucha, *Documents*, 281–291.

103. Senate Select Committee on Indian Affairs, *Hearing on Trust Status for the Pascua Yaqui Indians of Arizona*, statements by Sens. James Abourezk and Dennis DeConcini, 95th Cong., 1st sess., U-MSS, box 165, folder 14.

104. "Statement of Anselmo Valencia," ibid., 5–6.

105. *An Act to Provide for the Extension of Certain Federal Benefits, Services, and Assistance to the Pascua Yaqui Indians of Arizona, and for Other Purposes,* Public Law 95-375, 95th Cong., 2d sess. (September 18, 1978), U-MSS, box 165, folder 14.

106. Castile, "Yaquis," 406–410.

107. BIA, "Federal Acknowledgment of Indian Tribes," October 2, 1978, in Prucha, *Documents*, 289–290. Quotation from 289.

108. Public Law 95-375.

109. I learned this at a tribal council meeting in June 1994 in Guadalupe.

110. Bill Coates, "Yaqui Educator Battles Discrimination She Felt," *Tempe Daily News*, October 26, 1982, GTH.

111. Brenda Norrell, "Indigenous Women—Mexico's Emerging Power," *Indian Country Today*, November 15, 2004, 1.

112. Carpio and Valencia interview.

113. Smith to Udall, August 11, 1964, U-MSS.

CONCLUSION

1. Brenda Norrell, "Indigenous Women: Mexico's Emerging Power," *Indian Country Today*, November 15, 2004; Stephanie Innes, "New Tribal Look: Nine Reservations in Arizona Are Now Headed by Women," *Arizona Daily Star*, June 20, 2004.

2. Vivian Juan-Saunders and Ned Norris Jr. (Tohono O'odham vice president), "An Open Letter to the UN Regarding the Tohono O'odham Border," *Indian Country Today*, August 27, 2004.

3. Brenda Norrell, "Tohono O'odham and Yaqui: 'No More Walls,'" *Indian Country Today*, July 20, 2004. On the Indigenous Alliance Across Borders, see Brenda Norrell, "Native Groups Across U.S./Mexico Border Form Alliance," *Albion Monitor*, September 15, 1997.

4. *Guadalupe Organization Inc. v. Tempe Elementary School District*, 587 F.2d 1022 (1978), 1025.

5. Daniel González, "Arizona Win Encourages Bilingual-Ed Opponents," *Arizona Republic*, November 20, 2000, A1.

6. *Arizona Taxpayer and Citizenship Protection Act* (Prop. 200, 2004), sec. 2; Lawyers Committee for Civil Rights, "Arizona Voters File Lawsuit against Secretary of State Brewer," May 24, 2006, http://www.lawyerscomm.org; Margot Veranes

and Adriana Navarro, International Relations Center, Americas Project, "Anti-immigrant Legislation in Arizona: Leads to Calls for a State Boycott," June 1, 2005, http://americas.irc-online.org.

7. U.S. House, *A Bill to Amend the Immigration and Nationality Act to Strengthen Enforcement of the Immigration Laws, to Enhance Border Security, and for Other Purposes,* HR 4437, 109th Cong., 1st sess.

8. Howard Fischer, "100,000 Protest Immigration Legislation in Phoenix," *Arizona Daily Star,* 11 April 2006, http://www.azstarnet.com.

9. See James K. Galbraith, "The Kids Are All Right," *Mother Jones,* July/August 2006, 26–27.

10. *Tohono O'odham Citizenship Act of 2001,* HR 2348, 107th Cong., 1st sess.; *A Bill to Clarify the Citizenship Eligibility for Certain Members of the Tohono O'odham Nation of Arizona, and for Other Purposes,* HR 1502 IH, 107th Cong., 1st sess.; Carmen Duarte, "Tohono O'odham: Campaign for Citizenship; Nation Divided," *Arizona Daily Star,* May 30, 2001, A8.

11. *Tohono O'odham Citizenship Act of 2003,* HR 731 IH, 108th Cong., 1st sess.

12. See E. J. Hobsbawm, *Nations and Nationalism Since 1780: Programme, Myth, Reality* (Cambridge, UK: Cambridge University Press, 1990).

SELECTED BIBLIOGRAPHY

Abbott, Carl. *The Metropolitan Frontier: Cities in the Modern American West.* Tucson: University of Arizona Press, 1993.

Acuña, Rodolfo. *Occupied America: A History of Chicanos.* 3rd ed. New York: HarperCollins, 1988.

———. *Occupied America: A History of Chicanos.* 5th ed. New York: Pearson, 2004.

Aguilar Camín, Hector. *La frontera nomada: Sonora y la Revolución Mexicana.* Mexico City: Siglo Veintiuno Editores, 1977.

Almaguer, Tomás. *Racial Fault Lines: The Historical Origins of White Supremacy in California.* Berkeley: University of California Press, 1994.

Anderson, Benedict. *Imagined Communities: Reflections on the Origin and Spread of Nationalism.* London: Verso, 1991.

Anzaldúa, Gloria. *Borderlands/La Frontera: The New Mestiza.* 2nd ed. San Francisco: Aunt Lute Books, 1999.

Ascencio, Fernando Lozano, ed. *Sonorenses en Arizona: Proceso de formación de una región binacional.* Hermosillo, Mexico: Universidad de Sonora, 1997.

Banfield, Edward. *Government Project.* Glencoe, IL: Free Press, 1951.

Barrera, Mario. *Race and Class in the Southwest: A Theory of Racial Inequality.* Notre Dame, IN: University of Notre Dame Press, 1979.

Bell, Dennis. *Barrio Historico, Tucson.* Tucson: College of Architecture, University of Arizona, 1972.

Benton, Katherine A. "What About Women in the White Man's Camp?: Gender, Nation, and the Redefinition of Race in Cochise County, Arizona, 1853–1941." PhD diss., University of Wisconsin-Madison, 2002.

Berkhofer, Robert F., Jr. *The White Man's Indian: Images of the American Indian from Columbus to the Present.* New York: Vintage, 1979.

Berman, David R. *Reformers, Corporations, and the Electorate: An Analysis of Arizona's Age of Reform.* Niwot, CO: University Press of Colorado, 1992.

Bernal, Martin, and Louis Carlos Bernal. *Images and Conversations: Mexican Americans Recall a Southwestern Past.* 1983. Reprint, Tucson: University of Arizona Press, 1996.

Blaine, Peter, and Michael S. Adams. *Papagos and Politics.* Tucson: Arizona Historical Society, 1981.

Booth, Peter Macmillan. "Creation of a Nation: The Development of the Tohono O'odham Political Culture: 1900–1937." PhD diss., Purdue University, 2000.

Brooks, James F. *Captives and Cousins: Slavery, Kinship, and Community in the Southwest Borderlands.* Chapel Hill: University of North Carolina Press, 1992.

Byrkit, James. *Forging the Copper Collar: Arizona's Labor-Management War of 1901–1921.* Tucson: University of Arizona Press, 1982.

Cardoso, Lawrence A. *Mexican Emigration to the United States, 1897–1931.* Tucson: University of Arizona Press, 1980.

Castille, George Pierre, and Robert L. Bee, eds. *State and Reservation: New Perspectives on Federal Indian Policy.* Tucson: University of Arizona Press, 1992.

Castillo, Guadalupe, and Margo Cowan, eds. *It Is Not Our Fault: The Case for Amending Present Nationality Law to Make All Members of the Tohono O'odham Nation United States Citizens, Now and Forever.* Sells, AZ: Tohono O'odham Nation, Executive Branch, 2001.

Chafe, William H. *Civilities and Civil Rights: Greensboro, North Carolina, and the Black Struggle for Freedom.* Oxford: Oxford University Press, 1980.

Chaudhri, Joyotpaul. *Urban Indians of Arizona: Phoenix, Tucson, and Flagstaff.* The Institute of Government Research, Arizona Government Studies 11. Tucson: University of Arizona Press, 1974.

Chávez, Ernesto. *Mi raza primero: Nationalism, Identity, and Insurgency in the Chicano Movement in Los Angeles, 1966–1978.* Berkeley: University of California Press, 2002.

Clifford, James. *The Predicament of Culture.* Cambridge: Harvard University Press, 1988.

Coerver, Don M., and Linda B. Hall. *Texas and the Mexican Revolution: A Study in State and National Border Policy, 1910–1920.* San Antonio, TX: Trinity University Press, 1984.

Cohen, Lizabeth. *Making a New Deal: Industrial Workers in Chicago, 1919–1930.* Cambridge: Cambridge University Press, 1990.

Comaroff, John, and Jean Comaroff. *Ethnography and the Historical Imagination.* Boulder, CO: Westview Press, 1992.

Cook, Charles. *Among the Pimas; or, The Mission to the Pima and Maricopa Indians.* Albany, NY: The Ladies' Union Mission School Association, 1893.

Cooper, Frederick, Thomas C. Holt, and Rebecca J. Scott. *Beyond Slavery: Explorations of Race, Labor, and Citizenship in Post-emancipation Societies.* Chapel Hill: University of North Carolina Press, 2000.

Cornell, Stephen. *Return of the Native.* New York: Oxford University Press, 1988.

Cowger, Tomas W. *The National Congress of American Indians: The Founding Years*. Lincoln: University of Nebraska Press, 1999.

Cronon, William, George Miles, and Jay Gitlin, eds. *Under an Open Sky: Rethinking America's Western Past*. New York: W. W. Norton, 1992.

Crow, John E. *Mexican Americans in Contemporary Arizona: A Social and Demographic View*. San Francisco: R&E Research Associates, 1975.

Daniels, Roger. *Coming to America: A History of Immigration and Ethnicity in American Life*. New York: Harper Perennial, 1990.

Deloria, Philip J. *Playing Indian*. New Haven: Yale University Press, 1998.

Deutsch, Sarah. *No Separate Refuge: Culture, Class, and Gender on an Anglo-Hispanic Frontier in the American Southwest, 1880–1940*. New York: Oxford University Press, 1987.

Dobyns, Henry F. *Papagos in the Cotton Fields, 1950*. Tucson: University of Arizona Press, 1951.

———. *Spanish Colonial Tucson: A Demographic History*. Tucson: University of Arizona Press, 1976.

———. *The Papago People*. Phoenix: Indian Tribal Series, 1972.

Dudley, Shelly C. "Pima Indians, Water Rights, and the Federal Government: *U.S. v. Gila Valley Irrigation District*." MA thesis, Arizona State University, 1996.

Erickson, Winston P. *Sharing the Desert: The Tohono O'odham in History*. Tucson: University of Arizona Press, 1994.

Ferriss, Susan, and Ricardo Sandoval. *The Fight in the Fields: Cesar Chavez and the Farmworkers Movement*. San Diego: Harcourt Brace, 1997.

Fixico, Donald. *The Urban Indian Experience in America*. Albuquerque: University of New Mexico Press, 2000.

Flores, Raymond Johnson. "The Socio-economic Status Trends of the Mexican People Residing in Arizona." MA thesis, Arizona State University, 1951.

Flores, William V., and Rina Benmayor, eds. *Latino Cultural Citizenship: Claiming Identity, Space, and Rights*. Boston: Beacon, 1997.

Foley, Neil. *The White Scourge: Mexicans, Blacks, and Poor Whites in Texas Cotton Culture*. Berkeley: University of California Press, 1997.

Foner, Eric. *A Short History of Reconstruction: 1863–1877*. New York: Harper & Row, 1990.

Fontana, Bernard L. *Of Earth and Little Rain: The Papago Indians*. Tucson: University of Arizona Press, 1986.

Galarza, Ernesto. *Barrio Boy*. Notre Dame, IN: University of Notre Dame Press, 1971.

Gamio, Mario. *The Mexican Immigrant*. New York: Arno, 1969.

García, Mario T. *Desert Immigrants: The Mexicans of El Paso, 1880–1920*. New Haven: Yale University Press, 1981.

Getty, Harry T. *Interethnic Relationships in the Community of Tucson*. New York: Arno, 1976.

Giddings, Ruth Warner. *Yaqui Myths and Legends*. Tucson: University of Arizona Press, 1986.

Glaser, Leah. "The Story of Guadalupe, Arizona: The Survival and Preservation of a Yaqui Community." MA thesis, Arizona State University, 1996.

Glenn, Evelyn Nakano. *Unequal Freedom: How Race and Gender Shaped American Citizenship and Labor.* Cambridge: Harvard University Press, 2002.

Gómez-Quiñones, Juan. *Chicano Politics: Reality and Promise, 1940–1990.* Albuquerque: University of New Mexico Press, 1990.

González, Deena J. *Refusing the Favor: The Spanish-Mexican Women of Santa Fe, 1820–1880.* Oxford: Oxford University Press, 1999.

González, Gilbert. *Culture of Empire: American Writers, Mexico, and Mexican Immigrants, 1880–1930.* Austin: University of Texas Press, 2004.

Gordon, Linda. *The Great Arizona Orphan Abduction.* Cambridge: Harvard University Press, 1999.

Gorn, Elliott J., Randy Roberts, and Terry D. Bilhartz, eds. *Constructing the American Past: A Source Book of a People's History.* 4th ed. New York: Longman Press, 2002.

Griffith, James S. *A Shared Space: Folklife in the Arizona-Sonora Borderlands.* Logan: Utah State University, 1995.

Griswold del Castillo, Richard, and Richard A. García. *César Chávez, A Triumph of Spirit.* Norman: University of Oklahoma Press, 1995.

Gutiérrez, David G. *Walls and Mirrors: Mexican Americans, Mexican Immigrants, and the Politics of Ethnicity.* Berkeley: University of California Press, 1995.

Gutiérrez, José Angel. *The Making of a Chicano Militant: Lessons from Cristal.* Madison: University of Wisconsin Press, 1998.

Hahamovich, Cindy. *The Fruits of Their Labor: Atlantic Coast Farmworkers and the Making of Migrant Poverty, 1870–1945.* Chapel Hill: University of North Carolina Press, 1997.

Hall, Stuart, and Paul du Gay, eds. *Questions of Cultural Identity.* London: Sage, 1996.

Harmon, Alexandra. *Indians in the Making: Ethnic Relations and Indian Identities around Puget Sound.* Berkeley: University of California Press, 1998.

Harvey, David. *The Condition of Postmodernity: An Enquiry into the Origins of Cultural Change.* Cambridge, MA: Basil Blackwell, 1989.

Heyman, Josiah. *Life and Labor on the Border: Working People of Northeastern Sonora, Mexico, 1886–1986.* Tucson: University of Arizona Press, 1991.

Hobsbawm, E. J. *Nations and Nationalism Since 1780: Programme, Myth, Reality.* Cambridge: Cambridge University Press, 1990.

Hodes, Martha, ed. *Sex, Love, Race: Crossing Boundaries in North American History.* New York: New York University Press, 1999.

Hoffman, Abraham. *Unwanted Mexican Americans in the Great Depression: Repatriation Pressures, 1929–1939.* Tucson: University of Arizona Press, 1974.

Horr, David Agee, ed. *Papago Indians I.* New York: Garland, 1974.

———. *Papago Indians II*. Garland, 1974.

———. *Papago Indians III*. Garland, 1974.

Horsman, Mathew, and Andrew Marshall. *After the Nation-State: Citizens, Tribalism and the New World Disorder*. London: HarperCollins, 1994.

Hosmer, Brian. *American Indians in the Marketplace: Persistence and Innovation among the Menominees and Metlakatlans, 1870–1920*. Lawrence: University Press of Kansas, 1999.

Hosmer, Brian, and Colleen O'Neill. *Native Pathways: American Indian Culture and Economic Development in the Twentieth Century*. Boulder: University Press of Colorado, 2004.

Hoxie, Frederick E. *A Final Promise: The Campaign to Assimilate the Indians, 1880–1920*. Lincoln: University of Nebraska Press, 2001.

Hu-DeHart, Evelyn. *Missionaries, Miners, and Indians: Spanish Contact with the Yaqui Nation of Northwestern New Spain, 1533–1820*. Tucson: University of Arizona Press, 1981.

———. *Yaqui Resistance and Survival: The Struggle for Land and Autonomy, 1821–1910*. Madison: University of Wisconsin Press, 1984.

Hurtado, Al. *Intimate Frontiers: Sex, Gender, and Culture in Old California*. Albuquerque: University of New Mexico Press, 1999.

Ignatiev, Noel. *How the Irish Became White*. New York: Routledge, 1995.

Jacobson, Matthew Frye. *Whiteness of a Different Color: European Immigration and the Alchemy of Race*. Cambridge: Harvard University Press, 1998.

Jamieson, Stuart. *Labor Unionism in American Agriculture*. 1945. Reprint, New York: Arno, 1976.

Jenkins, Craig. *The Politics of Insurgency: The Farm Worker Movement in the 1960s*. New York: Columbia University Press, 1985.

John, Elizabeth A. H. *Storms Brewed in Other Men's Worlds: The Confrontation of Indians, Spanish, and French in the Southwest, 1540–1795*. Norman: University of Oklahoma Press, 1975.

Johnson, James. *Arizona Politicians: The Noble and the Notorious*. Tucson: University of Arizona Press, 2002.

Joseph, Gilbert M. *Revolution from Without: Yucatán, Mexico, and the United States, 1880–1924*. Durham: Duke University Press, 1988.

Josephy, Alvin M., ed. *America in 1492: The World of the Indian Peoples Before the Arrival of Columbus*. New York: Knopf, 1992. Distributed by Random House.

Kehoe, Alice B. *North American Indians: A Comprehensive Account*. 2nd ed. Englewood Cliffs, NJ: Prentice Hall, 1992.

Kelley, Jane Holden. *Yaqui Women: Contemporary Life Histories*. Lincoln: University of Nebraska Press, 1978.

Kelley, Robin D. G. *Hammer and Hoe: Alabama Communists During the Great Depression*. Chapel Hill: University of North Carolina Press, 1990.

Kingsolver, Barbara. *Holding the Line: Women in the Great Arizona Mine Strike of 1983*. Ithaca, NY: ILR Press, 1989.

Kluger, James R. *The Clifton-Morenci Strike: Labor Difficulty in Arizona, 1915–1916.* Tucson: University of Arizona Press, 1970.

Knight, Alan. *The Mexican Revolution.* Vol. 2, *Counter-revolution and Reconstruction.* Lincoln: University of Nebraska Press, 1986.

Knight, Rolf. *Indians At Work: An Informal History of Native Indian Labour in British Columbia, 1858–1930.* Vancouver, BC: New Star Books, 1978.

Kotlanger, Michael J. "Phoenix, Arizona, 1920–1940." PhD diss., Arizona State University, 1983.

Kroeber, Clifton B. *Man, Land, and Water: Mexico's Farmlands Irrigation Policies 1885–1911.* Berkeley: University of California Press, 1983.

Lamar, Howard R. *The Far Southwest: 1846–1912: A Territorial History.* New Haven: Yale University Press, 1966.

Lamb, Barry Edward. "The Making of a Chicano Civil Rights Activist: Ralph Estrada of Arizona." MA thesis, Arizona State University, 1988.

Lamb, Ruth. *Mexican Americans: Sons of the Southwest.* Claremont, CA: Ocelot, 1970.

Lauter, Paul, ed. Vol. 2 of *The Heath Anthology of American Literature.* 4th ed. Boston: Houghton Mifflin, 2002.

Leaming, George F. *Labor and Copper in Arizona.* Tucson: University of Arizona College of Business and Public Administration, 1973.

LeSeur, Geta. *Not All Okies Are White: The Lives of Black Cotton Pickers in Arizona.* Columbia: University of Missouri Press, 2000.

Levy, Jacques. *César Chávez: Autobiography of La Causa.* New York: W. W. Norton, 1975.

Lewis, David Rich. *Neither Wolf nor Dog: American Indians, Environment, and Agrarian Change.* New York: Oxford University Press, 1994.

Littlefield, Alice, and Martha C. Knack, eds. *Native Americans and Wage Labor: Ethnohistorical Perspectives.* Norman: University of Oklahoma Press, 1996.

"Los Mineros." Episode in the PBS series *The American Experience* (1991).

Lowe, Lisa. *Immigrant Acts: On Asian American Cultural Politics.* Durham: Duke University Press, 1996.

Lowe, Lisa, and David Lloyd, eds. *The Politics of Culture in the Shadow of Capital.* Durham: Duke University Press, 1997.

Luckingham, Bradford. *Minorities in Phoenix: A Profile of Mexican American, Chinese American, and African American Communities, 1860–1992.* Tucson: The University of Arizona Press, 1995.

———. *Phoenix: The History of a Southwestern Metropolis.* Tucson: The University of Arizona Press, 1989.

———. *The Urban Southwest: A Profile History of Albuquerque, El Paso, Phoenix, and Tucson.* El Paso: Texas Western Press, 1985.

Maldonado, José A. "¡Si Se Puede! The Farm Worker Movement in Arizona 1965–1979." MA thesis, Arizona State University, 1995.

Manje, Juan M. *Unknown Arizona and Sonora, 1693–1721.* Translated by Harry J. Karns. Tucson: Arizona Silhouettes, 1954.

Manuel, Frances, and Deborah Neff. *Desert Indian Woman: Stories and Dreams.* Tucson: University of Arizona Press, 2001.

Martin, Patricia Preciado. *Songs My Mother Sang to Me: An Oral History of Mexican American Women.* Tucson: University of Arizona Press, 1992.

McCarthy, James. *A Papago Traveler: The Memories of James McCarthy.* Edited by John G. Westover. Tucson: Sun Tracks and University of Arizona Press, 1985.

McCarty, Kieran. *A Frontier Documentary: Sonora and Tucson, 1821–1848.* Tucson: University of Arizona Press, 1997.

McLoughlin, Emmett. *People's Padre: An Autobiography.* Boston: Beacon, 1954.

Meeks, Eric V. "Border Citizens: Race, Labor, and Identity in South-Central Arizona, 1910–1965." PhD diss., University of Texas, 2001.

Mellinger, Philip. *Race and Labor in Western Copper: The Fight for Equality, 1896–1918.* Tucson: University of Arizona Press, 1995.

Menchaca, Martha. *Recovering History, Constructing Race: The Indian, Black, and White Roots of Mexican Americans.* Austin: University of Texas Press, 2001.

Michaelsen, Scott, and David E. Johnson, eds. *Border Theory: The Limits of Cultural Politics.* Minneapolis: University of Minnesota Press, 1997.

Miller, Tom. *On the Border: Portraits of America's Southwestern Frontier.* Tucson: University of Arizona Press, 1981.

Mirón, Rodolfo F., and Jonathan Xavier Inda. *Race, Identity, and Citizenship: a Reader.* Malden, MA: Blackwell, 1999.

Moisés, Rosalio, Jane Holden Kelley, and William Curry Holden. *A Yaqui Life: The Personal Chronicle of a Yaqui Indian.* Lincoln: University of Nebraska Press, 1971.

Montejano, David. *Anglos and Mexicans in the Making of Texas: 1836–1986.* Austin: University of Texas Press, 1987.

Montgomery, Charles. *The Spanish Redemption: Heritage, Power, and Loss on New Mexico's Upper Rio Grande.* Berkeley: University of California Press, 2002.

Montgomery, David. *Citizen Worker: The Experience of Workers in the United States with Democracy and the Free Market during the Nineteenth Century.* Cambridge: Cambridge University Press, 1993.

Montoya, Andrés E. Jiménez. *Political Domination in the Labor Market: Racial Division in the Arizona Copper Industry.* Berkeley: University of California, Chicano Studies Library, 1977.

More, John H. *The Political Economy of North American Indians.* Norman: University of Oklahoma Press, 1993.

Morley, David, and Kuan-Hsing Chen, eds. *Stuart Hall: Critical Dialogues in Cultural Studies.* New York: Routledge, 1996.

Muñoz, Carlos. *Youth, Identity, Power: The Chicano Movement.* New York: Verso, 1989.

Nabhan, Gary Paul. *The Desert Smells Like Rain: A Naturalist in Papago Indian Country.* San Francisco: North Point Press, 1982.

Nash, Gerald. *The American West Transformed: The Impact of the Second World War.* Bloomington: Indiana University Press, 1985.

Navarro, Armando. *La Raza Unida Party: A Chicano Challenge to the U.S. Two-Party Dictatorship.* Philadelphia: Temple University Press, 2000.

Neils, Elaine M. *Indian Migration and Federal Relocation.* Chicago: University of Chicago, Department of Geography, 1971.

Nichols, Roger, ed. *The American Indian: Past and Present.* 3rd ed. New York: Knopf, 1986.

Nichols, Roger. *American Indians in U.S. History.* Norman: University of Oklahoma Press, 2003.

Officer, James E. *Hispanic Arizona, 1536–1856.* Tucson: University of Arizona Press, 1987.

Olson, James S., and Raymond Wilson. *Native Americans in the Twentieth Century.* Chicago: University of Illinois Press, 1986.

Omi, Michael, and Howard Winant. *Racial Formation in the United States: From the 1960s to the 1990s.* 2nd ed. New York: Routledge, 1994.

O'Neill, Colleen. "Navajo Workers and White Man's Ways: Negotiating the World of Wage Labor, 1930–1972." PhD diss., Rutgers University, 1997.

Ortiz, Alfonso. *Handbook of North American Indians.* Vol. 10, *Southwest.* Washington: Smithsonian Institution, 1983.

Padfield, Harland, and William E. Martin. *Farmers, Workers, and Machines: Technological and Social Change in Farm Industries of Arizona.* Tucson: University of Arizona Press, 1965.

Painter, Muriel Thayer. *With Good Heart: Yaqui Beliefs and Ceremonies in Pascua Village.* Edited by Edward H. Spicer and Wilma Kaemlein. Tucson: University of Arizona Press, 1986.

Park, Joseph. "The History of Mexican Labor in Arizona during the Territorial Period." MA thesis, University of Arizona, 1961.

Parrish, Michael E. *Mexican Workers, Progressives, and Copper: The Failure of Industrial Democracy in Arizona During the Wilson Years.* San Diego: University of California, 1979.

Peck, Gunther. *Reinventing Free Labor: Padrones and Immigrant Workers in the North American West: 1880–1930.* Cambridge: Cambridge University Press, 2000.

Pfefferkorn, Ignaz. *Sonora: A Description of the Province.* Translated and annotated by Theodore E. Treutlein. Tucson: University of Arizona Press, 1989.

Pisani, Donald J. *Water and American Government: The Reclamation Bureau, National Water Policy, and the West, 1902–1935.* Berkeley: University of California Press, 2002.

Prucha, Francis Paul, ed. *Documents of United States Indian Policy.* 2nd ed. Lincoln: University of Nebraska Press, 1990.

Radding, Cynthia. *Wandering Peoples: Colonialism, Ethnic Spaces, and Ecological Frontiers in Northwestern Mexico, 1700–1850.* Durham: Duke University Press, 1997.

Ramenofsky, Ann. "The Rise of Guadalupe Yaqui Factions from Legal Claims to Plaza Land." MA thesis, Arizona State University, 1968.

Reisler, Mark. *By the Sweat of Their Brow: Mexican Immigrant Labor in the United States, 1900–1940.* Westport, CT: Greenwood, 1976.

Reitzes, Donald C., and Dietrich C. Reitzes. *The Alinsky Legacy: Alive and Kicking.* Greenwich, CT: JAI Press, 1987.

Reséndez, Andrés. *Changing National Identities at the Frontier: Texas and New Mexico, 1800-1850.* Cambridge: Cambridge University Press, 2005.

Reyhner, Jon. *Teaching Indigenous Languages.* Flagstaff: Northern Arizona University Press, 1997.

Ríos, Alberto Alvaro. *Capirotada: A Nogales Memoir.* Albuquerque: University of New Mexico Press, 1999.

Roediger, David. *The Wages of Whiteness: Race and the Making of the American Working Class.* London: Verso, 1991.

Ronstadt, Federico. *Borderman: Memoirs of Federico José María Ronstadt.* Edited by Edward F. Ronstadt. Tucson: University of Arizona Press, 2003.

Rosaldo, Renato, ed. *Cultural Citizenship in Island Southeast Asia: Nation and Belonging in the Hinterlands.* Berkeley: University of California Press, 2003.

Rosales, F. Arturo. *Chicano! The History of the Mexican American Civil Rights Movement.* Houston: Arte Público, 1996.

Rosenblum, Jonathan. *Copper Crucible: How the Arizona Miners' Strike of 1983 Recast Labor-Management Relations in America.* Ithaca, NY: ILR Press, 1995.

Ruiz, Ramón Eduardo. *The People of Sonora and Yankee Capitalists.* Tucson: University of Arizona Press, 1988.

Ruiz, Vicki L. *From Out of the Shadows: Mexican Women in Twentieth-Century America.* New York: Oxford University Press, 1998.

Russell, Frank. *The Pima Indians.* 1908. Reprint, Tucson: University of Arizona Press, 1975.

Sahlins, Peter. *Boundaries: The Making of France and Spain in the Pyrenees.* Berkeley: University of California Press, 1989.

Sánchez, George. *Becoming Mexican American: Ethnicity, Culture, and Identity in Chicano Los Angeles, 1900-1945.* Oxford: Oxford University Press, 1993.

Savala, Refugio. *The Autobiography of a Yaqui Poet.* Edited by Kathleen Sands. Tucson: University of Arizona Press, 1980.

Scott, James C. *Seeing Like a State: How Certain Schemes to Improve the Human Condition Have Failed.* New Haven: Yale University Press, 1998.

Servín, Manuel, ed. *An Awakened Minority: The Mexican-Americans.* Beverly Hills, CA: Glencoe, 1974.

Shaffer, Cathryn Retzlaff. "Preservation of Yaqui Language and Culture in Guadalupe, Arizona." MA thesis substitute, Arizona State University, 1986.

Shaw, Anna Moore. *A Pima Past.* 1974. Reprint, Tucson: University of Arizona Press, 1994.

Sheridan, Thomas E. *Arizona: A History.* Tucson: University of Arizona Press, 1995.

———. *Los Tucsonenses: The Mexican Community in Tucson: 1854–1941.* Tucson: University of Arizona Press, 1986.

Shoemaker, Nancy. *Negotiators of Change: Historical Perspectives on Native American Women.* New York: Routledge, 1995.

Shreve, Forest, and I. L. Wiggins. Vol. 1 of *Vegetation and Flora of the Sonoran Desert.* Stanford, CA: Stanford University Press, 1964.

Simpson, William. "An Ethnographic Account of Yaqui Guadalupe Compared With the Culture of Poverty." MA thesis, Arizona State University, 1969.

Slotkin, Richard. *Fatal Environment: The Myth of the Frontier in the Age of Industrialization: 1800–1890.* 1985. Reprint, New York: Harper Perennial, 1994.

Spicer, Edward H. *Cycles of Conquest: The Impact of Spain, Mexico, and the United States on the Indians of the Southwest, 1533–1960.* Tucson: University of Arizona Press, 1962.

———. *Pascua: A Yaqui Village.* Chicago: University of Chicago Press, 1940.

———. *People of Pascua.* Edited by Kathleen M. Sands and Rosamund B. Spicer. Tucson: University of Arizona Press, 1988.

———. *The Yaquis: A Cultural History.* Tucson: University of Arizona Press, 1980.

Spicer, Rosamund B., ed. *The Desert People.* Chicago: University of Chicago Press, 1949.

Stanley, Sam, ed. *American Indian Economic Development.* The Hague: Mouton, 1978.

Stern, Steve J., ed. *Resistance, Rebellion, and Consciousness in the Andean Peasant World, 18th to 20th Centuries.* Madison: University of Wisconsin Press, 1987.

Takaki, Ronald. *Iron Cages: Race and Culture in Nineteenth-Century America.* New York: Knopf, 1979.

Tapia, Nick. "Cactus in the Desert: The Chicano Movement in Maricopa County, Arizona 1968–1978." MA thesis, Arizona State University, 1999.

Taylor, Graham. *The New Deal and American Indian Tribalism: The Administration of the Indian Reorganization Act, 1934–1945.* Lincoln: University of Nebraska Press, 1980.

Taylor, Paul S. *Mexican Labor in the United States: Migration Statistics, IV.* University of California Publications in Economics 12, vol. 3. Berkeley: University of California Press, 1934.

Tinker Salas, Miguel. *In the Shadow of the Eagles: Sonora and the Transformation of the Border during the Porfiriato.* Berkeley: University of California Press, 1997.

Titcomb, Mary Ruth. "Americanization and Mexicans in the Southwest: A History of Phoenix's Friendly House, 1920–1983." MA thesis, University of California, Santa Barbara, 1984.

Tooker, Elisabeth J. "Papagos in Tucson: An Introduction to Their History, Community Life, and Acculturation." MA thesis, University of Arizona, 1952.

Trennert, Robert A., Jr. *The Phoenix Indian School: Forced Assimilation in Arizona, 1891–1935.* Norman: University of Oklahoma Press, 1988.

Truett, Samuel, and Elliott Young, eds. *Continental Crossroads: Remapping U.S.-Mexico Borderlands History.* Durham: Duke University Press, 2004.

Underhill, Ruth M. *Papago Woman.* Prospect Heights, IL: Waveland, 1979.

———. *Social Organization of the Papago Indians.* 1939. Reprint, New York: AMS Press, 1969.

Underhill, Ruth M., Donald M. Bahr, Baptisto Lopez, Jose Pancho, and David Lopez. *Rainhouse and Ocean: Speeches for the Papago Year.* Tucson: University of Arizona Press, 1997.

Utley, Robert. *The Indian Frontier of the American West 1846–1890.* Albuquerque: University of New Mexico Press, 1984.

Valle, Maria Eva. "MEChA and the Transformation of Chicano Student Activism: Generational Change, Conflict, and Continuity." PhD diss., University of California, San Diego, 1996.

Vélez-Ibáñez, Carlos. *Border Visions: Mexican Cultures of the Southwest United States.* Tucson: University of Arizona Press, 1996.

Wagoner, Jay J. *Arizona Territory, 1863–1912: A Political History.* Tucson: University of Arizona Press, 1970.

Webb, George. *A Pima Remembers.* 1959. Reprint, Tucson: University of Arizona Press, 1965.

Weber, David J. *The Mexican Frontier, 1821–1846: The American Southwest Under Mexico.* Albuquerque: University of New Mexico Press, 1983.

———. *The Spanish Frontier in North America.* New Haven: Yale University Press, 1992.

Weinstein, Laurie, ed. *Native Peoples of the Southwest: Negotiating Land, Water, and Ethnicities.* Westport, CT: Bergin & Garvey, 2001.

Weisiger, Marsha L. *Land of Plenty: Oklahomans in the Cotton Fields of Arizona, 1933–1942.* Norman: University of Oklahoma Press, 1995.

Weisman, Alan, and Jay Dusard. *La Frontera: The United States Border with Mexico.* San Diego: Harcourt Brace Jovanovich, 1984.

West, Robert C. *Sonora: Its Geographical Personality.* Austin: University of Texas Press, 1993.

White, Richard. *Roots of Dependency: Subsistence, Environment, and Social Change among the Choctaws, Pawnees, and Navajos.* Lincoln: University of Nebraska Press, 1983.

———. *The Middle Ground: Indians, Empires, and Republics in the Great Lakes Region, 1650–1815.* Cambridge: Cambridge University Press, 1991.

Wilber-Cruce, Eva Antonia. *A Beautiful, Cruel Country.* Tucson: University of Arizona Press, 1987.

Wilson, Charles Roderick. "Migration, Change, and Variation: A Papago Case Study." PhD diss., University of Colorado, 1972.

Wilson, Thomas M., and Hastings Donnan, eds. *Border Identities: Nation and State at International Frontiers.* Cambridge: Cambridge University Press, 1998.

Woodruff, Janette, and Cecil Dryden. *Indian Oasis.* Caldwell, ID: The Caxton Printers, 1939.

Worster, Donald. *Rivers of Empire: Water, Aridity, and the Growth of the American West.* New York: Pantheon Books, 1985.

Yans-McLaughlin, Virginia. *Immigration Reconsidered: History, Sociology, and Politics.* New York: Oxford University Press, 1990.

INDEX

Italic page numbers refer to figures.

Abourezk, James, 236, 237, 238
Acuña, Eva, 205
Acuña, Manuel, 205
Acuña, Rodolfo, 208
affirmative action, 201–202, 208
African Americans: as agricultural workers, 163; and Chicano movement, 195; and economic boom of 1960s, 158; Mexican American cooperation with, 179; migration to Arizona, 119; population of, 159; racial discrimination against, 155, 173; racial segregation of, 39, 119, 155, 156, 159–161, 177–179; stereotypes of, 126
Agricultural Employment Relations Act, 202–203, 208, 209
agricultural production: and assimilation, 51; crops of, 6–7; development of, 30–36; effect of urbanization on, 157; and Great Depression, 113; industrialization of, 31, 33, 34, 36, 66, 109–110, 165, 166–167, 168, 243; labor demands, 109–110, 166–167, 167; recruitment of labor for, 6, 117, 163–168, 204–205; and Salt River Project, 50, 111; and

San Carlos Project, 131–132; of Thono O'odham, 21, 54, 58–59, 136, 213–214
Aji, 32, 33, 50, 55, 56, 58, 135
Akimel O'odham. *See* Pimas
Alianza Hispano-Americana, 91, 94, 96, 116, 146, 173–179, 184–185
Alien Labor Law, 79, 94, 95, 98
Alonzo, Máximo, 114–115, 169, 172
Alvarez, Gabriel, 2–3, 231–232, 239
American Coordinating Council on Political Education (ACCPE), 184, 185, 187, 245
American Federation of Labor (AFL), 102, 103, 105, 113, 158–159, 170
Americanization programs, 11, 96–97, 116
Anderson, Benedict, 9, 15
Anglo Americans: as agricultural workers, 118, 125; and citizenship limits, 11, 43, 211–212, 244; and classification of immigrants, 102; defined, 13; as elites, 24; as ethnic category, 3; and federal labor camps, 123–124; marriages with ethnic Mexicans, 82; Mexicans degrading status of working class,